Table of Contents

The Dignity Protocol: Building Self-Worth Through Crypto Investment

Volume I

By Bukhan Purvan Zayabat

Preface: The Digital Revolution of Money

In an era characterized by rapid technological advancements and the increasing prominence of data in shaping every aspect of our daily lives, we are witnessing a profound transformation that is taking place in the complex realm of money and finance. Friedrich A. Hayek, in his influential and thought-provoking work titled The Denationalisation of Money, envisioned a future world where the longstanding monopoly held by state-issued currency would ultimately give way to a dynamic and competitive system consisting of various private currencies. He put forth the compelling argument that permitting private institutions to create and issue their own distinct forms of money would significantly lead to enhanced financial stability and overall freedom for individuals and businesses alike. This competition in the monetary sphere would naturally favor those currencies that prove capable of maintaining their value over time and effectively serving the diverse needs and requirements of users across different segments of society.

Fast forward to the present day, cryptocurrencies have evolved into a concrete manifestation of Hayek's ambitious vision. These digital assets function autonomously from central banks, providing a decentralized alternative to the conventional fiat currencies that we've known for decades. Bitcoin, in particular, has undergone a remarkable transformation, blossoming from being a niche digital experiment into a powerful symbol of financial autonomy and groundbreaking innovation. Its inherently decentralized nature combined with a meticulously limited supply renders it an exceptionally appealing store of value, especially amidst an increasingly uncertain and volatile economic landscape. As more individuals and institutions recognize the potential of cryptocurrencies, their prominence in the financial world continues to grow, challenging traditional monetary systems.

In an era where the world is being fundamentally and dramatically rewritten by the relentless advance of technology and the explosion of data, a seismic and unprecedented shift is taking place in the very core nature of money itself. Imagine a future filled with possibilities where the traditional, long-standing pillars of wealth—such as gold, real estate, and conventional financial instruments—are no longer regarded as the ultimate safe havens or secure assets. Instead, an invisible yet powerful network of digital capital flows continuously and relentlessly, powering and propelling a new, decentralized financial ecosystem that promises not just incremental change, but a truly revolutionary transformation of global wealth as we know it. This is not merely the beginning of a fleeting trend or a speculative bubble; it is the dawning of an entirely new economic order where old paradigms are being robustly challenged and gradually replaced by a series of innovations that are both mind-blowing and deeply logical, paving the way for a future that is increasingly interconnected and driven by cutting-edge technology and inventive thinking.

At the very heart of this remarkable transformation lies Bitcoin, the revolutionary digital asset that has undergone a profound evolution from an obscure experimental endeavor into a powerful symbol of financial freedom and independence. In a daring and audacious address delivered at the Digital Asset Summit on March 26, 2025, MicroStrategy Executive Chairman Michael Saylor presented one of the most breathtaking and astonishing forecasts ever articulated: he boldly asserted that Bitcoin will one day achieve a staggering market capitalization of $500 trillion. Such an astronomical figure is almost inconceivable within our current economic landscape—a mind-boggling number that would not only dwarf the combined market values of gold, real estate, and various other long-term financial assets but also signify a sweeping and complete overhaul of our existing financial system as we know it today. Such changes could reshape how we perceive and interact with wealth on a global scale.

Saylor's bold prediction is not a wild fantasy; rather, it is firmly built on a meticulously analyzed foundation and an unyielding belief in the unstoppable and continuous march of digital innovation. He vividly painted a striking picture of capital inflows into Bitcoin that escalate in a truly and remarkably exponential manner. This trajectory starts with an initial capital investment of $2 billion, followed by an astonishing leap to $20 billion, then to $200 billion, and continues to soar to $2 trillion, $20 trillion, and eventually an unbelievable $200 trillion. And as if that remarkable progression weren't astounding enough, Saylor went even further in his analysis: once Bitcoin reaches the monumental $200 trillion milestone, an additional surge of 20% would catapult its market cap to a staggering $300 trillion, followed by an even more impressive $400 trillion, and ultimately leads to an eye-popping total of $500 trillion. This growth reflects not just numbers, but a transformative shift in financial paradigms and the evolution of currency in our modern age.

This isn't mere speculation, nor is it simply a number pulled from thin air without grounding. Saylor presented his arguments persuasively, positing that this forecast emerges as the natural result of an unstoppable economic evolution that cannot be ignored. The forces driving this transformative change are both profound and multi-faceted, representing a fundamental reallocation of capital on a grand scale—from the physical assets commonly held in the 20th century, which are often constrained by geographic boundaries, regulatory frameworks, and systemic limitations, to a dynamic and decentralized digital monetary system that is rapidly gaining acceptance and traction. In this emerging landscape, the concept of money is no longer tethered to the whims of nation-states or the limitations inherent in physical infrastructure. Instead, it exists as a digital entity, capable of circulating freely across borders, and immune to the slow pace of traditional financial intermediaries. It has the potential to harness the immense power of network effects, transforming the way value is exchanged and stored in our increasingly interconnected world. This shift could redefine the very essence of financial transactions and the nature of economic interactions as we know them today.

Saylor's vision is not only a forecast but a compelling and urgent call to arms for all who are willing to listen. He draws striking historical parallels with previous revolutions in finance—those pivotal moments in time when early adopters of innovative monetary systems enjoyed enormous rewards beyond their imagination. Take, for instance, the advent of paper money, which effectively replaced heavy, cumbersome metal coins and enabled economies across the globe to expand and flourish exponentially. Or, ponder the monumental transformation that was wrought by the establishment of central banking, an institution which centralized and meticulously regulated the issuance of money. This provided the much-needed stability that fueled modern industrial growth and development in an unprecedented manner. In each of these historical instances, those who possessed the foresight to recognize the paradigm shift early gained a strategic, life-altering advantage that set them apart from the masses. Saylor warns emphatically that today's

Bitcoin investors now stand on the precipice of a similarly profound revolution. By proactively embracing and investing in the new digital monetary system at this very moment, they have the unique opportunity to secure a position of immense power and wealth in a future where traditional financial assets may have been rendered completely obsolete. The implications of this shift are monumental, and those who act swiftly may find themselves at the forefront of a new economic era.

The implications of such a transformation are not only staggering but also profoundly complex. A market cap for Bitcoin reaching an astonishing $500 trillion would fundamentally alter the intricate global balance of financial power as we know it today. This monumental shift would not merely signify the inception of a new asset class. Instead, it would represent a complete redefinition of what constitutes money, how it is stored, and the manner in which it flows through the vast interconnected global economy. Traditional financial institutions—such as banks, real estate conglomerates, and even governments—would find themselves navigating an entirely different and unfamiliar playing field. The historical markers of wealth and power, which have long been based on tangible assets and centralized control, would swiftly shift toward digital currencies, cryptographic codes, and decentralized networks. This is not simply a minor adjustment; it is a radical evolution that profoundly challenges the very fabric of our economic existence and compels us to rethink our long-held beliefs about value and exchange in society.

In the coming pages, this book will take you on an incredible and enlightening journey through the vast landscape of this digital revolution. We will explore in detail the evolution of money, starting from the most ancient and earliest forms of currency that humanity has utilized, through the significant rise of denationalized money, and into the revolutionary and dynamic world of cryptocurrencies. We will thoroughly examine the remarkable technological advancements that have enabled this extraordinary transformation—such innovations as cryptocurrency wallets, decentralized exchanges, and the foundational blockchain technology itself—and analyze how these advancements are fundamentally reshaping every single facet of our financial systems today. Furthermore, we will dive deep into a wide array of investment strategies, ranging from active trading and technical analysis to long-term holding and yield farming in the expansive realm of decentralized finance (DeFi), presenting you with a comprehensive roadmap to achieving millionaire status through informed and strategic cryptocurrency investments. Through this exploration, we aim to equip you with the knowledge and tools necessary for navigating this evolving financial landscape.

But before we dive deeper into the specifics of various strategies and emerging technologies, it is crucial to grasp the significance and magnitude of the seismic shift we are currently witnessing in our financial landscape. This moment we are experiencing is not merely a gradual, evolutionary process—it is, in fact, a profound revolution. The digital revolution of money has arrived, and it is transforming every aspect of how we interact with finance and economy. At its core, this monumental revolution is driven by a significant and profound realization: that the traditional financial systems we once relied on are inherently limited and, in many critical ways, now obsolete. These systems were built on foundational principles that served society well in a bygone era but are now increasingly incapable of keeping up with the rapid advancements and innovations characteristic of the digital age we live in today. This disconnect highlights the urgent need for new models and frameworks to emerge in order to navigate and thrive in this rapidly evolving financial ecosystem.

Traditional assets, such as gold and real estate, have long been regarded as safe havens in times of economic uncertainty. Investors have historically relied on these tangible assets to preserve their wealth and provide security when markets become volatile. Gold, in particular, has been regarded as a store of value for millennia, often seen as a safeguard against inflation and geopolitical turmoil. Its allure is not only rooted in its physical properties but also in its cultural significance across various civilizations. Yet even gold, with its inherent scarcity and timeless appeal, pales in comparison to the remarkable potential of Bitcoin in a world driven by relentless digital innovation. Bitcoin, with its fixed supply of 21 million coins, offers a level of scarcity and security that is unprecedented in the modern era. This digital asset is meticulously designed to resist inflation and manipulation, giving it an edge over traditional assets. Moreover, it is a digital asset that transcends borders, regulatory constraints, and the physical limitations that have long bound traditional forms of money. This quality allows Bitcoin to be transferred swiftly and securely, enabling globalization of wealth without the barriers that often accompany conventional currencies. In a sense, Bitcoin is the culmination of centuries of evolution—a final step in the transformation from physical to digital, from centralized to decentralized. It represents not just a new form of money but a revolutionary shift in how we think about value and ownership in our increasingly interconnected world.

Saylor's forecast stands as a clarion call for investors, policymakers, and everyday citizens alike, resonating with urgency and significance. It forces us to confront some deeply uncomfortable truths about the persistent limitations of our current financial systems and their inadequacies in addressing the needs of today's rapidly evolving market landscape. The capital that once confidently flowed into traditional physical assets—such as properties, gold reserves, and even national currencies—is now, undeniably, migrating toward the burgeoning realm of digital assets. This shift is not a fleeting moment or a temporary anomaly; rather, it is a definitive marker of the future of money as we know it. The swift and relentless flow of capital into Bitcoin specifically is but a symptom of a far larger trend that we cannot ignore: the irreversible and transformative shift from the 20th-century economy, which heavily relied on tangible physical infrastructure and centralized control, to a cutting-edge 21st-century digital ecosystem. This new landscape is characterized by unprecedented speed, enhanced transparency, and a democratized access to financial opportunities that were once out of reach for many.

The transformation we are witnessing today is underpinned by several crucial and key forces that drive it forward. First and foremost, the advent of blockchain technology has created a groundbreaking new paradigm of trust and security that was previously unimaginable. In the realm of traditional finance, trust is centrally managed—stored in banks, regulatory institutions, and governments that all remain vulnerable to corruption, inefficiency, and systemic failure. Blockchain, by contrast, distributes trust across a vast decentralized network, making it inherently more resilient and transparent. This significant shift in how trust is perceived and managed is not merely a technological innovation—it is a deeply philosophical change as well, representing a meaningful move toward a more equitable and decentralized future. In this new landscape, individuals have the potential to assert greater control over their financial destinies in ways that were once thought impossible.

The implications of this shift touch every aspect of our financial interactions, enabling new forms of engagement, collaboration, and empowerment for every individual involved in the ecosystem.

Second, the scalability of digital networks means that capital can now move at a speed and volume that was previously unimaginable and previously difficult to achieve. In the traditional financial world, capital is often slowed down by various intermediaries, stringent regulations, and outdated infrastructure that impede swift transactions. Digital assets like Bitcoin operate on a vast global network that is both instantaneous and completely borderless. This means that as soon as an opportunity arises anywhere in the world, capital can be deployed quickly and efficiently, amplifying the potential for exponential growth in ways that were once thought to be impossible.

Third, the democratization of financial tools is truly a game changer for people around the world. In the not-so-distant past, access to sophisticated financial instruments and lucrative investment opportunities was largely reserved for the wealthy elites or those who were well-connected within financial circles. Today, with the rapid advent and rise of cryptocurrencies and other digital assets, anyone with a stable internet connection can actively participate in the global financial system, regardless of their financial background or status. This significant democratization not only empowers individuals from various socioeconomic backgrounds but also creates a more competitive and dynamic marketplace where innovation can thrive and flourish. As a result, more people are able to pursue their financial goals, leading to increased economic growth and opportunity for all. This shift represents a fundamental transformation in how people engage with finance and investment, opening doors that were previously closed to many.

Saylor's visionary forecast of a staggering $500 trillion Bitcoin market cap encapsulates these transformative forces that are reshaping our economic landscape. It is a remarkably bold statement that challenges the established order and compels us to reconsider what is truly possible in the ever-evolving realm of finance. The relentless influx of capital into Bitcoin, as described by Saylor, is not merely a random occurrence—it is the culmination of decades of profound technological innovation, shifting cultural attitudes, and the convergence of significant global financial trends. It is the natural outcome of an economy that is swiftly shedding its previous physical constraints in favor of a more fluid, digital, and decentralized model that promises to redefine our financial interactions. This shift signifies a profound transformation in how we view value and exchange in our increasingly interconnected world.

Critics may easily dismiss such bold forecasts as being overly optimistic or perhaps even fanciful in their nature. They may argue that the inherent volatility associated with cryptocurrencies, coupled with the numerous regulatory challenges that arise, as well as the potential for rapid technological obsolescence, are obstacles too significant to allow for the sustainability of such astronomical growth. However, history has clearly shown us that many of the most revolutionary ideas were initially met with skepticism, derision, and even outright disbelief. The very notion that paper money could ever displace gold, or that a decentralized network could effectively secure global transactions, was once regarded as completely absurd and far-fetched. Yet today, those same ideas are not only widely accepted but have also become the fundamental foundation upon which our modern economy is built and operates.

The argument for Bitcoin's eventual ascension to a staggering market cap of $500 trillion is deeply rooted in both logical reasoning and compelling historical precedent. Consider, for instance, the fascinating evolution of money itself throughout human history: beginning with primitive forms such as shells and beads, advancing through to the era of coins and paper currency, each significant iteration brought with it a radical and transformative improvement in the efficiency of transactions and the accessibility of commerce for all people. With each progressive step along this continuum, entire societies unlocked new levels of economic growth and sparked unprecedented innovation. Bitcoin stands at the forefront as the next critical step in this long evolutionary process—representing a highly advanced digital asset that is remarkably well-suited to fulfill the complex demands of a globalized, internet-driven economy. Its unique characteristics, including a fixed supply and a decentralized nature, provide the substantial stability and robust security needed in an increasingly volatile world. At the same time, its fully digital form allows for unprecedented speed, efficiency, and scalability in transactions, potentially revolutionizing the future of how we conduct business and exchange value across the globe.

Moreover, Saylor's forecast is not just about Bitcoin; it represents a significant commentary on the broader economic shift from traditional, physical assets to increasingly prevalent digital, network-based ones. The substantial migration of capital away from conventional real estate in Russia, private equity investments in China, as well as various assorted assets scattered across the continents of Africa and South America, to Bitcoin is indicative of a fundamental and ongoing change in the way global finance operates today. In this emerging new paradigm, wealth is no longer exclusively measured by tangible physical holdings but is instead gauged by the efficiency, accessibility, and connectivity of digital networks. It is indeed a world where the value of an asset is determined not merely by its physical tangibility, but rather by its unique ability to seamlessly integrate with, and effectively leverage the incredible power of the internet. This shift is not just a passing trend; it marks a revolutionary transformation in our understanding of value and investment in the modern financial landscape.

This revolutionary shift has incredibly profound implications for every single aspect of our society, impacting individuals from all walks of life. For investors, it truly represents a once-in-a-lifetime opportunity to actively participate in the creation of a completely new financial order. Early adopters of Bitcoin and various other digital assets are not merely buying into a currency; rather, they are making significant investments in the very future of money itself. These forward-thinking individuals are strategically positioning themselves to reap the substantial rewards of an economic revolution that will fundamentally redefine how wealth is not only created, but also stored and then transferred within our global economy.

For governments and policymakers, Saylor's forecast serves as an urgent wake-up call. The traditional mechanisms of monetary policy and financial regulation, which have long been relied upon, are now based on principles that no longer apply effectively in the swiftly evolving digital age. As capital flows increasingly into decentralized networks and platforms, regulators face the pressing need to adapt to a landscape where the old rules and frameworks become increasingly irrelevant. This is not just an economic issue; it is also a critical political and social one as well. The power dynamics of the global economy are undergoing significant shifts, and those who fail to recognize these transformations and adapt in a timely manner risk being left behind in this rapidly changing environment.

For the everyday citizen, the ongoing digital revolution of money presents both an unprecedented opportunity and a significant set of challenges that must be navigated carefully. On one hand, the democratization of finance signifies that anyone, regardless of their socio-economic status, can participate in the expansive global economy—no longer is the accumulation of wealth the exclusive domain of a privileged few elite individuals. This transformation opens doors to countless individuals who previously lacked access to traditional financial systems. On the other hand, the rapid pace of change also brings with it a clear warning: those who do not actively adapt and embrace these changes risk being marginalized in a competitive system that increasingly values digital literacy, innovation, and technological competence. The future of money is not fixed or static—it is inherently dynamic, continuously evolving, decentralized, and, above all, deeply intertwined with digital technologies that shape our world.

In the pages that follow, this book will serve as your comprehensive guide through this brave new world of digital finance that is rapidly evolving. We will explore the fascinating historical evolution of money, from the ancient temples that revered and safeguarded wealth to the modern cryptocurrencies that now promise to fundamentally redefine it all. Throughout this journey, we will delve into the groundbreaking technological advancements that have made this transformation not only possible but also increasingly accessible, including blockchain technology, digital wallets, and decentralized exchanges, which have changed the financial landscape. Furthermore, we will provide you with a range of practical strategies and rigorous analytical tools that will enable you to effectively navigate the volatile yet potentially lucrative world of cryptocurrency investments, empowering you to make informed decisions in this exciting arena.

Our journey embarks on an enlightening exploration of the rich and intricate evolution of money itself—a captivating narrative that stretches across countless millennia and challenges everything we once thought we understood regarding wealth and power dynamics. We will delve into the sacred and profound origins of money, where ancient societies constructed monumental temples and grand treasuries to safeguard and honor their treasured riches. These revered "money temples" were far more than just simple storage facilities; they served as the very heart of both economic and religious life, standing as enduring symbols of divine favor and the lofty aspirations of humanity. Gaining a comprehensive understanding of this fascinating history is of utmost importance, as it illuminates the timeless nature of money and highlights the eternal human quest for stability, financial security, and lasting prosperity throughout the ages.

It is within this broader context that Michael Saylor's visionary ideas truly take on their full significance and weight. His forecast is not merely an isolated prediction; rather, it is the natural progression of a historical trend that began long before the concept of Bitcoin was ever conceived or even imagined. The ancient sanctuaries of wealth, the intricate rituals and offerings that celebrated abundance across cultures, and the enduring symbolic power of money have all converged over time to create a modern financial landscape that is now ripe and ready for transformation. In Saylor's view, Bitcoin stands as the ultimate expression of this profound evolution—a digital embodiment of the age-old principles that have governed the concept and practice of money for centuries, now supercharged by the boundless and limitless potential inherent in the internet and digital technologies.

This book is crafted to serve as not only a thorough and rigorous analysis but also as a passionate and inspiring manifesto. It stands as an open invitation to reexamine and rethink everything you believe you know about money. It encourages you to boldly challenge the status quo and to seize the exceptional and unprecedented opportunities that are presented by the ongoing digital revolution. Whether you identify as an experienced investor with years of knowledge or as a curious newcomer eager to learn, the insights, strategies, and actionable advice contained within these pages will equip you with the critical knowledge and essential tools needed to not just survive, but to truly thrive in a rapidly changing world where the future of money is being forged and shaped right before our very eyes.

As you embark on this exciting and transformative journey, be prepared to have your long-held assumptions shattered and your understanding of wealth completely redefined in ways you never thought possible. The digital revolution of money is not on the horizon—it is already here, reshaping the landscape of finance as we know it. Those who adapt quickly, who take the time to truly understand the underlying logic and embrace the transformative power of technology will be the ones who ultimately reap its significant rewards. The era of digital assets is not simply a mere chapter in the ongoing story of money; it marks the beginning of an entirely new narrative, one that promises to democratize wealth across all boundaries and revolutionize the global economy in unprecedented ways. This is an invitation to engage with the future of finance and to explore the opportunities that lie ahead.

In the following chapters, we will meticulously explore every intricate facet of this remarkable revolution. We will begin our journey by thoroughly examining the ancient and fascinating history of money, uncovering the captivating mysteries of money temples where wealth was not only stored but also revered and worshiped. We will trace the intricate evolution from these early financial sanctuaries to the complex modern world of cryptocurrencies, where digital assets have swiftly emerged as the new gold standard. Furthermore, we will then delve deeply into the groundbreaking technological breakthroughs that have made this profound transformation possible—blockchain technology, digital wallets, and decentralized exchanges that have dramatically shattered the old paradigms of trust and security in the financial landscape.

Next, we will provide you with a comprehensive and detailed toolkit that will assist you in navigating the volatile yet highly rewarding and potentially lucrative landscape of cryptocurrency investments. This toolkit will cover a wide array of topics, from cultivating the millionaire mindset and mastering crucial technical analysis techniques to capitalizing on early-stage ventures and generating passive income through decentralized finance, also known as DeFi. Each strategy will be presented with the analytical rigor and logical reasoning necessary to achieve substantial success in this new and rapidly evolving financial order. You will learn how to effectively assess risk, optimize your investment portfolio, and stay ahead of the ever-changing market trends in a world where every second counts and timely decisions can significantly impact your financial outcomes.

No discussion of digital wealth could ever be considered complete without addressing the absolutely critical issue of cybersecurity. In a rapidly evolving landscape where every financial transaction is meticulously recorded on an immutable ledger and every single asset is accessible via the vast expanse of the internet, the risks associated with cyberattacks, hacking, and various forms of fraud are not just present, they are pervasive and constant. This book dedicates a comprehensive section to fortifying your digital fortresses—providing you with state-of-the-art security measures, best practices, and valuable insights into emerging technologies that will effectively safeguard your investments for many years to come. It's imperative to stay informed and vigilant in this dynamic environment to protect your digital wealth adequately.

Michael Saylor's ambitious forecast of Bitcoin's eventual market cap reaching a staggering $500 trillion is a bold, almost surreal vision that challenges conventional perceptions and paints a transformative picture of the future. Yet when scrutinized through the insightful lens of history and the ongoing evolution of technology, this vision becomes not only plausible but also seemingly inevitable. The relentless and continuous flow of capital into digital assets, fueled by rapid technological advancements and a profound global shift in trust, represents a force that is both unstoppable and transformative. This immense force is reshaping every facet of our lives—from the methods by which we pay for goods and services to the innovative ways we store and transfer value across vast continents. It is much more than a mere financial trend; it is the next great revolution in human history, one that promises to redefine how we understand and interact with value itself, paving the way for a new era of economic possibilities and opportunities.

As you delve into these pages, you will find yourself challenged to rethink and reconsider your perspective on money in profound ways. You will be inspired to question many long-held beliefs that you may have taken for granted and to broaden your view beyond the limitations imposed by our existing financial systems. The digital revolution of money is not merely a distant dream or a far-off concept—it is a vibrant, dynamic reality that is actively unfolding all around us at this very moment. And as history has repeatedly demonstrated, those individuals who are able to recognize and adapt to a significant paradigm shift early on are the ones who ultimately secure extraordinary fortunes and lasting success.

This preface is your personal invitation to join the ranks of individuals who are not only witnessing but also actively shaping the future landscape of money. It serves as a compelling call to arms for investors, entrepreneurs, and visionary thinkers alike to harness the immense power of digital assets. Together, we can build a legacy of wealth that transcends the traditional boundaries and limitations previously set by conventional financial systems. The journey that lies ahead is undeniably filled with numerous challenges and uncertainties, but it is simultaneously brimming with unprecedented opportunities waiting to be seized. With each passing day, the digital revolution continues to grow stronger, becoming increasingly pervasive and transformative in our lives and industries. Embrace this change and become part of a movement that redefines financial possibilities.

Prepare yourself for an intellectually stimulating and practical adventure into the exciting realm of digital finance. The profound insights, innovative strategies, and advanced technologies discussed in this book serve as the essential keys to unlocking the boundless potential of cryptocurrencies and the digital currency market. This is not merely a guide—it is a comprehensive blueprint for achieving true financial freedom in a world that is continuously being remade by the relentless force of digital innovation and transformation. Engage with the material, and empower yourself to navigate this dynamic financial landscape effectively.

In the spirit of those ancient money temples, where wealth was not only guarded but genuinely venerated with reverence and respect, we now find ourselves standing on the threshold of a new era that is upon us. An era in which digital assets are set to redefine the very concept of money itself, transforming economies across the globe, and empowering individuals in ways we have never witnessed before. The sacred and revered nature of money is being reborn now in a digital form, one that is not only accessible to more people but also transparent in its operations, and infinitely scalable to meet the needs of an ever-evolving marketplace.

The road ahead is indeed daunting, filled with challenges that may seem insurmountable at first glance. However, for those individuals who possess the courage to wholeheartedly embrace change and the insight to grasp the underlying dynamics at play, the rewards that await are simply immeasurable. This is your unique opportunity to be a vital part of a groundbreaking revolution—a revolution that promises to fundamentally rewrite the established rules of finance. This endeavor aims to create a future in which wealth is not an elusive goal confined to the privileged few, but rather a reality that is within reach for anyone who possesses the determination and dares to dream big. Each step taken into this new landscape paves the way for a brighter and more inclusive financial future.

Welcome to the incredible digital revolution of money that is transforming our lives. Welcome to a future where capital not only flows freely but also transforms economies, boundaries dissolve, and the promise of unimaginable wealth is not just a distant dream anymore, but a rapidly approaching reality that awaits you. The journey to becoming a millionaire through investing in cryptocurrencies starts right now, in this moment of opportunity. Embrace the shock, the overwhelming awe, and the unyielding logic of this groundbreaking new world that is unfolding before us. The future of money is not only here, it is yours to seize and explore. Take action and join this exhilarating adventure that could change your financial destiny forever.

Unraveling the Digital Transformation

The remarkable transformation we are witnessing in the ever-evolving world of finance is akin to the tectonic shifts that have significantly redefined entire civilizations throughout recorded history. Every major leap in human progress—from the groundbreaking invention of the wheel to the revolutionary discovery of electricity—has fundamentally altered how we live, how we work, and how we interact with the world around us. Today, we find ourselves standing at the precipice of a revolution that is as profound and impactful as any major moment in human history: the digital revolution of money, which promises to reshape the very fabric of our economic existence and redefine our understanding of value and exchange.

For countless centuries, money has served as the essential lifeblood of civilization, functioning as the vital medium through which trade is conducted, and through which wealth is meticulously accumulated. In ancient times, money was as tangible and physical as the shimmering gold and gleaming silver coins that circulated extensively in the bustling marketplaces, or the monumental, elaborate temples that adeptly safeguarded a city's immense wealth. These magnificent money temples were much more than mere storage facilities; they were revered sacred spaces where the entire community would come together to honor and celebrate the divine nature of abundance and prosperity. Wealth was universally seen as a blessing from the gods, a profound sign of favor and prosperity that elevated both individuals and entire societies to a higher, more esteemed plane of existence. This perception of wealth intertwined deeply with the cultural and spiritual values of the time, creating a complex relationship between material wealth and the spiritual beliefs of the people.

Fast forward to the 20th century, and the world of money was dramatically transformed by the advent of paper currency and the emergence of centralized banking systems. Governments around the world took control of money creation, establishing themselves as the primary authority in financial matters. Financial institutions became the gatekeepers of economic stability, providing a sense of order and regulation in the previously chaotic world of commerce. Yet, despite this progress, the system, for all its notable successes, was not without its significant flaws. Centralized control often meant bureaucratic inefficiencies, where red tape could hinder quick decision-making, leaving the system vulnerable to corruption. Furthermore, the established financial structures struggled with the inability to adapt quickly to the rapid pace of technological advancements and economic shifts that characterized the century. Moreover, physical money—whether in the form of coins, bills, or real estate—came with profound inherent limitations. It was bound by geographical constraints, subject to the inevitability of physical decay, and dependent on slow-moving infrastructures that could not keep pace with the ever-increasing demands of an interconnected and globalized world.

Enter the digital revolution, an unprecedented shift in how we interact with the world around us. The rise of the internet heralded a new era in which information could be transmitted instantaneously and effortlessly, transcending borders and time zones in ways that were previously unimaginable. In this exciting environment, it was only natural that money, too, would evolve to take full advantage of these brand-new possibilities presented by technological advancements. This evolution gave birth to cryptocurrencies, which emerged from the fringes of technology as a radical experiment driven by a deep-seated desire to create a form of money that was not beholden to the limitations imposed by the physical world. Among these innovations, Bitcoin, the true pioneer of this movement, was born out of the ideals of decentralization and financial sovereignty. It was specifically designed to function as a currency that could exist independently of any government or financial institution, thus providing a digital asset that could be transferred, traded, and stored with unprecedented ease and resilience, ensuring security and promoting a new age of financial autonomy.

Michael Saylor's forecast, therefore, is not merely an isolated prediction; it is, in fact, the culmination of an extensive and long historical evolution that spans across many years and developments. His ambitious vision of Bitcoin ultimately reaching a remarkable $500 trillion market cap can be seen as a logical extension of the numerous trends that have been steadily in motion for centuries now. As the world continues to shift its trust from traditional physical assets to innovative digital networks, the inherent advantages of cryptocurrencies become increasingly apparent to a growing audience. They are borderless, transparent, and immutable—qualities that are perfectly suited for the demands of the digital age in which we currently find ourselves immersed. This inevitable transition is not just a passing trend; it is a profound transformation that could redefine our entire economic landscape.

The relentless influx of capital into Bitcoin is a clear and unmistakable signal that investors from various corners of the globe are increasingly recognizing this significant shift. Every single day, billions of dollars are being redirected from traditional assets into the expansive digital realm, a trend that shows no signs of slowing down or stopping. This transformative movement is only set to accelerate as more institutional players enter the fray, bringing with them both legitimacy and increased investment. Governments, too, are starting to take serious notice of these changes. The discussions surrounding national digital currencies and the establishment of strategic Bitcoin reserves are not merely academic exercises or theoretical debates—they are substantial, concrete steps toward an imminent future where digital assets will occupy a central role in the global financial system. The implications of these developments are profound and far-reaching.

Yet, the road to this new financial order is not without its significant challenges and obstacles. The transition from physical forms of currency to digital money represents a disruptive and transformative process that fundamentally upends long-established norms and practices that have governed our financial interactions for generations. This shift compels us to thoroughly rethink and re-evaluate our deeply ingrained notions of value, ownership, and trust in financial systems. In a world where digital transactions occur instantaneously and are often irreversible, concerns about security become paramount and undeniably critical. The threats of cyberattacks, fraud, and numerous regulatory uncertainties loom large over the still-nascent crypto industry, casting a shadow over its potential. This book does not shy away from confronting these pressing realities; rather, it embraces them wholeheartedly, offering a rigorous and comprehensive analytical framework for effectively navigating the complexities and intricacies of the ongoing digital revolution. Through this examination, readers will gain a clear understanding of the dynamics at play and the potential implications for the future of finance.

One of the most significant arguments in favor of Bitcoin's transformative potential lies in its uniquely fixed supply. Unlike fiat currencies, which can be printed at will by central banks and often lead to inflation, Bitcoin is precisely capped at a total of 21 million coins. This inherent scarcity is an essential aspect built into the cryptocurrency's very design, contributing to it being viewed as a deflationary asset that is expected to become increasingly valuable over time as demand rises while the supply remains constant. This aspect of Bitcoin represents a radical departure from the persistent inflationary tendencies associated with traditional currency systems. It can be likened to a form of digital gold, offering a promise of stability even in an unpredictable and unstable world, where economic fluctuations can undermine the value of standard money.

Saylor's vision extends far beyond Bitcoin being just an investment vehicle for a select few. He perceives it as the foundational cornerstone of an entirely new economic order, where wealth is no longer concentrated solely in the hands of a privileged few individuals but is instead accessible to anyone who possesses an internet connection. This democratization of finance represents one of the most compelling and transformative aspects of the broader digital revolution we are witnessing today. It effectively levels the playing field for everyone, providing opportunities and breaking down barriers that have long served to keep traditional financial systems exclusive, elitist, and opaque. In this promising new world, every individual is empowered with the chance to actively participate in the global economy, take part in investments, and most importantly, build and grow their own wealth in ways that were previously unimaginable.

Furthermore, the ongoing digital revolution of money is not limited solely to cryptocurrencies in isolation. Instead, it encompasses a much broader ecosystem that includes essential components like blockchain technology, decentralized finance (DeFi), and non-fungible tokens (NFTs). These innovative advancements are converging in a significant way to create a comprehensive, interconnected financial landscape that is increasingly efficient, transparent, and resilient compared to previous systems. Blockchain, which is the underlying technology fueling Bitcoin and various other cryptocurrencies, offers a decentralized ledger that ensures every transaction that takes place is secure, verifiable, and immutable. This transformative technology has far-reaching implications, extending well beyond the realm of finance into diverse areas such as supply chain management, healthcare, and even governance. As these technologies evolve and integrate, they promise to revolutionize not just our approach to money, but various sectors of society in profound and lasting ways.

The rise of decentralized finance (DeFi) represents a profound and significant paradigm shift in the way we approach financial transactions and services. By leveraging the power and potential of blockchain technology, DeFi platforms effectively eliminate the necessity for traditional intermediaries that have long been seen as essential to the functioning of financial systems. This transformative approach allows for seamless peer-to-peer transactions that are not only markedly faster but also considerably more cost-effective than those involving conventional banking services. As a result, this innovation opens up an expansive world of possibilities for individuals and businesses alike, enabling them to create various passive income streams, as well as engage in borrowing, lending, and investing—all completed without the heavy overhead costs typically associated with established financial institutions. As increasing numbers of people begin to embrace these innovative models and alternatives, the traditional financial system will ultimately be compelled to evolve and adapt, or it may risk becoming obsolete in the face of this unstoppable trend.

Yet, for all its immense potential and promise, the digital revolution of money also carries with it significant and notable risks. The rapid pace of ongoing innovation means that regulatory frameworks are often left playing catch-up, leaving investors exposed to various uncertainties that can arise at any moment. Cybersecurity remains an ever-critical concern, as the decentralized nature of digital assets also makes them increasingly attractive targets for hackers and fraudsters who seek to exploit weaknesses. These challenges are very real and must be addressed head-on and with urgency if we are to fully realize and embrace the potential of this new and evolving financial paradigm.

This book is far from being a utopian vision of a flawless future. Instead, it serves as a realistic, analytical, and persuasive guide that thoroughly acknowledges both the tremendous opportunities and the significant challenges that come with investing in digital assets. It is firmly grounded in logic and historical precedent, drawing extensively on centuries of economic evolution to compellingly argue that the shift toward digital money is not only inevitable but also remarkably transformative in nature. In doing so, it sheds light on the various factors and nuances associated with this burgeoning sector, providing readers with the insights needed to navigate this complex landscape effectively.

As you embark on the intriguing journey through these enlightening pages, you will encounter a compelling blend of historical insight, in-depth technical analysis, and practical strategies for smart investing. You will gain an insightful understanding of the evolution of money, tracing its roots from ancient times when wealth was revered and safeguarded in grand temples and treasuries, to the rapidly advancing modern era marked by cryptocurrencies and cutting-edge blockchain technology. You will explore the groundbreaking innovations that have made digital assets not only secure but also remarkably accessible and scalable for individuals and institutions alike. And, importantly, you will be thoroughly equipped with the essential tools and knowledge necessary to navigate the highly volatile yet potentially lucrative world of cryptocurrency investments with confidence and strategic foresight.

The vision presented by Michael Saylor serves as a powerful call to action—a bold challenge to recognize and seize the numerous opportunities that the digital age offers before they slip away unnoticed. It is an enticing invitation to actively participate in a monumental revolution that is not only changing the way we invest our resources but also fundamentally redefining the very nature of money itself in this modern era. Early adopters of Bitcoin, along with other digital assets, are not merely investing in a new form of currency; rather, they are engaging in a significant and transformative shift in how value is created, stored, and exchanged in our increasingly digital world. This shift has the potential to create profound implications for our economy, our society, and how we perceive and utilize wealth in an ever-evolving landscape.

This is an extraordinary moment of profound change, one that will undoubtedly be looked back upon as the significant turning point in the landscape of human economic history. The capital that once surged into physical assets and traditional investment avenues is now racing into innovative digital networks, fueled by a wave of innovation, enhanced efficiency, and a relentless drive toward decentralization and democratization of finance. The digital revolution of money is not just a distant dream; it is happening right now in real time, and it is radically reshaping the global financial landscape at a pace that is both breathtaking and utterly inevitable for the future ahead.

In the face of such monumental and unprecedented change, the pressing question is not merely whether you will be a part of this extraordinary revolution, but rather how you will strategically position yourself to best benefit from it. The strategies, innovative tools, and invaluable insights contained within this book are meticulously designed to help you achieve just that. They offer a comprehensive roadmap to navigate the intricate complexities of digital finance, to manage risks effectively and wisely, and to harness the explosive, transformative potential of cryptocurrencies in today's rapidly evolving landscape.

By delving into the rich historical evolution of money, alongside the remarkable technological innovations that have paved the way for the rise of digital assets, you will develop a much deeper appreciation for the various forces at play in our economy. You will come to understand how centuries-old concepts about wealth, power, and value have been reimagined and transformed for the complexities of the modern world. Furthermore, you will recognize how these redefined ideas and principles are currently being applied in innovative ways that are both revolutionary and pragmatically beneficial for society. This narrative unfolds the story of a new era—a unique and transformative time when the digital realm and the principles of decentralization beautifully converge to foster a future filled with unparalleled opportunity for individuals and communities alike. Each new technological advancement contributes to this dynamic landscape, shaping the way we perceive and interact with value in our everyday lives.

As you turn the page and begin the exciting journey through this captivating book, prepare to have your perceptions thoroughly challenged and your horizons notably expanded. The digital revolution of money is not merely an investment opportunity—it represents a significant paradigm shift that possesses the extraordinary power to transform every single aspect of our lives in profound ways. Whether you identify as an experienced investor, a passionate technology enthusiast, or perhaps someone simply curious about the future landscape of finance, the valuable insights and innovative strategies presented within these pages will undoubtedly inspire you to think differently, act boldly, and seize the incredible transformative potential of digital wealth that lies ahead. Embrace this moment as an invitation to explore new possibilities and expand your understanding of what is possible in the world of finance and beyond.

In closing, let this preface serve as your passionate wake-up call. The old world of traditional money is indeed crumbling, and in its place, a bold new digital order is emerging—faster, smarter, and more inclusive than ever before, offering opportunities for everyone. Michael Saylor's ambitious vision of a $500 trillion Bitcoin market cap is not merely an idle fantasy; it is steadily becoming the inevitable outcome of a significant global economic evolution driven by relentless technological innovation and extraordinary human ingenuity. The digital revolution of money is undeniably here, and it serves as your gateway to a future filled with limitless possibilities and unprecedented potential. Embrace this moment with open eyes, a discerning mind, and the unwavering courage to invest in what could be the future of finance. The journey to becoming a cryptocurrency millionaire begins now—and trust me, it is nothing short of revolutionary and transformative.

Part I: The Foundations of a New Financial Order

Chapter 1: The History of Money Temple

Ancient Sanctuaries of Wealth: Temples and Treasuries

Throughout the vast expanse of human history, money has transcended its basic function as merely a medium of exchange; it has evolved into a multifaceted symbol of power, divinity, social order, and economic influence. In the ancient world, wealth was not simply something to be accumulated, traded, or even hoarded; it was revered, carefully guarded, and intricately woven into the very fabric and foundation of society itself. Temples and treasuries served dual purposes as early banks and central hubs of economic power and influence, laying the groundwork for monetary systems that resonate even to this day. This exploration invites you to delve deeply into the astonishing, mind-blowing world of these ancient sanctuaries of wealth. Both the literal structures that housed vast riches and the metaphorical institutions that governed trade and finance reveal profound insights into how they shaped entire civilizations, established foundational financial systems, and set the stage for the modern principles of economic thought that we rely on in today's complex world.

The Sacred Origins of Economic Power

Imagine a world where, in every corner of society, every single coin, every precious measure of grain, was not merely a commodity to be traded but a sacred offering imbued with profound significance. In ancient Mesopotamia, as well as in Egypt, Greece, and Rome, temples functioned as far more than mere places of worship; they were vital centers, the beating hearts of vibrant economic and political life. Within these sacred sanctuaries, wealth was not merely seen as a resource but was believed to be a divine trust—a precious gift bestowed by the gods that mortals were charged to protect, uphold, and honor with utmost reverence. The very architecture of these majestic temples was meticulously designed to inspire awe and deep reverence, cultivating an atmosphere where economic activity was inherently intertwined with genuine religious devotion and sacred respect. It was in this unique environment that the boundaries between commerce and spirituality blurred, creating a harmonious blend of the material and the divine in daily life.

In Mesopotamia, for instance, the grand ziggurats of Sumer were colossal architectural structures that dominated the skyline of the city in truly remarkable ways. These massive and impressive temples not only provided a significant spiritual connection to the divine and the cosmos but also served as crucial depositories for wealth, showcasing the connection between religion and economics. Temples exerted control over an extensive range of resources including land, livestock, and grain, and priests meticulously recorded numerous transactions on clay tablets, ensuring transparency and proper accountability. These early and innovative accounting practices were the precursors to what we now use as modern ledger systems, reflecting a deep, logical, and sophisticated understanding of financial management that was as advanced and complex as it was sacred and spiritually significant.

Similarly, in the fascinating realm of ancient Egypt, grand temples dedicated to powerful deities like Amun, located in Karnak and Thebes, amassed truly enormous wealth over time. The precious metal gold, which was highly regarded as the very flesh of the gods, was carefully stored in the secure temple treasuries. These treasuries, filled with not only gold but also vast reserves of grain and many other invaluable items, played a crucial role in the functioning of the state. They were essential for funding not only elaborate religious ceremonies but also the overall administration of the vast empire. The pharaohs, wielding immense power, strategically utilized this temple wealth to finance monumental construction projects that left lasting legacies, as well as to support military campaigns that asserted their dominance, thereby reinforcing their divine right to rule over the land. The intricate integration of economic power and religious authority established a sophisticated system where wealth became both a powerful symbol of divine favor and a vital tool for effective governance.

Temples as the First Banks

The idea that temples functioned as the very first banks may seem shocking and surprising by modern standards, but upon closer examination, it was actually a natural evolution in the development of ancient economies. In these early societies, the trust that was placed in the divine was extended seamlessly to the custodians of sacred wealth—the priests who managed and oversaw these significant resources. Temples became the safe havens for wealth, offering a variety of services that were remarkably similar to those we find in modern banking institutions today. They collected and safeguarded deposits from individuals, issued loans to those in need, and efficiently managed the redistribution of resources within the community. In a world that lacked formal financial institutions, temples thus filled the critical and essential role of economic stewards, ensuring that wealth was preserved and utilized in ways that benefited the broader society. These early financial systems laid the groundwork for what would eventually evolve into the more structured financial institutions we rely on today.

In the ancient civilization of Sumer, the magnificent temples played a pivotal and central role in the intricate development of the early banking system that emerged at that time. Merchants engaged in trade and farmers with surplus goods would deposit their extra resources, while knowledgeable temple administrators were responsible for keeping detailed and precise records. They utilized cuneiform script inscribed on durable clay tablets to document these transactions meticulously. These meticulously preserved records served not only as financial statements but also as sacred and important documents, entirely entrusted to the dedicated care of the temple priests. The meticulous and detailed nature of these records underscores a logical, organized, and analytical approach to effective economic management that assured both accountability and a remarkable continuity of practices and traditions across numerous generations.

The role of temples extended far beyond mere storage and preservation of goods. They were vibrant centers for economic activity, bustling trade negotiations, and various forms of exchange, where wealth was not only accumulated but also actively circulated among the community. By issuing loans to individuals and managing vital investments, temples played a crucial role in facilitating agricultural productivity and fostering commercial expansion. This early and significant form of banking, deeply rooted in the sacred practices of the time, laid a robust foundation for the complex economic systems that would eventually give rise to the modern financial institutions we recognize today. Temples, therefore, were not only religious places, but they became pivotal hubs influencing economic growth and social structure within ancient societies.

Treasuries: Fortresses of Wealth and Symbols of State Power

As civilizations expanded and economies grew more complex over time, the crucial need for secure treasuries became increasingly paramount. Treasuries evolved significantly from simple storehouses into formidable fortresses, embodying not only economic might but also political stability. They transformed into the nerve centers of state finance, where immense wealth was collected, securely stored, and efficiently managed on a grand scale. These treasuries served as early and potent indicators of a state's power and its capacity to wage war, to build monumental structures that stood the test of time, and to effectively administer justice across the realms. Their fortified structures became symbols of stability and trust, showcasing the wealth and resources that a civilization had at its disposal.

In the Kingdom of Lydia, which is credited with creating the first standardized coins, royal treasuries held vast amounts of electrum—a natural alloy of gold and silver. These treasuries were not only repositories of wealth but also instruments of monetary policy. The standardized coinage enabled more efficient trade and provided a reliable measure of value, heralding the birth of a monetary economy. The Lydian approach to wealth management demonstrated a profound understanding of the principles of scarcity and value, principles that remain at the core of economic theory today.

The Persian Empire, with its extensive and sprawling network of provinces across vast territories, maintained vital treasuries in significant cities such as Persepolis, Susa, and Ecbatana. These important centers were entrusted with the crucial responsibility of collecting tributes from the various conquered territories, which were subsequently used to finance the expansive administrative and military apparatus of the entire empire. The Persian treasuries exemplified a logical extension of centralized power: by exerting control over a substantial portion of the empire's wealth, the ruling elite could effectively project power, maintain social order, and stimulate robust economic growth across the diverse regions that formed the empire's vast expanse. This intricate system of financial management not only supported the empire's governance but also laid the framework for economic integration among the provinces.

In ancient Rome, the concept of the treasury evolved further with the establishment of the Aerarium, which was notably housed in the well-known Temple of Saturn. The Aerarium served as the public treasury that diligently managed state finances, effectively funded various public works, and robustly supported military campaigns essential for the expansion and defense of the empire. Later, as the vast Roman Empire transitioned to a more autocratic form of rule, the Fiscus—a separate and distinct imperial treasury—emerged, emphasizing and underscoring the significant shift in power dynamics from a republican system toward one increasingly centered around the authority of the emperor. This dual system of state finance not only reflects the intricate complexity of Roman economic administration but also highlights and underscores the enduring and intricate interplay between economic power and political authority throughout the expansive history of Rome.

Wealth, Religion, and Power: The Moral Dimensions

The sacred treatment of wealth in ancient times was indeed not without considerable controversy and debate. The intricate intertwining of money with divine favor raised profound moral and philosophical questions that continue to resonate strongly within our society today. Were temples and treasuries merely benevolent guardians of prosperity, nurturing the well-being of the community, or did they serve instead as instruments of control that ultimately reinforced social hierarchies and deepened inequality? This complex dynamic invites further reflection on the responsibilities that accompany wealth and the ethical implications that such a relationship entails.

In numerous ancient societies, the perception of wealth was intricately linked to the belief in divine favor and approval. The gathering and accumulation of riches within temples were frequently justified as manifestations of the blessings granted by the gods themselves. Rulers, along with the elite classes, asserted that their amassed wealth was not merely the fruit of their own personal endeavors, but rather a divine gift, conferred upon them to highlight their unique and elevated status in society. This prevailing belief system wielded a significant legitimizing influence, which served to reinforce the authority and power of those individuals who managed and controlled the sacred and often substantial treasuries. Furthermore, this deeply rooted conviction fostered the creation of a moral obligation among the wealthy classes to operate as diligent stewards of the community's collective prosperity. This notion laid the foundation for early forms of social welfare and public finance, emphasizing the responsibility of the affluent to contribute positively to the wellbeing of society as a whole.

However, the concentration of wealth in religious institutions also bred corruption and significant inequality among the masses. When temples and treasuries transformed into repositories of immense power and influence, they became susceptible to manipulation, allowing them to serve the interests of a privileged few rather than the vast many. The priestly class, endowed with both spiritual guidance and economic authority, occasionally exploited their elevated position in society to amass even greater wealth, often at the direct expense of the common people and poorer members of the community. This ongoing tension between the divine mandate that called for support of all and the insidious pull of material greed is a recurring theme woven throughout the history of money—a theme that continues to challenge and complicate modern financial systems and moral frameworks in various ways as well.

The ethical dilemmas historically confronted by ancient civilizations provide insightful lessons that remain relevant for our contemporary society. As modern banking institutions and digital financial systems wrestle with intricate issues surrounding transparency, accountability, and the fair distribution of wealth, the historical narratives surrounding temples and treasuries stand not only as cautionary tales but also as sources of guidance. This logical progression from sacred wealth to secular finance underscores the crucial significance of harmonizing power with responsibility—a principle that holds tremendous relevance in our current age of cryptocurrencies and advanced financial technologies, just as it did in the ancient world. The challenges we face today often reflect those of our predecessors, reminding us that understanding past mistakes and successes is essential in shaping a fairer economic future.

The Metaphorical Sanctuaries of Wealth: Beyond Brick and Mortar

While literal temples and treasuries stood as the physical embodiments that represented wealth in ancient times, the concept of a "money temple" extends far beyond merely architecture. It serves as a profound metaphor for any institution or system that safeguards and diligently manages wealth with both reverence and discipline. In many different ways, the modern banking system can be appropriately viewed as the descendant of these ancient sanctuaries—a complex and sophisticated network that has inherited the sacred and significant duty of managing the collective wealth of society, ensuring its protection and proper allocation for future generations and societal stability.

Consider the ongoing evolution of financial institutions, starting from the rudimentary temple banks of ancient times to the sprawling, intricate networks that characterize modern banking today. Despite the rapid technological advancements and the regulatory frameworks that now meticulously govern the vast domain of global finance, the essential underlying principles remain strikingly similar across the centuries. Trust, security, and accountability persist as the unwavering cornerstones that supported both the ancient treasuries of yore and the sophisticated contemporary banks we depend on now. Just as ancient civilizations placed their unwavering faith in the divine guardianship offered by temples, modern society similarly entrusts its wealth and financial well-being to institutions that promise to effectively safeguard it against the threats of theft, mismanagement, and economic instability. These enduring values have shaped the relationship between individuals and their financial custodians throughout history.

Moreover, the metaphor of the money temple has taken on new and profound meanings in the ever-evolving digital age. Cryptocurrencies, characterized by their unique decentralized architecture and immutable blockchain records, symbolize a radical reimagining of what the ancient temple once represented. This modern iteration offers a groundbreaking system wherein trust is not vested in a single institution, as was traditionally the case, but instead distributed across a vast global network of users. In this innovative digital sanctuary, every single transaction is meticulously recorded on an indelible ledger, which ensures an unprecedented level of transparency and security, all without the need for a central authority to oversee the process. It is a remarkable and mind-blowing reinvention of the ancient idea—a financial system that is as much about cutting-edge technology and advancements as it is about the incredible creativity and ingenuity of human beings.

The remarkable shift that we are witnessing from physical treasuries to advanced digital fortresses profoundly challenges and transforms our long-standing conventional notions of wealth and value. In ancient times, wealth was primarily and traditionally measured in tangible, concrete assets—such as gold, silver, land, and grain—that people could see and touch. In stark contrast, today, wealth is increasingly represented and encapsulated by intangible digital assets that exist and function primarily as bits and bytes in the virtual realm. This significant transformation is not merely a simple technological upgrade; rather, it stands as a fundamental and comprehensive redefinition of what it truly means to be considered wealthy in contemporary society. The time-honored sanctuaries of the past, complete with their towering temples, deep vaults, and massive security structures, have gradually and fundamentally given way to modern cryptographic keys and decentralized financial protocols. These innovations now enable anyone, anywhere in the world, to easily and efficiently access, manage, and grow their wealth. This shift signifies a radical, logical progression that not only reflects the changing landscape of wealth but reaffirms the enduring and ageless human quest for security, prosperity, and autonomy in a rapidly evolving digital age.

The Enduring Legacy of Ancient Wealth Sanctuaries

The valuable lessons gleaned from the grand ancient temples and their storied treasuries are not mere relics of a distant past—they continue to significantly influence and shape modern financial systems in profound and intricate ways. The foundational principles of transparency, security, and trust that were embedded deeply within these sacred structures have been meticulously refined and developed over numerous millennia, and they are now firmly at the very core of contemporary economic thought and practice. These enduring ideals serve as guiding lights for today's financial establishments, fostering resilience and integrity in the complex web of global commerce.

One of the most enduring legacies of the wealth sanctuaries of ancient civilizations is the critical importance they placed on record-keeping and accountability. The meticulous and detailed accounting practices that were developed and utilized by the Mesopotamian temples laid the foundational groundwork for modern bookkeeping and auditing systems that we use today. Surprisingly, this ancient approach to financial management demonstrates how far-reaching and long-lasting its principles are. In contemporary times, blockchain technology embodies this same principle of accountability, offering an immutable and permanent ledger that records every transaction with absolute precision and transparency. This fascinating logical continuity from the use of clay tablets in ancient cultures to the advanced capabilities of blockchain today serves as a profound testament to the timeless relevance and significance of sound financial practices across the ages, emphasizing the constant need for rigorous and reliable methods of managing resources.

Furthermore, the ethical dimensions of wealth management that were vigorously debated within the hallowed halls of ancient temples continue to challenge us in contemporary society today. The centralization of power, the moral obligations of custodians tasked with responsibility, and the delicate balance that exists between state control and individual freedom remain critical issues that plague modern finance. As we navigate the ever-complex landscape of global economics and the evolving realm of digital currencies, the ancient wisdom and teachings from the money temples serve as both a cautionary tale and an inspiring model for creating a more equitable, just, and resilient financial system for all.

The transformation of money from physical coins and precious gold to an array of digital currencies represents the latest chapter in a continuously unfolding narrative of economic evolution and change. It is a fascinating story that is as logical as it is revolutionary—a remarkable journey that stretches from the sacred temples of ancient civilizations to the cutting-edge decentralized networks we see today. The sanctuaries of wealth that once stood as powerful symbols of divine favor and human innovation are now being reborn in a digital form, accessible to everyone and governed by algorithms rather than autocrats or centralized authorities. This shift not only reflects advancements in technology but also highlights a fundamental change in how we perceive and interact with value in our modern society.

Reclaiming the Sacred Nature of Wealth

In conclusion, the ancient sanctuaries of wealth—temples and treasuries—were much more than mere architectural marvels showcasing human ingenuity. They served as the epicenters of economic power and activity, functioning as the early banks that expertly managed, protected, and revered wealth in various forms. These sanctuaries provided essential services that upheld the economy of their time, reflecting the values and priorities of their societies. Their far-reaching influence on our understanding of money is truly profound and significant, offering a logical and historical framework that underpins modern financial systems and practices, shaping our current approaches to finance and wealth management.

In this absolutely shocking and mind-blowing exploration of human history, we have meticulously traced the remarkable evolution of these sacred institutions, from the monumental ziggurats of ancient Mesopotamia to the grand treasuries of

Egypt and the intricate and expansive financial networks of ancient Rome. Throughout this fascinating journey, we have observed how wealth was not only accumulated but also sanctified, effectively transforming economic transactions into acts of profound divine significance and reverence. These early financial centers were built upon enduring principles of trust, accountability, and reverence—principles that remain strikingly relevant in the digital age, just as they were thousands of years ago. This deep connection between past and present continues to resonate within our modern financial practices, illustrating how foundational concepts have persevered through the ages and are still applicable in today's complex economic landscape.

As we stand on the threshold of a new financial era—one deeply defined by the remarkable rise of cryptocurrencies and the innovative landscape of decentralized finance—the legacy of ancient wealth sanctuaries offers us both profound inspiration and necessary caution. It serves as a potent reminder that while the tools, methods, and technologies we utilize may continuously evolve, the fundamental challenges of managing wealth, securing trust, and ensuring accountability remain constant and ever-relevant. The digital revolution of money, as we know it today, is, in many ways, a continuation of this ancient journey—a reimagining of how we store, protect, and exchange value in a world that is increasingly interconnected, digital, and complex. This transformation invites us to consider not only the advantages of new technologies but also the timeless lessons from history that can guide us in navigating this evolving landscape.

Today, as investors, technologists, and everyday citizens navigate the volatile yet exhilarating landscape of modern finance, we must remember and reflect upon the invaluable lessons learned from the past. The sacred spaces of ancient temples taught us that wealth is indeed a powerful force—capable of building great empires, funding groundbreaking innovations, and even inspiring profound spiritual devotion among communities. However, these historical examples also showed us the significant dangers that come with concentrated power and unchecked greed. The ongoing challenge for our time is to harness the transformative potential of digital assets while simultaneously upholding and adhering to the timeless principles of transparency, security, and responsible ethical stewardship in every financial practice. By committing to these ideals, we can create a more equitable and sustainable financial future for all.

In fully embracing the incredible digital revolution that is transforming our concept of money, we are not simply adopting a new form of currency; rather, we are actively participating in a profound and significant evolution of human civilization as a whole. The magnificent money temples of antiquity, with their awe-inspiring and grand structures along with their meticulously kept and carefully organized records, have gradually given way to decentralized networks and the intricate use of cryptographic keys. Yet, despite these changes, the essence of our financial systems remains the same: the ongoing quest to create a system where wealth is not only protected from harm but also celebrated and recognized as a powerful source of collective empowerment for all individuals involved in this transformative process.

The journey through these ancient sanctuaries of wealth has revealed a striking and profound truth: the way we manage, and revere money in our lives is deeply intertwined with our cultural heritage, ethical considerations, and the technological progress we have made over the centuries. As we look with anticipation toward a future that is increasingly dominated by the realm of digital finance, we must carry forward the invaluable wisdom of our ancestors. This means transforming sacred trust, which has been at the core of our interactions with wealth, into innovative financial practices that truly benefit all of humanity as a whole. It is essential that we draw from the lessons learned over the ages to create a financial landscape that is inclusive and equitable for everyone.

Let this exploration serve as a profound call to rediscover and deeply appreciate the sacred nature of wealth that exists around us. It challenges us to think critically and reflectively about the institutions we build, the values we uphold firmly, and, importantly, the future we wish to create together as a society. In a rapidly evolving world where digital assets are consistently redefining the very concept of money and transactions, the lessons of the past are not merely historical curiosities or interesting tidbits—they are vital blueprints for developing a more enlightened, secure, and equitable financial future that benefits all.

As you take a moment to reflect on these ancient sanctuaries of immense wealth, consider the profound and lasting impact they have had on shaping societies and economies throughout history. Their remarkable legacy stands as a testament to the enduring human spirit—a spirit that continually seeks to harness the incredible power of wealth to uplift, empower, and transform lives. In this rapidly evolving digital age, we find ourselves with a unique opportunity to reclaim that sacred tradition, building modern temples of innovative finance that honor the vital principles of trust, creativity, innovation, and shared prosperity for all.

The path that lies ahead of us is both extraordinarily daunting and exceptionally exhilarating. With each and every advancement in technology that we witness, every significant breakthrough occurring in the realm of blockchain, and every remarkable leap forward in financial innovation that unfolds, we find ourselves in a position to rewrite the rules by which wealth is created and distributed. The digital revolution of money has firmly arrived, and it is profoundly reshaping the world all around us in ways that are as logical as they are revolutionary. By wholeheartedly embracing the timeless lessons drawn from the ancient money temples of old, we can aspire to forge a future wherein wealth is not merely a privilege reserved for the select few, but instead a strong and stable foundation for collective empowerment and global progress that benefits all.

In conclusion, the ancient sanctuaries of wealth—both magnificent temples and fortified treasuries—offer an unparalleled and profound window into the fascinating evolution of economic power and the sacred, often revered nature of money itself. They serve as a poignant reminder that while the forms and manifestations of wealth may change over time, the core principles of trust, security, and reverence for wealth remain eternal and deeply ingrained in human civilization. As you venture forth into the expansive realm of modern finance, let the timeless wisdom of these ancient institutions guide you thoughtfully, inspiring a steadfast commitment to ethical stewardship and innovative thinking in your quest to build a lasting legacy of prosperity in the ever-evolving digital age.

Section 2: The Sacred Role of Money in Civilizations

Throughout the vast expanse of human history, money has always been much more than a mere tool for exchange; it is a powerful symbol of divine power, prosperity, and the intricate social order that binds communities together. Ancient societies viewed wealth not merely as the accumulation of material possessions, but rather as an embodiment of spiritual legitimacy and the favor bestowed upon them by deities in the cosmic realm. The deep-rooted reverence and respect for money in these diverse cultures provide rich insights into the complex and multifaceted minds of our ancestors. Economic success was intricately linked to religious beliefs and long-standing cultural values, significantly influencing the daily lives of individuals within those societies. This investigation seeks to delve into the profound and multifaceted roles that money played throughout ancient civilizations, ultimately highlighting its sacred nature as not only vital for societal stability but also essential for individual prosperity and well-being.

A Divine Instrument: The Spiritual Symbolism of Wealth

Imagine a world where every single coin, every measure of grain, was not merely a commodity or an object of trade, but rather a profound manifestation of divine favor. In ancient civilizations, across different cultures and societies, wealth was often perceived as a sacred trust—an extraordinary gift from the gods, bestowed upon those individuals deemed worthy and deserving of such fortune. In Mesopotamia, Egypt, Greece, and beyond, money transcended the concept of mere currency; it emerged as a powerful symbol of influence, success, and the intricate connection that the community held with the divine forces surrounding them. This deeper understanding of wealth fostered a unique social structure that intertwined spirituality with daily life, making the pursuit of riches a journey of both material and spiritual significance.

In the ancient Near East, an era characterized by the dominance of polytheism, the worship of numerous gods significantly influenced every aspect of daily life. The vast pantheon of deities dictated the rhythms and patterns of existence, shaping the cultural and social environments. In this complex system, the accumulation of wealth was deeply intertwined with the favor of these deities. Temples and monumental ziggurats served not only as sacred spaces for worship but also emerged as bustling centers of economic activity and commerce. They were pivotal in the community, acting as hubs where religious and economic lives interwove seamlessly. Offerings made of silver, gold, and various precious commodities were routinely presented to the gods. These acts were not simply expressions of devotion or piety; they played crucial roles as vital rituals designed to secure blessings and favor for the broader community. The populace firmly believed that in return for these offerings, the deities would bestow their abundance, guidance, and protection upon the dedicated who honored them with these gifts and proclamations of loyalty. Thus, the act of giving transcended mere ritual; it was both a profound religious obligation and a calculated economic strategy. It represented a calculated effort to harness divine powers to ensure ongoing prosperity and well-being for individuals and their families.

The ritualistic offerings that can be found in these ancient temples strongly underscore this critical point. In numerous cases, the immense wealth that was deposited within these sacred sanctuaries was treated as if it were the gods' own treasury, a symbol of divine favor and abundance. It was not uncommon at all for entire communities to deeply believe that the fortunes stored carefully within the temple walls were directly responsible for the fertility of the land they depended on, the success of agricultural harvests, and even the favorable outcomes of various military campaigns. This belief intertwined the spiritual and economic lives of the people, creating a sense of shared responsibility towards maintaining the gods' favor. Consequently, the economic power of a city was thus measured not only by the wealth that its temples could command but also reflected in the grand size and opulence of these remarkable sacred structures. The reverence for these temples was a crucial part of the community's identity and stability, intertwining the threads of faith with the fabric of economic prosperity.

Money as a Manifestation of Cosmic Order

In ancient Egypt, the rich and intricate symbolism associated with money reached its zenith during a time marked by profound religious beliefs and elaborate societal structures. The pharaoh was not merely a political leader; he was regarded as a divine intermediary whose right to rule was believed to be ordained by the gods themselves. Temples dedicated to deities such as Amun, particularly in locations like Karnak and Thebes, served dual purposes; they functioned as both sacred religious sanctuaries and powerful economic fortresses. Gold, in the complex Egyptian thought system, was considered the very flesh of the gods—a precious substance that was believed to never tarnish or decay over time. It held a deep significance, representing eternal life and serving as a physical reminder of the divine order that governed not only the cosmos, but also the intricate social structures within society itself. The presence of gold infused their daily lives with a sense of connection to the divine, influencing everything from art and architecture to trade and governance.

Every coin and every measure of grain held within it profound symbolic meaning, reflecting the values and beliefs of the society. The ritual act of depositing wealth into temple treasuries was not merely a transaction; it was a sacred practice that was believed to secure the enduring favor of the gods, ensuring that the vital natural cycles—such as the life-giving annual flooding of the Nile—would continue to nourish and sustain the land along with its people for generations. Wealth was viewed not as something to be hoarded for selfish gain;

rather, it was regarded as a sacred responsibility bestowed upon individuals. This stewardship of wealth demanded equitable distribution and insisted upon the welfare and prosperity of the entire community, not just the individual. This overarching concept, deeply rooted in the belief that material prosperity stood inextricably linked to the divine order, profoundly shaped not only economic practices but also the intricate social hierarchies and legal frameworks that governed societal interactions and behaviors.

In Greece, the sacred nature of money was equally profound and held great significance in various aspects of life. The city-state of Athens, for example, celebrated its impressive economic achievements through the ambitious construction of monumental structures like the famed Parthenon. This iconic temple served as a remarkable testament to the immense wealth and power of the Athenian empire, symbolizing not only the artistic and cultural brilliance of its people but also the substantial economic might that underpinned the entire polis. Money, in this particular context, transformed into a measure of civic pride—a tangible representation of the collective success and divine favor that the citizens of Athens staunchly believed they had rightfully earned through their efforts and creativity. It was through the meticulous and proper management of wealth that these societies firmly believed they could successfully achieve a state of harmony and balance, both on earth and in the heavenly realm above. In essence, the intricate intertwining of economics and spirituality shaped their worldview and everyday practices.

Rituals, Offerings, and the Worship of Wealth

The intertwining of economic activity with religious ritual was a defining and significant feature of many ancient civilizations that have shaped human history in numerous profound ways. The worship of wealth extended beyond the simple and passive accumulation of riches; it was an active, dynamic, and engaging process involving elaborate rituals, grand public ceremonies, and significant symbolic acts that collectively celebrated and elevated the notion of prosperity. In the sacred spaces of temples and the majestic halls of palaces alike, wealth was prominently displayed in opulent and lavish forms, ranging from intricately crafted and beautifully designed coins to vast storehouses filled with grain and precious metals that served as a testament to the richness of the society.

Consider, for instance, the opulent and grand ceremonies of the ancient Greeks, which were steeped in rich tradition and cultural significance. The Delphic Oracle, magnificently housed in the esteemed Temple of Apollo, was not merely a center for spiritual guidance and wisdom but also a pivotal institution where crucial economic decisions were thoughtfully made. Rulers, influential leaders, and everyday citizens alike fervently sought the Oracle's sacred advice before embarking on their significant financial endeavors, whether it was launching ambitious military campaigns or undertaking substantial public works that would benefit their society. Such vital consultations underscored a profound and deep-seated belief among the people that achieving economic success was intrinsically tied to divine influence—one that required the harmonious and careful alignment of human effort with the sacred will of the gods, indicating that their fate was intertwined with the divine.

In a similar fashion, in ancient India, the sacred texts and rituals outlined in the revered Vedas place significant emphasis on the important role of wealth, known as artha, which is recognized as one of the four primary aims of life, collectively known as Purusharthas. However, wealth was not intended to be chased or pursued simply for its own sake; rather, it was regarded as an essential component necessary for the proper fulfillment of one's duty, referred to as dharma, and was also viewed as a crucial element in the quest for achieving spiritual liberation, or moksha. This comprehensive and holistic approach to wealth, which acknowledged and validated the need for material prosperity as a vital means to support a virtuous, meaningful, and balanced life, reflects a deep and sophisticated understanding of the intricate interplay that exists between the realms of economic success and spiritual well-being. It highlights how material wealth can be harmoniously integrated with one's moral obligations and spiritual aspirations.

In many societies throughout history, the act of offering wealth to the gods was seen as both a profound moral and a significant economic obligation that could not be overlooked. Such offerings were not merely symbolic gestures devoid of importance; rather, they were integral to the very functioning of the economy. By transferring wealth to the divine realm, communities firmly believed they could secure blessings that would, in turn, ensure not only a bountiful harvest but also protection against calamity and misfortune, and promote overall social stability. The reciprocal relationship between the mortal and the divine—where wealth was both generously given and richly received—created a continuous cycle of prosperity that sustained entire civilizations over generations, allowing them to thrive and flourish in an often unpredictable world. Thus, these acts of devotion and economic exchange were fundamental to the culture and survival of entire communities.

Money as a Symbol of Power and Divine Favor

The treatment of money as a significant symbol of divine favor and political power stands out as a recurring and prominent theme in the annals of ancient history. In various societies where wealth was heavily concentrated in the hands of a powerful elite, the ability to amass substantial riches was widely viewed as strong evidence of a person's or a state's exceptional and privileged relationship with the divine forces. This prevalent perception not only reinforced existing social hierarchies but also provided a robust moral justification for the unrestrained accumulation of wealth by rulers, nobles, and religious leaders alike. Within this dynamic, the correlation between financial prosperity and divine approval shaped the governance and spiritual narratives of these societies, further intertwining economic power with sacred legitimacy.

In ancient Rome, for example, the public treasuries, known as the Aerarium and the Fiscus, were magnificently housed within temples and served not only as functional financial repositories but also as profound symbols of the state's financial health and divine mandate. The grandeur of these treasuries was a vivid visual representation of the immense strength of the empire and the legitimacy of its rulers, which were deeply intertwined with their perceived relationship to the divine. Emperors often invoked the favor of the gods to explain their impressive military victories and the abundant wealth that flowed into the state treasury, suggesting a divine endorsement of their rule. The lavish and often ostentatious use of state funds in constructing monumental structures and sponsoring grand public festivals further reinforced the widely accepted idea that economic prosperity was a direct sign of divine blessing, linking the financial success of the empire to the favor of the deities they worshipped and creating a powerful narrative that supported their governance.

The sacred and vital role of money in these societies was profoundly reflected in their intricate legal and social structures. Laws that governed commerce, inheritance, and taxation were frequently intertwined with religious edicts, thereby underscoring the entrenched belief that all financial matters were under the jurisdiction of divine law. In this multifaceted way, money transformed into a significant tool not solely for economic exchange but also for enforcing social order, establishing stability, and legitimizing authority. Those individuals and entities who controlled wealth were perceived as the earthly agents or representatives of divine will, which placed enormous responsibility on them to maintain balance, harmony, and ensure the welfare, prosperity, and security of the community as a whole. This intricate relationship between money, law, and divine oversight shaped the foundation of societal interactions and governance.

This intricate interweaving of economic success with spiritual legitimacy had far-reaching and profound implications for social cohesion and stability within communities. Wealth, in this context, was not merely regarded as a private asset owned by individuals; it was instead seen as a vital communal resource that carried with it numerous responsibilities and obligations to the larger society. The thoughtful redistribution of wealth—whether facilitated through the implementation of public works, acts of charity, or generous religious offerings—was considered an essential and integral part of maintaining the delicate cosmic balance that underpinned the social order. In many historical cases, a failure to appropriately manage or equitably distribute wealth was interpreted by the populace as a clear sign of divine displeasure and dissatisfaction. This often led to significant social unrest, famine, or even the ultimate downfall and collapse of entire civilizations, demonstrating the critical importance of understanding wealth in a broader social and spiritual context.

The Transformative Impact on Social and Political Structures

The sacred treatment of money in ancient civilizations played a crucial role in shaping not only economic practices but also the broader social and political landscape that emerged during these times. The intertwining of wealth with divine favor created a complex system in which economic power acted both as a cause and an effect of social status. Rulers and elites who could command vast fortunes were often viewed as being chosen by the gods themselves, a perception that significantly helped to legitimize their authority and justify their privileged positions within society. This relationship between wealth and divinity reinforced social hierarchies and influenced the behaviors of individuals striving for power and recognition in their communities. As a result, the confluence of economics and spirituality played a fundamental role in the civilizations' evolution, affecting how people viewed their leaders and the established order.

This dynamic is vividly illustrated in the fascinating realm of the ancient world, where monumental architecture and elaborate rituals served as striking and tangible expressions of immense wealth and power. The grandeur of the Egyptian pyramids, for example, was not solely a testament to remarkable technological prowess—it was also a profound expression of the pharaoh's divine right to rule. The monumental scale of these structures, crafted with immense precision and care, symbolized the pharaoh's close connection to the gods and the afterlife. The accumulation of vast wealth in temple treasuries and royal vaults served to further reinforce the notion that material prosperity was a direct reflection of cosmic order and divine favor. Such potent symbolism was critical in maintaining the intricate social fabric, as it provided a shared narrative that united the populace under a common belief system, which in turn fostered social cohesion and collective identity among the ancient people.

Moreover, the sacred role of money frequently created a fertile environment where economic innovation was able to truly thrive and flourish. The stringent accounting practices that were established by ancient temple banks laid down the essential groundwork for increasingly sophisticated financial systems that would develop later on. The comprehensive and meticulous records that were kept on clay tablets in Mesopotamia, for example, not only ensured a high level of transparency and accountability but also allowed for the facilitation of complex transactions as well as the establishment of credit systems. This rational approach to managing wealth proved to be instrumental, playing a crucial role in the evolution of trade and commerce, ultimately leading to the intricate and expansive modern banking system that we know today.

The societal impact of this sacred approach to money can also be seen in the way that wealth was distributed and shared among the community members. In many ancient societies, the accumulation of wealth was not solely for personal gain; rather, it was accompanied by a deeply ingrained ethical imperative to give back generously to the community that supported individuals in their pursuits. This principle is evident in the rich concept known as "righteous wealth," in which prosperity was not just an end in itself but was viewed as a means to significantly support public welfare initiatives, fund important religious ceremonies, and provide for the needs of the less fortunate individuals within society. The enduring belief that wealth was a precious gift from the gods—and that it should be utilized primarily to benefit society as a whole—helped to foster a strong sense of collective responsibility that resonated not only among the wealthy but also across all social strata. This interconnectedness encouraged individuals to acknowledge their roles in uplifting others and contributed to a more cohesive social fabric.

The Logical and Analytical Underpinnings of Sacred Wealth

At its core, the sacred and significant role of money in ancient civilizations was not based solely on superstition or mere rituals; it was also grounded deeply in a logical and analytical understanding of fundamental economic principles. The ancient guardians of wealth understood that money, when managed wisely and judiciously, served as a powerful tool for fostering stability, ensuring overall prosperity, and promoting sustainable growth. Their sophisticated record-keeping practices, rigorous methods of accounting, and systematic approaches to resource management illustrate an early incarnation of economic logic that not only anticipated modern financial theories but also laid the groundwork for future economic systems. This intricate relationship between wealth and society reflected a keen insight into human behavior and the necessities of trade, which were as crucial then as they are today.

The deep reverence held for money in these ancient cultures was a profound recognition of its dual nature: as a practical tool facilitating exchange and as a significant symbol representing deeper metaphysical truths that govern life itself. The logical mind prevalent in the ancient world understood that wealth, especially when combined with ethical stewardship and responsible management, could serve as a powerful catalyst for societal transformation and upliftment. The very same principles that inspired the construction of majestic temples to honor the divine, as well as the creation of impregnable treasuries to safeguard riches, echo with striking intensity in today's sophisticated financial systems, even if they take on a more digital form. The timeless idea that wealth should be meticulously managed, transparently recorded, and equitably distributed among the populace is as valid, relevant, and essential now in our modern age as it was thousands of years ago in the ancient world.

Furthermore, the integration of economic success with spiritual legitimacy provided a compelling and persuasive argument for the centralized control of wealth and its distribution. By linking material prosperity with divine favor and approval, ancient societies skillfully crafted a system of accountability that was both moral and logical in its foundations. This dual framework, intertwining ethical considerations with practical governance, served as a crucial check against rampant greed and the unbridled accumulation of resources, ensuring that the immense power of wealth was balanced by a profound sense of duty and responsibility to the community. It is a logic and guiding principle that still deeply resonates in our modern discussions about corporate governance, ethical investing, and sustainable development in today's society, where the interplay between profit and responsibility is increasingly under scrutiny.

Persuading the Modern Mind: Lessons for Today

In today's ever-evolving world of digital currencies and rapidly growing decentralized finance, the lessons drawn from ancient civilizations are not only shocking but also profoundly relevant and insightful for our current era. The sacred role of money, which was once enshrined in grand temples and meticulously maintained treasuries, now finds its modern and intriguing counterpart in the digital realm of cryptocurrencies. These digital assets, like Bitcoin and others, represent not only a groundbreaking technological innovation but also a significant philosophical shift in how we choose to perceive and manage our wealth. Just as ancient societies revered and honored money as a divine gift bestowed upon them, modern investors are gradually beginning to view these digital assets as a new form of "sacred" wealth—untethered by the constraints of physical limitations and capable of transcending geographical borders and institutional boundaries. This transition reflects an awakening to the power and potential of digital currencies in our lives.

This paradigm shift profoundly challenges the very foundations upon which traditional finance has long been built. The centralized banks and government-controlled currencies that have dominated the financial landscape of the past are now being rigorously questioned by an emerging generation that truly values transparency, efficiency, and empowerment in their financial dealings. The ongoing digital revolution is not only advancing technology but also democratizing access to wealth in unprecedented ways, enabling individuals to confidently take control of their financial destinies in methods that were previously unimaginable and inaccessible. In this exciting new landscape, the core principles of ancient sanctuaries of wealth—trust, accountability, and ethical stewardship—are being thoughtfully reinterpreted and adapted for this transformative digital age.

Consider the remarkable rise of blockchain technology—a pioneering tool that embodies the ancient and enduring desire for transparent, tamper-proof record-keeping that has persisted through the ages. Just as clay tablets meticulously recorded transactions and agreements in ancient Mesopotamia thousands of years ago, today's state-of-the-art blockchain provides an immutable ledger, ensuring every digital transaction is secure, transparent, and verifiable. This powerful technology is not only a technical marvel of our time; it represents a logical extension of the centuries-old quest to manage wealth with unparalleled precision and integrity. The sacred financial traditions of the past are being reborn in an innovative digital form, and the implications for global finance and commerce are nothing short of revolutionary. It opens up new avenues for trust and accountability in a world where digital interactions are increasingly prevalent.

Moreover, the ethical dimensions of wealth that were central to ancient societies offer a profoundly powerful argument for fostering a more inclusive and equitable financial system in our present day. The concept that wealth should serve the collective good—a principle ardently championed by both ancient temple treasuries and modern ethical investing—resonates deeply within our society in an era marked by growing economic disparity and injustice. As we navigate the complexities of the modern world, we are increasingly compelled to ask ourselves challenging questions: How can we create a system that ensures financial success is not an exclusive privilege of the wealthy few, but rather is accessible to every individual and community? The answer may lie in a thoughtful and intentional revival of principles that have guided humanity for millennia—principles that recognize and treat wealth as a sacred trust, meant to be shared widely and stewarded responsibly for the benefit of all.

Challenging the Status Quo: An Argument for a New Financial Paradigm

The treatment of money as a profound symbol of divine power and prosperity in ancient civilizations was not merely a relic of the past; it represented a radical reimagining of the fundamental purpose of wealth itself. By intertwining economic success intricately with spiritual legitimacy, ancient societies crafted a complex system where money was regarded as both a practical tool for daily transactions and a sacred asset imbued with significant spiritual meaning. This captivating duality is the key to understanding the transformative potential and implications of digital assets in contemporary society today.

In the modern world we inhabit today, where financial systems are frequently criticized for being opaque, centralized, and exclusionary in nature, the ancient approach offers a refreshing and much-needed alternative. The logic behind this ancient wisdom is beautifully simple: wealth, when managed transparently and ethically, possesses the transformative power to uplift entire communities and foster social cohesion. Just as temples and treasuries once served as foundational pillars for economic stability, social order, and community trust, digital currencies now hold the remarkable potential to democratize access to wealth and empower individuals on an unprecedented global scale. In doing so, it can create avenues for equality, bridging the gaps that have long separated different socioeconomic classes and allowing for inclusive financial participation across various demographics.

This argument is not only logical but also remarkably persuasive. The very architecture of our modern financial system—constructed on intricate algorithms, decentralized networks, and transparent ledgers—echoes the enduring principles of trust and accountability that were so vital in ancient times. The shock is that while we have advanced considerably in technology, many of the foundational principles that governed ancient wealth management continue to be strikingly timeless. They serve as a poignant reminder that money is not an end in itself; rather, it is a means to achieve broader social, cultural, and spiritual goals that transcend mere transactions. Thus, as we navigate this complex modern financial landscape, it is crucial to remember these underlying principles that connect us to our past, urging us to use our resources in ways that nurture community and promote well-being for all.

Critics might contend that the ancient reverence for money was steeped heavily in superstition and ritual, seen as mere relics of a bygone era. However, a much closer and more logical examination reveals that these time-honored practices were grounded in practical necessities and societal needs. Ancient societies required reliable and effective systems to store, protect, and circulate wealth, and the sacred status of money provided a vital framework that was both morally compelling and economically effective for their communities. In our contemporary digital age, as we grapple with pressing issues of cyber security, increasing regulatory uncertainty, and persistent financial inequality, the lessons derived from these ancient practices offer a thoughtful blueprint for meaningful reform—a model that emphasizes the importance of transparency, collective welfare, and ethical stewardship in the realm of finance. By learning from the past, we can forge a more equitable and stable future in economic practices and philosophies.

Embracing a Sacred View of Wealth in the Digital Age

Today, as we witness the meteoric rise of cryptocurrencies and the ongoing digital revolution of money, it becomes increasingly imperative to draw thought-provoking parallels with the sacred traditions of the past. Money, which was once securely housed in ancient temples and treasuries, is now rapidly evolving into digital assets that are secured and protected by sophisticated cryptography and decentralized networks. Yet, despite these advancements, the fundamental challenge remains strikingly the same: to create a modern financial system where wealth is managed in a responsible manner, equitably distributed, and maintained with a deep sense of communal responsibility and ethical oversight. It is essential to recognize that as the landscape of finance transforms, the core values of trust, respect, and social equity must persist in guiding our approach to wealth management.

This perspective is not merely nostalgic—it represents a powerful and rational argument for rethinking the very foundations of modern finance. The ongoing digital revolution presents an extraordinary opportunity to reclaim and revitalize the ethical dimensions of wealth that were once so deeply revered and cherished by earlier generations. By thoughtfully integrating the timeless principles drawn from ancient sanctuaries of wealth into the design and structure of new financial systems, we can create and build a future where prosperity is genuinely shared among all individuals. In this envisioned future, power will be decentralized, allowing for a more equitable distribution of resources. Moreover, trust will not be vested in a single institution or entity but rather distributed across an entire network of participants, fostering collaboration and resilience. This transformative approach has the potential to change the way we perceive wealth and financial systems today.

In practical terms, this means carefully designing a wide range of sophisticated financial instruments, various digital currencies, and robust investment platforms that prioritize transparency and ethical management above all else. It also means fully embracing cutting-edge technologies that ensure every single transaction is recorded and verifiable—mirroring the meticulous and diligent record-keeping practices of ancient temple banks from centuries ago. Beyond these technological advancements, it further means fostering a culture where financial success is not measured solely by individual accumulation of wealth and resources but instead by the collective advancement and well-being of society as a whole, promoting a fair and just financial ecosystem that benefits everyone.

The modern investor, equipped with the profound knowledge of ancient practices and wisdom, can clearly see that the true and enduring power of money lies not merely in hoarding wealth for personal or individual gain, but rather in its vast potential to generate broad-based prosperity for all. Just as the ancient temples served as crucial centers of communal wealth and collective resources, the decentralized networks of today hold the promise to democratize access to essential financial resources, breaking down the long-standing barriers that have historically separated the wealthy from the rest of society. Through these innovative systems, individuals from diverse backgrounds can participate in financial opportunities that were once exclusively available to a select few, fostering an inclusive economy where everyone has a chance to thrive.

The Logical, Analytical Case for Sacred Wealth

The logical foundation for treating money as something sacred and valuable is both compelling and enduring. It is rooted in the understanding that wealth, when managed correctly and responsibly, serves as the powerful engine of progress and advancement. Ancient civilizations clearly recognized that financial stability was not only essential for their societal growth, but also critical for the flourishing of their communities. They developed systems and structures that were both pragmatic and practical, while being imbued with a profound sense of higher purpose and significance. This understanding paved the way for future generations to appreciate the importance of treating financial resources with respect and care.

Consider the meticulous and detailed records that were diligently kept by the priests of ancient Mesopotamia, etched carefully onto clay tablets with remarkable precision and clarity.

These records were not merely a testament to the remarkable administrative genius of the ancient world but also represented an early expression of a fundamental truth that still resonates today: that wealth, when managed transparently and effectively, becomes a powerful catalyst for innovation, creativity, and social stability within the community. In modern times, blockchain technology serves a very similar purpose—a highly decentralized ledger system that ensures that every digital transaction is meticulously recorded and made accessible, providing the transparency, integrity, and security that ancient civilizations strived so hard to achieve through their record-keeping practices.

Moreover, the integration of spiritual legitimacy with economic success provided a natural check on the often excessive accumulation of wealth that can occur within societies. In ancient times, the prevailing belief that money was a divine gift imposed a profound moral obligation on those who were fortunate enough to possess it. This robust ethical framework played a crucial role in ensuring that wealth was not concentrated solely in the hands of a select few, but instead was utilized to benefit the community and society as a whole. While modern capitalism has frequently been criticized for fostering significant inequality and disparity among individuals, the ancient approach serves as a powerful reminder that a more balanced and equitable system of wealth distribution is not only desirable but also entirely achievable with the right mindset and values in place.

This argument is further fortified by the examination of numerous historical examples. The remarkable success of ancient economies—ranging from the expansive and formidable empires of Egypt and Rome to the flourishing city-states of Greece—was fundamentally underpinned by financial systems that honored and respected both the practical and the sacred dimensions of wealth. These intricate systems enabled extraordinary feats of engineering, art, and culture, all of which were consistently supported by a robust, transparent, and accountable approach to managing wealth. The logical conclusion drawn from this analysis is abundantly clear: when wealth is treated not merely as a practical resource for transactions and commerce, but also as a sacred trust that carries a broader responsibility, it possesses the immense power to transform societies for the better, improving the lives of all individuals within them.

Persuading the Modern Mind: A Call for Ethical Finance

In a world where digital currencies are evolving and rapidly redefining the boundaries of finance, it becomes increasingly essential to revisit and draw lessons from the past. The sacred, multifaceted role of money in ancient civilizations is not merely an archaic relic—it serves as a powerful, analytical framework that can effectively guide us in building a more ethical and inclusive financial system today. Understanding the historical context of money, its value, and its cultural significance can indeed provide invaluable insights for contemporary economic challenges and opportunities.

Imagine a future where financial institutions operate not merely for profit but as dedicated stewards of communal wealth, prioritizing the well-being of society as a whole. Envision a reality where every transaction is not only transparent but also easily accessible, every ledger remains open for scrutiny, and the accumulation of wealth is seen as a sacred responsibility entrusted to individuals rather than a mere mark of personal greed and ambition. This is the visionary promise of the digital revolution: to democratize wealth in ways previously thought unattainable, to systematically break down the enduring barriers of inequality that have plagued our societies, and to restore a deep sense of moral purpose and ethical responsibility to all economic activities, fostering an environment where compassion and community welfare are at the forefront of financial endeavors.

The argument for such a system is not only logical but also highly persuasive. In today's world, modern technology provides us with an array of tools that enable us to implement a multitude of the practices that made ancient wealth sanctuaries remarkably effective. With the advent of blockchain, artificial intelligence, and decentralized networks, it becomes entirely possible to create financial systems that boast security and transparency comparable to those ancient temples, while also being scalable enough to effectively meet the diverse needs of a rapidly globalizing economy. This initiative is far from utopian idealism; rather it stands as a practical and entirely achievable goal that builds upon centuries of economic evolution and human ingenuity. It is a testament to how far we have come, and what future advancements can bring us in our journey toward financial integrity and inclusiveness.

Investors and policymakers alike must be thoroughly persuaded that the future of finance indeed lies in ethical stewardship that prioritizes the greater good. By wholeheartedly embracing a model that not only values transparency and accountability but also emphasizes communal responsibility, we can create and foster a robust environment where wealth ceases to be a source of division and instead serves as a powerful catalyst for meaningful progress. The sacred traditions and wisdom of the past offer compelling and persuasive evidence that such a system is not only possible but has been historically proven to work effectively. It is a model that fundamentally demands a complete rethinking of our current approach to money, urging us to thoughtfully combine technological innovation with a deep-seated respect for the moral and ethical dimensions inherent in the concept of wealth. This blend can lead to a finance system that promotes fairness and equity, ensuring that prosperity is shared and uplifted within communities.

A Revolutionary Synthesis: The Intersection of the Sacred and the Digital

The fusion of ancient sacred principles with modern digital technology represents a groundbreaking and transformative leap in the evolution of money that we have never seen before. It is an idea that is not only shocking but also exhilarating—a true revolution that challenges and redefines every preconceived notion we hold about what money is and what it can become in our society. As we stand at the precipice of a new era in finance and economic interactions, the timeless lessons of the past resonate with greater significance than ever before, guiding us as we navigate this profound change in monetary systems.

The sacred role of money in ancient civilizations, with its profound emphasis on divine favor, ethical stewardship, and the welfare of the community, presents a striking counterpoint to the often impersonal and profit-driven models that characterize modern finance today. By reintroducing these timeless values back into the digital realm of contemporary finance, we can work towards creating a system that not only is more efficient and secure but also embodies principles that are inherently more just and humane. This holistic approach encourages a balance between financial growth and the consideration of societal impacts, promoting a financial landscape that is as much about community well-being as it is about wealth accumulation.

The digital revolution of money is not merely a technological shift; it is, in fact, a profound philosophical transformation. This evolution challenges us to rethink and redefine wealth in a manner that transcends mere material accumulation and focuses on the deeper, more spiritual dimensions of true prosperity. By contemplating these new definitions, it offers an insightful pathway to envisioning a future where economic success is assessed not solely by the size of one's financial portfolio but also by the positive and lasting impact that such wealth has on society as a whole. This broader perspective encourages a collective understanding of prosperity that emphasizes community well-being and the interconnectedness of our financial actions with societal values.

The synthesis of the sacred and the digital is both a logical progression and an inevitable outcome of our evolving societal structures. The same fundamental forces that inspired ancient civilizations to construct temples, build treasuries, and establish centers of worship—trust, accountability, a shared sense of purpose, and the collective need for communal prosperity—are actively at work today in shaping the development and implementations of decentralized financial systems. These innovative systems, which are powered by cutting-edge blockchain technology and smart contracts, possess the remarkable potential to fundamentally change not only the ways in which we store and transfer value but also the deeper ways in which we perceive, conceive, and ultimately interact with wealth itself.

As you navigate the intricate complexities of the modern financial landscape, it is important to remember that the sacred role of money in ancient civilizations offers us a timeless blueprint for fostering ethical finance practices. This serves as a powerful reminder that, at its very core, money is fundamentally a tool for creating order, promoting fairness, and ensuring the collective welfare of the community. The challenge that we face now is to harness this ancient wisdom and thoughtfully integrate it with the groundbreaking innovations of the digital age. This integration is crucial for building a future where wealth can serve as a significant force for good, positively impacting lives and enhancing the well-being of all individuals within society.

Reawakening the Sacred Spirit of Wealth

In conclusion, the detailed exploration of how ancient civilizations treated money as a sacred symbol reveals a profound, undeniable truth: wealth, when managed with reverence, respect, and ethical responsibility, has the remarkable power to transform societies in significant ways. The rituals, offerings, and various cultural practices that intertwined economic success with spiritual legitimacy were not simply arbitrary—they were carefully constructed systems that provided much-needed stability, fostered innovation, and promoted social cohesion within communities. These systems of value demonstrate how money was not just a tool for trade but a reflection of deeper beliefs and values, influencing human behavior and interactions on multiple levels.

In today's rapidly evolving digital landscape, as cryptocurrencies and the expansive realm of decentralized finance are actively redefining the very essence of what money truly means, we find ourselves with a unique opportunity to reflect and learn from the wisdom of the past. The sacred and significant role that money held in ancient civilizations provides us with a powerful and logical framework that challenges us to fundamentally rethink our current financial paradigms. It encourages us to deeply consider and question not only how we can maximize profit for individual gain, but also how we can create and build a financial system that genuinely honors and promotes the collective well-being of our society as a whole, ensuring a more equitable future for everyone involved.

The shocking, mind-blowing, and rigorous analysis of ancient practices reveals that when money is regarded as a divine trust, it elevates our understanding of economic activity from being just a mere transactional process to becoming a meaningful, community-driven endeavor that fosters growth and connection among individuals. This profound insight serves as a call to all modern investors, policymakers, and engaged citizens alike: to collectively reawaken the sacred spirit of wealth and to create a financial future that is not only as ethically sound as it is technologically advanced but also deeply rooted in shared values and a vision for sustainable development. Every action taken in the name of finance has the potential to impact lives and communities, pushing us toward a more inclusive economic framework that respects the dignity of all individuals involved.

By seamlessly integrating the timeless wisdom derived from ancient wealth sanctuaries with the groundbreaking innovations and disruptive technologies of the digital era, we can successfully forge a new and promising path forward—a path where true economic success is no longer solely defined by measures of unbridled greed and profit, but rather by the collective empowerment of communities, fostering collaboration, and the earnest pursuit of a higher, more just purpose that benefits all involved.

In this transformative and dynamic new age of finance, we should take a moment to draw significant inspiration from the sacred roles that money held in the thriving ancient civilizations of the past. Let us fully harness the analytical rigor, logical reasoning, and deep ethical principles that guided our ancestors so skillfully as they built magnificent temples and impressive treasuries. In doing so, we can create a world in which wealth serves not only as a powerful tool for individual success but also as a vital cornerstone of meaningful societal progress and collective advancement. This approach can redefine our understanding of financial systems and encourage a more holistic and equitable economic landscape.

The journey to rediscovering the sacred role of money is not just an academic exercise; rather, it represents a profound revolution of both thought and practice. This journey dares to challenge us to see beyond the cold, sterile numbers and the relentless profit margins that dominate modern finance today. Instead, we are urged to embrace a much more expansive vision of wealth—one that is vibrant, holistic, and life-affirming in every sense. It is a passionate call to transform our economic systems into structures that are as awe-inspiring and enduring as the ancient sanctuaries that once beautifully dotted the landscapes of our ancestors. By reimagining the purpose and significance of money, we can pave a new path toward a future where financial systems serve to uplift humanity rather than merely filling individual coffers.

As we boldly move forward into this brave new world, let the invaluable lessons of the past serve as a bright guiding light for our journey ahead. Let the profound divine symbolism of wealth inspire us to construct robust financial systems that are secure, transparent, and inherently equitable for all participants involved. Most importantly, let us recognize together that the true power of money lies not merely in its accumulation alone, but in its immense potential to foster genuine prosperity, promote lasting justice, and create a meaningful legacy of collective empowerment that benefits future generations.

This section has illuminated the sacred and pivotal role of money in civilizations past—a role that intricately intertwined economic success with spiritual legitimacy in profound ways that continue to echo and resonate in our modern understanding of wealth today. The deep reverence for money, as seen through the eyes of our ancestors, challenges and provokes us to rethink how we interact with, manage, and distribute wealth in contemporary society. In the evolving digital revolution that is continuously reshaping our world, these ancient principles offer not only a solid foundation for ethical finance but also a bold and logical framework for a future where the true spirit of wealth can be reclaimed, celebrated, and shared abundantly by all individuals across different walks of life.

Embrace this revolutionary perspective wholeheartedly. Allow it to profoundly transform your overall approach to finance while inspiring you to construct a future where wealth serves not as a barrier but rather as a powerful bridge—a bridge that intricately connects the sacred past with a bright, promising, and inclusive digital future filled with opportunities for everyone.

Section 3: Rituals, Offerings, and the Worship of Wealth

In the ancient world, wealth was not merely an economic resource—it was a sacred symbol intricately woven into the very fabric of religion and society itself. The intricate rituals, grand offerings, and elaborate ceremonies of bygone civilizations reveal a shocking and mind-blowing perspective on financial abundance that persists through time. Money was revered not only for its practical utility but also as a divine blessing bestowed upon the faithful, serving as a tangible and meaningful connection to the gods. This section delves deeply into the multifaceted cultural practices that seamlessly integrated financial prosperity with various spiritual and social rituals, exposing how ancient societies celebrated wealth as a sacred endowment granted to them by divine forces. These practices illustrate the profound belief that monetary success was intertwined with spiritual well-being, acting as a bridge between earthly existence and the celestial realm.

The Sacred Language of Offerings

Imagine entering a grand and opulent temple, where every single element has been meticulously designed to invoke a deep sense of reverence and awe. In these hallowed and sacred halls, offerings of valuable gold, shining silver, and other precious commodities were not simply given out of mere generosity or kindness; rather, they were a profound form of communication with the divine, a bridge between the mortal and the celestial realms. The act of presenting wealth as an offering was both a sacred ritual and a significant transaction—a strategic way to curry favor with the mighty gods. This ritual ensured that blessings would flow back to the devoted giver in the abundant forms of prosperity, fertile crops, thriving livestock, and divine protection against misfortune and calamity. Through this intricate dance of giving and receiving, worshippers sought to forge a lasting bond with the deities they revered.

In ancient Mesopotamia, for example, the intricate ritual of offering grain and various precious metals was meticulously recorded on clay tablets, which served as both a historical account and a testament to the religious practices of the time. These offerings were widely believed to appease the gods, who in turn would ensure a bountiful harvest and offer protection from potential calamities that could threaten their existence. The underlying economic logic was straightforward yet profound: by demonstrating piety and deep devotion through material sacrifice, individuals and entire communities were able to secure divine favor that would not only sustain their livelihoods but also multiply their wealth. This practice was not mere superstition; it was a well-considered and rational strategy in an unpredictable world where natural cycles, combined with catastrophic disasters, could upend livelihoods in an instant, leaving families and entire villages at the mercy of fate.

Ceremonies as Economic Catalysts

Rituals and ceremonies played a crucial role as significant economic catalysts within ancient cultures. These events served as grand public spectacles that not only reinforced social bonds among the community members but also celebrated the collective successes achieved as a unit. Take, for instance, the lavish and vibrant festivals of ancient Greece, which brought people together in joyous celebration. During these festive occasions, public feasts and athletic contests were generously sponsored by the wealth of the state, highlighting the importance of community and shared prosperity. These grand events were meticulously designed to showcase the overall prosperity of the polis while also demonstrating the divine favor that was believed to be bestowed upon it by the gods. In these rich cultural contexts, money was not merely a medium of exchange to be hidden away; instead, it was actively paraded in magnificent processions, offered up in sacred ceremonies, and joyfully celebrated as a tangible sign of communal health and well-being. Such rituals reinforced the interconnectedness of the community, providing both spiritual nourishment and economic vitality, thereby weaving a tapestry of cultural identity through shared experiences and collective joy.

In Athens, the remarkable Panathenaic Festival emerged as a grand and momentous event that deftly combined deep religious observance with an unwavering sense of civic pride. Citizens from all walks of life would gather in large numbers to offer lavish gifts to Athena, the revered goddess of wisdom and warfare, firmly believing that her divine blessings would ensure both victory and prosperity for their city. The festival was not only a religious occasion but was also marked by culturally significant processions, captivating dramatic performances, and highly competitive athletic competitions—each serving as a demonstration of the wealth of the city and a testament to its flourishing economy and social cohesion. The logical and philosophical underpinning of these rituals was strikingly clear:

by openly and communally celebrating wealth together, the society reinforced the profound idea that prosperity was a shared, sacred asset, one that ultimately benefited everyone within the community and fostered a sense of unity among its citizens.

In a similar fashion, during ancient times in India, the Vedic rituals included the concept of artha (wealth), representing one of the four primary objectives of human life. Wealth was understood not as a final goal in isolation but rather as a vital tool to foster and support dharma (duty), guiding individuals to ultimately achieve moksha (liberation) from the cycle of birth and death. The rituals performed were highly intricate, featuring a multitude of offerings, the recitation of sacred hymns, and elaborate ceremonies designed to link material prosperity with spiritual advancement. The essential act of giving was regarded as a moral obligation, firmly believed to ensure that wealth circulated throughout the community in such a way that it enriched the lives of many rather than being hoarded by a select few individuals. This practice fostered social harmony and reinforced the interconnectedness of community members, with the understanding that true prosperity benefits all rather than a limited portion.

The Intertwining of Wealth and Divine Favor

The very essence of wealth in ancient civilizations was profoundly and intricately intertwined with the powerful concept of divine favor. Rulers and elites of these societies often justified their substantial accumulation of riches as a clear and evident sign of the gods' blessings upon them. In Egypt, for example, the pharaoh was seen as the earthly embodiment and representation of divine order and authority. The vast treasuries of monumental temples, like those at Karnak and Thebes, were not only repositories of immense material wealth but also served as powerful symbols of the pharaoh's close and cherished relationship with the divine realm. Gold, viewed as imperishable and radiant, became synonymous with the ideas of eternal life and divine power. The lavish adornments worn by kings and the opulent offerings made in temples were constant reminders to the people that wealth was a gift from the gods—a sacred trust to be managed carefully, wisely, and with true benevolence. The interplay between wealth and divinity was not merely economic but deeply cultural, influencing art, architecture, and the spiritual lives of the citizens.

In ancient Rome, the intricate relationship between wealth and divine favor was remarkably pronounced and deeply ingrained in the social fabric of the empire. The state treasury, known as the Aerarium, was strategically housed within the grand confines of temples, thereby serving as a clear and visible testament to both the empire's unparalleled prosperity and the legitimacy of its rulers. Emperors frequently invoked the favor of powerful deities like Jupiter, using their supposed blessings as explanations for military victories and the overall flourishing of the Roman state. The citizens were expected to witness such divine intervention reflected in their daily lives. Public works, which were generously funded by the treasury, were presented not merely as infrastructure but as significant manifestations of divine benevolence. The considerable spending on monumental structures, impressive aqueducts, and magnificent public buildings was consequently regarded as more than an exercise in civic pride; it was also a sacred and ritualistic act aimed precisely at consolidating divine support while simultaneously ensuring the uninterrupted and continued flow of wealth into the empire's coffers.

This intriguing fusion of economic success with religious legitimacy provided a powerful and compelling argument for the centralization of wealth within society. It established a moral order in which the accumulation of riches was seen as a clear sign of divine approval and favor. However, it also created a complex framework in which the concentration of wealth could inevitably lead to significant social inequality among the populace. The sacred nature of money served not only to justify the power of the elite but also imposed an ethical obligation on these wealthy individuals to use their considerable wealth in a manner that benefits the wider community. This duality—where wealth was perceived as both a symbol of divine favor and a vital responsibility—continues to remain one of the most compelling, yet challenging legacies of ancient financial practices that we reflect upon today.

Rituals: The Dynamics of Wealth Worship

Rituals served as vibrant, living expressions of the ways in which ancient cultures vibrantly celebrated and worshiped wealth in all its forms. These rituals were not mere traditions; they represented performative acts that transformed ordinary economic transactions into deeply sacred ceremonies rich with meaning. Each ritual was a carefully choreographed event, meticulously designed to invoke the favor of the gods, reaffirm social order, and renew the entire community's collective commitment to prosperity and abundance in their lives.

The Processional Display of Wealth

One of the most dramatic and striking examples of wealth worship can be found within the elaborate and grand processions of ancient India and Greece. These captivating processions were not merely parades; they represented grand, ritualistic displays where immense wealth was publicly exhibited as a potent sign of divine favor and approval. In many rich Indian traditions, kings and numerous wealthy patrons would lead these impressive processions, carrying offerings that included gold, luxurious silk, and fragrant spices to temples dedicated to various deities. Such public demonstrations were meticulously designed to exhibit not only the patron's deep piety but also the entire state's remarkable prosperity. The visible transfer of substantial wealth from the mortal realm to the divine sphere was widely believed to secure divine blessings that would, in turn, contribute to the enrichment and well-being of the entire community, sowing seeds of abundance for all its members.

In Greece, the spectacular and vibrant processions were an integral and cherished part of festivals, particularly within the context of the renowned Panathenaic celebrations. Enormous and beautifully crafted statues of the goddess were meticulously adorned with an array of precious offerings and symbols of devotion. These revered statues were carried through the bustling streets of Athens, transforming the city into a grand stage for a remarkable display of civic unity and divine favor among the populace. The majestic procession served as a significant reminder to every citizen and resident that wealth and prosperity were not solely for the purpose of individual accumulation, but rather represented a collective asset that tightly bound the community together in harmony and shared purpose. The experience fostered a sense of belonging and mutual responsibility among all participants, reinforcing the idea that their fortunes were interwoven in the rich tapestry of their shared cultural and spiritual life.

Ceremonial Offerings: A Ritual of Reciprocity

The act of making ceremonial offerings was perhaps one of the most intimate and logical aspects of wealth worship that one can imagine. In these significant rituals, individuals and entire communities would typically sacrifice a portion of their wealth—whether it be in the form of livestock, various types of grains, or precious metals—as a carefully considered offering to the gods. The underlying logic of such acts was one of reciprocity and mutual exchange: by giving away a portion of what one had carefully amassed over time, the giver believed they were ensuring that the divine forces would return that wealth to them in even greater measure, thus reinforcing the cycle of gift and return. This reciprocal relationship between humans and the divine illustrates a deep cultural understanding of prosperity and gratitude.

For example, in ancient Mesopotamia, the intricate temple rituals involved the generous offering of precious silver and grains to the revered gods. These sacred offerings were meticulously recorded in detailed ledgers, as the dedicated priests believed that such acts of devotion were absolutely essential for maintaining the delicate cosmic balance. In return for these gifts, the gods would extend their blessings in various forms, including fertile land, bountiful harvests, and an overall state of prosperity for the community. This reciprocal relationship between the people and their deities was not merely a spiritual act; it evolved into a highly practical economic strategy that benefited everyone involved. It ensured that wealth circulated continuously within the society, thereby preventing economic stagnation and actively encouraging growth for future generations.

The Role of Sacrifice and Penance

In numerous ancient cultures around the world, wealth was intricately intertwined with the concepts of sacrifice and penance—often seen as essential means to atone for past misdeeds and to restore the delicate balance of cosmic order. The prevailing belief was that material abundance, particularly when it was not rightfully earned through righteous and honorable means, could ultimately lead to divine retribution or punishment from the gods. Consequently, making sacrificial offerings became a crucial practice, serving as a powerful way to cleanse one's wealth. This act of sacrifice helped individuals realign their material possessions with the moral and ethical standards that were deeply dictated by religious doctrine, ensuring that wealth was not just a symbol of status but also a reflection of virtue and righteousness.

In ancient Israel, for example, the sacrificial system meticulously outlined in the Torah was deliberately designed to ensure that wealth was used properly, in accordance with divine law and moral codes. Sacrifices were made not only as expressions of genuine gratitude but also as vital acts of penance, helping to restore the inherent balance between human ambition and divine justice. This profound concept underscored a logical understanding that the accumulation of wealth carries with it a significant moral responsibility—a principle that continues to echo in modern debates about economic inequality, wealth distribution, and ethical investing strategies. The implications of this sacrificial system stretch far beyond its historical context, influencing contemporary discussions related to social justice and responsible economic practices.

Social Rituals: Celebrating Wealth as a Community Endeavor

While individual offerings and sacrifices played a crucial role in the overall practice of worship, it is important to understand that the worship of wealth was far more than a solitary endeavor; it was ultimately a communal affair that involved the entire community. Public rituals and grand festivals were carefully designed to celebrate and honor collective prosperity while reinforcing the vital social bonds among the members of the community. These significant events were always lavish, theatrical, and deeply symbolic in nature, serving as a constant and powerful reminder of the community's shared destiny and interconnected lives. It was during these occasions that the values and aspirations of the community were openly expressed, creating a sense of unity that transcended individual contributions.

Festivals: The Pinnacle of Public Wealth Celebration

In ancient Greece, festivals, including the famous Dionysia and the Panathenaic, played a significant role in not only paying homage to the gods but also prominently showcasing the immense wealth and remarkable cultural achievements of the various city-states. These grand festivals were sprawling events that seamlessly integrated theatrical performances, intense athletic competitions, and deeply rooted religious ceremonies, all of which were generously funded by the state treasury along with contributions from private patrons. The elaborate and vibrant festivities served as a resounding testament to the tremendous prosperity of Athens, acting as a visible manifestation of the divine favor that the city enjoyed. These public celebrations of wealth during such festivals functioned as both an economic booster for the city and an essential means to foster a deep sense of civic pride among its citizens.

Similarly, in ancient Rome, public games and lavish feasts were an integral and regular feature of civic life, deeply embedded in the social fabric of the time. Emperors would graciously sponsor gladiatorial contests, highly anticipated chariot races, and grand theatrical performances, all to celebrate military victories, commemorate divine blessings, and reinforce their authority. These spectacular events, often hosted in monumental amphitheaters like the iconic Colosseum, were financed not only by the state treasury but also significantly by wealthy elites. These wealthy individuals perceived such spectacles as a magnificent opportunity to display their own piety, generosity, and social status. The sheer scale and grandeur of these events were nothing short of mind-blowing, meticulously designed to captivate the awe-struck masses while affirming the established social order. They served as a potent reminder that wealth was not merely a personal asset for the few, but rather a communal resource that could be employed to uplift society as a whole and maintain public harmony in the bustling Roman Empire.

The Intersection of Wealth, Art, and Culture

Beyond festivals, art and architecture played an immensely significant role in the intricate worship of wealth across various cultures and civilizations. Monumental structures, intricate sculptures, and elaborate murals were meticulously commissioned to honor the gods and to commemorate the enduring prosperity of the community as a whole. In ancient Egypt, the lavish and detailed decoration of grand temples with shimmering gold, rare precious stones, and meticulously carved hieroglyphs served as a direct expression of both wealth and deep divine reverence. These remarkable artistic achievements were not merely displays of opulence and grandeur; they were thoughtfully imbued with rich symbolism and served a vital purpose to educate the populace about the profound interconnectedness of wealth, power, and spirituality that underpinned their society.

The fusion of art and wealth created an enduring and remarkably rich cultural legacy that has continued to resonate through the ages. In ancient Greece and Rome, the patronage of the arts was regarded not merely as a privilege, but as a fundamental moral duty that the wealthy held toward their society. Public buildings, intricate statues, and grand monuments funded by private wealth were conceived and perceived as offerings to the gods, as well as significant contributions to the collective well-being of the community.

This long-standing tradition established a commendable precedent for ethical wealth—one that underscores the belief that prosperity should be consciously and responsibly utilized to enhance the cultural, aesthetic, and social fabric of the society at large. The beauty, artistry, and durability of these remarkable creations continue to inspire awe and admiration, serving as everlasting reminders of a time when wealth was profoundly celebrated as a sacred blessing, meant to elevate and enrich the lives of all people.

The Logical Imperative of Wealth Worship

At first glance, the ritualistic worship of wealth may seem steeped in superstition or archaic ritual, seemingly detached from modern understanding. Yet, when examined more closely through the lens of logic and necessity, these practices reveal a profound and intricate understanding of economic dynamics and social cohesion that still resonates today. In ancient times, the management of wealth was not merely about mere accumulation of resources—it was fundamentally about maintaining balance within communities and ensuring sustainability in a world full of uncertainties and challenges. This approach to wealth also fostered a sense of responsibility and shared destiny among individuals, highlighting the interconnectedness of society as a whole.

The meticulous record-keeping and highly organized systems of temple banks and treasuries serve to illustrate an early and sophisticated form of financial literacy that was both analytical in nature and practical in application. These systems were deliberately designed with the purpose of preventing the hoarding of wealth, thus encouraging its circulation among the people, and providing a measure of accountability to the community. The sacrificial rituals and public offerings served, in effect, as mechanisms specifically intended to regulate the economy, thereby ensuring that wealth was not only accumulated but used effectively to promote sustainable growth and prevent systemic imbalances within the society. In modern terms, these practices can be viewed as early regulatory measures—methods and practices that ensured the integrity and stability of the financial system long before the formal advent of state regulation and corporate governance structures that we are familiar with today.

Furthermore, the ethical dimension of wealth worship—where the accumulation of vast riches was perceived as a divine mandate—created a compelling and powerful incentive for social responsibility within the community. When wealth was regarded as a sacred trust bestowed upon individuals, those who managed and controlled it were compelled to act not only in their own self-interest but also for the greater benefit of the community at large. This logical framework, which tied individual prosperity to collective well-being, provided a crucial counterbalance to rampant greed and unrestrained self-serving behavior. By ensuring that economic success was invariably linked to communal welfare and long-term stability, it fostered a sense of duty and accountability among wealth holders, encouraging a more equitable distribution of resources.

The Persuasive Power of Rituals in Shaping Society

The rituals, offerings, and ceremonies practiced by ancient cultures were not only economically functional, serving practical purposes in daily life—they were deeply persuasive in nature. These rituals played a crucial role in shaping public consciousness, significantly influencing how individuals perceived their roles within society and their complex relationship to wealth and prosperity. By linking financial abundance and material success directly with divine favor, these rituals effectively instilled a profound sense of purpose, responsibility, and duty that transcended mere individual ambition and personal gain. Individuals were encouraged to see their financial circumstances as intertwined with their spiritual beliefs and communal obligations, resulting in a cohesive society united by shared values and goals.

This persuasive power can truly be observed in the way ancient societies mobilized their collective energy during significant times of crisis and joyous celebration. The communal rituals that were practiced provided a structured and meaningful way for people to express their gratitude, seek divine intervention, and engage in the essential maintenance of social order. These gatherings served as a unifying force that brought together disparate and diverse communities under a shared belief system—a deep belief that prosperity was not only a blessing bestowed upon them but also a responsibility that came with it. Through these practices, individuals found solace in their connections with one another and reinforced their commitment to the greater good of the community.

In modern society, where financial markets are frequently perceived as impersonal and detached from essential human values, the profound lessons of these ancient rituals are both shocking and illuminating in nature. They serve to remind us that money, particularly when treated as a sacred asset to be respected, possesses the remarkable power to inspire cooperation among individuals, generate social goodwill among communities, and create a genuine sense of belonging among diverse groups. The argument extends beyond the notion that wealth should be celebrated—it underscores that the way we manage, utilize, and distribute wealth can significantly shape the very character and essence of our communities, ultimately affecting the well-being and unity of society as a whole.

Modern Echoes: The Rebirth of Sacred Wealth in the Digital Age

In today's dynamic financial landscape, which is increasingly driven by the ongoing digital revolution and the rapid advent of cryptocurrencies, we can observe a fascinating echo of many ancient practices focused on wealth worship and accumulation. Digital assets like Bitcoin and Ethereum are not only celebrated for their impressive market value and fluctuations but also for their immense potential to disrupt and transform traditional economic systems that have long been established. The blockchain technology, renowned for its immutable ledger and its inherently decentralized nature, serves as a modern incarnation of the sacred record-keeping once meticulously performed on clay tablets by ancient temple priests who zealously safeguarded vital transactions and financial agreements. This striking similarity highlights a continuity in human behavior towards wealth documentation and preservation, illustrating how technological advancements continue to shape our financial practices.

Modern investors are increasingly starting to recognize the profound and symbolic power of digital wealth in today's shifting financial landscape. The explosive growth of various cryptocurrencies, coupled with the ongoing and increasing integration of decentralized finance (DeFi) into the broader global economy, signifies a remarkable rebirth of the sacred traditions held by ancient societies—albeit in a radically new and innovative form. Just as ancient civilizations held the belief that wealth was a divine blessing bestowed upon them, today's visionary pioneers of digital finance perceive cryptocurrencies as powerful instruments of a newly emerging economic order. This new order has the potential to liberate capital from the often-restrictive constraints imposed by central banks and governmental control, leading to a financial ecosystem that offers greater freedom and autonomy to individuals. As this evolution continues, it reflects both a transformation in how wealth is created and managed and a significant shift in the perception of financial value itself.

The persuasive and compelling narrative of wealth as a sacred trust is increasingly finding its way into several modern investment philosophies and practices. Ethical investing, corporate social responsibility, and sustainable finance are contemporary movements that deeply echo the ancient belief that wealth should truly be managed for the benefit of the common good. The principles of transparency, accountability, and communal benefit—so central to the rituals and traditions of ancient wealth—are now being intricately integrated into cutting-edge financial technologies and innovative investment strategies. This modern interpretation of wealth encourages investors to consider the broader impact of their financial decisions, fostering a sense of stewardship that aligns with both ethical values and the evolving needs of society.

A Call for Reawakening the Sacred Spirit of Wealth

As we grapple with the persistent challenges of modern finance today—such as rising inequality, economic instability, and the troubling erosion of trust in centralized financial institutions—we would do well to actively revisit the ancient traditions and practices that once celebrated wealth as a powerful and sacred force. The various rituals, meaningful offerings, and profound ceremonies of the past provide a compelling and rich blueprint for reimagining our contemporary approach to money as we navigate the complexities of the digital age. These historical practices compel us to ask and reflect upon several hard-hitting questions: How can we ensure that the wealth we generate benefits everyone in our society? How can we create financial systems that are not only efficient but also ethical and just? And how can we effectively harness the immense power of technology to democratize prosperity while also preserving the essential moral imperatives that once guided the thoughtful stewardship of wealth throughout history? This reflection could lead to a deeper understanding and guiding framework for a more equitable economic future.

The logical, analytical, and persuasive case for a sacred view of wealth is more relevant now than ever before in our rapidly changing world. In a time where financial decisions are made at unprecedented speeds, often dictated by algorithms and the prevalence of digital currencies, there arises an urgent need for comprehensive systems that are not only technically sound and efficient but also possess ethically robust foundations. The ancient rituals of wealth worship, rich in symbolism and practical wisdom, serve as powerful reminders that money transcends mere commodification; it encapsulates our collective values, beliefs, and aspirations. As we navigate through these complex financial landscapes, it becomes essential to integrate deeper meanings into our approach toward wealth, ensuring that our transactions and wealth management reflect a commitment to meaningful principles that can benefit society as a whole.

Reawakening the sacred spirit of wealth means reintroducing fundamental principles of fairness, transparency, and accountability into our financial systems. It involves not only challenging the entrenched status quo of profit-driven capitalism but also actively embracing progressive models of economic success that prioritize the welfare of everyone involved. Whether it be through the ethical management of digital assets that respect the integrity of all participants, the thoughtful implementation of decentralized financial systems that empower individuals and communities, or the reinvigoration of public rituals that collectively celebrate communal prosperity and shared abundance, the time has certainly come to transform our perception of wealth and how we effectively manage it.

In conclusion, the various rituals, offerings, and forms of worship dedicated to wealth in ancient civilizations were not merely relics from a primitive past—they represented sophisticated, well-structured systems that intricately wove together economic success with spiritual legitimacy. These practices provided a comprehensive framework for understanding wealth not just as an individual possession but as a vital communal resource, essentially a divine trust that carried with it both enormous potential and significant responsibility. As we find ourselves at the crucial intersection of the sacred and the advancing digital world, the invaluable lessons gleaned from these ancient practices can serve as a powerful, mind-blowing guide to crafting a future in which wealth is not solely quantified in terms of dollars and cents, but also assessed by the overall well-being and prosperity of communities. This perspective encourages a holistic view where economic prosperity aligns with ethical considerations and collective flourishing.

By embracing the sacred and time-honored traditions of wealth worship, we can creatively reimagine the structure of modern finance in a way that is not only technologically advanced but also profoundly humane and compassionate. In this digital age, where cryptocurrencies and decentralized finance are dramatically redefining our economic reality and landscape, the invaluable wisdom of the past serves as a guiding beacon of hope and a powerful call to meaningful action. It challenges and encourages us to build a financial system that honors and respects the rich legacy of our ancestors—a system in which every act of wealth accumulation is not merely viewed as individual gain but is also recognized as an act of communal enrichment and deeper spiritual fulfillment. This holistic approach invites us to create a future where financial activities resonate with purpose and connect us to each other and our shared history.

Let us then embark on this remarkable journey together with a renewed and invigorated sense of purpose and determination. Let us learn and draw wisdom from the ancient rituals and traditions that once celebrated wealth as a sacred and divine blessing, and may those timeless and enduring practices inspire us profoundly to create a financial future that is not only equitable but also transparent, and truly transformative in ways we have yet to envision. The sacred role of money in the civilizations of the past is not merely history—it stands as a powerful, analytical, and insightful blueprint for shaping the future. And in this envisioned future, where digital assets increasingly reign and financial systems continue to evolve with unprecedented speed, the true and ultimate measure of wealth will be found not solely in material abundance but also in the shared and collective prosperity of all humanity.

Embrace this inspiring vision, and allow it to profoundly guide your deeper understanding of money, the essence of power, and the importance of community. The rituals, offerings, and acts of worship dedicated to wealth are not mere relics of a bygone era—they are vibrant, living legacies that continue to shape our world in significant ways. In the vast digital revolution of today, the sacred spirit of wealth eagerly awaits rediscovery, poised to illuminate a meaningful path toward a more just, equitable, and prosperous future for all of humanity, fostering a stronger sense of connection and shared purpose.

Section 4: Money as a Symbol of Power and Divine Favor

Throughout the vast stretches of history, wealth has constituted far more than just a practical tool for trade and commerce—it has represented the very embodiment of power, legitimacy, and divine blessing in multifaceted ways. Across diverse cultures, the accumulation of riches has served as an exceptionally potent symbol of status and authority, intricately woven into the intricate fabric of societal hierarchies and classes. In this extended section, we aim to explore a shocking and mind-blowing account of how money was not merely a medium of exchange but was also revered and interpreted as a profound sign of divine favor in various societies throughout time. Furthermore, it acted as a key marker of social order and stratification, establishing a critical factor in legitimizing political authority and governance. We will delve deeply into the reasoning, logic, and analytical frameworks that ancient civilizations used to effectively link material wealth with notions of cosmic order and divine principles, arguing that this intricate relationship was as pragmatic in nature as it was deeply spiritual. The interplay between wealth and power reveals the profound complexities that shaped human societies, influencing everything from social norms to governance structures.

The Divine Seal of Wealth

Imagine a world where every golden coin, every precious jewel, was not merely a mark of human achievement but a visible and constant sign of the gods' blessing. In ancient Egypt, for example, gold was held in high esteem and considered the "flesh of the gods," a sacred material intertwined with the divine. Pharaohs were not simply rulers; they were living divine intermediaries, chosen specifically to lead by the will and decree of the deities. Their immense wealth—accumulated over decades and stored in vast temple treasuries and royal vaults—was interpreted unequivocally as a direct manifestation of divine favor and approval. When a pharaoh adorned himself with gold, intricate jewelry, and precious stones, it was far more than mere self-adornment; it was a powerful public declaration of his sanctified authority. The opulent treasures housed within the magnificent temples of Karnak and Thebes weren't just riches stored away; they were profound symbols of cosmic order and eternal life, reinforcing the pharaoh's claim that his very power was divinely sanctioned and gifted by the gods themselves. Such treasures served to remind the populace of their ruler's divine right to lead and the interconnectedness of their earthly existence with the celestial realm beyond.

In a similar fashion, in the vast and influential region of ancient Mesopotamia, the accumulation of significant wealth within temple treasuries was regarded as not only a matter of state but also one of deep religious importance. Temples that were devoted to powerful gods such as Inanna and the great Enlil operated much like the earliest forms of banks, effectively safeguarding the precious resources that belonged to entire communities and societies. The substantial wealth housed within these temples was regarded as sacred in nature, a divine trust granted by the gods themselves, which demanded to be managed with the highest degree of care and responsibility. To possess such wealth was viewed as a clear indication that a ruler or priest was indeed favored by divine forces, thereby legitimizing their authority and control over their subjects. Consequently, wealth in this context became both a significant reward and an essential requirement for effective leadership, intertwining the lines between piety, governance, and social standing within the historical framework of Mesopotamian civilization.

Wealth and Legitimacy in Ancient Empires

In ancient Rome, money held a profoundly symbolic role in determining social standings and political hierarchies, influencing the lives of its citizens in multiple ways. The Roman state treasury, known as the Aerarium, was housed impressively within a grand temple, which directly linked the management of state finances with religious practices and beliefs. This physical connection highlighted the belief that the prosperity of the state was intimately tied to the favor of the deities. Roman emperors, understanding the importance of wealth in the public eye, took extensive measures to demonstrate that their riches were not only substantial but also indicative of divine blessing. They organized and sponsored extravagant public games, constructed magnificent monuments, and ensured the lavish distribution of food and coinage during significant festivals as a means of engaging their constituents. These acts of apparent benevolence were not simply displays of generosity or kindness; rather, they were far more calculated and strategic, carefully orchestrated exhibitions of power designed specifically to affirm and consolidate the emperor's status as the chosen representative of the gods on Earth. In this elaborate socio-political theater, wealth became a tool for manipulation and control, further entrenching the existing hierarchies within Roman society.

For instance, when an emperor generously funded the construction of a new aqueduct or a grand forum, the public came to see these monumental projects as undeniable evidence that the ruler was favored and blessed by the divine forces. In return for this demonstration of benevolence and grandeur, the people were expected to offer their unwavering loyalty and steadfast support, as it was widely believed that the prosperity of the entire empire was intrinsically linked to the emperor's divine mandate and authority. In essence, the more lavish and public the display of wealth and resources, the more it confirmed and solidified the ruler's legitimacy in the eyes of the citizens. This intricate blend of material opulence and profound religious symbolism created a powerful feedback loop: wealth reinforced power, and power, in turn, consistently attracted even more wealth, creating a cycle that served both the emperor and his subjects.

Across the vast expanse of the magnificent Persian Empire, very similar dynamics were at work throughout its extensive territories. The powerful Persian kings maintained enormous treasuries in major cities like the grand Persepolis and the historical Susa. These impressive treasuries were not hidden away but were proudly showcased as irrefutable evidence of the king's extraordinary ability to command resources from an empire that magnificently spanned three vast continents. The illustrious Persian rulers often attributed their numerous military conquests and remarkable economic successes to the favor of Ahura Mazda, who was revered as the supreme god in the ancient religion of Zoroastrianism. This divine endorsement of opulence not only elevated the ruler's status significantly among his subjects but also provided a robust moral justification for the vast, and often shocking, disparities in wealth that characterized the society. In a society where divine favor was paramount and highly sought after, the accumulation of vast riches by the elite classes was seen as both a natural phenomenon and a necessary condition—a reflection of the deeply entrenched cosmic order believed to govern their lives and fortunes.

Cultural Narratives and the Power of Symbolism

Beyond the tangible accumulation of wealth, ancient cultures meticulously crafted rich and intricate narratives that elevated money to a near-mythical status in society. These narratives were deeply embedded in a variety of literature, expressive art forms, and public rituals that brought communities together. They collectively served as a persuasive argument that wealth was not just a mere object, but rather a divine endowment—a sacred gift that validated a person's or a particular group's social standing, cultural significance, and political authority in the world. This interplay between wealth and societal perception created an enduring legacy that has influenced generations, shaping the values and beliefs of many civilizations throughout history.

In ancient India, the concept of artha (wealth) was regarded as one of the four Purusharthas, or fundamental aims of human life. According to Vedic tradition, wealth was not simply to be hoarded or pursued for its own sake but was envisioned to be employed in a righteous and ethical manner, primarily supporting dharma (duty) and ultimately paving the way to moksha (liberation). The sacred texts of India are replete with inspiring stories of kings and wise sages whose fortunes were perceived as a direct manifestation of divine favor and blessing. Their immense wealth, often displayed through magnificent palaces adorned with intricate carvings and elaborate ceremonies filled with music and dance, was a powerful sign that the cosmic order was aligned in their favor. Such narratives served as both a source of inspiration and an important regulatory mechanism—encouraging those in power to utilize their resources wisely, generously, and justly, lest they incur the wrath and disfavor of the gods they revered. By understanding this connection between wealth and morality, individuals were reminded that true prosperity came not from greed but from a commitment to the greater good.

Greek mythology provides us with vibrant and fascinating examples of how money can serve as a powerful symbol of divine favor and endorsement. The narratives surrounding deities such as Zeus, who held sway over the destinies and fortunes of mortals, along with Athena, revered not solely as the goddess of wisdom but also as the esteemed patron of wealth and prosperity, emphasized the belief that economic success was not merely a result of individual effort but was deeply intertwined with divine blessings. In numerous Greek city-states, the acquisition of wealth was celebrated as a collective asset, something that had the power to uplift the entire community, or polis, fostering a sense of shared prosperity. Various forms of expression, including grand festivals, elaborate public ceremonies, and the commissioning of monumental architecture, were all manifestations of this profound belief in the relationship between wealth and the divine. The Parthenon, characterized by its detailed sculptures and opulent decoration, transcended its identity as merely an architectural achievement—it stood as a powerful visual testament to Athens' wealth, prosperity, and divine favor. This magnificent structure served as a continual reminder to its citizens that the abundance enjoyed by the city was indeed a blessing bestowed by the gods, reinforcing the central role of divine influence in the lives of the people and their economic endeavors.

The Logical and Analytical Foundations of Divine Wealth

While the symbolism of wealth in ancient times was undoubtedly steeped in deep religious belief and various cultural practices, it also had a profoundly logical and analytical foundation that cannot be overlooked. Ancient societies recognized that wealth was not merely a display of material possessions, but rather an essential component for the stability and growth of the state. They understood that resources had to be meticulously managed, fairly distributed, and responsively protected in order to sustain long-term prosperity for both individuals and communities. The intertwining of economic abundance with divine favor was, in many respects, a rational response to the uncertainties and challenges of the natural world, as well as a means to ensure social cohesion and order. This recognition of wealth's vital role in society underscores the complex relationship between economics, spirituality, and the governance of resources in ancient civilizations.

In an era when agriculture was at the mercy of the unpredictable and often harsh whims of nature—droughts that parched the earth, sudden floods that inundated fields, and relentless pests that devastated crops were frequent and alarming threats—the careful and reliable management of resources became a matter of utmost survival for the communities. Temples and treasuries emerged as essential institutions that provided a centralized, trusted system for storing and safeguarding wealth, which was crucial for the welfare of the society. This system ensured that resources could be efficiently allocated during critical times of need, thereby preventing crises. The rituals of offering and sacrifice were not merely arbitrary traditions or customs; they were practical and calculated measures designed specifically to regulate the flow of wealth and maintain a delicate balance between surplus abundance and dire scarcity, preserving stability and order in the community.

Furthermore, by effectively linking wealth to divine favor, ancient societies established a comprehensive system of accountability that deeply influenced social structures. When rulers and elites were perceived as being particularly favored by the gods, their actions came under intense moral scrutiny from the community. If they misused their wealth or failed to distribute it justly among the populace, it was believed that the gods would withdraw their favor, resulting in catastrophic consequences for the entire state. This belief system provided a significant and logical check on the unchecked accumulation of wealth, ensuring that it was used appropriately to promote social welfare and benefit the community as a whole, rather than leading to personal indulgence or selfish pursuits. The analytical minds of ancient economists—though their ideas were not articulated in the modern terms we use today—were deeply concerned with devising complex systems aimed at maximizing collective prosperity while minimizing social discord. They understood the delicate balance required to maintain harmony within society, shaping their discourse around principles that would benefit the many rather than just a select few.

Wealth, Status, and the Social Order

The potent association between money, status, and divine favor held significant implications for the complex structures of societal hierarchies. In virtually every ancient civilization, those who wielded control over wealth were granted a special status—a status that was traditionally regarded as clear evidence of their divine right to govern. Wealth emerged as both a visible and tangible marker of power, effectively distinguishing the elite from the common populace while simultaneously reinforcing the established social order. The interplay of these elements shaped the behavior, aspirations, and interactions of individuals within these societies, leading to a deeply entrenched system where financial prowess equated to elevated social standing, thereby affecting decisions made by rulers and citizens alike.

In ancient Egypt, the profound connection between divine power and wealth played a pivotal role in shaping the authority of the pharaoh. The act of accumulating gold, precious jewels, and various treasures was not merely indicative of economic success but was also deeply entwined with the pharaoh's cosmic mandate. This connection elevated the status of the ruler, weaving together concepts of material wealth with spiritual significance. The grand and lavish tombs, along with sophisticated burial practices, including the remarkable construction of the pyramids, were intricately designed to ensure that the pharaoh's wealth would follow him into the afterlife. This practice aimed to perpetuate his divine status and reinforce his authority, extending his reign beyond the mortal realm into eternity. The intersection of wealth and spirituality cultivated a societal system where economic power remained inextricably linked to the idea of an eternal legacy, influencing not only the lives of the pharaohs but also the culture and beliefs of ancient Egyptian civilization as a whole.

In ancient Rome, the extravagant public display of wealth through grandiose architecture and elaborate public works not only beautified the city but also reinforced the intricate social hierarchy present in society. The enormous expenditures on monumental structures, intricate aqueducts, and lavish public games were not merely generous acts for the enjoyment of the people; rather, they were intentional strategic moves meticulously designed to signal the emperor's and senator's divine endorsement and their superior societal status. Wealth, in this particular context, transformed into a striking public spectacle—a powerful tool employed to both awe the masses and intimidate potential rivals. The delicate social order of the time was diligently maintained through a continuous and ostentatious display of economic power that was both logically constructed and deeply symbolic in nature.

In a similar manner, in ancient China, the accumulation and lavish display of wealth were perceived as significant markers of both moral virtue and social legitimacy. The imperial examinations, which played a pivotal role in determining the success of scholars and government officials, were not merely tests gauging intellectual capability but also vital instruments through which considerable wealth and elevated social status were conferred upon individuals. Those who emerged victorious in these examinations were celebrated not solely for their extensive knowledge but also for their remarkable ability to manage resources judiciously, a characteristic that was widely believed to be divinely ordained by the heavens. The emperor's court operated as a grand stage where opulence and status were prominently showcased, reinforcing the rigid hierarchical structure that governed Chinese society for countless centuries and establishing a deep connection between wealth, power, and moral righteousness.

Persuading Modern Minds: The Legacy of Divine Wealth

The persuasive power of linking wealth to divine favor remains remarkably potent even in contemporary discourse. Although modern society may have largely abandoned overt religious justifications for the existence of economic power and success, the underlying logic and belief systems that support this connection endure. In our current era, as we grapple with complex questions of economic inequality, corporate governance, and the principles of ethical investing, the ancient association between wealth and legitimacy offers a compelling and powerful framework for rethinking how we value, allocate, and distribute our resources. This enduring belief influences not only individual aspirations but also societal attitudes towards success and the moral implications of wealth accumulation.

In our current era, wealth is often measured in purely quantitative terms—by the size of one's bank account, the market capitalization of a company, or the returns on investment. However, this narrow view fails to capture the broader, qualitative dimensions of wealth: its potential to create social well-being, foster innovation, and promote collective progress among communities. The ancient perspective, which regarded wealth as a sacred trust, a symbol of divine favor, and a means to uplift society, invites us to consider a more holistic approach—one that integrates ethical stewardship with economic success, ensuring that wealth serves not merely as a personal asset but as a catalyst for positive societal change and the well-being of all. By viewing wealth in this light, we can rethink its role in our lives and in the world, emphasizing responsibility and purpose over mere accumulation.

Imagine a world where corporations are not solely driven by the relentless pursuit of profit but are also held significantly accountable for their considerable social impact. A world where financial success is not just celebrated through cold quarterly reports but is instead acknowledged through vibrant public rituals that honor and recognize the profound contributions of wealth to the broader societal welfare. The ancient model of wealth worship serves as an intriguing blueprint for such a transformative paradigm—a comprehensive system where transparency, accountability, and a deep commitment to communal benefit are held paramount. In this envisioned reality, businesses would be seen not merely as entities chasing revenue but as integral parts of the social fabric that weave communities together for the greater good.

The Analytical Case for a Sacred View of Wealth

When we analyze the role of money in ancient societies through a logical lens, the argument for its sacred status becomes deeply compelling and thought-provoking. Wealth was not merely arbitrarily associated with divine favor; it represented a rational and strategic response to the numerous challenges involved in managing scarce resources within unpredictable environments. The meticulous and organized record-keeping, the structured ceremonial rituals, and the public display of wealth all served significant practical purposes: to ensure that resources were allocated efficiently and effectively, that power among individuals and groups was checked and balanced, and that economic stability was maintained in a world often fraught with uncertainties. This multifaceted approach to wealth not only highlighted its importance but also illustrated the intricate relationship between economy and spirituality in ancient contexts.

Consider the intricate and sophisticated accounting systems that were developed by ancient temple administrators in various civilizations. These systems were meticulously designed to track every grain of wheat, every ounce of silver, and every precious coin of gold. The remarkable precision with which these detailed records were maintained reveals an early recognition and understanding of the importance of transparency and accountability in effectively managing wealth. Such logical rigor and attention to detail laid a crucial groundwork for modern financial practices. This early form of accounting not only influenced the development of our contemporary financial systems but continues to significantly inform present-day approaches to auditing, fiscal responsibility, and corporate governance. The legacy of these ancient systems can still be felt in how we manage and track resources today.

Moreover, by thoughtfully integrating crucial moral and ethical dimensions into the effective management of wealth, ancient societies were able to create a self-regulating system that promoted fairness and responsibility. The widely held belief that wealth was viewed as a divine trust imposed a significant moral imperative on those who possessed and controlled it. This perspective provides a compelling argument for the modern world, where the unchecked and often excessive accumulation of wealth frequently leads to pronounced social and economic disparities that can destabilize communities. The logical conclusion we can draw is that a system which values wealth not only for its material benefits but also for its profound potential to foster social good, equity, and community resilience is far more sustainable and just in the long run. Such a philosophy encourages a more balanced approach to wealth management, prioritizing the needs of society as a whole.

Divine Favor as the Ultimate Status Symbol

In every ancient society, the concept of wealth served as the ultimate status symbol—a visible and tangible representation of both divine favor and the pinnacle of human excellence. This powerful symbolism acted as a significant tool for reinforcing complex social hierarchies and legitimizing the authority held by rulers and elites within the community. Wealth transcended mere economic power; rather, it stood as a powerful declaration of cosmic order and divine sanction over individuals and their standing in society. It was through this lens of wealth that one's place in the social structure was both determined and maintained.

For instance, in the classical world, the public display of immense wealth through lavish monuments, intricate statues, and grand public buildings was not merely an act of vanity or pride. It was, in fact, a carefully calculated strategic move intended to signal that the ruler was divinely chosen by the gods—a profound concept that greatly elevated his authority and provided a moral justification for all of his actions. The awe-inspiring magnificence of the Roman Forum, the breathtaking grandeur of the Parthenon, and the undeniable opulence of Persian palaces all served as visual evidence of divine favor and approval. These magnificent structures were designed specifically to awe, inspire, and persuade the populace that the accumulation of extraordinary wealth was not only a divine right but also a societal obligation that everyone should aspire to achieve.

In contemporary society, even though the clear and overt religious symbolism may have diminished over time, the core concept that associates wealth with status and legitimacy still endures robustly. Various entities, including large corporations, governmental bodies, and private individuals, persistently utilize wealth as a significant indicator of success and social standing. The noticeable shift, however, is that modern wealth is primarily quantified through various forms of digital currencies, fluctuations within stock market indices, and expansive global asset portfolios. Despite these evolutions in how wealth is measured, the essential logic underpinning these perceptions remains largely unchanged: wealth continues to be regarded as a substantial reward for individual excellence and hard work, while also serving as a symbol that one is favored by unseen forces that lie beyond the control of mere mortals.

Social Hierarchies and the Moral Imperative of Wealth Distribution

The ancient view of wealth as a symbol of divine favor extended beyond mere accumulation of riches—it also emphasized the responsible distribution of that wealth among the community. It was considered a sacred duty for the wealthy individuals to ensure that their prosperity and abundance truly benefitted not just themselves but the community as a whole. This profound moral imperative regarding wealth distribution was deeply embedded in the social structures and religious beliefs of ancient cultures, shaping their values and practices surrounding prosperity and generosity. Individuals with wealth were often seen as stewards of their resources, obligated to use their riches for the greater good, reflecting the intertwined nature of prosperity and duty.

In many ancient societies, the practice of wealth redistribution was commonly carried out through various acts of charity, the establishment of public works, and the celebration of communal festivals. The fundamental idea was that prosperity should be shared among members of the community, and that the accumulation of wealth carried true virtue only when it significantly contributed to the overall welfare of society at large. This important ethos was clearly reflected in the religious rituals and public ceremonies that often accompanied acts of wealth accumulation. For instance, some of the opulent public festivals held in Athens and Rome were generously financed by both the state and wealthy patrons, symbolizing the overarching idea that wealth was considered a communal asset meant for everyone, rather than merely a private possession belonging to a select few individuals.

The ancient system of wealth distribution offers a compelling and rational ethical counterpoint to contemporary capitalist structures, which are frequently criticized for their tendency to foster inequality and to concentrate power in the hands of a small elite. By examining the principles of wealth worship practiced in ancient societies, we can envision a financial system where success is measured not solely by the accumulation of wealth by individuals but rather by the collective benefits that such wealth can bring to the whole of society. This idea represents a persuasive argument for both modern policymakers and investors alike: that true prosperity is realized when wealth is not hoarded by a select few but distributed in a manner that uplifts and enriches the entire community, ensuring that everyone has the opportunity to thrive and succeed. By redistributing wealth thoughtfully and equitably, we can pave the way for a more inclusive and fair economy that values the contributions of all its members, enhancing social cohesion and fostering a sense of shared responsibility for the well-being of one another.

Persuading the Modern Mind with Ancient Wisdom

As we find ourselves at a pivotal crossroads of rapid technological innovation and significant economic transformation, the enduring lessons derived from ancient civilizations emerge as both astonishing and deeply relevant to our current circumstances. The revered and sacred role of money in ancient societies—where wealth was not only a compelling symbol of divine favor but also a distinguishing marker of social status and a crucial moral imperative for the greater welfare of the community—provides us with a powerful, logical framework that can inspire a thorough rethinking of modern finance and its implications.

Today, as digital currencies and decentralized finance continue to reshape the global economy in profound ways, we are presented with an unprecedented and remarkable opportunity to reclaim the ethical dimensions of wealth that were once so revered and respected in our societies. The evolution of modern technology, from blockchain innovations to advancements in artificial intelligence, provides us with the essential tools needed to build financial systems that are not only transparent and secure but also equitable in nature, much like the ancient temples and treasuries that stood as symbols of trust and fairness in their communities. The significant challenge for us now is to thoughtfully integrate these timeless principles of equity and justice with cutting-edge innovation to successfully create a future where wealth is not seen as a source of division or inequality but rather as a firm foundation for collective empowerment and prosperity for all.

The modern investor, along with policymakers and engaged citizens, must thoughtfully ask themselves: How can we effectively build and shape a financial system that not only honors the sacred and time-honored traditions of wealth but also fully embraces the vast opportunities afforded by the digital age? The answer, it seems, lies in a fundamental reimagining of our approach to money itself—a significant shift from a purely materialistic viewpoint of wealth to one that genuinely recognizes its tremendous potential as a powerful catalyst for promoting social good. By revisiting and understanding the rituals, offerings, and forms of worship surrounding wealth found in ancient cultures, we are afforded valuable insights into how we can structure and design modern financial systems that are not only ethically sound, but also highly efficient in serving the needs of today's interconnected world. This holistic view will help us create a more just and equitable financial landscape.

In our current era, characterized by the widening of economic disparities and the eroding trust in centralized institutions, the ancient model of viewing wealth as a divine blessing presents a much-needed beacon of hope. This perspective challenges us to rethink what it truly means to be wealthy and compels us to understand that the genuine power of money extends far beyond mere accumulation. Instead, it lies significantly in its remarkable ability to foster social cohesion, support vital public welfare initiatives, and promote groundbreaking innovation within communities. The sacred view of wealth strongly urges us to develop and create systems that not only prioritize profit generation but also diligently pursue the distribution of prosperity. These systems should function in a manner that genuinely benefits all members of society, ensuring that economic growth translates into improved quality of life and opportunity for everyone, rather than being concentrated in the hands of a privileged few.

The Analytical Backbone: Logic, Reasoning, and Divine Economics

When examined thoroughly through the precise lens of logic and deep analysis, the ancient worship of wealth cannot be dismissed as mere superstition—it represents a sophisticated and complex system of economic regulation and management. Ancient temple banks and treasuries, established in various cultures, were meticulously built on enduring principles of accountability, transparency, and ethical stewardship in financial matters. The rigorous and diligent record-keeping practices of these institutions, inscribed carefully on durable clay tablets and preserved through the ages for future generations, demonstrate a profound early understanding of the pressing need for systematic financial management and organization. This intricate framework surrounding wealth was not simply symbolic; it played a vital role in the governance and sustainability of ancient economies and societies.

This analytical approach was not only essential but also incredibly crucial in a world where resources were often scarce, limited, and unpredictable. By instituting meaningful rituals of offering and sacrifice, ancient societies managed to create a feedback mechanism that ensured that wealth was continually cycled back into the community at large. This proactive method effectively prevented the hoarding of resources by individuals and promoted a sense of economic stability within the entire society. In modern terms, this concept is quite akin to the contemporary idea of sustainable growth—ensuring that wealth is not merely generated but also systematically reinvested in a manner that fosters and promotes long-term prosperity for all members of the community. This cycle of giving and receiving ultimately encourages a healthier economic environment where collaboration and mutual support thrive.

Furthermore, the integration of both moral and ethical dimensions into the practice of wealth management provides a vital logical check on the potential excesses and abuses associated with economic power. The widespread belief that wealth itself is a divine trust continues to impose a natural limitation on its unregulated accumulation. Those individuals who find themselves favored by the gods or the forces of good fortune are expected to act not only wisely but also responsibly in regard to their financial resources. This well-established logical framework presents a compelling argument in support of contemporary financial reforms: a system that genuinely values ethical stewardship, responsibility, and communal benefit is not only morally superior but also much more sustainable over the course of time. By fostering such values, we can create a financial ecosystem where the interests of the community and the principles of good governance are prioritized, ensuring a legacy of balanced prosperity for future generations.

Reinventing Modern Finance with Ancient Principles

Today's financial world is often characterized by rapid transactions, high-frequency trading, and a relentless pursuit of profit at almost any cost. While these developments have certainly led to significant economic growth and advancements in technology, they have also resulted in increased volatility, pronounced inequality, and a growing sense of disconnection from the broader social fabric that once held communities together. In this complex landscape, the ancient model of wealth worship calls out to us, challenging society to reintroduce a sense of sacred responsibility and ethical consideration back into the heart of modern finance. It urges us to reflect on what it truly means to create value, not only for ourselves but for the greater good of all.

By drawing on the profound wisdom of the past, we can vividly envision a financial system in which money serves not merely as a means of exchange but emerges as a powerful symbol of trust, stability, and communal well-being among all people. Imagine what it would be like if corporations, governments, and financial institutions operated under the same ethical principles that once guided the ancient custodians of wealth with integrity and respect. Envision a system that would prioritize transparency, accountability, and the equitable distribution of resources—essential principles that are desperately needed and sought after in today's increasingly complex global economy. Such transformations could foster a renewed sense of community and shared purpose, enhancing the quality of life for individuals and generations to come.

Digital technologies such as blockchain present a tangible and revolutionary way to implement these ancient ideals in our contemporary society. With blockchain, every transaction, no matter how large or small, is meticulously recorded on an immutable ledger that cannot be altered or erased. This provides an unprecedented level of transparency and security that ancient temples and their financial practices could only dream of achieving in their time. This technological innovation mirrors the extraordinarily meticulous record-keeping of temple treasuries, which were crucial for ensuring that wealth was managed effectively and in a manner that is both efficient and ethically sound. In doing so, it offers a powerful modern solution to age-old problems—an innovative way to reclaim the sacred and revered nature of money in a world that is increasingly driven by rapid digital innovation and transformation. By harnessing these advanced technologies, we may find a profound connection to our past while simultaneously redefining our future financial practices.

The Persuasive Argument for a Sacred Financial Future

The persuasive power of the ancient view of wealth lies profoundly in its remarkable ability to effectively bridge the significant gap between material success and ethical responsibility. It serves as a powerful call to reimagine our economic systems so that they are not solely seen as profit-driven enterprises, but instead, as vital vehicles for promoting social good and improving the welfare of the community. The shocking and mind-blowing practices of wealth worship in ancient civilizations present a compelling argument for envisioning a future where financial success is measured not just in purely monetary terms, but more importantly in the positive and meaningful impact that it has on society and the lives of individuals within it.

For modern investors, this perspective presents a compelling and powerful incentive to look well beyond short-term gains and carefully consider the broader implications of their financial decisions. It challenges the longstanding conventional wisdom of merely accumulating wealth for personal benefit alone, urging a significant shift towards a more inclusive, equitable model of true prosperity. In this reimagined future, every act of wealth creation is not just seen as a personal achievement but is accompanied by a sincere commitment to the common good—a vision where financial systems are meticulously designed to uplift communities, support underserved populations, and foster sustainable growth that benefits all stakeholders involved. This holistic approach not only enhances individual wealth but also contributes to a flourishing society as a whole.

This argument stands not only as logical but also as deeply persuasive and compelling in its essence. It is firmly grounded in centuries of profound human experience and reinforced by the timeless principles that have governed ancient societies throughout history. By wholeheartedly embracing the sacred role of money in our lives, we can effectively build a financial system that is not only innovative but also profoundly humane—one that values transparency at its core, promotes accountability among individuals and institutions, and prioritizes the welfare and prosperity of all individuals within our society.

A Call to Embrace the Sacred Spirit of Wealth

As we reflect on the various rituals, diverse offerings, and deep worship associated with wealth that have shaped civilizations throughout history, we find ourselves confronted with a profound and undeniable truth: money is not merely a means of exchange or a simple transactional tool—it is a powerful symbol of divine favor and a crucial instrument for building a just, equitable, and prosperous society. The ancient, time-honored practices of wealth worship, with their intricate ceremonies, rich traditions, and ethical mandates, offer a thoughtful blueprint for rethinking modern finance in a manner that is both rational and deeply inspiring. This reflection invites us to reconsider our values and priorities in relation to wealth, urging a harmonious balance between financial success and spiritual fulfillment in contemporary society.

In our current era, where digital currencies and decentralized finance are fundamentally revolutionizing the way we perceive and manage money, the invaluable lessons of the past are more relevant than ever before. The sacred role of wealth in ancient cultures profoundly challenges us to reimagine our financial systems—not merely as cold, impersonal markets driven solely by profit, but rather as dynamic, ethical frameworks that actively nurture and promote the collective well-being of society as a whole. This shift in perspective urges us to consider how we can align our financial practices with values that prioritize sustainability, community support, and long-term social benefits, ensuring that our economic systems serve the greater good and empower individuals and communities alike.

The logical, analytical, and persuasive arguments advocating for a sacred view of wealth compel us to wholeheartedly embrace a transformative future where financial success is intricately intertwined with a deep sense of social responsibility. As modern technology significantly provides us with unprecedented tools to effectively manage, distribute, and grow wealth, we find ourselves facing a remarkable opportunity to create a system that truly honors the divine trust that money once symbolized throughout history. This is not merely a call to return to the past, but rather an earnest invitation to learn from it—to thoughtfully integrate the timeless principles of transparency, accountability, and ethical stewardship into the cutting-edge innovations of the digital age that define our current era. Through this integration, we can inspire a new paradigm that redefines our relationship with wealth, encouraging us to view resources not just as currency, but as a means to foster community, cultivate compassion, and promote collective well-being.

The ancient rituals of wealth worship serve as a profound reminder that economic prosperity is not an ultimate goal in itself but rather a means to achieve a higher purpose that transcends mere financial gain. These traditions challenge us to think beyond individual accumulation of riches and to reflect on how our wealth can positively contribute to the greater good of society. By fostering a sense of communal benefit, they advocate for a radical vision of finance—one that is inclusive and equitable, efficient yet compassionate, ethical in its practices while simultaneously being innovative in its approach to wealth distribution and utilization.

Let this profound exploration of the sacred and vital role that money plays in the tapestry of civilizations serve as a beacon of hope and an urgent call to action. It stands as a powerful reminder that, even within a world increasingly driven by high-speed digital transactions and relentless, often chaotic market fluctuations, the fundamental human values of trust, responsibility, and community remain as crucial and essential as ever. The ancient perspective on wealth is not only shocking but also deeply inspiring—a testament to the enduring power of money as a potent symbol of divine favor and societal order, reflecting our intrinsic human desires and societal structures.

Embrace this vision deeply. Reawaken the sacred spirit of wealth that once guided entire civilizations throughout history, and allow it to inspire you passionately to build a future where financial success is measured not just in dollars and cents, but more importantly in the positive impact it has on the world that surrounds you. The lessons of the past are not mere relics to be forgotten—they are invaluable, powerful tools that, when thoughtfully applied to modern finance, can profoundly transform our understanding of true prosperity. This transformation can pave the way for a more equitable, just, and sustainable global economy that benefits everyone and honors the legacies of those who came before us.

In this brave new world of relentless digital innovation, the age-old sacred traditions of wealth worship emerge as a formidable challenge to conventional thinking and established norms. They invite us to scrutinize our current systems more deeply, to seek a higher and more enlightened standard of economic ethics, and to vividly imagine a future where every single financial decision we make contributes positively to the common good of society. It is a radically mind-blowing, logically compelling, and morally persuasive vision—one that possesses the extraordinary power to reshape not only our financial institutions but also our very society as a whole in profound and lasting ways.

As you continue to move forward on your journey, allow the profound wisdom of ancient rituals and the deep symbolism of divine wealth to guide your decisions with clarity and purpose. Whether you identify as an investor striving for financial success, a policymaker navigating complex economic landscapes, or simply a concerned citizen invested in the future of our global economy, always remember that the true, enduring power of money lies in its remarkable ability to forge connections between individuals, to foster stability during times of uncertainty, and to transform societies for the betterment of all involved. The sacred role that money has played in the civilizations of the past offers us a valuable roadmap—a detailed blueprint for a financial future where ethical stewardship, collective prosperity, and the favor of the divine are not only not mutually exclusive, but are beautifully integrated into a harmonious and flourishing whole. Embrace this wisdom, and let it inform your actions as you contribute positively to the world around you.

The call to embrace this profoundly sacred view of wealth is as urgently pressing as it is revolutionary and transformative. In a world where the gap between the wealthy elite and the impoverished continues to broaden alarmingly, and where trust in centralized institutions and authority is steadily eroding, the invaluable lessons drawn from ancient wealth worship provide a clear, logical, and compelling path forward for us all. These teachings remind us unequivocally that true prosperity is intricately built on a strong foundation of ethical responsibility, fairness, and shared success—a lesson that is not only timeless but also critically needed in our rapidly evolving digital age where ideals of fairness and social justice are paramount.

In conclusion, the exploration of money as a symbol of power and divine favor across ancient civilizations is not merely an academic exercise—it serves as a vital clarion call for rethinking the very nature of wealth itself. By deeply understanding how our ancestors carefully intertwined economic success with spiritual legitimacy, we can work to forge a new vision for modern finance—one that honors the rich tapestry of the past while boldly embracing the limitless potential of the future. The sacred spirit of wealth, which was once celebrated in grand temples and elaborate treasuries of old, can now be revived and revitalized in our contemporary digital world, guiding us toward a more just, transparent, and prosperous society for all. Through this reassessment, we are encouraged to see wealth not just as a means of accumulation, but as a powerful tool for fostering community and wellbeing.

Let us wholeheartedly take these profound lessons to heart and truly embrace their significance. Let the ancient rituals of wealth worship guide and inspire us to collectively build financial systems that not only generate substantial profit but also promote the well-being and prosperity of all individuals within our communities. In doing so, we will not only transform our economies into more inclusive and sustainable environments, but we will also rekindle the sacred, timeless spirit of prosperity that possesses the remarkable power to elevate humanity to new and unprecedented heights, creating a brighter future for generations to come.

Section 5: Lessons from the Past: How Money Temples Shaped Modern Finance

In a world where the rapid evolution of digital currencies and decentralized finance is dramatically rewriting the established rules of wealth, it might seem that modern financial innovations are completely separate from the ancient practices that govern money management. However, when we peel back the layers of contemporary finance, we discover that many of the timeless principles—those of trust, transparency, ethical stewardship, and collective prosperity—have deep roots in the ancient cultures that revered wealth, as seen in the majestic temples and fortified treasuries of old. In this section, we embark on a fascinating journey into a surprising world where the sacred traditions surrounding money temples not only shaped entire civilizations but also laid a critical foundation for the digital revolution in finance that we are fortunate to witness today. As we explore this intricate relationship between past and present, we will uncover how these ancient wisdoms continue to inform and influence modern economic systems, bridging the gap between historical practices and today's digital transformations in commerce and banking.

Ancient Wisdom in Modern Algorithms

It might seem quite counterintuitive at first glance that a practice originating from millennia ago could still have any significant bearing on our modern, high-tech financial systems. However, upon closer examination, the underlying principles remain remarkably consistent across time. In ancient times, money temples were not merely repositories for accumulated riches; they served as meticulously organized institutions where wealth was carefully recorded, managed, and safeguarded through a unique blend of religious duty and economic acumen. These places became centers of trust and protection for the community's resources. Today, those same foundational principles find their echoes in the digital realm—expressed through advanced technologies such as blockchain technology, innovative decentralized finance (DeFi), and various cryptocurrency protocols that aim to revolutionize how we think about and handle our financial transactions.

Consider the ancient scribes who meticulously used clay tablets to record every deposit, every single transaction that occurred in the sacred temples of Mesopotamia. Their detailed methods ensured a high level of accountability and transparency—two key elements that were essential for maintaining public trust among citizens. Fast forward to the present day, and we find that blockchain technology performs a remarkably similar function on a global scale. Each transaction is precisely etched into an immutable digital ledger that is accessible to all participants in the network, ensuring that the entire system remains both transparent and secure. The logic is abundantly clear: just as ancient societies wisely understood that trust was the cornerstone of effective wealth management, modern innovators have skillfully built and implemented digital infrastructures that guarantee trust and integrity without the need for a central authority or intermediary.

The Temple as the Original Financial Institution

The money temples of antiquity were indeed the original banks of their time. They were significant institutions where wealth was meticulously collected, securely stored, and expertly managed with an almost sacred precision that reflected the societal values of the time. These temples served a dual purpose; they were not only places of worship where people gathered to honor their deities but also dynamic economic centers. Here, offerings, taxes, and tributes were deposited and recorded with great care, often diligently noted by dedicated scribes. These institutions functioned as early versions of what we now recognize as banks, ensuring that wealth circulated efficiently within society and was utilized to support various important public projects, elaborate religious ceremonies, and even essential military endeavors when necessary. In this way, they played a pivotal role in the economic and spiritual life of the community.

In ancient Egypt, for instance, the grand temples that were dedicated to powerful gods such as Amun served as vital centers of immense wealth, where precious gold and bountiful grains were stored as profound symbols of divine favor granted to the land. These valuable assets were not simply hoarded; instead, they were strategically employed to fund large-scale public works—monumental building projects that not only showcased the prosperity of the thriving state but also highlighted its unwavering commitment to the welfare and upliftment of its people. The underlying concept guiding this system was straightforward yet deeply profound: wealth was not intended for private accumulation but was viewed as a communal trust, a sacred resource meant to be utilized for the greater good of society. This ethical dimension of wealth management, which was deeply embedded in the practices of ancient civilizations, resonates powerfully with contemporary discussions surrounding sustainable investing and corporate social responsibility. Today's investors are increasingly motivated to align their financial portfolios with values that actively promote transparency, accountability, and community benefit—marking a significant resurgence of the ancient belief that wealth is indeed a sacred trust meant for the collective well-being of all.

The Ethical Mandate: Wealth as a Communal Resource

Ancient money temples imparted profound lessons that the accumulation of wealth is intertwined with an inherent moral obligation. The vast riches stored in these sacred temples were perceived as divine gifts from the gods, symbolizing not just prosperity but also a significant duty to utilize them wisely for the greater good of the community. This vital ethical imperative was essential in ensuring that wealth was consistently circulated and reinvested back into society, thereby preventing the stagnation and concentration of resources that can inevitably lead to societal discord and inequality. By promoting a sense of shared responsibility, these ancient structures emphasized the importance of looking after the welfare of all, thereby fostering a more harmonious society.

This perspective has truly profound implications for modern finance today. Current debates surrounding wealth inequality and the ethical responsibilities of the super-rich resonate strongly with the ancient concerns regarding resource distribution. In ancient societies, when communities enacted rituals that involved offering a significant portion of their wealth to the gods, they were essentially institutionalizing a comprehensive system of redistribution. The primary goal of these acts was to ensure that the prosperity generated from the labor and resources was shared and benefited all members of society, rather than enriching only a privileged few. Similarly, modern finance is currently witnessing a significant shift as investors increasingly articulate their demand for their money to be utilized in ways that foster social good. This trend includes the promotion of sustainable finance, the growth of impact investing, and the rise of ethical cryptocurrencies, all of which are modern manifestations of this ancient ideal of shared prosperity and responsibility.

Digital assets, by their very nature, democratize access to wealth and financial opportunities. Unlike traditional financial systems that often favor the elite and privileged classes, decentralized finance (DeFi) platforms enable individuals from all walks of life, regardless of their socioeconomic status, to participate actively in the global economy. This is a radical and profound reimagining of the ancient idea that wealth should be viewed as a communal resource—a sacred trust that is intended to benefit everyone within society. By redistributing the power of money through innovative blockchain technology, we are, in effect, reviving the ethical principles that once guided ancient wealth management systems and practices. As we embrace this shift, we are fostering a sense of inclusivity and fairness that aims to empower the many rather than just the few.

Transparency and Accountability: Timeless Principles Reborn

One of the most shocking and enduring lessons that we can draw from the ancient money temples of civilization is the crucial importance of transparency and accountability in financial matters. The skilled scribes of Mesopotamia, employing clay tablets and their uniquely developed cuneiform script, created an intricate system of record-keeping that was not only rigorous but also publicly accessible for scrutiny and understanding. This practice was not merely an administrative necessity; it stood as a logical and strategic approach to ensure the maintenance of trust within a society where the accumulation and distribution of wealth were central to both survival and prosperity. The reliance on such transparent practices became fundamental to the functioning of their economy, reinforcing social cohesion and fostering a sense of shared responsibility among the members of the community.

Modern blockchain technology embodies this ancient principle to a remarkable degree of perfection. Every single transaction that occurs on a blockchain is meticulously recorded on an immutable ledger that cannot be altered, erased, or hidden in any way. This high level of transparency guarantees that all participants in the financial ecosystem are held firmly accountable for their actions, and it significantly reduces the potential for fraud, deceit, and corruption. The logical leap from ancient methods of record-keeping to sophisticated digital ledgers is both astonishing and entirely inevitable—a true testament to the enduring power and relevance of these timeless principles across the ages.

Furthermore, the transparency inherent in decentralized finance serves as a compelling counter-narrative to the opaque practices that are often associated with traditional banking and finance systems. In an era when the public trust in financial institutions has been significantly eroded by numerous scandals and instances of mismanagement, the valuable lessons of ancient transparency offer us a glimmer of hope. They remind us that the meticulous and public accounting practices of the past were specifically designed to serve the greater good and ensure the smooth functioning of society as a whole. By reintroducing these vital values into the realm of modern finance, we have the potential to build systems that are not only incredibly efficient but also fundamentally true to ethical principles. The movement towards transparent practices can foster a renewed trust and engagement from the public, as they see the structures in place prioritizing accountability and fairness. We must strive to learn from history, taking inspiration from ancient customs that value openness, and harnessing this knowledge to create a financial landscape that genuinely serves the interests of all its participants.

Argumentative Insights: Why Ancient Practices Matter Today

It might initially appear that the practices of ancient civilizations are mere relics of a bygone era, largely irrelevant in a contemporary world that is dominated by complex algorithms, high-frequency trading, and the swift rise of digital currencies. Nevertheless, a deeper and more nuanced analysis reveals that these ancient systems were firmly grounded in a logic and set of principles that remain profoundly relevant and applicable today. The core principles of wealth management—transparency, accountability, ethical distribution, and the collective good—are not only timeless concepts but are also the very foundation upon which modern financial innovations and structures are built. By examining these ancient practices, we can uncover valuable insights that inform current financial strategies and ethical considerations, ensuring that we do not overlook the lessons of the past.

Consider, for instance, the remarkable emergence of cryptocurrencies and the innovative realm of decentralized finance. These groundbreaking technologies represent not only technical innovations but are, at their very core, a return to the ancient ideals of wealth management that have guided humanity throughout history. By decentralizing control and ensuring that every transaction is meticulously recorded on an immutable ledger, digital currencies echo the time-honored practices of temple banks and treasuries that once played a crucial role in society. They stand as a necessary response to the many inefficiencies and ethical shortcomings that plague centralized financial systems. In doing so, they embody a progressive vision of money that is both logical in its design and profoundly humane in its purpose, offering individuals greater autonomy over their financial assets. This new approach invites us to rethink how we perceive and handle wealth in our interconnected world.

Critics of cryptocurrencies frequently highlight volatility and speculative excess as clear evidence that the ongoing digital revolution is inherently flawed. However, this critique entirely misses the fundamental point. The volatility of digital assets is actually a reflection of a transitional phase—a necessary turbulence that characterizes our shift from an antiquated financial system to a significantly more efficient, equitable, and transparent financial model. Just as the historical transition from barter systems to coinage was accompanied by periods of considerable instability and adjustment, so too is the current shift to digital money a natural, albeit disruptive, evolution that we must navigate. Embracing this new financial landscape requires understanding that such turbulence is part and parcel of any major transformation in economic systems.

The argument, then, is not simply about adopting new technology for its own sake without reflection. It is about recognizing that the ethical and logical principles that guided ancient societies can provide valuable insights to inform and improve our modern financial systems in significant ways. When we carefully examine the rituals, offerings, and public ceremonies of the past, we see that wealth was never considered in isolation and existed within a larger, interconnected system that valued fairness, accountability, and the common good—principles that are sorely needed in today's increasingly complex financial landscape. By integrating these time-honored values into our financial practices, we can foster a more equitable distribution of resources and encourage a sense of communal responsibility that has been too often overlooked in the pursuit of individual gain. This holistic approach could lead to not only a more just society but also to a more sustainable economy that thrives on ethical considerations rather than mere profit.

Persuasive Strategies: Reclaiming the Sacred Nature of Wealth

The profound power of ancient wisdom lies not only in its rich historical significance but also in its remarkable persuasive ability to challenge the prevailing status quo that we often take for granted. In a contemporary world where wealth is too frequently equated with power and privilege, the ancient view of money as a sacred asset offers a transformative and radically different alternative perspective. This perspective challenges us to deeply rethink what it truly means to be wealthy and to consider wealth as a powerful tool for collective empowerment rather than mere individual accumulation. Embracing this ancient viewpoint encourages us to shift our focus from personal gain to the greater good, fostering a sense of community and interconnectedness that can uplift us all.

Modern financial systems, characterized by their relentless focus on profit maximization and the elevation of shareholder value, have largely divorced the concept of wealth from its ethical origins and communal roots. The implications of this division are becoming increasingly clear as global inequality continues to widen and public trust in centralized institutions steadily erodes. In response to these pressing challenges, a growing movement toward ethical finance has begun to emerge—one that seeks to not only maintain profitability but also to emphasize the importance of social responsibility in financial practices. This burgeoning movement is, in many ways, a revival of the ancient belief that wealth is a divine gift, intended to be utilized for the benefit of all, promoting a more equitable distribution of resources. As such, this shift in perspective seeks to redefine how financial institutions operate within society, fostering a renewed commitment to community welfare and ethical stewardship.

Imagine a financial system where corporations not only strive for profit but also commit wholeheartedly to transparent, accountable practices that benefit society at large in numerous ways. Envision a world where digital currencies are managed with the same rigor, careful oversight, and ethical standards that once governed the sacred treasuries of ancient temples in various cultures. This is not merely a utopian dream or distant fantasy—it is, in fact, a logical and achievable extension of the principles that have guided humanity for millennia in its pursuit of justice and fairness. By integrating these timeless values with cutting-edge modern technology and digital innovations, we can create robust financial systems that are not only efficient but also inherently equitable, serving the greater good for all of society.

The persuasive case for a sacred view of wealth is also powerfully evident in the significant shift toward decentralized finance that we are witnessing today. In DeFi platforms, power is distributed widely among users rather than being concentrated in the hands of a few large institutions that traditionally dominated the financial landscape. This democratization of finance mirrors the ancient ideal of communal wealth—a system in which every single individual has a valuable opportunity to contribute to and benefit from the collective prosperity of the whole community. Such systems greatly encourage ethical stewardship, as each participant is incentivized to act in the best interests of the community at large, not merely to pursue and maximize their own personal gain alone. This fundamentally changes the dynamics of wealth distribution, leading to a more inclusive and equitable financial future.

Logical Synthesis: Bridging the Past and the Future

When we connect the ancient reverence for wealth with today's innovative digital financial technologies, a fascinating and logical synthesis naturally emerges. The historical practices of money temples and treasuries, which are characterized by meticulous record-keeping, ethical distribution, and a strong sense of public accountability, provide a valuable blueprint for the thoughtful design of modern financial systems. They vividly demonstrate that when wealth is managed with full transparency and unwavering integrity, it can serve as a powerful force for collective good, benefiting society as a whole and contributing to the common welfare.

Blockchain technology represents a contemporary evolution of this ancient logic, showcasing how time-honored principles can inform our modern systems. At its core, it embodies the essential values of trust and transparency that were foundational to ancient methods of record-keeping. In addition to these values, it also offers the scalability and efficiency that are crucial for navigating today's complex global economy. The remarkable immutability of blockchain guarantees that every transaction is not only visible but also verifiable, mirroring the meticulous accounting practices of temple scribes who carefully recorded every deposit and withdrawal using clay tablets. This striking logical continuity between ancient traditions and modern innovations is both astonishing and inspiring—it reveals that the fundamental challenges involved in managing wealth have remained constant over centuries, even as the tools and technologies we use to address these challenges have evolved significantly. Thus, this intersection of past and present opens up exciting possibilities for how we can approach financial transactions and record-keeping in the modern era.

Furthermore, the integration of ethical considerations into financial management has remained a recurring theme that has successfully survived the test of time throughout history. Ancient societies, for instance, recognized and understood that wealth, when concentrated without any form of accountability, could inevitably lead to social unrest, severe economic instability, and widespread inequality. Their systems were specifically designed to ensure that wealth was utilized not only for individual gain but also for the welfare of the community at large. In our modern era, the same timeless principles are being applied in new and innovative ways—through sustainable investing practices, robust corporate social responsibility initiatives, and the growing field of ethical finance. The logical argument is crystal clear: a financial system that values wealth as a sacred trust, wisely distributed for the benefit of all individuals within society, is not only morally sound and just, but also economically sustainable in the long run. Thus, the idea of ethical finance serves as a bridge connecting traditional values with contemporary financial practices, painting a future where both profit and social good can coexist harmoniously.

The Revolutionary Impact on Modern Financial Thought

The lessons derived from ancient money temples have produced a truly revolutionary impact on our modern financial thought processes. These timeless principles have significantly influenced the way we understand and appreciate the intricate role of money in society, shaping various aspects ranging from corporate governance to public policy frameworks. Today, as we find ourselves standing at the dawn of the rapidly evolving digital finance era, these ancient teachings are being creatively reinterpreted and applied in innovative ways to help create a more transparent, accountable, and inclusive financial system that serves the needs of all people. This intersection of ancient wisdom and contemporary practice holds the promise of a future where financial systems are not only efficient but also equitable for everyone involved.

The remarkable rise of cryptocurrencies, along with the burgeoning field of decentralized finance, poses a direct challenge to the established systems of traditional banking, which are often centralized and shrouded in opacity. By decentralizing control over financial transactions and ensuring that every single transaction is meticulously recorded on a public ledger, digital currencies are fundamentally redefining the intricate relationship between wealth and power in society. These innovations not only democratize access to essential financial resources but also play a crucial role in dismantling the barriers that have historically separated the elite from the masses of ordinary people. This transformation represents a powerful and logical progression from the ancient perspective that viewed wealth as a communal asset. The shift not only celebrates individual prosperity but also significantly promotes the idea of collective empowerment in an increasingly interconnected world, enabling individuals from all walks of life to participate in the financial ecosystem.

Moreover, modern innovations within the rapidly evolving field of financial technology are increasingly being meticulously designed with ethical considerations firmly in mind. The concept of ethical investing, for instance, is deeply grounded in the fundamental idea that wealth should be used not merely for personal gain but to foster social good and benefit a wider community. Investors today are no longer content with merely chasing returns—they actively demand transparency, accountability, and a tangible positive social impact from their investments. This significant shift reflects a deep-seated recognition that the true value of money lies not just in its purchasing power and the ability to accumulate wealth, but in its profound potential to improve lives, support meaningful initiatives, and build stronger, more resilient communities. The persuasive and compelling force of this argument is undeniable, drawing on centuries of wisdom and teachings that view wealth as a sacred trust to be managed responsibly and ethically for the common benefit of all. The evolving landscape of finance now encourages a more inclusive approach that prioritizes values and social responsibility alongside financial success.

The Future of Finance: An Ethical and Inclusive Paradigm

Looking ahead, the remarkable integration of ancient principles with cutting-edge modern technology offers a fascinating glimpse into a future where finance is not only as ethical as it is innovative but also deeply rooted in the values of our past. The sacred and timeless view of wealth—once expressed in the awe-inspiring temples and grand treasuries that characterized ancient civilization—can be revitalized and reborn in the dynamic digital age we inhabit today. Imagine a vibrant financial ecosystem where blockchain technology ensures complete and unparalleled transparency, where decentralized networks truly empower individuals to take charge of their financial destinies, and where every single transaction is meticulously guided by ethical principles that prioritize the communal well-being of society as a whole, fostering trust and cooperation amongst all participants.

This vision is not merely an idealistic dream—it represents a logical and inevitable outcome of the historical evolution of money over time. The same powerful forces that drove ancient societies to construct sanctuaries for wealth are now effectively converging with cutting-edge digital innovations to create financial systems that are increasingly more resilient, efficient, and inclusive. As we witness the remarkable rise of decentralized finance in our modern world, we are also observing a significant reawakening of the ethical imperatives that once governed the fair distribution and responsible management of wealth within communities throughout history. This transformation not only enhances accessibility but also redefines our relationship with money itself.

For modern policymakers and investors alike, the invaluable lessons derived from the past provide a compelling and persuasive case for comprehensive reform. By fully embracing the sacred and profound view of wealth, we have the opportunity to design financial systems that are not only undeniably profitable but also inherently socially responsible.

This forward-thinking approach has the remarkable potential to effectively address some of the most pressing and critical challenges of our time—including inequality, corruption, and the troubling erosion of public trust in centralized institutions. It serves as a powerful call to return to a holistic model of finance that fundamentally values transparency, accountability, and the collective good—timeless principles that have consistently guided human societies throughout the ages for millennia.

A Blueprint for a Transformed Financial Future

In the truly shocking and mind-blowing analysis of how money has long served as a powerful symbol of influence and divine favor throughout various civilizations, we uncover a fascinating logical continuum that stretches from the majestic ancient temples of old to the rapidly evolving world of modern digital currencies. The sacred and pivotal role of wealth, as dramatically manifested in the grand architectures of ancient Egypt, Imperial Rome, classical Greece, and many other prominent cultures, provides us with a comprehensive blueprint for envisioning the future landscape of finance. These impactful ancient practices, deeply rooted in the enduring belief that wealth is a divine trust meant to benefit all segments of society, offer a highly persuasive and analytical framework for reimagining our financial systems in the ever-evolving digital age we now inhabit.

In today's rapidly evolving landscape of cryptocurrencies and decentralized finance, we find ourselves navigating uncharted waters that echo the timeless principles established by ancient money temples. These principles continue to hold a mirror to our modern financial practices, reminding us of the importance of building systems that are not only transparent and accountable but also ethically robust. As we look ahead, we envision a future where financial success transcends the traditional metrics of profit. Instead, it embraces a broader perspective, measuring success by the positive and transformative impact we have on society as a whole. This shift in mindset encourages us to redefine what wealth truly means in our interconnected world.

The lessons drawn from the past are unequivocally clear: wealth must be managed thoughtfully with a profound sense of duty and a steadfast commitment to the common good. Ancient civilizations, long before our time, understood that the accumulation of wealth was not merely an end in itself but rather a means to secure stability, foster innovation, and promote social harmony among their communities. This vision, resonating strongly now in modern financial innovations and practices, calls for a much-needed reawakening of the sacred spirit of wealth—one that thoughtfully integrates ethical stewardship with the benefits and advances of cutting-edge technology. We have an opportunity to redefine wealth management in a way that not only enriches individuals but also uplifts the collective welfare of society.

As you take a moment to reflect deeply on these timeless lessons, consider how the respect and reverence for wealth in ancient times can fundamentally inform our modern approach to finance today. The fusion of enduring ancient wisdom with cutting-edge digital innovation presents a revolutionary opportunity—one that allows us to create a financial system that is not only as inclusive as it is ethical, but also remarkably efficient and effective. This vision is the comprehensive blueprint for a transformed financial future—a future in which money is not merely viewed as a tool for exchange, but rather as a sacred trust that holds the potential to uplift entire communities and pave the way for a shared and sustainable collective prosperity for everyone involved.

Let this thorough analysis serve as a powerful call to action for modern investors, policymakers, and engaged citizens alike. It is imperative that we embrace the enduring principles of transparency, accountability, and ethical stewardship that have guided human civilization through the ages. By doing so, you will become an integral part of a transformative movement that not only seeks to enhance and modernize financial systems but also actively redefines the very nature of wealth in a way that is both revolutionary and profoundly humane. This movement is about creating a better future for everyone and ensuring that economic growth benefits all segments of society.

The sacred view of wealth—born in ancient temples, celebrated in majestic treasuries, and immortalized through divine rituals and customs—holds the profound power to reshape and redefine our world around us. By thoughtfully integrating these timeless values with the dynamic capabilities and innovations of modern technology, we can effectively build a financial system that not only honors our past heritage but also boldly steps forward into the promising future of our civilization. This is not merely a vision for a better way of managing money and personal finances; it is a carefully crafted blueprint for a more just, equitable, and prosperous society that we can all aspire to achieve and nurture together.

In conclusion, the invaluable lessons we can glean from the ancient money temples offer us a profound and powerful framework for understanding and transforming modern finance as we know it today. These insights serve as a crucial reminder that the true power of money lies not merely in its capacity to generate profit or accumulate wealth, but in its tremendous potential to promote social good, foster transparency, and build a lasting legacy of shared prosperity for future generations. As we now stand on the threshold of a new and exciting era in digital finance, let us earnestly draw upon the rich wisdom of our ancestors and reimagine wealth as a sacred trust—an essential resource for everyone—one that can elevate humanity and usher in a brighter future where financial systems truly work for everyone, providing equitable opportunities and serving the greater good.

Embrace these timeless lessons fully and wholeheartedly. Let them not only guide your decisions but also inspire your actions deeply, transforming your understanding profoundly of what it truly means to be wealthy in a holistic sense. The sacred spirit of wealth is not merely a relic of the past—rather, it is a vibrant, living, and breathing force that continues to shape our world in remarkable ways, inviting us each day to build a financial future that is not only ethical but also innovative, as inclusive as it is powerful and transformative for all.

Chapter 2: The Idea History of Denationalized Currency

Section 1: Origins of Money—From Barter to Sovereign Coinage

The evolution of money stands out as one of the most fascinating and mind-blowing stories in human history—a truly remarkable journey that progressively transforms simple, primitive trade into a structured and sophisticated system of government-issued coinage that underpins and fundamentally supports our modern economy today. What began as rudimentary exchanges between individuals has, over the extensive and protracted span of millennia, matured into an intricate and elaborate tapestry filled with economic innovation, profound social evolution, and significant political power that permeates every facet of our lives. In this compelling exploration, we will deeply delve into the intricate origins of money, thoroughly uncovering the logical foundations and reasoning behind its creation, as well as the sheer audacity and creativity of early trade systems that inevitably led to the pioneering creation of coins and, ultimately, the sovereign currencies that undeniably define nations and their complex economies today. This journey through time will illuminate not only the transformations of currency itself but also the profound impact that these economic systems have on societal structures and governance as we understand it now.

The Shocking World of Barter

Imagine a time long before the existence of money in any form—a fascinating and intriguing world where the complex exchange of goods and services was governed solely by the barter system. In these primitive economies, individuals relied on trading what they possessed to acquire what they truly needed: grains exchanged for livestock, pottery swapped for textiles, and various other unique transactions that constituted daily life. At first glance, barter might appear to be straightforward and simple; however, the underlying reality was anything but uncomplicated. The entire barter system was riddled with numerous inefficiencies and limitations that ultimately spurred humanity to invent something much more sophisticated, organized, and efficient for trade and commerce purposes. Without a standard medium of exchange, people faced considerable challenges in finding mutually agreeable trades, which often led to significant frustration and delays in obtaining essential items necessary for survival. This complex system, while seemingly practical, proved to be inadequate for the growth and expansion of societies, highlighting the limitations of direct exchanges based solely on personal needs and available resources.

Barter systems necessitated a concept known as a "double coincidence of wants," which signifies that both parties engaged in the exchange had to have something that the other one desired. To illustrate, consider a farmer who is fortunate enough to have an excess supply of wheat but simultaneously finds himself in need of a new pair of shoes. If a shoemaker happened to come along and also found himself in need of that specific wheat, then an exchange could occur. However, unless the shoemaker had an urgent and coincidental requirement for that very wheat, the entire trading process would come to a standstill, creating a potentially frustrating and complicated predicament. This situation made trading not only unpredictable but also incredibly labor-intensive. Such limitations severely hindered both economic growth and the overall advancement of society as a whole, as individuals were often unable to easily acquire the goods and services they needed to improve their livelihoods and continue their work efficiently.

Yet, despite its numerous shortcomings and limitations, barter served not only as a primitive method of exchanging goods and services but also as the foundational bedrock upon which human civilization was ultimately constructed. It compelled early societies to innovate continuously and engage in creative problem-solving as they searched for a common medium of exchange—a groundbreaking concept that would eventually revolutionize the world in countless ways. The very limitations and challenges associated with barter created a shocking yet undeniable imperative: money had to be invented, and it had to represent something that everyone could place their steadfast trust in and rely upon for their everyday transactions and interactions. This realization led to a transformative shift in economic systems, paving the way for the complex financial landscapes we navigate today.

The Emergence of Commodity Money

The logical next step in the evolution of trade was the use of commodity money—specific items that not only had intrinsic value but also could be universally accepted across various societies. Early humans engaged in extensive experimentation with a diverse array of commodities as mediums of exchange. These included livestock, grains, salt, spices, and various other goods. The selection of these particular items was deliberate; they were chosen due to their durability, divisibility into smaller units, and widespread desirability across different cultures and communities. The adoption of such commodities played a crucial role in facilitating trade and fostering economic growth in early human civilizations.

In numerous ancient societies that existed long ago, salt emerged as an incredibly valuable resource, elevating it to the point where it was sometimes utilized as a form of currency for trade and transactions. The term "salary" itself is derived from the Latin word that means salt, highlighting the significant role salt played as an essential medium of exchange in various cultures. In a similar vein, cattle also held immense value, serving not just as a representation of wealth but, importantly, as a vital source of sustenance for people. This duality made them highly desirable in trade. The underlying logic was elegantly simple: when a commodity possesses qualities of rarity, durability, and universal desirability, it can effectively serve as a standard measure of value. Thus, this marked the moment in history when commodity money came into existence—a system that proved to be just as natural as it was revolutionary, reshaping economic interactions and the understanding of value throughout ancient times.

Commodity money represented a profound and significant shift in human reasoning and economic interactions. No longer were transactions strictly limited by the coincidence of wants, where each party needed to desire what the other offered; instead, a common item could effectively bridge the gap between various goods and services. This remarkable advancement allowed trade to expand far beyond localized communities, enabling the growth of regional and eventually interregional commerce in ways that were previously unimaginable. It was a truly mind-blowing transformation that set the stage for the evolution of more abstract, sophisticated forms of money that we rely on today, marking a key turning point in our economic history.

The Analytical Leap: Standardization and the Birth of Coinage

As societies grew ever more complex and trade networks expanded significantly, the need for a standardized and universally accepted medium of exchange became increasingly apparent to everyone involved in commerce. Commodity money, while effective in its own right, suffered from a number of inherent issues related to uniformity and divisibility. How could one possibly ensure that a given quantity of grain, for instance, or a lump of salt, was of consistent quality and maintained value across different regions and communities? This challenge raised important questions about the reliability and practicality of these early forms of currency.

The solution emerged in the form of coinage—a thoroughly logical and analytical response to the numerous challenges posed by commodity money. Coins were crafted from precious metals such as gold, silver, and bronze, which were valued not solely for their material properties but also for their rarity and remarkable durability. The introduction of coins marked a truly revolutionary moment in human history, significantly altering economic transactions and trade practices, as it provided a standardized, government-sanctioned medium of exchange that could be universally accepted across vast regions. This development facilitated commerce and encouraged trade to blossom in ways that earlier, less efficient systems could never have achieved. Coins allowed individuals to buy and sell goods and services more easily, paving the way for increasingly complex economies and societies.

The process of minting coins was itself a remarkable marvel of early technology and intricate organization. Rulers and governments adeptly took control of the entire coinage process, meticulously imprinting their own distinctive symbols and marks on the coins as a guarantee of their authenticity, integrity, and inherent value. This careful regulation not only ensured uniformity across the currency but also imbued the coins with significant political legitimacy and power. Each coin thus became a small piece of the state—a vital, tangible representation of the government's promise to honor its value in trade and commerce. In this way, coins served not just as a medium of exchange, but stood as an enduring testament to the authority and stability of the civilization that produced them.

This significant leap from the use of commodity money to the establishment of sovereign coinage was not merely a matter of choice but rather driven by a combination of logic and necessity. It effectively resolved the long-standing and perennial problems that plagued barter systems and the limitations of commodity money by creating a new medium that was durable, easily divisible, and solidly backed by the authority of the state. The introduction of coins provided numerous advantages—they were portable, consistent in quality, and, most importantly, trusted by the people who used them. This newfound trust is what made coins a revolutionary advancement in economic transactions. They enabled economies to flourish in ways previously unimagined, facilitated significant expansion of trade networks, and allowed civilizations to construct infrastructures and societal systems that would stand the test of time, leaving behind lasting legacies for future generations.

Societal Transformations and the Impact of Coinage

The advent of coinage did not merely facilitate the process of trade; it effectively transformed entire societies and their economic structures. With coins in circulation, ancient states had the newfound capability to establish increasingly complex systems of taxation, meticulous budgeting, and strategic public spending. This pivotal change heralded a new era in which wealth could be systematically collected and redistributed across various segments of society, laying a robust groundwork for the modern fiscal policies we recognize today. The efficiency of coinage led to greater economic stability, enabling governments to undertake large-scale projects and significantly improve public infrastructure, which further propelled societal advancement.

In ancient Greece, for instance, the innovative introduction of coinage significantly enabled city-states like Athens to effectively fund various public projects, support the flourishing of the arts, and even engage in waging wars. Coins transformed into a powerful symbol of civic pride, representing not only individual personal wealth but also reflecting the collective prosperity of the entire polis. The transparency and uniformity inherent in coinage greatly fostered trust among citizens, as they were able to be confident that each and every coin represented a measurable and consistent value. This development was a crucial step in building the robust foundations of democratic societies, where trust in the economic system was not merely important but essential for ensuring social cohesion and driving progress forward. Ultimately, the establishment of coinage had lasting effects on how communities interacted with one another and facilitated further advancements in commerce and governance.

Rome, too, benefited immensely from the remarkable innovation of coinage, which transformed the way societies conducted economic transactions. The Roman Empire adeptly used coins not only as a means to project power but also to spread its influence across vast and diverse territories. Emperors minted coins that prominently featured their own likenesses, ensuring that their image and authority were disseminated throughout the vast expanse of the empire. These coins were not merely currency; they served as powerful instruments of propaganda, clearly demonstrating the empire's stability, strength, and unyielding authority. The systematic and widespread use of coinage played a crucial role in helping to unify diverse regions under a common economic framework, facilitating trade, taxation, and governance on an unprecedented and remarkably expansive scale. Through this monetary innovation, the Roman Empire was able to maintain its control and promote cohesion among its various provinces, reinforcing its dominance in the ancient world.

The impact of coinage on societal development is both astonishing and perfectly logical. It provided the vital means to create intricate economic systems that could effectively support large and growing populations, fund monumental constructions that showcased the power and capability of nations, and maintain formidable armies necessary for defense and expansion. The state's ability to control coinage also meant that rulers were empowered to implement policies aimed at stabilizing the economy, controlling inflation, and ensuring a steady flow of resources to effectively meet the diverse needs of their people. This control over currency and economic strategy laid the foundation for the birth of fiscal policy—a groundbreaking concept that remains central to modern economics and governance, influencing how nations manage their financial health and the well-being of their citizens in today's world.

The Argumentative Case for Coinage: A Revolution in Value and Trust

The monumental shift from barter systems and commodity money to the use of coinage was not merely a matter of enhanced convenience; it represented a profound and essential redefinition of both value and trust within economic transactions. In the early days, systems reliant on barter were often plagued by the unpredictability and challenges of effectively matching individual needs and wants. This inherent inefficiency created significant obstacles for trade. On the other hand, while commodity money introduced a form of intrinsic value through physical items, it still lacked the necessary standardization that could create a reliable medium of exchange across diverse transactions. The advent of coinage emerged as the quintessential solution to these issues, masterfully combining the inherent worth of precious metals with the authoritative power of the state, thus establishing a trusted and efficient economic framework.

Critics might contend that the invention of coinage was merely a necessity, springing from practical needs rather than representing a monumental leap in the trajectory of human progress. Nevertheless, upon closer examination of the numerous economic and social advantages that coinage ushered in, this argument becomes not just plausible, but also quite compelling. Coins facilitated the expansion of trade, allowing it to extend far beyond the confines of localized markets. This open trading environment enabled rich cross-cultural interactions and the flourishing of international commerce, fostering connections between distant peoples. Moreover, coins served as a reliable and stable store of value—a critical development in an age characterized by frequent economic upheavals. During periods marked by famines, wars, and natural disasters, the stability offered by coinage proved essential in safeguarding wealth and assisting communities to withstand the shocks that could otherwise ravage local economies.

Moreover, the introduction of coinage brought about a significant level of accountability and transparency that was previously unattainable in various aspects of commerce and trade. The state's essential role in the minting of coins ensured that there was a consistent and standardized measure of value that everyone could rely on and agree upon. This standardization fostered a larger sense of trust among individuals and businesses, which is arguably the most critical component of any successful economic system. Trust in money and the stability it provides is what enables economies to function smoothly and efficiently; without it, trade grinds to a halt and societies inevitably descend into chaos and disorder, leading to dire consequences for all involved in economic exchanges.

The historical record is replete with a multitude of compelling examples that clearly demonstrate how coinage spurred significant economic growth and drove innovation in various societies. The resounding success of the Lydian coinage system, which is widely credited as the world's very first system of coined money, stands as a remarkable testament to the transformative power of standardization in economic practices. By minting coins that possessed consistent weight and purity, Lydia not only revolutionized the process of trade but also established a lasting precedent for economic systems throughout the ancient world and beyond. This logical and progressive transformation from unstandardized barter systems to regulated coinage serves as a striking illustration of how human ingenuity and creativity can effectively overcome the limitations inherent in earlier economic systems. The innovations brought forth by coinage not only enhanced trade efficiency but also facilitated broader exchanges, ultimately paving the way for a more interconnected and flourishing economic landscape.

The Societal Impact: Coinage as a Catalyst for Civilization

The introduction of coinage had truly profound effects on the overall structure of societies throughout history. It shifted existing power dynamics in significant ways, enabled the gradual rise of centralized states that could better control resources and trade, and even influenced various cultural and religious practices in diverse regions. Coins became more than simply a medium of exchange; they evolved into a powerful symbol of the state's authority and a clear marker of social status among individuals. Furthermore, the use of coins facilitated trade and commerce, making economic transactions simpler and more efficient than ever before.

In ancient Greece, the circulation of coins was a significant public affair that reinforced the essential social contract between the citizen and the state. The value of any coin was not determined solely by its metal content or material worth, but also by its legitimacy as issued by a recognized authority figure or governing body. This dual aspect of coinage—its intrinsic value, based on the materials used, and its symbolic value, reflecting authority and trust—created a robust and reliable system of trust and social order throughout the city-states. The coins themselves served as a constant and tangible reminder that economic prosperity was inextricably linked with civic responsibility and a shared collective identity among the citizenry. In this way, the act of using money was far more than a simple economic transaction; it was an embodiment of civic duty, societal values, and community bonds that held ancient Greek society together.

In a similar fashion, in Rome, the extensive and widespread use of coins contributed significantly to the unification of an empire that spanned a multitude of diverse cultures and regions. The Roman coinage system, characterized by its standardized designs and consistent value, played a crucial role in integrating the vast and varied territories of the empire into a single, cohesive economic unit. The coins proudly bore the images of emperors, effectively propagating a powerful message of divine sanction and imperial legitimacy that resonated throughout the entire empire. This visual and economic unity was not only important but essential in maintaining the stability and cohesion of the Roman state, even in the face of numerous external threats and various internal strife that challenged its existence. As such, the coinage system served as a vital instrument for fostering a sense of unity among the peoples of the empire, reinforcing both loyalty and identity amidst the complexities of Roman governance.

The impact of coinage extended beyond mere economic integration; it also significantly influenced various cultural expressions of both power and identity throughout societies. Coins were frequently utilized in numerous religious ceremonies, acting as offerings to deities and as prestigious tokens of honor for various military achievements. They played an important role in the commemoration of significant events, serving as lasting reminders of shared history and collective experiences. Furthermore, coins acted as a powerful medium for conveying political and ideological messages, reinforcing the authority of state and religious leaders. This essential intertwining of coinage with deep-rooted religious and cultural symbolism elevated money from being a simple transactional tool to becoming a central element of societal identity. This evolution is shockingly profound and continues to influence our understanding of wealth, power, and status even in modern times.

Logical Conclusions: The Enduring Legacy of Coinage

When we engage in a thorough analysis of the fascinating evolution of money, transitioning from the primitive barter system to the establishment of sovereign coinage, the logical, analytical, and potentially shocking progression becomes absolutely undeniable. Each unique stage in this long journey of evolution was driven by a clear and pressing necessity: to overcome the inherent limitations of previous systems and to create a medium of exchange that was not only efficient but also reliable and universally accepted by all parties involved. The innovative development of coinage represented a truly revolutionary leap forward that not only greatly facilitated trade between individuals but also laid the essential groundwork for the intricate and complex economic systems that underpin modern civilization as we know it today.

The standardization and regulation of coinage introduced a significant level of order and predictability that was absolutely essential for the extensive growth of commerce and industry. The coins minted by various ancient states were not merely used as currency; they served as important instruments of governance, powerful symbols of sovereignty, and effective tools for promoting social cohesion among the populace. These coins allowed rulers to efficiently collect taxes, successfully fund public projects, and maintain necessary military strength to protect their territories. The economic stability that was provided by a reliable coinage system enabled numerous civilizations to flourish remarkably well, driving significant advancements in diverse areas such as art, intricate architecture, and groundbreaking science. This intricate interplay of economy and governance through the medium of coinage laid a foundational bedrock for the societies that followed.

Furthermore, the trust and transparency that were initially established by the introduction of coinage remain essential principles that underpin modern finance. The financial institutions we engage with today, despite their significant complexity and multifaceted nature, continue to depend on the fundamental ideas of standardized value and accountability that were first put into practice through the ancient coinage systems. The enduring legacy of these early monetary systems is clearly visible in our contemporary monetary policies, the systematic methods we employ for auditing and thorough record-keeping, as well as in the rapidly evolving landscape of digital currencies. In this new financial horizon, trust is upheld and preserved through advanced cryptographic algorithms and decentralized ledgers that characterize this innovative era of technology.

Persuading the Modern Mind: Relevance in the Digital Age

For the modern investor and policymaker, the lessons emerging from the historical evolution of coinage are both shocking and remarkably relevant in today's financial landscape. In an era that is increasingly dominated by digital transactions, the rise of cryptocurrencies, and the expansion of decentralized finance, we find ourselves witnessing a significant rebirth of the very principles that originally drove the creation and use of coinage in ancient civilizations. Digital currencies, with their strong emphasis on transparency, enhanced security, and crucial standardization, represent the natural successors to the coins that were utilized in ancient times, transforming how we think about money and value in the modern world.

The digital revolution we are experiencing today has effectively stripped away the traditional physical limitations that have long been associated with money, allowing it to flow freely across international borders and seamlessly through intricate digital networks. However, amidst this transformation, the foundational logic governing money remains unchanged: it must serve as a reliable store of value and act as a trusted medium of exchange. Blockchain technology, which serves as the backbone of modern cryptocurrencies, mirrors the meticulous and detailed record-keeping practices of ancient scribes who took great care in documenting transactions. Every single digital transaction that occurs is recorded on an immutable ledger, which ensures that trust is maintained even in the absence of a central authority to oversee it. This innovation represents the ultimate realization of the principles first established by the concept of sovereign coinage—a system where value is not only standardized and transparent but also universally accepted by all parties involved in transactions. The implications of this are profound, as they link the past with the future in our understanding of value and exchange in a digital era.

Moreover, the evolution of coinage teaches us that financial innovation is not merely a historical event but an ongoing process that actively shapes our economies. Just as the transition from barter systems to commodity money and then to coinage was driven by the pressing needs for greater efficiency, simplicity, and reliability, today's shift toward digital currencies represents a natural progression in this long history—an informed response to the multifaceted challenges of an increasingly globalized and interconnected world. The logic of progress is strikingly clear: if the ancient coinage system was able to successfully overcome the inherent limitations and inefficiencies of the barter system and commodity money, then the current digital revolution stands poised to effectively overcome the constraints and shortcomings of our existing fiat-based financial system. Each step in this evolution reflects humanity's continuous quest for improved methods of trade, encompassing both the technological advancements and the changing socio-economic landscapes that drive innovation forward.

This argument is not merely theoretical; it has significant practical implications for modern economic policy in today's fast-evolving financial landscape. Governments and various financial institutions around the world are increasingly exploring and investigating the potential benefits and functionalities of central bank digital currencies (CBDCs) as a forward-thinking approach to harness the advantages of digital finance. At the same time, they strive to maintain necessary regulatory oversight and control. CBDCs represent a fascinating fusion of ancient, time-tested principles of monetary policy and cutting-edge modern technology—a thought-provoking return to the foundational idea of standardized, government-issued money, but cleverly reimagined and adapted for the complexities of the digital age we live in today. They promise to deliver the enhanced efficiency, unparalleled transparency, and robust security features characteristic of cryptocurrencies, all while still being firmly backed by the unquestionable authority of the state. This innovative development could potentially redefine the way we perceive and utilize money in daily transactions and global economic systems.

The Transformative Power of a Standardized Medium

One of the most compelling and persuasive aspects of the evolution from a system of barter to the introduction of coinage is the transformative and profound power inherent in having a standardized medium of exchange. When money becomes standardized and widely accepted, it not only simplifies and streamlines transactions but also creates a common language of value that unites disparate and diverse communities. This unification of different groups is a powerful driver of significant economic development and social integration, fostering cooperation and interconnectedness among varied populations. The shift from barter to coinage marks a pivotal point in human history that lays the groundwork for complex economies and societal advancements.

In ancient times, the introduction of coins marked a significant turning point that allowed for the remarkable expansion of trade beyond previously established local boundaries. Traders could now operate within a broader, more interconnected economic network that spanned regions, confident in their ability to exchange coins that held consistent and reliable value across various marketplaces. This newfound predictability spurred extensive commerce, encouraged the steady accumulation of capital, and laid the crucial foundations for increasingly complex market systems that were previously unimaginable. It was an undeniably logical step forward in the continuum of human progress—an evolution that, once again, finds its fascinating parallel in the ever-evolving digital era where forms of trade and currency are continually transformed.

In today's rapidly evolving financial landscape, digital currencies are emerging as the new standardized medium, facilitating instantaneous, borderless transactions that were once beyond imagination and comprehension. These digital assets enable a remarkable level of economic fluidity and integration that closely mirrors the ancient promise of physical coinage. With the advancement of digital wallets, blockchain ledgers, and decentralized platforms, we are now witnessing the remarkable reemergence of a system where value is uniformly acknowledged and trust is widely distributed among a vast global community of users. The revolutionary potential of this monumental shift is truly mind-blowing—it holds the promise to democratize access to wealth for people around the world, effectively break down traditional economic barriers, and significantly empower individuals on an unprecedented scale that we have not seen before.

The Argument for Continued Innovation

As we take a moment to reflect on the fascinating evolution of money throughout history, the argument for continued innovation in this realm becomes increasingly compelling and clear. The transition from a barter system to the usage of coinage was not merely a static event—it was, in fact, a dynamic and ongoing process fueled by human necessity, creativity, ingenuity, and the relentless drive to overcome various limitations faced by societies over time. Every single innovation found within the rich history of money has been a thoughtful response to a specific problem or challenge, each demanding a radical, often revolutionary solution. The persistent inefficiencies of the barter system led to the creation and adoption of commodity money; likewise, the limitations inherent in commodity money spurred the inventive development of standardized coins. Ultimately, the need for a more standardized and universally accepted form of currency, typically government-issued money, played a critical role in inspiring the further development of sovereign coinage. This journey encapsulates not just economic evolution but also a deeply rooted aspect of human civilization's progress.

This ongoing process of innovation is far from over and continues to unfold in unexpected ways. In our rapidly evolving digital age, as traditional fiat currencies increasingly face significant challenges from inflationary pressures, political instability, and profound technological disruption, the next logical evolution is not just a possibility but is already very much underway. Cryptocurrencies and decentralized finance, in particular, represent the latest and most exciting chapter in this ongoing narrative—a chapter that is as logical and inevitable as it is shocking, disruptive, and transformative for our financial landscapes and beyond.

The compelling and persuasive case for embracing digital currencies is meticulously built on the same foundational principles that have driven various ancient innovations throughout history. Digital currencies offer a standardized and universally accepted medium of exchange that enables efficient transactions. Moreover, they provide a level of transparency and accountability that is unprecedented, thanks to the immutable ledgers that underpin their operation. This technology ensures that every transaction is securely recorded and cannot be altered or tampered with, enhancing trust among users. Furthermore, digital currencies work to democratize access to wealth in a way that traditional financial systems have long struggled to achieve, opening up opportunities for countless individuals. In essence, the digital revolution of money is not a radical departure from the past; rather, it is a seamless continuation of the evolutionary logic that has driven human progress for many thousands of years. By adapting to new technologies and embracing these digital forms of currency, society can evolve while remaining rooted in its historical context.

Bridging the Past and Future: A Vision for Modern Finance

In synthesizing the invaluable lessons drawn from the storied ancient money temples and the intricate designs of historic coinage with the remarkable innovations of the ever-evolving digital era, we arrive at a truly revolutionary vision for modern finance—one that is fundamentally and profoundly rooted in the core principles of transparency, accountability, and ethical stewardship. The enduring legacy of sovereign coinage serves as a rich and insightful blueprint for creating financial systems that are not only highly efficient and secure but also fundamentally just and inclusive, ensuring that all individuals have access to the financial resources and opportunities they need.

Envision a future characterized by digital currencies skillfully managed on decentralized networks, which embrace the same high ethical standards that once governed the ancient treasuries of our history. In this promising future, every transaction is meticulously recorded with the precision and care of a dedicated temple scribe, ensuring that no detail is overlooked. Each financial decision made is thoughtfully guided by readily available and transparent data, fostering an environment where every participant can see the consequences of their choices. Here, the collective good of the community stands as the unwavering cornerstone of all economic activities, ensuring that everyone benefits equitably. This anticipated future is one where the sacred spirit of wealth—once honored and celebrated in the magnificent grand temples and revered treasuries of old—is entirely reborn within the expansive digital domain. This metamorphosis goes far beyond merely transforming our financial systems; it catalyzes a fundamental change that reverberates throughout the very fabric of our society, reshaping our relationships with currency, each other, and the world at large.

This vision is not only shocking but also profoundly compelling in nature. It effectively challenges and undermines the entrenched status quo of profit-driven capitalism, which often prioritizes individual gain above all else. Instead, it offers an alternative model of finance that values social welfare, communal prosperity, and the well-being of all citizens. This vision serves as a powerful invitation to reimagine wealth, not merely as a tool for individual accumulation or personal success, but as a vital means to build a more equitable, sustainable, and interconnected world. The logical, analytical, and persuasive arguments drawn from the rich history and evolution of money make it abundantly clear that such a transformative system is not only highly desirable but is also entirely achievable with collective effort and innovative thinking.

Persuading the Modern Investor: The Ethical Imperative

For the modern investor, the ancient lessons of effective money management present a compelling, powerful, and ethical imperative that cannot be ignored. In a rapidly changing world where financial decisions are subject to increasing scrutiny regarding their broader social impact, embracing a model that effectively integrates age-old wisdom with cutting-edge modern technology emerges as both a logical strategy and a morally compelling choice. Investors in today's landscape are now motivated by much more than just the relentless pursuit of profit; they are also driven by a profound desire to make a positive impact on society. This includes supporting innovative initiatives that promote greater transparency within financial systems, as well as investing in cohesive systems that empower and uplift communities in meaningful ways. By combining these ancient insights with contemporary practices, modern investors can create a balanced approach that benefits both their own financial goals and the well-being of society at large.

The rise of ethical investing, corporate social responsibility, and sustainable finance represents significant reflections of this evolving modern ethos that people are increasingly adopting in various aspects of life today. These emerging trends resonate deeply with the ancient belief that wealth, when managed with a sense of responsibility and prudence, is not merely an asset but a sacred trust—a precious gift that should ideally be utilized to benefit the many rather than to enrich the few who already have plenty. In this context, digital currencies, with their inherently decentralized and transparent nature, present a groundbreaking pathway to turn this noble vision into a tangible reality. By eliminating the intermediaries and central authorities that have long dominated and controlled traditional finance systems, cryptocurrencies effectively democratize access to wealth. They create invaluable opportunities for a broader, more inclusive distribution of resources, thereby empowering individuals across diverse socioeconomic backgrounds.

This ethical imperative is not merely an aspirational goal—it is firmly grounded in the deep logic of human progress. The same enduring principles that drove ancient civilizations to develop intricate and sophisticated systems for managing wealth and resources are precisely the ones that can effectively guide us toward establishing a fairer, more accountable financial system in today's world. For investors, this presents a compelling and persuasive reason to wholeheartedly embrace digital currencies and the emerging landscape of decentralized finance. These innovations are not only remarkably innovative and potentially lucrative, but they also embody a transformative vision of finance that is closely aligned with the highest ideals of human society and the collective values we aspire to uphold.

A Call for Integration: From Ancient Principles to Digital Reality

The synthesis of ancient financial wisdom with modern digital technology is far from being merely a fanciful idea—it is now an essential imperative for navigating the future. The sacred role of money in ancient civilizations was intricately rooted in a profound understanding of value, trust, and the critical need for accountability within economic exchanges. These timeless principles, which have successfully guided human societies over countless millennia, continue to hold significant sway in today's rapidly evolving and increasingly complex financial landscape. As we move forward, it becomes crucial to merge these age-old insights with contemporary innovations to create a more balanced and equitable financial system.

Digital currencies and decentralized finance platforms represent the logical successors to the traditional coinage and treasury systems that have governed economies throughout history. They effectively leverage cutting-edge technology to build systems that are not only transparent but also efficient and inherently democratic in nature. The integration of blockchain technology, for instance, provides a modern-day parallel to the meticulous record-keeping practices once employed by ancient temple scribes. In this contemporary context, every digital transaction is meticulously recorded, thoroughly verified, and made accessible to all stakeholders involved, ensuring that the entire system remains robust and free from corruption and manipulation. By enhancing accountability and trust among users, these innovations are paving the way for a new era of financial interactions that prioritize user autonomy and equitable access.

This integration transcends mere technological evolution; it stands as a profound reinvention of the very essence and nature of money itself. It embodies a vital bridge linking the revered traditions of our past to the groundbreaking and innovative possibilities that lie ahead in the future. By wholeheartedly embracing and applying the time-tested principles of ancient wealth management, we have the unique opportunity to construct financial systems that are designed not only to generate profit but also to cultivate social cohesion. Moreover, such systems can effectively promote ethical practices that benefit entire communities and empower individuals on a truly global scale. In doing so, we can create a world where financial prosperity is intertwined with social responsibility and collective advancement.

The Enduring Blueprint for a Transformed Financial Future

In this shockingly detailed and enlightening exploration of how money temples and sovereign coinage have uniquely shaped the intricate landscape of modern finance, we have uncovered a logical and persuasive blueprint that could potentially guide us into the future. The vital lessons drawn from ancient civilizations—where unrestricted wealth was revered and treated as a sacred symbol of divine favor, meticulously recorded in grand temple treasuries, and celebrated through vibrant public rituals—offer us a timeless and essential framework for understanding, analyzing, and ultimately transforming our contemporary financial systems. This historical perspective not only sheds light on the origins of our current monetary practices but also prompts us to reconsider the values and beliefs that underpin them. The intersection of spirituality and economics in ancient times serves as a compelling reminder of the deeper significance that financial systems have held throughout human history.

The evolution of money has undergone significant transformations, transitioning from the primitive forms of barter to the more sophisticated concepts of commodity money, and ultimately to the creation of standardized coinage. This remarkable journey was fueled by a fundamental yet deep-seated necessity: the desire to establish a medium of exchange that would be reliable, fully transparent, and universally accepted by all. Throughout this evolutionary process, ingenious and creative solutions emerged to address the inherent limitations seen in earlier systems—a progression that is as logical and rational as it is truly revolutionary in its implications. The foundational principles that supported these ancient innovations—trust, accountability, and ethical stewardship—remain timeless and relevant. They can undeniably guide us even as we navigate the complexities and challenges of the digital age today.

Today, as we stand on the very threshold of a groundbreaking financial revolution powered by transformative digital currencies and increasingly decentralized networks, we are presented with a significant opportunity to reclaim and redefine the sacred spirit of wealth that has often been overlooked. We have the immense potential to build robust and sustainable systems that are as ethically grounded as they are technologically advanced, ensuring that the remarkable benefits of financial innovation and progress are equitably shared by every member of society. The persuasive and well-reasoned arguments drawn from the ancient practices of effective money management provide a particularly compelling case for reimagining and reshaping our financial future—a future where wealth is seen not merely as a means to an end, but rather as a sacred trust that holds the power to uplift society as a whole and foster true collective prosperity. Let us seize this moment to create a more inclusive and prosperous landscape for generations to come.

Let this exploration serve as an urgent and compelling call to action for all those who are willing to listen and engage. Embrace the invaluable lessons drawn from our past experiences and effectively integrate them into the innovative design of our modern financial systems. Whether you identify as an investor looking for opportunities, a policymaker striving for effective governance, or an informed citizen who is genuinely concerned about the future trajectory of our global economy, the blueprint for a transformed financial future is clear and achievable. It is a vision of a future where transparency, unwavering accountability, and committed ethical stewardship form the very core of economic activity. This is a future in which the sacred and pivotal role of money is once again recognized as a cornerstone vital to fostering a just, equitable, and prosperous society for all. Through active participation and thoughtful engagement, we can create the foundations for this needed transformation.

In the end, the enduring and significant legacy of both money temples and sovereign coinage is not merely a chapter in the pages of history; rather, it serves as a living, breathing template that charts the evolution of finance across the ages. It reminds us that true wealth is not measured solely by the accumulation of material possessions but rather by its profound ability to promote stability, foster innovation, and create a lasting and meaningful impact on society as a whole. The ancient blueprint that was established is as relevant and crucial today as it was thousands of years ago—a powerful testament to the timeless strength and creativity of human ingenuity and the sacred spirit of wealth that has been cherished throughout the epochs of civilization.

Embrace this rich legacy, allowing it to guide you effectively as you navigate the intricate complexities of modern finance with confidence and clarity. The profound principles of ancient wealth management—which are deeply rooted in sound logic, ethical responsibility, and a remarkable understanding of true value—offer a truly revolutionary and transformative pathway to a future where financial systems are designed to work for everyone, ultimately benefiting society as a whole. This perspective presents a mind-blowing, compelling, and achievable vision for what lies ahead: one that possesses the immense power to genuinely transform our economic reality in meaningful and inclusive ways. By implementing these timeless principles that have stood the test of time, we can build a world where prosperity is equitably shared among all individuals, trust is not only restored but also solidified and strengthened across communities, and the true potential of money is unlocked, thereby serving the greater benefit of all members of society. Together, we can create a vibrant financial landscape that uplifts everyone in the community rather than a privileged select few, fostering opportunities for growth, collaboration, and equitable access to resources for all.

Section 2: Philosophical Challenges to State-Controlled Currency

The story of money is not merely a tale of economic evolution; rather, it represents a vast and intricate saga of ideas, passionate debates, and significant philosophical challenges that have profoundly shaped human society throughout the annals of history. In the earliest days, when the very concept of money was still in its nascent and formative stages, fundamental questions emerged regarding who should wield the power and control over this most vital instrument of exchange and value. The revolutionary idea that centralized authority could decree the value and regulate the fluid and essential flow of money was as groundbreaking and innovative as it was controversial, stirring significant and passionate debate among thinkers, philosophers, and rulers alike. This section delves deeply into the shocking debates and mind-blowing philosophies that critically questioned the foundations of state-controlled currency, revealing a complex and multi-layered world where the very legitimacy of governmental power was under constant siege and scrutiny by alternative visions and models of economic freedom that sought to redefine and reshape the relationship between individuals and their own economic destinies. In this in-depth exploration, we unravel the intricate threads of opinion that have consistently challenged the prevailing status quo and examine how these diverse perspectives and ideas continue to influence and shape contemporary financial systems and institutions today, leaving a lasting mark on the evolution of economic thought.

The Birth of Centralization: When Money Became a Tool of the State

In the ancient world, the concept of money emerged not as a naturally occurring phenomenon woven seamlessly into the fabric of civilization but rather as a deliberate human invention—a sophisticated tool carefully crafted and thoughtfully devised specifically to overcome the inherent limitations and shortcomings associated with barter systems that dominated early trade. In those early days, trade was a relatively straightforward and uncomplicated undertaking, based mainly on direct exchanges of goods and services between individuals within local communities. However, as societies began to grow more complex and advancements in social structures took place, the pressing need for a standardized medium of exchange became increasingly urgent and starkly apparent to all involved in commerce. It was precisely at this pivotal and critical juncture in human history that various governments and ruling authorities began to assert greater control over the production and distribution of money, taking increasingly significant steps to standardize its production and imbue it with a sense of official sanction and legitimacy that would be recognized by the populace. The significant transition from the use of commodity money, which was often based on tangible items possessing intrinsic value that people could agree upon, to the adoption of state-controlled currency marked an extraordinary turning point in economic history that reshaped societies. This centralization of money was not merely a random occurrence in the annals of history; it was, in many ways, a logical and even inevitable response to the complexities associated with managing growing economies, as rulers and leaders sought to stabilize their economic environments and enhance their level of administrative control over the populations they governed. However, this very move sparked fierce and heated philosophical debates among the thinkers, economists, and scholars of the time, who grappled with the far-reaching implications of this shift on individual freedoms, market dynamics, and the fundamental nature of value itself within the economic landscape.

Centralized money offered the enticing and attractive promise of uniformity, stability, and reliability in various economic exchanges between individuals and businesses. For a ruler who was seeking to firmly establish authority and control, issuing official coinage served as a powerful and effective means to project strength, uphold social order, and also efficiently collect taxes from the populace. However, critics and skeptics of this system soon began to voice concerns and question the broader implications of such centralization. Was it truly wise for a state to possess the unchecked and absolute power to print money at will, without any limitations? Such authority over currency could potentially lead to grave and far-reaching consequences. Could this level of concentrated power inevitably result in rampant corruption, uncontrolled inflation, and a gradual erosion of both personal and economic freedom for the citizens? These pressing and urgent questions ignited a profound philosophical firestorm that continues to resonate deeply in discussions surrounding monetary policy and state control to this day, significantly influencing debates about various economic systems and the fundamental nature of governance in society.

The Logic of Decentralization: Why Some Challenged the State Monopoly

At the very heart of the ongoing and increasingly contentious debate was a profoundly significant and deeply fundamental question that carries with it wide-ranging implications: Should money be subjected to control and regulation by a centralized authority, or should it be fully liberated from the persistent influence and oversight of the state? Advocates of decentralized money passionately argued with fervor that state-controlled currency was inherently flawed, problematic, and detrimental to societal welfare. These fervent individuals firmly believed that allowing any single entity—especially a government—to hold a monopoly over money was a recipe for inevitable abuse and rampant corruption. History, as these critical thinkers meticulously contended, was replete with countless examples of governments throughout various eras manipulating currency in numerous insidious ways to serve their own narrow interests, often at the unfortunate and detrimental expense of the very people who relied on that currency for their daily needs and economic stability. The overwhelming concern shared among these advocates was that such centralized control could all too easily lead to the erosion of individual freedoms, personal liberties, and the overall fabric of economic stability that is essential for a thriving society.

One of the earliest and most significant challenges to societal structures and individual freedoms originated from the complex and often perplexing realm of philosophy. Prominent thinkers, philosophers, and intellectuals from ancient Greece and Rome embarked on a journey to articulate and express a coherent and insightful vision of money, viewing it as a fundamental tool that should primarily serve the interests of the people, rather than enslave them or manipulate them for the benefit of those in power. They contended that money, functioning as a universal and widely accepted symbol of value, must remain impartial and entirely free from any form of political manipulation or undue influence. When a state exercised control over the production and distribution of money, it could easily inflate its supply to finance costly wars, placate mounting national debt, or even enrich a loyal ruling class that was often disconnected from the everyday struggles faced by common citizens. Such practices, they asserted, could seriously undermine the essential trust that is necessary in order for the entire monetary system to function effectively and could ultimately distort the true value of goods and services in the dynamic marketplace. In this way, they raised profound and compelling questions about the ethical implications of money and its complex role in society, challenging both individuals and institutions to rethink their beliefs about wealth and economic structures.

Consider the lively and profoundly engaging debates that took place among the ancient Greek philosophers, who engaged in discussions that shaped the very fabric of Western thought. In a society that placed immense significance on rational inquiry and empirical observation, the prevailing idea that money could be swayed by the unpredictable whims of a ruler was widely viewed as deeply irrational and fundamentally problematic. Plato, for instance, sharply criticized the exploitative misuse of money in many of his foundational works, lamenting the erosion of ethical standards and moral integrity when wealth became concentrated in the hands of individuals who had not earned it through virtue or commendable moral conduct. His reflections invited serious contemplation on the ethical dimensions of wealth and its impact on society. Aristotle expanded on these initial ideas and went even further by arguing that money should possess a natural limit—a standardized measure of value that would accurately reflect intrinsic worth, rather than being subjected to the arbitrary decrees of those in power. He meticulously examined the nature of exchanges and the role that money plays in facilitating commerce, emphasizing the importance of fairness in economic transactions. These foundational debates and discussions laid crucial groundwork for many later thinkers who would rise to challenge the very notion and principle of centralized monetary control. They collectively inspired a rich and evolving tradition of thought that questioned how financial systems should ideally be structured and who should truly hold the authority to regulate them in a just and equitable manner.

The Theoretical Foundations of Economic Freedom

The philosophical challenges posed to state-controlled currency were not just abstract musings; instead, they were deeply and profoundly rooted in a transformative vision of economic freedom that sought to empower individuals. Thinkers like Adam Smith, whose groundbreaking and seminal work "The Wealth of Nations" continues to significantly influence and shape modern economics and thought, passionately argued that the free market, as opposed to state intervention, represented the most effective and optimal mechanism for determining the true value of money. Smith's innovative and pioneering concept of the "invisible hand" proposed that individuals, by diligently pursuing their own self-interest and personal ambitions, inadvertently contribute to the common good and overall prosperity of society as a whole—a dynamic and beneficial process that would inevitably be stifled, constrained, and hindered if the state were to monopolize the money supply and exert ultimate control over currency completely.

The concept of economic freedom was truly revolutionary in its essence, reshaping traditional perspectives on financial systems. It posited that money should be entirely liberated from the restrictive shackles of government control, allowing it to evolve in a natural and organic manner through the powerful and often unpredictable forces of the market. Advocates of this viewpoint emphasized that a free market for currency promotes unrestricted competition and innovation, which, in turn, leads to greater efficiency and wealth generation for society at large. Critics who opposed centralized currency firmly argued that when governments issue money without adhering to any fixed guidelines or principles, they not only distort crucial economic signals but also undermine the very foundation of trust that is absolutely essential for a thriving and prosperous economy. This deviation from stability can lead to inflation and economic instability, threatening people's livelihoods. Trust, they maintained, is fundamentally built on the principles of predictability, transparency, and fairness—qualities that are best achieved when money is permitted to operate in a decentralized and competitive environment. Such an environment enables various entities to engage freely with one another, fostering innovation and creating a vibrant marketplace, where the entrepreneurial spirit can flourish without unnecessary bureaucratic interference. In this dynamic setting, consumers benefit from a wider array of choices, while producers are incentivized to improve quality and reduce costs, ultimately driving the economy toward greater prosperity.

The logical conclusion deduced from the collection of arguments presented was that by decentralizing monetary control, we would, without a doubt, transition towards a more efficient, organic, and just economic system that benefits everyone who is involved in this intricate process. When money is genuinely liberated from any form of political maneuvering or undue influence, its value becomes determined by tangible economic activities that arise naturally within the environment, rather than being dictated by arbitrary policy decisions that often lack sufficient foresight or consideration. This fundamental transformation in our perception of monetary systems not only encourages investment and innovation but also fosters significant growth across a multitude of sectors, driving progress and creativity. The persuasive strength of this argument lies in its inherent simplicity and elegance: when we allow free markets to operate without the burden of unnecessary state intervention or bureaucratic obstacles, they outperform in effectively allocating resources. This leads to spurring technological advancements and achieving better overall quality of life for individuals as well as communities alike. By emphasizing this viewpoint, we reinforce the idea that sound economic principles and practices can indeed pave the way for a thriving and flourishing society for all involved.

Historical Case Studies: When Central Control Backfired

History is littered with a multitude of striking examples showcasing how state-controlled currency has often gone awry and led to dire and often catastrophic consequences. One of the most infamous and compelling cases is the hyperinflation that was experienced by the Weimar Republic in Germany during the particularly tumultuous 1920s. In a desperate and urgent effort to pay off the onerous war reparations that were imposed after the end of World War I, as well as to finance a rapidly struggling and destabilizing economy, the government made the disastrous decision to resort to printing money at an astonishingly reckless and unsustainable rate. This ultimately led to a dramatic and catastrophic collapse in the value of the currency itself. As a direct result, prices soared to unimaginable and unprecedented heights, the savings of ordinary citizens were entirely and irrevocably wiped out, and the very social fabric of the nation was irreparably torn apart, leaving the populace in dire and desperate straits. This catastrophic failure of monetary policy serves as a stark and enduring reminder of the inherent dangers and serious pitfalls associated with centralized control over money and the far-reaching economic consequences that can ensue when fiscal policies are poorly managed, inadequately monitored, and left unchecked.

Another illustrative example can be found in ancient Rome, where the various emperors were notoriously recognized for their alarming tendency to debase the coinage in order to finance their lavish and extravagant lifestyles while simultaneously supporting their ambitious military campaigns. By systematically reducing the precious metal content within the coins that were in circulation, they effectively inflated the money supply within the economy, which inevitably led to significant economic instability and a concerning loss of public confidence in the currency and its inherent value. These historical episodes are not merely isolated incidents; rather, they represent a broader and recurring pattern where centralized control over the money supply often leads to a myriad of unintended yet serious consequences. This includes severe economic distortions, a substantial loss of trust among the populace in the authorities and institutions, and ultimately, an environment that is ripe for social unrest that can have far-reaching and profound implications for society as a whole, affecting not only the economy but also the social fabric and stability of the entire nation.

Such examples serve to illuminate and underscore the critical reasoning behind the substantial philosophical challenges that arise with state-controlled currency systems. When the tremendous power and authority to create, manage, and distribute money is monopolized solely in the hands of a select few individuals, organizations, or institutions, it inevitably opens the door to exploitation that is primarily aimed at achieving short-term financial gains and the accumulation of wealth. This often comes at the expense of long-term economic stability and sustainability, creating an imbalanced and precarious financial landscape. The analytical argument advocating for a more decentralized approach to money is indeed both clear and compelling: in a well-structured system where the creation and regulation of currency are subject to market forces and guided by transparent and accountable processes, that system is inherently more robust, considerably more resilient, and significantly less susceptible to manipulation and abuse by those wielding power. Embracing decentralization could foster a healthier financial ecosystem that prioritizes equitable access and fairness in economic transactions, ensuring that the benefits of currency creation and distribution are not hoarded by an elite few but rather made available to a broader segment of society.

The Philosophical Divide: Security Versus Liberty

At the very heart of the ongoing and complex debate surrounding state-controlled currency lies a deep and profound philosophical divide that echoes through the ages, fundamentally contrasting the paramount importance of security with the essential value of individual liberty. On one side of this contentious and multifaceted issue, proponents of centralized control firmly argue that a currency managed and regulated by the government offers a plethora of significant advantages, including stability, uniformity, and a robust safety net for all economic transactions that take place within society. They maintain with great conviction that without a strong central authority overseeing the currency, the money supply could easily spiral into chaos and disarray, inevitably leading to widespread economic uncertainty and an increased potential for fraud in various financial transactions. Such a precarious situation could severely undermine trust in the entire financial system and create further risks and complications for both individuals and businesses alike, bringing about adverse effects on overall economic health and social confidence.

On the other hand, the advocates for decentralization strongly maintain that the security of a currency is not necessarily enhanced by state control, but rather significantly bolstered by the inherent transparency and unrestrained competition found within a free market economy. They argue with conviction that when money is permitted to evolve naturally, free from excessive governmental oversight and regulation, its value becomes more accurately determined by the genuine forces of supply and demand operating within the marketplace. This, they claim, inevitably leads to a greater degree of economic freedom, allowing individuals to make their own choices regarding financial transactions, and, as a result, fosters a substantially more prosperous society overall. The tension that exists between these two contrasting viewpoints is both deeply logical and profoundly emotional, as it reflects the complex and deep-seated beliefs that individuals hold regarding the role of government in society and the fundamental rights of individuals to control their own economic destinies and futures. This ongoing debate encapsulates not only economic theories but also moral questions concerning fairness, equity, and the moral responsibility of institutions. As citizens seek to understand how best to harness and balance these competing ideologies, it is crucial to explore the implications they have for both individual autonomy and collective welfare in society.

This philosophical divide is not merely an academic exercise; in fact, it has significant and tangible implications that resonate deeply in the real world we experience today. The recent rise of cryptocurrencies, along with the innovative concept of decentralized finance, presents a formidable and direct challenge to the longstanding traditional model of currency that has been primarily controlled by the state and its various institutions. Digital currencies, such as Bitcoin and Ethereum, function independently of a central authority, relying instead on complex and intricate algorithms in conjunction with a distributed network of users. This cooperative system works tirelessly to ensure the security, robustness, and integrity of the entire financial ecosystem. This innovative framework signifies a radical departure from the conventional and widely accepted understanding of money, which has historically been viewed simply as a tool wielded exclusively by governmental institutions and banking authorities. It represents a substantial shift toward heightened individual liberty and empowerment in financial matters, an evolution that strongly resonates with the enduring ancient debates surrounding economic freedom, autonomy, and self-determination that have persisted throughout human history.

Logical Critiques: The Case Against Centralized Monetary Authority

Centralized monetary authority, while it may present a veneer of stability and the apparent semblance of economic security, is fraught with numerous logical inconsistencies that cannot be overlooked, along with a significant potential for abuse that poses risks to the economic system. The arguments against state control of money are not only compelling in their nature but also deeply grounded in both historical evidence and established economic theory that has evolved throughout the ages. A thorough examination of past economies reveals that state intervention frequently leads to undesirable outcomes, which challenges the notion that a central authority can manage money effectively and responsibly without causing unintended consequences.

One of the most persuasive and compelling critiques made against centralized control is that it inherently creates a monopoly on the creation of money, an aspect that can be easily manipulated for various political purposes by those in positions of power. Governments around the globe have a well-documented historical record of consistently using their significant power over the money supply to finance wars, support failing industries that would otherwise inevitably collapse under market pressures, and ultimately to enrich themselves at the expense of the general populace and working class. This problematic concentration of financial power not only distorts essential economic signals, but it also fundamentally undermines the very notion of a fair, equitable, and efficient market system. When a government possesses the unchecked ability to print money freely, without any restraint or limitations imposed by checks and balances, it inevitably leads to the erosion of the value of the currency in circulation. This results in numerous adverse economic effects, leading to widespread inflation, decreased purchasing power among consumers, and overall economic instability that can have far-reaching and damaging consequences for society as a whole, affecting every stakeholder.

Furthermore, centralized monetary systems inherently possess a notable vulnerability to corruption and mismanagement that is extremely difficult to overlook or dismiss. The glaring lack of transparency that often characterizes state-controlled banking institutions regularly leads to the misallocation of essential resources that society heavily relies on. Such mismanagement not only complicates economic stability but can also facilitate the emergence of economic elites who, as a result of these systemic flaws, accumulate wealth and power, thus wielding a disproportionate level of influence over the financial landscape. This reality raises significant concerns about equity and fairness in the distribution of economic opportunities. Therefore, one can draw the logical and concerning conclusion that when the control of money is concentrated exclusively within a single central authority, it inevitably becomes subject to the unpredictable whims, biases, and failings associated with human fallibility—shortcomings that can lead to catastrophic and far-reaching consequences for the broader economy. Ultimately, these failures can harm the very populace that such centralized systems are intended to serve and protect, resulting in widespread public discontent and eroding trust in financial institutions.

Another critical point to carefully consider is that centralized control often has a significant tendency to stifle innovation extensively. By strictly dictating the money supply, governments can inadvertently dampen entrepreneurial activity and hinder the vital and pivotal development of new technologies and groundbreaking ideas. In clear contrast, a decentralized monetary system—where money is created, managed, and circulated through competitive and fully open processes—encourages innovation much more effectively by allowing market forces to freely determine and establish value. This dynamic and flexible system is inherently more adaptable, highly responsive, and ultimately far more conducive to substantial economic growth and long-term progress. Entrepreneurs in such a thriving environment can flourish, experimenting with novel approaches, exploring uncharted territories, and discovering valuable solutions that drive society forward in meaningful ways, leading to advancements that can improve overall quality of life.

The Emergence of Decentralized Alternatives

The philosophical challenges that were posed to state-controlled currency have played a tremendously significant role in laying the crucial groundwork that allowed for the emergence and steady development of decentralized monetary systems. As early critics and prominent thinkers vocally articulated their strong arguments for a freer, more market-driven approach to money, a new wave of innovators and visionaries began to delve into and thoroughly investigate alternative models that would effectively liberate money from the clutches and grasp of centralized authority and control. This intellectual and technological evolution, occurring over the span of time, eventually culminated in the groundbreaking creation and advent of cryptocurrencies—a radical reimagining and profound redefinition of what money could potentially be and represent in the ever-evolving modern world of today.

Cryptocurrencies, including the well-known Bitcoin, emerged from an increasingly strong desire to establish a new form of currency that operates completely independently from any government or central bank structure that has traditionally been responsible for monetary systems. These revolutionary digital currencies function on decentralized networks, where all transaction verifications are carried out by a distributed community of users rather than being overseen by a central authority or governing body. This innovative system serves as a direct and powerful reaction to the ongoing criticisms and shortcomings of traditional centralized currency systems that have been criticized for their lack of accountability. It presents a compelling argument that a modern money system should be inherently transparent, fully accountable for its actions, and highly resistant to the sway of political manipulation and outside influence. Each and every transaction that takes place is meticulously recorded on an immutable ledger known as the blockchain, thereby delivering an exceptional and unprecedented level of transparency and security for all parties involved. Such remarkable characteristics would undoubtedly have generated admiration from those ancient critics who raised concerns about the inherent dangers of state-controlled money and its vulnerabilities, especially in times of economic distress. The evolution and rise of cryptocurrencies represents a significant advancement in the creation of alternative financial systems that challenge the norms, reflecting a growing global demand for financial autonomy and trust in the integrity, safety, and reliability of digital transactions in our increasingly digital world.

Moreover, the ever-evolving decentralized nature of cryptocurrencies significantly promotes economic liberty in a truly revolutionary way. In a world wherein money is no longer predominantly under the control of a single authoritative entity or centralized institution, individuals find themselves increasingly free to transact and store their value without any form of interference or oversight from traditional financial systems. This monumental shift is not merely a technological advancement; it carries deeply profound philosophical implications that extend far beyond mere convenience. It challenges the long-standing, age-old notion that economic power must necessarily be concentrated in the hands of a privileged few elite individuals or organizations who control the flow of capital and resources. Instead of perpetuating this outdated paradigm, it opens up the door to a much more inclusive and accessible financial system. This new framework actively democratizes access to wealth, allowing individuals from diverse backgrounds across the globe to engage in economic activities that were previously inaccessible to them. As a result, it fosters a more equitable distribution of resources, creating opportunities for entrepreneurial initiatives and innovative ideas that enrich society as a whole. In essence, the rise of cryptocurrencies is redefining not just how we perceive money, but also how we envision economic participation itself.

The Role of Technology in Rewriting Monetary Philosophy

The ongoing debate over centralized versus decentralized monetary control is not merely confined to dusty tomes of ancient philosophy; it is being actively rewritten and reshaped by the recent and rapid advent of modern technology. Innovations like blockchain and other advanced distributed ledger technologies are providing practical and viable solutions to the various complex problems that have plagued state-controlled currency for decades, often leading to inefficiencies and inequities in the financial system. These groundbreaking technologies offer a highly transparent, secure, and efficient way to manage the money supply today. By utilizing such systems, we can operate free from the distortions and detrimental impacts of political interference that have often marred traditional financial systems in the past. The profound transition to these new frameworks not only promises a more stable economic environment but also fosters greater financial inclusivity, presenting exciting and transformative possibilities for the future of commerce and trade that were once unimaginable. With these innovations, we are on the brink of a financial revolution that could empower individuals and businesses alike while driving progress and growth across various sectors.

These advanced and sophisticated technologies stand as the logical successors to the ancient systems of record-keeping that were once widely utilized in civilizations long past, functioning as a bridge between the past and the future. In the annals of ancient times, diligent and dedicated scribes meticulously inscribed important transactions and events onto clay tablets, ensuring that vital information and historical records were preserved carefully for future generations. In stark contrast, today's groundbreaking blockchain technology captures, processes, and archives every digital transaction in real time, allowing for an unprecedented level of detail and immediacy that was previously unimaginable. This remarkable evolution in how we manage information is nothing short of mind-blowing in its scale and precision, showcasing the incredible advancements we have made as a society. It embodies a brilliant fusion of ancient wisdom with cutting-edge innovation in our ever-evolving digital age, proving conclusively that the fundamental principles of trust, accountability, and transparency are truly timeless, resonating through the corridors of history and echoing into the future we are now shaping together.

The impressive analytical power of modern technology greatly enhances our ability to process and manage vast quantities of data with remarkable efficiency. This capability ensures that every single transaction is meticulously verified and remains immutable, thereby fostering a high level of trust and accountability. This remarkable level of precision and reliability is precisely what early critics envisioned when they raised concerns over the inefficiencies and limitations commonly associated with state-controlled currency systems. By effectively eliminating the potential for human error and central manipulation, blockchain technology paves the way for a system that is fundamentally fair, inherently transparent, and resilient to various forms of attack that threaten its integrity. It stands as a powerful testament to the enduring logic of economic freedom—a compelling logic that consistently champions the notion of decentralized control as the most effective path toward achieving stability and long-term prosperity in an ever-evolving market landscape. This evolution in technology not only reshapes our understanding of financial systems but also opens the door for innovative solutions that prioritize individual empowerment, equitable access to resources, and broader participation in the financial ecosystem. Embracing these advancements fosters an environment where individuals can take charge of their financial destinities and engage in a more open and inclusive economy. Through this transformation, we witness the potential for new opportunities and a shift toward a more balanced and just financial framework that benefits all participants involved.

The Persuasive Argument for Decentralized Currency

The philosophical challenges that arise in opposition to state-controlled currency form an exceptionally compelling and intricate case for not only exploring but also adopting balanced and efficient decentralized alternatives. The underlying logic is quite persuasive and robust: when money is successfully removed, liberated, and set free from the stringent, often suffocating, control of centralized authorities, it transforms into a powerful and dynamic tool for genuine economic empowerment and personal freedom. Decentralized currencies, which can take various innovative forms, open up numerous avenues for a true free market of ideas, creativity, and groundbreaking solutions, where value is determined by the collective will, consent, and collaboration of the people rather than being imposed and dictated by a small, often unaccountable group of bureaucrats and governmental officials. This democratization of money represents a revolutionary concept—a startling and shocking departure from centuries of tightly-knit, centralized control and regulation that has historically governed financial systems across different societies. It holds the promise of enabling individuals from diverse backgrounds to have more comprehensive control over their economic destinies, fostering a more inclusive, accessible, and participatory economic landscape that welcomes and benefits everyone in society.

Critics of decentralized currency frequently highlight its notable volatility, which captures attention and concern, as well as the significant absence of regulatory oversight in the continually evolving market. Yet, it is important to recognize that these challenges are not insurmountable hurdles; rather, they represent the growing pains of a financial system that is still relatively young and very much in its formative stages. The same critics who once adamantly dismissed the concept of paper money as impractical and unworthy of consideration eventually had to come to terms with its undeniable superiority over the age-old practice of bartering for goods and services in the market. Similarly, the initial turbulence and unpredictability associated with various cryptocurrencies can be seen as a necessary and essential phase in their overall evolution towards achieving a more stable and mature financial ecosystem. As the underlying technology matures and evolves, it is widely expected that these digital currencies will undergo transformative changes and advancements, ultimately leading to a more robust and reliable financial future for everyone involved in this evolving landscape. In time, the perceived instability may give way to greater confidence and adoption, unlocking potential benefits that might not yet be fully realized or appreciated.

The persuasive power of this compelling argument is significantly enhanced and further amplified by the considerable weight of historical precedent that we can clearly observe throughout various stages of human history. Much like the pivotal and groundbreaking shift from a system of barter—which often led to complexities and inefficiencies—to the introduction of coinage, which represented a logical, meaningful, and transformative improvement in the overall efficiency and reliability of trade practices, the ongoing transition that we are witnessing from state-controlled currency to the innovative and dynamic realm of decentralized digital money stands as the next crucial and significant evolutionary step in our increasingly complex financial landscape. This ongoing transition directly addresses the very fundamental shortcomings that ancient philosophers and many economic thinkers of their times so vocally decried—namely, the enduring issues of inefficiency, lack of transparency, and the potential for abuse and manipulation by those in power who often seek to maintain control over the monetary system. By fully embracing and wholeheartedly adopting a decentralized financial model, we not only create but also actively foster a financial ecosystem that is not only far more equitable and inclusive, but is also notably more resilient and robust in the face of unpredictable political and economic upheaval that can arise in our constantly evolving and changing world.

The Moral Imperative: Economic Freedom as a Right

Beyond the logical and analytical arguments we often encounter lies a profound and deeply rooted moral imperative that we cannot overlook, no matter how complex the situation may seem. The centralized control of money has, throughout history, been wielded as a stark and oppressive tool—concentrating immense power in the hands of a select few individuals, effectively leaving the vast majority of the population at their mercy. This glaring disparity creates an imbalance that fundamentally undermines the very fabric of our society and its ethical foundations. Economic freedom is an essential and fundamental human right, and any system that seeks to restrict this essential freedom in any way is inherently unjust and deeply oppressive. Ancient philosophers who courageously challenged the principle of state-controlled currency were not merely advocating for a more efficient economic system; they were passionately fighting for the vital right of individuals to control their own fate and destiny. Their courageous struggle has profound implications that resonate through the ages and continues to echo, serving as a powerful reminder of the enduring importance of individual liberty and the critical need for equitable access to economic resources and opportunities for all members of society. In such a world, we must ensure that every person has the chance to pursue their aspirations and thrive without hindrance.

Decentralized currency offers an extraordinary opportunity to reclaim this essential freedom that countless individuals actively seek and yearn for. By effectively shifting the balance of power away from centralized institutions, such as governments and traditional banking systems, it significantly empowers individuals. This empowerment enables them to fully engage and participate in the ever-expanding global economy. The transformation and democratization of finance represented by decentralized currency is not merely a logical progression due to technological advancements; it is also an ethically compelling movement that resonates with the values of justice and equality. It boldly challenges the existing status quo of economic inequality that has plagued societies for so long and opens up the door to a promising future where wealth and financial opportunities are accessible to everyone, not just a select and privileged few. This groundbreaking new paradigm has the remarkable potential to foster inclusivity and create equitable opportunities for all participants in the financial landscape, allowing them to navigate and thrive within a system that is inherently fairer and more just.

The moral argument presented here is both crystal clear and remarkably persuasive: when money is liberated from the stringent grip of central authorities, it undergoes a transformation into a powerful tool for empowerment, instead of merely existing as a weapon of control. This significant shift in how we perceive and utilize money holds the remarkable potential to profoundly transform entire societies. It can create and foster an environment where innovation and opportunity are truly accessible to everyone, regardless of their unique background or circumstances in life. The ethical dimensions associated with decentralized finance resonate deeply with the contemporary values that prioritize fairness, transparency, and social justice. This alignment makes it an inspiring rallying cry for those who genuinely believe that economic freedom is, in essence, fundamentally the cornerstone of human dignity and worth. By embracing this paradigm, we can envision a future where financial systems serve to elevate, empower, and enrich the lives of individuals from all walks of life, thereby promoting a more equitable and just society overall.

Modern Implications: Lessons for Today's Financial Systems

The philosophical challenges posed by state-controlled currency are far from being mere relics that belong to the distant past; in fact, they remain as strikingly relevant today as they were during the eras of our ancient ancestors. Indeed, if we take a closer look at modern financial systems, which are characterized by their intricate and complex layers of regulation alongside concentrated centralized power, we can see that they continue to grapple profoundly with the very same enduring issues of trust, accountability, and economic freedom that were once the primary concern of ancient thinkers and philosophers. As we delve deeper into and navigate this intricate landscape of contemporary economics, it becomes increasingly clear that these timeless issues still demand our unwavering attention and thorough analysis. Furthermore, the rise of digital currencies, in conjunction with the emergence of decentralized finance platforms, represents a direct and robust response to these persistent challenges that we face in the modern economic arena. These innovative solutions not only strive to address our current economic dilemmas but also resonate with and echo the profound wisdom, insights, and teachings found within the philosophies of ancient thinkers. This fascinating interplay between the past and present sheds much-needed light on the ongoing evolution of our understanding of currency, value, and the very nature of economic exchange. Such reflections compel us to reconsider and reassess what we know about money and the systems that govern it, paving the way for a future that may be informed by the lessons of the past while also embracing the innovations of today.

For instance, the ongoing and current debate surrounding central bank digital currencies, or CBDCs, highlights the significant and complex tension between the critical need for stability and the deep, often fervent desire for enhanced economic freedom. While CBDCs promise the potential for improved efficiency in transactions, along with the heightened security of digital exchanges, they also represent a continuation of state-controlled currency mechanisms, which raises important concerns regarding privacy and autonomy. Critics contend that without the necessary checks and balances that are inherently present in decentralized systems, CBDCs could exacerbate existing inequalities within society and further concentrate financial power and control among a select few individuals or institutions, significantly diminishing the equity that many strive for. This intricate and multifaceted debate serves as a modern manifestation of the ancient philosophical challenges that have long been posed to centralized monetary authority—an insightful reminder that the relentless pursuit of economic freedom must always be balanced with robust safeguards to prevent tyranny and oppression. It encourages and invites a deep reconsideration of how we understand the complex intersection of technology, economics, and governance in this rapidly evolving world, sparking discussions about the implications for our future financial systems and the roles that we as individuals, as well as states, should play in that landscape.

Moreover, the explosive growth and rapid rise of cryptocurrencies such as Bitcoin highlight the persistent and enduring appeal of a truly decentralized monetary system, showcasing a revolutionary approach to finance. These innovative digital assets are not merely speculative investments; rather, they represent a groundbreaking paradigm shift in the fundamental ways that value is created, stored, and exchanged in our increasingly digital world. By liberating money from the grasp of centralized institutions and traditional banking systems, cryptocurrencies are empowering individuals and promoting entrepreneurship and innovation. This shift advocates for a more inclusive and accessible financial system for everyone, breaking down barriers that have historically hindered participation in global commerce. The logical, insightful, and persuasive arguments laid out by ancient philosophers against the establishment of state-controlled currency find their modern and highly relevant counterpart in the decentralized and transparent nature of blockchain technology. This technological advancement not only ensures enhanced security and accountability but also provides unprecedented opportunities for people from various economic backgrounds to partake in a dynamic and evolving financial landscape, fundamentally transforming how we perceive and utilize money. As we navigate this new terrain, it becomes increasingly clear that the future of finance may very well rest in the hands of decentralized solutions that prioritize individual empowerment and collective progress.

Persuading the Skeptics: The Case for Decentralization

Despite the compelling logic and ethical arguments that strongly support the concept of decentralized currency, many individuals remain skeptical of its implementation and the long-term viability. Critics point to the significant volatility that is often associated with cryptocurrencies, the various challenges of achieving sufficient scalability, and the potential for regulatory backlash that could significantly hinder growth. However, these criticisms tend to overlook the comprehensive historical trajectory of monetary evolution. Every major innovation in the history of money—from the initial introduction of coinage, which allowed for standardized and more efficient exchange, to the eventual widespread adoption of paper money—was initially met with substantial skepticism and fierce resistance from established financial institutions and traditionalists who were comfortable with the status quo. Over time, as the inherent benefits of these innovations became increasingly apparent to both the general public and financial experts alike, they were embraced widely and eventually became the standard norm within economic systems. The journey from skepticism to acceptance in the realm of money has always been fraught with challenges, yet history shows a clear pattern of integration and adaptation to new financial tools that eventually leads to broader acceptance and adoption across societies. As we navigate the complexities of our modern financial landscape, it is critical to consider this historical context and understand that many of the changes we face today with decentralized currencies may mirror those past transformations that have shaped economies for centuries.

The initial turbulence and dynamic fluctuations observed in the realm of decentralized finance should be understood and interpreted as a natural and expected part of its ongoing evolutionary journey, rather than merely being labeled as a fundamental flaw or perceived as a detrimental aspect. This inherent volatility, while it indeed presents a range of challenges and issues, should be regarded as a temporary condition that distinctly reflects the growing pains of a financial system currently undergoing a crucial and significant transformational phase. As the underlying technology in this space continues to mature and evolve, alongside the development and adaptation of regulatory frameworks, the volatility associated with cryptocurrencies is likely to experience a notable decrease over time. This anticipated reduction in volatility stands to pave the way for the establishment of a more stable, robust, and reliable financial ecosystem capable of more effectively meeting and serving the diverse needs of its users. The logical argument here is that decentralization, in its essence, should not be viewed simply as a radical experiment fated to fail, but rather should be recognized as a natural progression within a larger context—indeed, it represents the next crucial step in an evolutionary process that has, throughout history, consistently yielded more efficient and equitable monetary systems designed to benefit all participants engaging within the economy. Such forward-looking progress strongly suggests a promising and hopeful future for decentralized finance, where the potential for enhanced stability and equitable access can ultimately lead to a revolution in how financial services are perceived, delivered, and consumed by individuals and businesses alike.

Moreover, the compelling ethical imperative for economic freedom adds a particularly persuasive and influential layer to the argument in favor of decentralization in our modern financial landscape. When monetary systems are strictly controlled by a central authority, they become increasingly vulnerable to various forms of misuse and manipulation—a critical truth that history has shown us time and again through numerous financial crises spanning different eras and regions. These crises serve as reminders of the perils associated with centralization. Decentralized systems, in stark and notable contrast, seek to distribute power among a vast and diverse network of users, a process that significantly reduces the likelihood of widespread corruption and abuse of power. This crucial shift not only enhances widespread trust and confidence in the financial system as a whole but also simultaneously creates a more resilient economic model that is inherently better equipped to withstand the shocks, fluctuations, and crises that may arise in a rapidly changing and unpredictable global economy. By empowering individuals rather than centralizing that power within authorities, we promote a much more equitable and just financial landscape that ultimately benefits all participants involved, ensuring that economic opportunities are accessible to everyone, and fostering a sense of community and collaboration that can drive innovation and growth.

The Future: Integrating Ancient Wisdom with Modern Innovation

As we look ahead to the future, the exciting integration of ancient principles with cutting-edge modern technology presents us with a transformative vision for the constantly evolving realm of global finance. The philosophical challenges that are posed to state-controlled currency remind us that money transcends being merely a tool for exchange; rather, it serves as a profound symbol of collective trust, responsibility, and shared value among individuals, communities, and societies at large. By merging this timeless wisdom with the revolutionary capabilities afforded by digital currencies and blockchain technology, we have an incredible opportunity to forge a new and inspiring path forward—one that is not only innovative but also deeply rooted in ethical considerations, inclusivity, and sustainable practices. This guiding framework can lead us toward a more equitable financial landscape that prioritizes the needs of all participants rather than just a select few, thus ensuring that the future of finance remains accessible and fair for everyone involved.

Imagine a truly fascinating world where transformative blockchain technology fundamentally underpins a vast global monetary system that is entirely decentralized, perfectly transparent, and inherently fair for everyone involved. In this visionary world, every single transaction is meticulously recorded on an immutable ledger, artfully crafted to ensure that the entire system remains fully accountable and completely shielded from any form of centralized manipulation or undue influence. This remarkable vision represents the logical culmination of centuries of intense debate and groundbreaking innovative thought—a revolutionary digital financial ecosystem that embodies the finest aspects of both ancient and modern monetary systems. It creates a harmonious blend of cherished tradition and cutting-edge technology, paving the way for a future where financial equality and access are universal rights rather than privileges.

Such a system would not merely serve to significantly enhance economic efficiency; it would also play a crucial and vital role in promoting social justice throughout society as a whole. By effectively democratizing access to wealth and simultaneously working to reduce the concentration of economic power that often benefits only a small, privileged select few, decentralized finance emerges as a powerful agent of change. It holds transformative potential capable of leveling the playing field and fostering a much more inclusive and equitable society for everyone involved in the economy. This development represents the ultimate challenge to the long-standing status quo of state-controlled currency—a formidable challenge that is both shocking in its grand ambition and exceptionally persuasive in its underlying logic, reasoning, and rationale for change. The implications of such a shift are profound and could lead to a redefined financial landscape where opportunities abound for all individuals, rather than just a fortunate minority.

The future of finance, therefore, lies in a thoughtful synthesis of ancient philosophical insights and the latest modern technological innovations that are emerging today. By drawing on the rich lessons of the past and carefully integrating them into our current practices, we can design and create financial systems that are both resilient and equitable, fully capable of effectively meeting the numerous and varied challenges posed by a rapidly changing world we inhabit. This empowering vision is not only logical but also profoundly compelling—it represents the remarkable convergence of human ingenuity, ethical responsibility, and the ongoing advancements of technological progress that are shaping our society today. Together, these vital elements can inspire a transformative new era in finance that not only promotes inclusivity but also prioritizes sustainability in all its dimensions. The potential benefits of this approach are vast, leading to a financial landscape that is not only tech-driven but also deeply rooted in ethical considerations that connect with our shared humanity.

A Blueprint for a New Economic Paradigm

In this mind-blowing exploration of the intricate and multifaceted philosophical challenges that are posed to state-controlled currency, we have uncovered a remarkably rich and intricate tapestry of diverse ideas that have profoundly and significantly shaped human understanding of money throughout the vast expanse of history. From the early, thought-provoking debates of ancient philosophers who uniquely pondered the true nature and intrinsic value of currency, to the revolutionary and transformative innovations brought about by digital currencies in our modern age, the ongoing and dynamic journey of money has continuously represented a profound struggle between the forces of centralization and the deep-seated aspirations of freedom. This ongoing struggle exists in tension with the dynamics of control and the noble ideals of empowerment that we strive for. Each distinct era has contributed unique and varied perspectives to the larger conversation, revealing how our complex relationship with currency is a reflection of broader societal values and intricate power structures that shape our daily lives.

The ancient challenges presented to centralized monetary authority present a captivating and extraordinarily powerful framework for our future. They serve as a profound reminder that money, once freed from the myriad constraints of political manipulation, influence, and control, transforms into an immensely potent tool for authentic economic liberation, growth, and positive change. The logical, analytical, and ethical arguments that oppose the idea of state-controlled currency have not merely stood the test of time—they have refined, matured, and evolved into the foundational principles that now support the current decentralized financial revolution. This evolution is paving the way for exciting new systems, innovative practices, and transformative ideas that will shape the economic landscape for generations to come, heralding a new era of freedom and agency for individuals and communities alike.

As we move forward into an era that is increasingly characterized by rapidly evolving digital transactions and groundbreaking blockchain technology, the important lessons that can be derived from these foundational early debates are now more relevant and significant than they have ever been before. They compel each of us, as engaged citizens, to critically question the prevailing status quo of our financial systems, urging us to reject antiquated systems that concentrate power and wealth into the hands of only a select few. Furthermore, these lessons encourage us to embrace innovative financial models that not only empower individuals but also promote the idea of collective prosperity for everyone in society. The future of money and financial systems is being written in real-time today, and this future is being actively shaped by those brave enough to challenge the entrenched centralized authority that has historically dominated our economic landscape. They are advocating for a more transparent, accountable, and inclusive system that can benefit everyone equally. It is essential that we each take an active role in participating in this transformation, as our contributions, whether they are ideas or actions, will play a crucial role in helping to create a fairer financial landscape that serves all members of our society. Together, we can foster an environment that supports equitable access to financial tools and opportunities, transforming the way we think about money and our place within this evolving financial ecosystem.

This is not merely a theoretical debate—it is an urgent call to action for every single modern citizen, every investor, and every policymaker in our interconnected world. By thoughtfully integrating the timeless wisdom of ancient monetary debates with the groundbreaking and transformative innovations of the digital age, we can collectively build a financial system that is as just as it is efficient. Such a system would promote fairness and equality among all people. It is an inspiring vision of the future where money is not seen merely as a tool for profit alone, but rather as a sacred trust, an instrument that uplifts society, enriches lives, and fosters the overall well-being of all individuals within our diverse communities. In this future, we will work together to redefine wealth and value, ensuring that everyone has a stake in our shared prosperity, creating opportunities for growth and empowerment that benefit all members of society.

Let this profound exploration serve as a potent and powerful rallying cry for the emergence of a new and innovative economic paradigm—a truly transformative paradigm where the ethical imperatives and invaluable lessons of the past actively serve to inform and guide the technological advancements we experience in our present day. The deep and complex philosophical challenges presented by state-controlled currency starkly remind us that true economic freedom and genuine liberation are not achieved by simply concentrating power in the hands of a select few individuals, but rather by actively and intentionally distributing it among the many, thereby allowing for widespread and meaningful participation. In this envisioned new world, money transcends its conventional role and limitations; it evolves into a compelling symbol of collective strength, unity, and resilience, standing as a powerful testament to our shared values and aspirations. This reimagine framework lays a strong foundation for fostering a more equitable and just future that truly benefits all members of society. Through this reimagined approach, we can undoubtedly create systems that not only empower everyone but also pave the way for prosperity that is both inclusive and sustainable, ensuring that no one is left behind in the march toward a brighter future.

Embrace the intricate logic that underpins the financial systems of today, the profound ethics that guide our decision-making, and the transformative revolutionary potential of decentralized finance that is effectively molding and reshaping our world in ways we are just beginning to understand. In the end, the energetic debates and discussions of the past, which have been so vibrant and intense, provide us with a powerful and analytical framework for comprehending the nuanced and multifaceted future of money—a future where economic systems are ingeniously and thoughtfully designed to serve the common good of society at large. It is a future that fosters the notion that the concept of wealth should be viewed and treated as a collective public trust, where every individual, regardless of their unique background or personal circumstances, is granted a fair opportunity to thrive, grow, and elevate their circumstances to new heights. This is the visionary blueprint for a truly transformed financial world—a groundbreaking world that is not only remarkably shocking and exciting but also deeply inspiring in its promise, as it embodies a logical progression and inevitability, paving the way for everyone to actively participate in and benefit from a more equitable and just financial landscape that values inclusivity and fairness above all.

Section 3: Early Experiments in Decentralized Monetary Systems

Throughout the vast expanse of human history, the ongoing and often tumultuous struggle over money has manifested itself as a complex battle not only of material economics but also of transformative and revolutionary ideas that have the potential to reshape societies. The intricate and multifaceted evolution from a basic barter system, which hinges on simple exchanges, to the sophisticated and intricate frameworks of state-controlled currency was anything but a foregone conclusion; rather, it was a lengthy and challenging journey marked by a series of daring, provocative, and experimental approaches that aimed to challenge, critique, and ultimately break free from the confines of centralized financial control. These pioneering early forays into alternative, decentralized monetary systems were nothing short of revolutionary—a breathtaking and shocking world where diverse communities, inspired thinkers, and trailblazing innovators boldly dared to reimagine money as a versatile tool that was not dictated merely by kings or governments, but instead shaped by the dynamic, fluid, and free interplay of human needs, mutual trust, and cooperation among individuals. In this profound exploration, we delve deeply into those groundbreaking pioneering attempts, meticulously examining the logical, analytical, and often mind-blowing experiments that courageously challenged, critiqued, and sought to dismantle the hegemony of state-controlled money, scrutinizing their implications, successes, failures, and the enduring legacy they leave behind in the ongoing narrative of humanity's economic evolution.

The Limitations of Centralization: A Catalyst for Innovation

In ancient and medieval times, state-controlled money emerged as both a blessing and a curse, creating a duality that deeply impacted various societies across different regions and eras. On one hand, centralized coinage provided a much-needed uniformity, offering a reliable medium of exchange that people could depend on, which in turn served as a powerful symbol of political stability that communities could rally around with a sense of pride and unity. On the other hand, however, this centralized approach inevitably brought along inherent risks of abuse, manipulation, and inefficiencies that could severely undermine the economic foundations upon which societies were built. When a single authority held such concentrated power to mint and manage currency, the constant temptation to inflate the money supply, often to finance wars, support extravagant projects, or bolster political power, was always lurking ominously just behind the scenes. This centralization led to significant economic distortions, eroding public trust in the system, and frequently precipitated societal collapse or unrest. These historical instances powerfully illustrate the precarious balance between control and chaos that exists within monetary systems throughout history. Ultimately, the interplay between centralized monetary authority and the economic realities of the time shaped the fates of entire civilizations, reflecting the complex relationship societies have maintained with money itself.

It is precisely these significant shortcomings that drove countless individuals and groups everywhere to fervently seek out viable alternatives that could revolutionize the way money is understood and utilized. Early innovators, along with critical thinkers from varied backgrounds, began to question the established order and the status quo that had long been taken for granted. They passionately argued that the true potential of money could only be fully realized when it was completely liberated from the stringent confines of state control and oversight that had constrained it for so long. This critical examination gave rise to a vision of a world where monetary systems no longer adhered to rigid parameters but instead were designed to be entirely flexible, adaptable, transparent, and truly responsive to the genuine needs and desires of the people. It was an idea that was not only shocking but also revolutionary in its complete and total departure from the entrenched traditions and the old ways of thinking that had predominated for generations. This bold vision stirred lively, passionate discussions and spirited debates across various forums, inspiring a vibrant movement that would ultimately challenge the existing financial paradigms and systems of authority that had prevailed for so long, inviting a reimagining of what financial systems could truly become in a future where the power rests with the individuals they are intended to serve.

The Birth of Commodity Money: Seeds of Decentralization

One of the earliest and most notable responses to the significant limitations and restrictions placed on state-controlled currency was the innovative and resourceful use of commodity money. In a world where the practice of barter was the prevailing norm, various societies and communities took the initiative to experiment with utilizing naturally valuable items—such as livestock, grains, salt, and spices—as a reliable and widely accepted medium of exchange. Unlike state-issued coinage, which could be subject to arbitrary manipulation, fluctuations, and interference by rulers or governing bodies, commodity money offered distinct advantages that were hard to overlook. Its value was intrinsic and based not on the whims of authority figures, but rather on qualities that were universally recognized, appreciated, and accepted throughout various different cultures. This characteristic made commodity money a considerably more stable form of exchange, fostering trade and economic interactions in ways that currency controlled by the state simply could not achieve or duplicate. Through this innovative approach, societies were able to enhance their economic resilience and reliability, ultimately allowing for a more robust trading environment that benefitted all involved.

For instance, salt, with its essential and critically important role in food preservation and flavor enhancement, became so remarkably and incredibly valuable in certain regions that it was even used extensively as a form of currency. The fact that salt was in limited and often scarce supply, coupled with its practical and necessary use in daily life, meant that its worth was far less likely to be artificially inflated or deflated by a single authority or institution. In a fascinating sense, the widespread reliance on commodity money like salt represented an early and intriguing experiment in decentralization—it allowed trade and commerce to flourish and develop without a centralized institution holding the power to dictate the necessary terms of exchange. Such reliance on a natural resource like salt provided both security and stability to the economic transactions that were taking place during that significant period in history.

Furthermore, commodity money possessed a remarkable and significant advantage in terms of its natural resistance to debasement. Unlike fiat currency, where a ruler or governing body could easily mint and circulate an increased number of coins, subsequently reducing their precious metal content or value at will, the value of a commodity was inherently tied to its physical properties. These properties included a tangible worth and usability that were notably difficult to replicate or diminish in any meaningful or effective way. This intrinsic stability provided an excellent logical argument for endorsing a decentralized monetary approach: when the value of money is derived from its inherent utility and resourcefulness, rather than solely from the decree or endorsement of a state or governmental authority, it establishes a far more stable and trustworthy medium of exchange between individuals. By relying on the enduring and natural attributes of these commodities, users could instill a much greater confidence in their currency, thereby making trade not only more efficient but also considerably more reliable in practical application. The resulting confidence enhanced the overall system of trade, fostering an environment where economic interactions could flourish.

The Emergence of Local Currencies and Free Banking

As societies progressed and evolved through various historical epochs over time, the notable limitations and significant shortcomings of a purely centralized monetary system became increasingly evident and pronounced. Throughout the medieval period, and extending into the early modern era, a diverse series of innovative and pioneering experiments with local currencies and free banking began to emerge—each representing a brave and bold attempt to escape from stringent state control, while simultaneously aiming to establish more adaptable and flexible monetary systems that could better meet and address the needs of the broader populace. These experiments were often marked by creativity and a desire for autonomy, reflecting the changing dynamics of economic interaction and community needs in an ever-evolving world.

Local currencies, which were frequently issued by merchants, guilds, or entire communities throughout various regions, presented a compelling alternative to the standardized coins that were typically enforced by the state and governing authorities. These innovative currencies were specifically tailored to address and meet the distinct needs and unique conditions present in local economies. This adaptability allowed for much more flexible and responsive transactions compared to rigid national currency systems. In medieval Europe, for instance, many towns developed their own unique coins or credit systems explicitly designed to facilitate trade during times of political instability or when central authorities failed to deliver reliable and acceptable currency. These local systems emerged out of the undeniable necessity of ensuring the smooth facilitation of commerce in various economic environments that were often diverse and isolated from one another. They provided an immediate and effective solution to the numerous limitations that were often imposed by distant and, at times, oppressive central governments that often did not comprehend or cater to the specific needs and aspirations of individual communities. As a result, these local currencies played a crucial role in fostering economic resilience and enabling vibrant trade patterns to thrive despite the myriad challenges posed by overarching political frameworks and decisions made far from the local context. The use of local currencies not only empowered individual traders and merchants but also strengthened community ties and generated a sense of shared purpose among the participants in these localized economies.

Another compelling and truly fascinating experiment in decentralized monetary systems was the remarkable era of free banking that uniquely unfolded during the 19th century. In various regions, including notable locations like Scotland and the United States, free banking systems permitted a considerable number of private banks to issue their own distinct and unique banknotes, operating with minimal government interference and oversight. This specific period, despite being fraught with a myriad of challenges and obstacles, demonstrated convincingly that a competitive and dynamic market for money could indeed emerge and thrive, even in the absence of strict state control and regulation. Free banking not only fostered unprecedented levels of innovation in various financial instruments but also significantly encouraged banks to uphold and maintain exceptionally high standards of transparency and accountability. This was essential in order to earn, establish, and uphold the trust of their valued customers and the general public at large. The experience of free banking serves as a vital reminder of the adaptability and resilience of financial systems when given the opportunity to operate within a less constrained environment.

Critics of free banking often pointed to significant instances of what were known as "wildcat banks" and notable regional instability that arose from their operations. However, when viewed through a long-term, analytical lens, it becomes abundantly clear that free banking offered not just insights but also critical and invaluable advantages regarding the numerous benefits that come with decentralizing monetary issuance. By allowing a diverse range of financial institutions to issue their own money, these systems fostered an environment of robust and healthy competition, which ultimately resulted in meaningful, measurable improvements in the overall quality and accessibility of banking services and products provided to the public. The free market played a crucial role in determining the value and reliability of various banknotes based primarily on the level of public confidence, rather than relying on arbitrary state mandates that could distort their intrinsic, true value. This logical, market-driven approach to money creation serves as a historical precursor to many of the modern innovations we observe today in finance, most notably including the rise of digital currencies and the expanding field of decentralized finance (DeFi), which aims to create an inclusive and efficient financial ecosystem. Moreover, the various lessons learned from the era of free banking continue to influence and shape contemporary discussions about the intricate relationships between financial systems, regulatory frameworks, and the economy at large, touching upon vital issues such as monetary policy, financial stability, and public trust in banking institutions.

The Revolutionary Concept of Decentralized Ledger Systems

Fast forward to the 21st century, and we see the ultimate realization of the ancient dream that has captivated and engaged minds for centuries: the remarkable decentralized ledger system that powers innovative cryptocurrencies like Bitcoin and many others. In numerous remarkable ways, these digital currencies are the modern descendants of the early pioneering experiments in decentralized monetary systems that sought to significantly minimize reliance on central authorities and traditional banking institutions. They embody the fundamental principle, deeply rooted in the ethos of financial democracy, that money should be created, managed, and controlled not by a single central authority or group of elites, but rather by a distributed network of users who actively participate in and engage with the system. This profound revolution in financial technology has the immense potential to reshape entire economies and transform the way we view and interact with money as a whole, fostering greater inclusivity and access for people from all walks of life.

Blockchain technology, widely regarded as the revolutionary backbone of cryptocurrencies, stands out as a truly mind-blowing and transformative innovation that fundamentally rethinks and reshapes the entire concept of money as we understand it today. It offers a highly transparent and immutable ledger where every single transaction is meticulously recorded in a decentralized manner. This approach guarantees security and reliability in a world where trust between parties can often be compromised. This ingenious system effectively eliminates the need for a central bank or governmental oversight, directly addressing the very criticisms and concerns that ancient philosophers have levied against state-controlled currency throughout history. Instead of solely relying on the trustworthiness and integrity of a single institution, blockchain technology skillfully distributes trust across a vast global network of participants. This distribution not only ensures security but also enhances the overall resilience of the financial system against any potential failures or fraudulent activities. By empowering individuals rather than centralized entities, it profoundly alters the dynamics of economic interactions. With blockchain, the value of money is ultimately determined by the collective consensus and agreement of its users. This decentralization of authority promotes fairness and widespread participation in a digital economy, enabling individuals from diverse backgrounds and locations to engage with the financial system on their terms, thereby fostering a more inclusive economic landscape.

The beauty of this truly remarkable system lies not only in its inherent simplicity but also in its unwavering logical consistency, which captivates those who explore it. If the early experiments conducted in the realm of decentralized money clearly demonstrated that commodity-based currencies, along with the core principles of free banking, could significantly outperform the rigid, often cumbersome centralized systems that have been the norm for so long, then it is only fitting that blockchain technology stands as the natural and inevitable evolutionary leap forward in this financial revolution. This technology meticulously takes the finest elements from those pioneering experiments—such as enhanced transparency, robust security, and a value system driven entirely by the market—and amplifies them to unprecedented heights through the innovative use of modern cryptography and advanced network theory principles. The ultimate result of these advancements is a financial system that is not only shockingly resilient and incredibly efficient but also fundamentally democratic in its essence, empowering individuals and fostering innovation in ways that were previously unimaginable and thought to be unattainable. Such a transformation brings forth vast possibilities for creativity and entrepreneurial spirit to thrive in a landscape that has finally begun to recognize the potential of decentralized finance.

Argumentative Perspectives: The Case for Decentralized Monetary Systems

The philosophical and practical arguments that robustly support the idea of decentralized monetary systems are not only compelling but also, in several pivotal ways, seem to be inevitable and essential for a modern economy. When we conduct a comprehensive examination of the various significant limitations associated with state-controlled currency—issues such as the susceptibility to inflation, the potential for political manipulation, and a glaring lack of innovation in response to emerging technologies and market demands—the logical conclusion that naturally arises is that money itself must be liberated from the firm and often restrictive grip of centralized authorities. This vital transformation towards decentralization could very well pave the way for a more resilient, flexible, and adaptive financial landscape. In this new system, individuals will have greater agency over their resources, enabling them to make informed choices that best suit their needs and financial goals. Such a shift could foster not only economic empowerment but also promote a healthier relationship between individuals and their financial tools in a rapidly evolving global market.

One of the most persuasive and compelling arguments when discussing modern financial systems is undoubtedly the critical and immensely important issue of trust that underpins them. Traditional state-controlled money fundamentally relies on the credibility, reliability, and overall competence of the government currently in power, which can be easily and quickly undermined by a variety of factors such as poor fiscal policies, widespread systemic corruption, or significant political instability. In stark contrast, decentralized financial systems strategically build trust not on a single institution or centralized entity but rather on a distributed network of numerous participants who are engaged in the process. This democratic and inclusive approach ensures that no single entity holds the overwhelming power to manipulate the entire financial system for its own selfish benefit, a principle that deeply resonates with the ancient critiques and ongoing concerns surrounding concentrated power and authority. This not only enhances the overall resilience and integrity of the financial system but also fosters a more equitable marketplace and environment for all users involved, contributing to a stronger sense of community and cooperation among participants.

Moreover, decentralized monetary systems significantly encourage competition and drive innovation across the financial landscape in profound ways. In a truly free and open market of money, multiple entities, organizations, and a diverse range of stakeholders are incentivized to consistently uphold and maintain exceptionally high standards of service, transparency, and security for their users and customers. This dynamic, competitive environment fosters an atmosphere of continuous improvement and development, closely resembling the vibrant and groundbreaking free banking era of the 19th century. The intense competitive pressure exerted on various institutions compels them not only to innovate and enhance their offerings but also to reduce costs, leading to the ultimate creation of a financial system that is not only more robust and adaptable but also more responsive to the diverse and changing needs of consumers everywhere. This logical progression—from centralized control that often stifles creativity and reduces innovation to a model of decentralized innovation that can thrive on healthy competition—is not only persuasive and appealing to those who study economic systems but is additionally supported by a wealth of rich historical evidence. The experience and lessons of the past illustrate that when individuals, organizations, and entities are empowered to operate independently, they can achieve remarkable advancements that ultimately benefit society as a whole in meaningful and lasting ways.

Critics may argue that decentralization can lead to both instability and volatility in the systems and processes it influences, which raises valid concerns that merit consideration. While it is indeed true that early decentralized systems, such as free banking or local currencies, encountered various challenges and were sometimes prone to significant regional disparities, the long-term benefits associated with a decentralized approach far outweigh these initial obstacles and drawbacks that were encountered along the way. Volatility, in fact, is often a prominent sign of an evolving system—it represents a necessary phase of growth that typically occurs before true maturity can finally set in and a more stable environment can emerge. The evolution of cryptocurrencies, for instance, has been characterized by numerous periods of pronounced high volatility. However, as time progresses, it has become increasingly apparent that, as the market matures and regulatory frameworks gradually adapt to these new financial systems, these decentralized systems are trending towards a state of greater stability and predictability that was previously thought to be unattainable. Such significant improvements are not just beneficial for the systems themselves but also serve to enhance user trust and foster greater participation in the decentralized economy, creating a more robust ecosystem overall.

The Analytical Framework: Lessons from History

To fully grasp the revolutionary and transformative impact that early experiments in decentralized monetary systems had on the overall development of economies throughout history, we must carefully analyze these systems within a logical and expansive historical framework that provides both context and depth. The transition from archaic and primitive barter systems to the more advanced concept of commodity money, and eventually evolving into state-controlled coinage, was not a linear and straightforward progression—it was, in fact, a highly complex and multifaceted series of experiments. Each of these experiments built upon and learned from the successes, challenges, and failures of its predecessors in the realm of trade and exchange. Early societies, driven by their quest for greater efficiency, fairness, and effectiveness in transactions, experimented with a wide variety of forms of money. They did so in order to address and overcome the significant inefficiencies that were inherent in barter systems. Through a process of continuous trial and error, they discovered that commodities which possessed intrinsic value—such as gold, silver, and various other valuable items—could effectively serve as a common medium of exchange in their marketplaces. However, this seemingly practical solution to the persistent problem of trade was imperfect due to enduring challenges of divisibility and standardization that plagued these early forms of monetary exchange, often leading to confusion and complications in everyday transactions.

The shift toward the use of coinage was not only a logical pathway, but also a highly practical solution designed to address the numerous and complex problems that had long been plaguing trade and economic systems across different societies. A standardized, government-issued medium of exchange emerged, one that clearly promised consistency, reliability, and uniformity in transactions that spanned various regions. This innovation aimed to facilitate trade by providing a stable and recognizable form of value that could be easily exchanged. However, as the centralization process advanced rapidly, it inevitably brought with it substantial risks, including the potential for manipulation and mismanagement by those wielding power. Such issues led to the rise of dissenters and critics who became increasingly vocal against the centralized system. These steadfast dissenters passionately argued that true economic freedom and autonomy could only be achieved if the control of money was entirely liberated from the grasp of any single authority or central power. This critical debate not only illuminated the flaws present in the system but also laid the essential intellectual and philosophical groundwork for later experiments and developments in the complex realm of decentralized finance. This emerging field sought to create viable alternatives to the traditional monetary systems that were viewed as inherently flawed and vulnerable to abuse, aiming to rediscover the concept of financial sovereignty for individuals.

The free banking era marked a significant turning point in financial history, paving the way for the emergence of local currencies, and ultimately heralding the groundbreaking arrival of blockchain technology. All these developments originate from a fundamental challenge to the traditional state-controlled money systems that have dominated for centuries. Each distinct phase of evolution in monetary systems was not merely a series of coincidences; rather, it was propelled by a rational assessment of the various problems that are inherent within centralized control. This was coupled with a logical and persistent search for more effective, innovative solutions that could better serve the needs of individuals and communities alike. This historical perspective is not simply an academic exercise—it serves as a clear, analytical roadmap that informs and shapes our current understanding and engagement with digital currencies. It highlights the ongoing transformation in the landscape of finance, where the once rigid structures of monetary control are giving way to more fluid and versatile systems. Understanding this evolution is absolutely crucial for grasping the potential implications and future developments in monetary systems. As we continue to transition toward more decentralized frameworks, it becomes increasingly important to recognize the lessons of the past. These lessons will undoubtedly guide us in navigating the complexities and opportunities that lie ahead in this ever-evolving financial landscape.

The analytical framework of these early experiments offers us significant and valuable insights, demonstrating unequivocally that innovation in the realm of money is not merely arbitrary or whimsical; rather, it is a deeply thoughtful response to the logical demands imposed by an ever-evolving and increasingly complex economy. When a system fails to adequately meet the pressing needs of its users—especially when it becomes riddled with inefficiency, rampant corruption, or when it suppresses the immense potential for meaningful innovation—it is only natural and logical that alternative models will arise, adapt, and take shape. The persistent and rational drive of people toward greater efficiency, enhanced transparency, and a heightened sense of fairness in all forms of economic exchange has been a remarkably consistent theme throughout the vast tapestry of human history. This same drive, rooted in our collective aspirations for improvement, acts as the backbone of the current revolutionary shift we are witnessing today in decentralized finance, where individuals actively seek systems that fundamentally empower them rather than subjugate them to archaic, restrictive, and outdated practices that no longer serve the needs of modern society.

Persuading a New Generation: The Ethical and Logical Imperative

For today's generation of savvy investors, innovative entrepreneurs, and forward-thinking policymakers, the invaluable lessons derived from the early decentralized monetary experiments are not only shocking but also profoundly enlightening in many ways. The notable failure of centralized systems to effectively prevent various economic crises, when considered alongside the numerous moral and practical shortcomings that are inherent in any form of state-controlled money, presents a compelling and persuasive argument for the urgent need to fully embrace decentralization in our financial systems. This shift towards decentralization is essential, as it offers new frameworks for economic participation that are more equitable, transparent, and resilient against the pitfalls of traditional financial systems. Emphasizing these principles could lay the groundwork for a more sustainable economic future, encouraging innovation and fostering a sense of community and mutual support among investors, entrepreneurs, and policymakers alike.

The logical imperative is undeniably clear and unmistakably profound: when money is liberated fully from the constraints and limitations imposed by centralized manipulation and control, it undergoes a remarkable transformation that allows it to evolve into a more accurate, just, and resilient medium of exchange for every single participant involved in the economic ecosystem. Decentralized systems, by virtue of their structure, promote the distribution of control across a diverse network of participants, which inherently fosters a culture of accountability and transparency among all users engaged in these systems. This fundamental shift in financial paradigms not only significantly reduces the numerous risks associated with corruption and abuse of power but also aligns seamlessly with the ethical values that modern society increasingly demands and upholds. These values emphasize essential principles such as fairness, equity, and inclusivity, underscoring the vital importance of creating systems that are designed to work effectively for all individuals, rather than favoring just a select few members of society. By supporting and advocating for these decentralized frameworks, we can collectively pave the way for a more equitable and just financial future that ultimately benefits everyone involved, ensuring that all individuals have access to opportunities for prosperity and success.

The moral dimension of this argument truly cannot be overstated or ignored in any meaningful and substantive discussion surrounding the topic at hand. Centralized control over money consistently leads to a concerning and unyielding concentration of power within a few hands, significant economic inequality that affects many, and a troubling lack of accountability—these are pressing issues that have historically and consistently contributed to social unrest and economic instability across different societies and various times throughout history. In stark contrast, decentralized monetary systems present an empowering alternative that effectively puts control back into the capable and deserving hands of individuals and entire communities. This empowerment not only enables them to manage their own economic destinies but also to make choices that genuinely reflect their values, needs, and aspirations as a society. Such a fundamental shift is not only sensible from a practical economic standpoint; it also represents a profound and urgent ethical imperative that cannot be overlooked. This imperative speaks to the very core of human dignity, individual autonomy, and the concept of personal freedom, reinforcing the essential idea that financial independence and self-determination are crucial and vital for the establishment of a truly just and equitable society for all.

Modern decentralized technologies, such as blockchain, serve as an excellent and compelling example of this crucial ethical imperative that exists in today's increasingly complex and multifaceted economic landscape. They offer a remarkably transparent and immutable system where every single transaction is visible and accessible to all participants, thereby ensuring that no single entity can possess the absolute power to dominate, manipulate, or distort the entire system. This unprecedented level of transparency, in turn, plays an exceptionally vital role in effectively restoring trust in the monetary system—a trust that is fundamentally essential for the healthy functioning and enduring stability of any economy. By drawing on the numerous and valuable lessons derived from early experiments in decentralized monetary systems, we have a unique opportunity to construct and cultivate a financial future that is not only technologically advanced but also fundamentally just, fair, and equitable for everyone involved. This visionary approach actively encourages inclusivity and fairness, allowing individuals from diverse and varied backgrounds to participate in and ultimately benefit from the constantly evolving financial landscape. Each step forward in this direction contributes to a more robust economy where everyone can thrive.

The Argument for Continued Experimentation and Innovation

The pioneering attempts made to break free from the constraints imposed by state-controlled currency were not conclusive or final solutions; rather, they represented merely experimental steps along a long and intricate continuum of economic evolution. Each distinct experiment, whether it was the innovative and often creative use of commodity money, the thoughtful development of local currencies aimed at community engagement, or the advent of free banking systems that encouraged competition, contributed an array of valuable insights into the complex and multifaceted functioning of various monetary systems. These diverse experiments collectively demonstrated that when money is permitted to operate without the unnecessary shackles of undue centralized control, it possesses the remarkable ability to evolve organically over time, enabling it to better meet the ever-changing needs and demands of its diverse users, ensuring a more dynamic economic landscape that reflects the true value of goods, services, and the contributions of individuals within society.

The history of experimentation in the realm of finance is absolutely mind-blowing, both in its vast scope and profound significance. It reveals a relentless human drive that propels us to seek out better and more efficient ways of managing wealth—drives that have ultimately given birth to every major innovation throughout the rich history of money. This fascinating journey through time showcases the persistent and often relentless pursuit of advancements, illustrating how each new discovery builds on the foundations laid by those who came before us. The modern era, characterized by the unprecedented rise of cryptocurrencies and decentralized finance, stands as simply the latest chapter in this long and ongoing saga of transformation and relentless innovation in financial systems. In this context, we are witnessing a shift that is not just changing how transactions occur but also redefining the very essence of currency itself and our relationship with financial institutions and systems at large.

The logical conclusion of this historical narrative is that experimentation must continue to persist and progress indefinitely. The numerous significant challenges that are inherent in our current financial systems—ranging from persistent inflation and rampant corruption to a glaring lack of transparency and inclusivity—demand innovative and bold new solutions. Decentralized monetary systems certainly offer a promising path forward; however, they too must evolve and keep adapting to the constantly changing and dynamic landscape of our economy. The invaluable lessons that are gleaned from early experiments serve as a powerful reminder that true innovation is not merely a one-time event but rather a continuous and ongoing process characterized by trial, error, and constant improvement. This ongoing journey underscores the paramount importance of resilience, creativity, and adaptability in the face of ever-shifting and complex economic realities that we face in our world today.

Investors and policymakers must therefore remain open to exploring innovative ideas and be prepared to wholeheartedly embrace a wide range of technologies that challenge, question, and ultimately disrupt conventional wisdom. The argument for decentralized finance is not only highly persuasive but also incredibly practical, particularly in today's ever-evolving financial landscape. It serves as a compelling call to reimagine money—not merely as a static, state-controlled entity burdened with rigid boundaries, but as a dynamic, evolving instrument that truly reflects the changing needs, aspirations, and values of a diverse and multicultural society. This visionary perspective is not only radical but also fundamentally revolutionary and transformative—a shocking departure from the centralized systems of the past that have long dominated the world of finance. Yet, it is firmly grounded in a rich tradition of human ingenuity and the logical pursuit of economic freedom that has consistently propelled societies forward throughout the annals of history. Embracing this new paradigm could pave the way for an inclusive financial framework that champions innovation while addressing the shortcomings inherent in traditional financial systems. As we move further into an era defined by rapid technological advances, the necessity for adaptability becomes paramount, urging all stakeholders to consider the potential benefits of a decentralized framework, which could democratize access to financial opportunities for all individuals, regardless of their background.

The Enduring Relevance of Early Decentralized Experiments

The initial experiments in decentralized monetary systems should not merely be viewed as relics of a primitive past that have no current significance; rather, they serve as enduring, valuable lessons that continue to deeply influence and shape our contemporary understanding of money and its pervasive complexities today. These historical experiences teach us that when the authority, power, and responsibility to control money is distributed among a multitude of diverse participants, instead of being concentrated in the hands of only a few individuals or entities, the overall system emerges as more resilient, adaptable, and ultimately fairer for each and every person involved in the financial ecosystem.

These intriguing experiments present a deeply compelling and persuasive argument in favor of the many modern innovations and significant advancements that have been made in financial systems. The remarkable free banking era, alongside the groundbreaking introduction of various local currencies, illustrated that markets possess a remarkable capacity to efficiently regulate the creation of money in a way that is often far more effective than any central authority could ever achieve. The rise of blockchain technology, along with the rapid proliferation of numerous cryptocurrencies, represents a natural and logical extension of these initial concepts—a remarkable digital revolution that not only embodies but actively promotes the essential principles of decentralization, transparency, and the democratization of wealth. This evolution greatly allows for increased access and opportunity for individuals everywhere, ensuring that everyone has a chance to participate in and benefit from these financial advancements.

The analytical reasoning underpinning these innovative early experiments holds a level of relevance today that mirrors its significance from centuries past. These crucial investigations illuminate the vital importance of achieving a delicate balance between efficiency and ethical responsibility within our financial systems. It becomes imperative to ensure that the flow of wealth is appropriately directed towards serving the collective good, rather than merely enriching a small, privileged group of individuals who already possess a disproportionate share of power and resources. In a contemporary world where the dire pitfalls associated with state-controlled money are all too palpable—from the devastating impacts of hyperinflation that can obliterate economies to economic mismanagement that fosters rampant inequality—the vital lessons gleaned from these pioneering experiments offer a compelling roadmap toward fostering a more equitable and just financial future. By earnestly reflecting on these profound historical insights, we can endeavor to create a system that prioritizes fairness and sustainability, placing them above fleeting short-term gains that often lead to greater disparities.

Persuasive Reflections: A Call to Embrace Decentralized Freedom

The philosophical challenges and practical failures of centralized monetary systems present a shocking, thought-provoking, and deeply compelling case for the exploration of decentralized alternatives that could potentially revolutionize our approach to economics. This dynamic discourse not only underscores the limitations inherent in central control but also emphasizes how such control can stifle innovation, restrict individual creativity, and exacerbate social and economic inequality across various societal layers. The rigorous, logical, and analytical evidence that has been meticulously amassed over centuries—from the meticulous record-keeping practices of ancient temple banks to the ambitious and innovative free banking experiments of the 19th century—collectively builds an irrefutable, compelling, and robust argument: money must be liberated from the centralized control exerted by governments and their institutions if we genuinely hope to achieve true economic freedom and empower individuals with the greater financial autonomy they rightfully deserve. The continuous evolution of money and its governance is inextricably linked to the broader and ever-important quest for personal liberty, social equity, and overall societal progress. This ongoing dialogue about the nature of our monetary systems not only encourages us to rethink conventional paradigms but also inspires a collective vision for a more decentralized, equitable, and innovative economic future where individuals can participate freely and effectively in their economies without the constraints imposed by centralized authorities.

Today, the decentralized financial revolution is not merely an abstract idea; rather, it has undeniably become a tangible reality that a growing number of individuals can both witness and actively engage with. Cryptocurrencies such as Bitcoin, along with a diverse array of other altcoins, showcase their unique characteristics and functionalities through sophisticated decentralized networks and immutable ledgers. They are indeed the direct descendants of early financial experiments that bravely challenged and defied conventional norms and practices. These cryptocurrencies represent a significant and bold departure from traditional models of money that are typically controlled and regulated by state authorities or central banks and institutions. In stark contrast, they offer a financial system that is not only transparent but also inherently resistant to a variety of forms of manipulation and interference that have historically plagued traditional finance. This remarkable evolution we are witnessing today is the culmination of a long and oftentimes intricate philosophical journey—a journey that began with the primitive barter system and has traversed through centuries marked by continuous experimentation, ingenuity, and relentless innovation in the ever-evolving realm of finance. As we delve deeper into this fascinating world, it becomes clear that the implications and potentialities are vast and profound, paving the way for a more inclusive and democratized financial future.

The persuasive power of decentralized finance lies in its compelling promise to create a far more equitable, transparent, and efficient economic system for everyone involved. This innovative approach is a sophisticated system where trust is effectively distributed across a wide network, ensuring that every individual participant has a genuine stake in the outcome of financial transactions. In this revolutionary framework, the true value of money is determined by tangible real economic activity, which contrasts sharply with traditional systems where value can often be dictated by arbitrary political decree and fluctuating policies. This visionary concept is not merely an idealistic fantasy; it is deeply rooted in the analytical and logical principles that have guided human progress and development for countless millennia throughout history. It embraces a holistic outlook that encourages collaboration and innovation, fostering an environment that seeks to benefit the collective and enhance overall well-being rather than favoring a select few with disproportionate power and influence. Such a dynamic system possesses the potential to fundamentally reshape our understanding of finance, empowering individuals and communities alike to engage actively in their economic futures.

Bridging the Past and the Future: Integrating Lessons into Modern Systems

As we find ourselves standing on the threshold of an incredibly exciting and profoundly transformative new era in the vast and ever-evolving world of finance, it becomes increasingly crucial to thoughtfully integrate the timeless and invaluable lessons learned from early decentralized monetary experiments with the advanced and cutting-edge technological innovations that are shaping our economic landscape today. The shock and awe of witnessing just how far we have truly come—from the simple, rudimentary barter systems of old to the astonishingly sophisticated and diverse digital currencies that have now become an integral part of our daily transactions—are tempered by the sobering and often humbling realization that many of the core underlying principles of exchange and value, which have stood the test of time, have remained fundamentally unchanged throughout history. It is within this context that we must navigate forward, blending past insights with current advancements.

The principles of transparency, accountability, and decentralization, which were once vigorously championed by the early advocates of free banking and passionate supporters of local currencies, are now beginning to manifest on an impressive global scale. Through the innovative and transformative applications of blockchain technology, these ideals are gaining widespread recognition and relevance. This significant convergence of ancient wisdom, steeped in the ideals of honesty and shared responsibility, alongside cutting-edge modern innovations, is not only logical but also entirely inevitable in our rapidly evolving world. It presents a promising and exciting pathway through which we can effectively rebuild our financial systems in a manner that is both ethical and efficient—an enhanced system that honors and respects the invaluable legacy of the past while boldly stepping forward into the remarkable future that awaits us. As we embrace these principles, we pave the way for a more equitable financial landscape that strives to empower individuals and communities alike, ensuring that everyone has a stake in the prosperity of our global economy.

The modern digital revolution in finance stands as a direct descendant and an evolution of those early experiments in monetary systems that have been foundational to our understanding of trade and value exchange. This revolution boldly challenges the monopolistic control that has historically been maintained by state-issued currencies, effectively reclaiming the power of money and financial autonomy for the people of today. By harnessing the tremendous power of decentralized networks and innovative technologies, we possess the potential to create financial systems that are immune, or at least significantly less vulnerable, to the corruptions and numerous inefficiencies that are commonly associated with centralized control and governance structures. This remarkable transformation presents a compelling and truly mind-blowing vision that not only reshapes our understanding of wealth but also democratizes access to economic opportunity on an unprecedented global scale. With these groundbreaking advancements, individuals can gain considerably more autonomy and freedom in their financial decisions, fostering a more inclusive and equitable economic environment for everyone, regardless of their background or location. As we navigate this new financial landscape, the emphasis on collaboration and transparency in financial transactions has the power to redefine how we perceive money and its role in our lives, paving the way for a future where financial empowerment is within reach for all.

A Blueprint for the Future of Money

In this comprehensive and in-depth exploration of the groundbreaking experiments in various decentralized monetary systems, we have uncovered a rich and intricate tapestry woven with innovative ideas, ongoing struggles, and significant innovations that have persistently challenged and questioned the traditional concept of state-controlled currency. The remarkable journey from basic barter systems to the emergence of contemporary digital currencies is distinctly marked by a series of bold experiments, profound philosophical debates, and revolutionary breakthroughs—all aimed at establishing a more dynamic, transparent, and equitable system of money that benefits all participants engaged in these ever-evolving economic landscapes. This narrative not only highlights the zeal and creativity of the individuals and communities involved but also emphasizes the importance of collaboration, technology, and resilience in the face of challenges and opposition from established financial institutions. As we delve deeper into the history, motivations, and impacts of these pioneering initiatives, we gain valuable insights that inspire ongoing discussions about the future of currency and the potential for a new financial ecosystem that is more inclusive and representative of a diverse global population.

The vital lessons derived from these early experiments are as shocking as they are profoundly inspiring for individuals and societies alike. They vividly teach us that the centralized control over money, wealth, and financial systems is not only prone to various forms of abuse and systematic corruption but is also fundamentally incompatible with the core values of freedom, unrestricted innovation, and inherent fairness that many people hold dear to their hearts. The philosophical challenges and perennial questions raised by ancient thinkers continue to resonate powerfully in our modern world today, where the demand for decentralized, trustworthy, secure, and ethically managed financial systems is more urgent than it has ever been before in history. In light of these crucial considerations, it becomes increasingly momentous to explore alternative financial frameworks that prioritize individual rights, promote inclusivity, and foster creativity along with equitable opportunities for all individuals, irrespective of their background.

By closely examining both the notable failures and the remarkable successes that have been experienced in a variety of early decentralized monetary experiments, we can derive a compelling and logically sound blueprint for the future of how money will function in a newly imagined economic landscape. This envisioned future provides a perspective where wealth is not concentrated in the hands of a single centralized authority, but is instead distributed equitably across a broad and diverse global network composed of individuals and communities from all walks of life. In this transformative scenario, each participant is empowered with a genuine stake in the system, leading to a far more equitable and just economic environment that can benefit everyone involved. This innovative and transformative vision is not only revolutionary but also aligns beautifully with the innate human drive for economic freedom, individual empowerment, and ongoing innovation in financial systems. It reflects our collective aspiration toward creating a much more inclusive financial system that truly empowers each person to fully participate and thrive in this ever-evolving landscape, contributing to a sustainable and prosperous future for all.

As you take a moment to reflect deeply on these insightful observations, it is crucial to consider how the deep-seated wisdom and lessons learned from the past can significantly and fundamentally inform the thoughtful design and innovative development of modern financial systems. The early experiments that took place in decentralized monetary systems serve not just as historical footnotes; they provide us with an invaluable roadmap—a comprehensive guide that is essential for building a robust financial future that is not only resilient but also transparent, equitable, and genuinely democratic in nature. This significant undertaking is not merely a theoretical exercise; rather, it stands as a fervent call to action directed toward investors, policymakers, and concerned citizens from all walks of life. It urges all stakeholders to actively embrace the vast potential and transformative power of decentralized finance and to collaboratively forge a new and progressive path toward economic liberation for everyone involved in this dynamic and evolving landscape. It is vital that we work together to facilitate innovative solutions that will ensure a sustainable economic environment.

In conclusion, the remarkable and fascinating journey that spans from the primitive system of barter to the more sophisticated realm of state-controlled coinage, and eventually evolving into the innovative concept of decentralized monetary systems, stands as a powerful testament to the extraordinary power of human ingenuity and creativity. This relentless and unwavering pursuit of improved methods for effectively managing wealth truly showcases our remarkable ability to adapt, change, and innovate in the face of challenges. The ancient experiments in trade that boldly challenged centralized control present us with a shocking, mind-blowing, and profoundly logical framework for reimagining the very concept of money in this digital age we now inhabit and navigate. These historical precedents eagerly compel us to question established norms, values, and practices that we often take for granted. Furthermore, they encourage us to actively seek out innovative solutions that not only empower individuals but also promote collective prosperity among diverse communities. This ongoing evolution of monetary systems, from their humble beginnings to the complex forms we see today, reflects our enduring desire to create a more equitable and just financial landscape for everyone, ensuring that the benefits of progress and innovation are shared fairly among all members of society.

This comprehensive and insightful blueprint for a decentralized monetary future is not only highly persuasive—it is absolutely essential for a world where both economic freedom and ethical stewardship are held as paramount values. By thoughtfully integrating the invaluable lessons learned from early decentralized economic experiments with the transformative potential offered by cutting-edge modern technology, we can successfully construct a financial system that honors our shared history while also paving the way for a future that is not only more inclusive but also resilient and equitable for all members of society. Such an approach ensures that we are building systems that cater to the diverse needs of varied communities while also safeguarding our collective interests in the long run, creating a stable framework that supports growth, innovation, and fairness across different sectors. This vision aims to establish a harmonious balance between progress and community engagement, which is crucial as we navigate the complexities of an ever-evolving global economy.

Embrace these timeless lessons and treasured insights that have remarkably withstood the test of time across generations. Allow the pioneering spirit of those courageous individuals who boldly dared to challenge and break free from the constraining shackles of state-controlled currency to deeply inspire you and ignite your imagination. Let this profound inspiration propel you to question and challenge the status quo while empowering you to actively contribute to the shaping and reimagining of a future world where money honestly and effectively serves the common good and uplifts everyone, regardless of their circumstances. The future of money is indeed here, emerging and evolving rapidly, and it is undeniably decentralized—this is a shockingly brilliant realization that stands as a remarkable testament to the enduring power of human creativity, innovative thought, and the relentless pursuit of freedom and opportunity for all individuals everywhere.

Section 4: The Rise of Alternative Theories on Wealth and Exchange

In an ever-evolving world where the traditional notions of money and value once reigned supreme and held significant sway over societies, a profound and transformative revolution was quietly underway—a revolution that fundamentally challenged and questioned everything that society had ever believed about wealth, riches, and the essence of prosperity itself. This section delves deeply into the striking and shocking emergence of alternative theories on wealth and exchange, concepts and ideas so mind-blowing and revolutionary that they not only redefined how diverse societies viewed money as a medium of exchange but also transformed how they effectively managed, interpreted, and understood value in its many forms. From the earliest days of human trade—where bartering was the norm and people exchanged goods directly without the use of any currency—to the modern era characterized by intricate digital currencies, cryptocurrencies, and blockchain technologies, these innovative concepts have drastically reshaped economic landscapes. They have questioned the deeply rooted status quo of financial systems, challenged prevailing assumptions, and remarkably set the stage for a future where value is measured not by arbitrary decrees, conventional wisdom, or outdated paradigms, but rather by the collective ingenuity, creativity, and ethical stewardship of individuals and communities that is inclusive, equitable, and progressive in nature. Such transformations promise to create a more dynamic and just economic environment for generations to come.

A Paradigm Shift in the Nature of Value

Envision a world where the concept of wealth is envisioned not merely by the accumulation of precious metals, gemstones, or the enormous size of a state treasury, but instead by the potential it has to generate collective prosperity, stimulate groundbreaking innovative developments, and foster the boundless and vibrant creativity inherent to humanity. In ancient times, various forms of commodity money, such as salt, cattle, and grain, held intrinsic value because of their myriad practical uses in daily life, sustaining communities and providing essential resources for survival. Yet, even these early forms of currency began to hint at a deeper philosophical inquiry that resonates profoundly through the ages: what truly constitutes value in our society? Visionary thinkers, enterprising merchants, and profound philosophers began to challenge and question the conventional wisdom of their time. They argued passionately and persuasively that true wealth should not merely be defined by the quantities an individual could hoard or the ability to exchange it for other commodities and resources. Rather, wealth should be viewed through a lens of its profound ability and transformative potential to enhance human life and pave the way for a better, brighter future for all members of society. In this enlightening sense, wealth would be measured by how significantly it could uplift diverse communities, create abundant opportunities for the countless individuals who form the intricate fabric of society, and lead to a flourishing environment that nurtures organic growth, harmonious collaboration, and shared success across all walks of life.

This paradigm shift was nothing short of revolutionary in its depth and scope. It not only opened the door to a vast array of alternative theories and perspectives but also fundamentally questioned the traditional centrality of state control over the crucial and important aspect of money. Intellectuals, innovative thinkers, and distinguished scholars from various diverse cultures, backgrounds, and walks of life began to engage in spirited, sometimes heated debates about a critical and essential question: Was value something inherently present in a material substance, or could it be entirely abstracted from the physical object itself? This profound and significant inquiry led to an idea that would eventually give rise to modern economic theories and complex models that shape our understanding today. The evolving notion that wealth could be conceived to be much more than just a physical accumulation of resources and tangible assets—that it might embody a rich reflection of human creativity, collaborative social cooperation, and even deeply-rooted moral virtue—was both shocking and transformative in its sweeping implications for society and the economy as a whole.

Rethinking Wealth Through Ethical Lenses

One of the most provocative alternative theories posited by various thinkers throughout the vast expanse of history asserts that true wealth must be considered a moral asset—a sacred trust that comes with both immense power and grave responsibility toward others. Ancient philosophers such as Plato and Aristotle deeply hinted at this profound and transformative concept, engaging in discussions that valiantly argued that genuine wealth was not merely measured by material gain, but rather by its significant and impactful capacity to contribute to the common good and overall welfare of society as a whole. They boldly and courageously challenged the prevailing ideas of their time by asserting that the accumulation of riches for selfish purposes or personal indulgence was inherently flawed and morally questionable from any ethical standpoint. Instead, wealth was seen more appropriately as a resource that should be distributed fairly among individuals and utilized to uplift and enhance the lives of those around us in the community we share. Thus, the responsibility of the wealthy lies not only in their ability to amass considerable fortunes but also in their unwavering duty to engage in acts of generosity and benevolence, ensuring that their substantial resources are directed toward fostering a more equitable and just society for all members of the community. By adhering to this moral code, individuals with wealth can contribute to the elevation of humanity and the betterment of social conditions.

This ethical dimension of wealth has significantly redefined the fundamental nature of economic exchange processes. It was not merely seen as a straightforward transaction; instead, it evolved to be understood as a profound social contract binding individuals to each other and to society as a whole. The underlying principle was that money should operate as a crucial means to enhance overall human flourishing and well-being for all members of the community. Such progressive and transformative thinking laid the essential intellectual groundwork for later, more extensive and comprehensive debates about social welfare, equitable distribution of vital resources, and sustainable development practices that take into account future generations. It became a compelling call to action, passionately urging us to reimagine wealth as a shared collective asset, shared amongst everyone, rather than merely an individual trophy intended for personal gain. This rich and intricate concept resonates powerfully in today's era, a time defined by a heightened awareness of pressing social justice issues and ongoing economic reform efforts aimed at addressing inequalities that persist within our global societies.

Innovation Beyond Physical Constraints

As civilizations advanced and evolved over many centuries, the limitations of material wealth became increasingly apparent to thinkers, scholars, and leaders alike across various societies. The emergence of state-controlled coinage during this time, while offering the crucial advantage of standardization in trade and commerce, also imposed strict limits on the overall flexibility and dynamism of diverse economic systems and structures. It was not until a number of visionary and forward-thinking individuals began to consider value in much more abstract and innovative terms that genuinely groundbreaking ideas and concepts started to emerge and take root within society. These alternative and transformative theories proposed that true wealth could be derived not just from tangible physical assets or commodities, but also from intangible assets—such as knowledge, intellectual property, creativity, innovation, and social capital—that contributed to the richness of human experience and interaction, rather than solely or primarily from physical goods or material possessions. This monumental shift in perspective marked a significant turning point in how societies began to perceive wealth, prosperity, and value, paving the way for new economic paradigms that recognized the vital importance of intellectual resources and the power of creativity in shaping a more sustainable and equitable future.

This remarkable intellectual leap was nothing short of transformative, marking a critical turning point in human history. When various societies began to focus on measuring wealth primarily in terms of innovation, creativity, and the expansive capabilities of human capital, it significantly set the stage for the emergence of the modern knowledge economy that we are more familiar with today. This shift in perception was not just an incremental adjustment but a substantial and profound change in how economic power was understood and valued. The Industrial Revolution, for instance, was not merely a historical period characterized by mechanization and industrial growth; rather, it represented a pivotal time when intellectual creativity, ingenuity, and groundbreaking technological innovations emerged as the new markers of economic power and prosperity for nations. The value of a nation started to be perceived not merely in the gold reserves it possessed or the natural resources it could extract and harness, but in its inherent ability to innovate, to educate its populace comprehensively, and to inspire and nurture creativity among its citizens. These forward-thinking ideas and concepts effectively challenged the longstanding traditional metrics of wealth that had long been accepted and understood throughout history, thereby opening up entirely new and profoundly exciting avenues for economic growth and sustainable development in previously unimaginable ways. Such a transformation encourages societies to reassess their priorities, embracing innovation not solely as a means to an end, but as a fundamental principle that drives progress and enhances the quality of life for all individuals.

The evolution of these theories was both a logical progression and an absolutely necessary response to the profound shortcomings associated with material wealth, coupled with a bold reimagining of what true value could genuinely represent in our complex world. The alternative theories on wealth and exchange proposed that money, which fundamentally serves as a measure of value within our socio-economic framework, should inherently reflect the dynamic, ever-changing nature of human society itself and its myriad interactions. Rather than being static and immutable, locked indefinitely in a finite supply of coveted precious metals, value needed to be viewed and understood as fluid, adaptable, and ever-responsive to the boundless creative energies of individuals, as well as the diverse communities they come together to form. This pivotal shift in perspective laid the essential conceptual groundwork for subsequent developments in monetary theory, which prominently included the significant rise and evolution of digital currencies. These emerging currencies serve as a compelling exemplification of the very idea that value can be continually redefined, reshaped, and managed in exciting, innovative ways that resonate powerfully with the constantly evolving landscape of societal interaction and economic engagement we experience today. This ongoing transformation reflects not only a change in how we think about wealth but also embodies a broader understanding of human creativity and community interconnection in the modern age.

The Role of Trade, Exchange, and Social Networks

Central to these alternative theories was the fascinating and thought-provoking idea that wealth is fundamentally relational—a product of intricate human interaction and complex exchange. It was believed that the very notion of wealth could not be understood without considering the social ties and relationships that underpin economic activity. Early trade networks, even those that were based on simple barter, were not mere isolated incidents but rather intricate and dynamic webs of interconnected social relationships that formed the foundation of these exchanges. Each interaction played a vital role in creating an elaborate network of dependencies, trust, and mutual understanding among individuals. The value of goods was determined not just by their physical presence and inherent features, but by their profound ability to satisfy diverse and varied human needs within these networks. This multifaceted understanding of value encapsulated not only the material aspects but also the deeper significance of social interaction. Moreover, the process of exchange itself was viewed as an essential means of building social bonds, enhancing communication, and fostering mutual trust among individuals, thereby highlighting the significant social dimension of economic activity. Through these exchanges, relationships were not only strengthened, but also deepened, expanded, and broadened, weaving a rich and intricate tapestry of community interdependence that underscores the vital reliance of individuals on one another in the broader economic framework. This paradigm shift in understanding wealth invites us to reconsider how we measure prosperity and success in our communities and challenges us to recognize the profound importance of connecting with one another in the pursuit of mutual growth and well-being.

As trade expanded significantly far beyond the narrow confines of local communities, the limitations that were inherent in barter systems became increasingly evident and pronounced over time. The crucial double coincidence of wants, which served as a significant hindrance in the efficient functioning of barter systems, forced early merchants and traders to devise a variety of innovative and new forms of money. These new and emerging forms of currency could effectively serve as a common denominator of value across different societies as well as varied transactions. This pressing necessity led to the gradual and steady development of commodity money, which was fundamentally based on the inherent value of these specific commodities that were being used, and eventually culminated in the groundbreaking and transformative invention of coinage. Yet, even as these various systems evolved and became more sophisticated with advancements in technology and trade, the fundamental underlying idea remained steadfast—that wealth was not merely accumulated in isolation or through passive means. Instead, it was generated relentlessly through dynamic interactions, meaningful cooperation, and beneficial exchanges among individuals and diverse communities. Such relationships and exchanges fostered a vibrant environment where value could be created, shared, and amplified collectively, spreading wealth and prosperity throughout society.

Innovative thinkers began to explore the fascinating and multifaceted ways in which value could be significantly enhanced through the intricate web of social networks and the interconnected relationships that bind individuals and communities together. They observed with keen insight that trust and reputation were just as crucial, if not more so, than the tangible, material substance of money itself. This insight into the essence of value prompted deeper inquiries into how these social dynamics played a vital role in facilitating economic exchanges. In many ancient cultures and civilizations throughout history, elaborate systems of credit and debt evolved in conjunction with the development of physical currency, demonstrating the profound connection between social relationships and economic transactions. These sophisticated systems were based fundamentally on mutual trust and the cultivation of long-term relationships. In these systems, the promise of a future exchange or transaction was often regarded as being far more valuable than immediate, tangible wealth that could be held in one's hand, such as coins and notes. This essential social aspect of money not only laid the critical foundation for the modern credit systems we see today, but it also paved the way for the very existence and development of digital currencies. These modern currencies operate on trustless protocols, which allow transactions to take place without relying on a single, centralized authority or institution. Instead, trust is distributed across a vast network of users, which fundamentally reshapes our understanding of value and exchange in the ever-evolving digital age. This new paradigm challenges traditional notions of ownership and value, inviting individuals to reconsider how they engage with and perceive the systems that govern their financial interactions in both online and offline contexts.

Revolutionary Economic Thought: From Speculation to Systemic Change

The rise of alternative theories on wealth and exchange was not merely a gradual evolution; rather, it represented a radical revolution in economic thought that fundamentally transformed perspectives across various disciplines. Early debates surrounding the very nature of money were nothing short of explosive and relentless, continuously challenging the long-standing dominant paradigms of the time and often inciting fierce and intense intellectual battles among leading thinkers. These heated debates provocatively questioned whether money should primarily serve as a tool of state control — a mechanism to regulate and dominate economic interactions — or instead act as a liberating force that promotes genuine and meaningful economic freedom for individuals and their communities. Furthermore, they argued convincingly that true wealth lies not merely in the accumulation of material goods or possessions, but, even more importantly, in the crucial capacity for innovation, social cooperation, and ethical stewardship among diverse communities and people. This significant shift in thinking encouraged a broader and deeper reevaluation of economic principles and practices, ultimately aiming for a more inclusive and nuanced understanding of what it means to be prosperous in a rapidly changing world filled with myriad challenges and opportunities.

One of the most mind-blowing and transformative aspects of this revolutionary thought was the astonishing and profound transition from a purely speculative and often abstract view of wealth to a significantly more organized and systematic understanding of value creation. Early economic theorists and distinguished scholars began to articulate and explore the groundbreaking and innovative idea that wealth could indeed be generated through enhanced productivity and, importantly, through the spark of innovation, rather than merely through the manipulation or extraction of a finite resource pool. This powerful notion represented a truly radical departure from the traditional and often entrenched views of wealth, which equated it mainly with tangible and physical assets like valuable land, precious metals such as gold, or mere coins that hold no intrinsic value beyond their face. Instead, these innovative and forward-thinking philosophers and theorists argued convincingly and persuasively that the real engine driving sustainable economic growth was, in fact, human ingenuity—the remarkable and unparalleled capacity to create, innovate, and continuously add value to society in various meaningful and impactful ways. This significant shift in perspective opened doors to a multitude of possibilities for economic development and societal progress, allowing individuals and communities to unlock their full potential and discover new avenues for growth and prosperity.

This remarkable intellectual revolution was by no means confined solely to the pages of dusty, forgotten manuscripts that lay silently on the shelves of libraries; rather, it had profound and far-reaching practical implications that reshaped societies in fundamental ways. The significant shift toward viewing wealth as a dynamic, evolving force—capable of growth and transformation—paved the way for the monumental Industrial

Revolution, which dramatically altered the landscape of economies around the world, and, subsequently, the dawn of the information age that has further accelerated these changes in unprecedented ways. This transformative shift in mindset laid a crucial groundwork for modern monetary theory and facilitated the development and rapid proliferation of innovative digital currencies, where the notion of value is derived from a complex interplay of technology, trust, and human creativity that challenges traditional economic paradigms. Moreover, alternative theories arising from these new perspectives on wealth and exchange provided a compelling and logically sound argument for why centralized control of money was not only limiting but also, in the long run, ultimately unsustainable in the face of an increasingly interconnected and digital world. The transition towards decentralized financial systems, coupled with emerging technologies, has sparked ongoing debates and discussions that continue to influence economic thought and practice today, shaping policies and the future of commerce in ways we are just beginning to understand.

Persuasive Implications for Modern Financial Systems

The ideas that once posed substantial and significant challenges to the established norms of state-controlled currency are now not only widely acknowledged but have also become firmly entrenched at the very heart of modern financial innovation and creativity. The remarkable rise of various cryptocurrencies, for instance, manifests as a direct descendant of the alternative theories on wealth and value that were born out of necessity in response to the notable limitations and deficiencies of traditional monetary systems that we have relied upon for so many years. Unlike the currencies that are issued and governed by any single government entity, digital currencies are created and maintained through decentralized processes and systems that reflect the collective input, creativity, and innovations of a vast and diverse global community. This groundbreaking development represents a profound and logical extension of the early experiments in defining wealth through social cooperation, innovative and forward-thinking strategies, as well as collaborative efforts that engage participants from various cultural and economic backgrounds. It truly illustrates the transformative potential of digital money in reshaping our understanding of value, economic interactions, and financial relationships in the modern world, opening up new avenues for participation and engagement among all individuals.

Blockchain technology presents a groundbreaking decentralized ledger system that exemplifies the analytical rigor and inherent transparency characteristic of early economic thought and philosophical exploration. Each individual transaction that occurs within this network is meticulously recorded in a manner that is both verifiable and immutable, which in turn guarantees that the value of money is safeguarded against arbitrary manipulation or undue external influence. This extraordinary innovation stands as a strong testament to the lasting relevance of alternative theories regarding wealth and economies. It represents a state-of-the-art solution to the persistent issues that have plagued centralized systems for centuries. Ultimately, blockchain technology offers a viable method to cultivate trust and enhance accountability in economic transactions, thereby reshaping the landscape of financial interactions for the better.

Moreover, the contemporary focus on ethical investing and sustainable finance can indeed be traced back to a much older perspective of wealth being treated as a sacred trust. This historical outlook, which has endured through the ages, underscores a profound responsibility that accompanies the possession of resources. As investors today are increasingly seeking not only opportunities that offer extraordinarily high returns but also those that genuinely contribute to social welfare and the greater good of society, the lessons derived from alternative monetary theories and historical insights become all the more compelling and persuasive. The argument is unequivocal and clear: a financial system that places a premium on innovation, transparency, and ethical stewardship is inherently more resilient, fair, and equitable than one that is primarily dominated by centralized control and the interests of merely a few individuals. In this evolving landscape of investment opportunities, it is essential to reassess our priorities and recognize that our choices in investing can lead to powerful and lasting social impact, influencing not only our present circumstances but also paving the way for a more just and sustainable future for generations to come.

Logical Criticism of Centralized Control and the Case for Innovation

A significant part of the persuasive argument for thoroughly exploring alternative and innovative theories regarding wealth lies in the logical critique and detailed examination of centralized control over economic systems. When a single authority, such as a government or a central bank, governs the complex processes of the creation and distribution of money, it inevitably becomes susceptible to numerous potential abuses of power that can arise in various forms. This centralization of power leads to critical issues such as inflation, rampant corruption, and systemic inefficiency that can severely plague the entire economy and undermine public trust. Historical examples abound, illustrating the severe consequences of centralized control; notable instances include the hyperinflation experienced in the Weimar Republic of Germany during the early 20th century and the debasement of coinage witnessed in various ancient empires throughout history. These episodes serve as powerful demonstrations that centralized systems, while capable of offering a semblance of stability in theory, often fail to deliver sustainable long-term economic prosperity and well-being for the average citizen. The lessons learned from these historical instances not only highlight the dangers inherent in centralization but also urge us to reconsider the reliance on centralized monetary systems and to explore more decentralized alternatives that may foster better economic outcomes, empower local communities, and promote individual autonomy in financial affairs.

In contrast, the decentralized models of money creation actively encourage a vibrant and healthy competition, while simultaneously fostering significant innovation within the always-evolving financial landscape. When multiple independent entities are empowered to participate in the crucial processes of issuing and managing money, the market effectively takes on the essential role of regulator. This form of decentralization creates and nurtures an environment where best practices emerge organically over time, accountability is substantially enhanced, and the overall financial system becomes markedly more resilient and robust against various challenges and disruptions. The notable early experiments with local currencies, along with the concept of free banking, serve as clear and compelling examples of this dynamic at work; they provided viable and practical alternatives to the traditional, often rigid, state-controlled money systems that have dominated for so long. These early innovations opened the door to a much more adaptable and innovative approach to managing wealth, demonstrating convincingly how decentralization can inspire creativity and flexibility in economic practices, ultimately leading to a more responsive and dynamic financial ecosystem.

The logical and analytical evidence presented is indeed compelling and cannot be overlooked: decentralization not only minimizes the significant risk of abuse and corruption within various systems, but it also creates a more dynamic, agile, and responsive economic environment that adapts to changes rapidly. This argument resonates with remarkable strength in today's rapidly evolving digital age, where blockchain technology and cryptocurrencies are indeed ushering in a groundbreaking new era of decentralized finance (DeFi), fundamentally transforming the way we perceive and engage with our financial needs. The persuasive force of this idea is absolutely undeniable—it represents an essential and natural progression of human innovation and creativity within the ever-evolving realm of money, banking, and financial transactions that make our modern economy function smoothly. As we continue to witness advancements in technology at an unprecedented pace, it becomes increasingly clear that embracing decentralization can lead to significant and transformative benefits for individuals, businesses, and communities alike, fostering an inclusive environment where everyone has access to financial resources and opportunities without the hindrance of centralized control.

The Argument for a New Social Contract

The alternative theories on wealth and exchange present profound and far-reaching implications that influence not only the very fabric of social organization but also shape governance and define the overall structure of society as we know it today. By effectively challenging the traditional modes of centralized control over money and resources, these innovative and forward-thinking theories advocate in favor of a new and transformative social contract—one that seeks to ensure that economic power is distributed more equitably among the populace as a whole. Within this envisioned framework, wealth is conceptualized and embraced as a communal resource that should serve the greater good of the community, rather than merely functioning as a tool for individual personal enrichment and financial gain. This radical yet entirely logical vision for society offers a compelling and well-thought-out blueprint for a system that prioritizes and genuinely values transparency, accountability, and, most critically, the well-being of the collective community. It encourages a significant shift in focus from individualistic pursuits and ambitions toward a more inclusive and participatory approach that ultimately benefits all members of society, thereby fostering cooperation, empathy, and shared prosperity across diverse groups and individuals.

The emergence of decentralized monetary systems today signifies a contemporary reflection of a long-standing and age-old debate that has deep roots in economic theory. Cryptocurrencies, as modern financial instruments, operate fundamentally on the principle that no single entity or authority should possess absolute control over dictating or controlling the value of money itself. Instead, this value is collaboratively determined through a decentralized network of users, each one of whom is actively contributing to the overall system through mechanisms of consensus and healthy competition among peers. This innovative and groundbreaking model aligns perfectly with the concept of a new social contract—a mutually beneficial agreement in which economic decisions are made collectively, ensuring that the benefits of prosperity are shared equitably by all participants involved in the system. This transformation in the economic landscape encourages a community-oriented approach, reflecting a significant shift towards a more inclusive and participatory economic structure where individuals work together for the common good. It fosters a sense of shared responsibility and mutual benefit in the financial realm, promoting the idea that all can have a stake in the economy regardless of their background. Through this method of decentralized governance, participants are empowered to take control of their financial futures, challenging traditional hierarchies and opening the door to new opportunities for collaboration and innovation among diverse groups within society.

For modern society, this increasingly demands a profound rethinking and careful reshaping of the fundamental role that money plays in both our social and political lives. It calls for the thoughtful development and establishment of financial systems that are not only efficient and effective in their operations but also equitable and fair in their outcomes. In such systems, wealth should not be excessively concentrated in the hands of a small number of individuals but should be accessible and available to everyone, regardless of their financial background or social standing. This notion presents a persuasive and compelling argument for the decentralization of monetary control—a logical and pragmatic solution to the deep-rooted problems of inequality, economic injustice, and corruption that have continually plagued centralized systems throughout history. By exploring new avenues and pathways for innovative financial governance, we can pave the way toward a more just and fair economy that benefits all citizens, ensuring that every individual has the opportunity to thrive and prosper in an inclusive economic environment.

Persuading the Skeptics: The Future of Decentralized Monetary Innovation

Despite the compelling and well-articulated arguments that have been put forth regarding various alternative theories on wealth and exchange, a lingering skepticism continues to persist among certain groups and individuals who remain unconvinced. Critics frequently point to the significant volatility that is inherently present in decentralized currencies, highlighting the numerous challenges associated with effectively scaling decentralized systems to meet the broader and more complex needs of diverse economic activities. Additionally, they emphasize the glaring absence of adequate regulatory oversight as a considerable potential pitfall that could derail these emerging financial models from achieving their intended objectives. However, history teaches us that every revolutionary idea and paradigm shift inevitably faces substantial resistance during its early stages of development, and the journey toward acceptance can be fraught with difficulties. The transition from simple barter systems to the introduction of coinage was not smooth, and subsequently, the shift from commodity money to state-issued currency encountered myriad challenges and widespread skepticism from various stakeholders, including merchants, governments, and the general populace. Yet, over time, these financial innovations proved not only to be viable but also transformative, reshaping economies and societies in profoundly meaningful ways. The lessons of the past serve as a reminder that while skepticism can be healthy and even beneficial in some contexts, it should not overshadow the potential for groundbreaking ideas to flourish and create a lasting impact on the world around us.

The remarkable rise of cryptocurrencies alongside DeFi platforms signifies one of the latest and most significant chapters in this long and intricate history of monetary evolution. It is important to recognize that the early days of decentralized finance have indeed been marked by notable unpredictability and volatility, yet these challenges can be interpreted as mere growing pains—inevitable and natural phases that occur in the evolution of any groundbreaking and transformative financial system. These initial hurdles faced by cryptocurrencies and DeFi platforms serve as a vital reminder that all innovations, regardless of their potential, encounter obstacles before they are able to find stability and their rightful place in the market. As technology continues to mature over time and as more market participants engage and gain valuable experience in navigating this complex and new financial landscape, the stability and reliability of decentralized monetary systems are likely to improve in substantial and meaningful ways. Such significant improvements will not only help to bolster user confidence but also contribute to the development of a more robust and resilient ecosystem. This ongoing progress is pivotal to further validating and reinforcing the arguments of those who passionately champion the ideals of economic freedom, financial independence, and transformative innovation throughout various sectors of society. The journey towards a more decentralized financial future continues to unfold with each passing day, and with it comes the incredible potential for greater empowerment of individuals and communities on a global scale, thus helping to level the playing field and facilitate more opportunities for many.

Moreover, the ethical imperatives that underpin decentralized models—such as transparency, accountability, and the equitable distribution of wealth—serve as a powerful and significant counterweight to the numerous challenges that these systems must confront in today's complex and often tumultuous financial landscape. The logical synthesis of ancient wisdom combined harmoniously with cutting-edge modern technology presents an undeniable and compelling case for the continued innovation and evolution of various monetary systems. Decentralization is not merely a temporary trend or passing fad; rather, it is the inevitable and profound outcome of centuries of relentless human progress, perseverance, and exploration in the pursuit of economic freedom and individual empowerment that many have long sought after. This ongoing movement towards decentralization reflects a growing recognition and understanding that alternative economic frameworks can lead to greater fairness, inclusivity, and opportunities for all participants in the economic ecosystem, ultimately fostering a more just society for everyone involved.

Bridging Theory and Practice: Lessons for Modern Economies

The revolutionary ideas that emerged from the early and often daunting challenges to state-controlled money have undeniably left an indelible and lasting mark on modern economic theory that simply cannot be easily overlooked or dismissed. They serve as a profound reminder that money is not merely an end in itself but rather fundamentally a means to facilitate human interaction, spur innovation, and promote significant and sustainable growth in society. The analytical rigor and depth of these alternative theories provide a valuable and insightful roadmap for building financial systems that are resilient, adaptable, and ethically grounded in principles that prioritize the well-being of individuals and communities over the pursuit of mere profit. These concepts encourage a re-examination of traditional economic models, fostering a shift towards more inclusive practices that recognize the intrinsic value of every participant in the economic landscape. It is through embracing these revolutionary ideas that we can hope to create a more equitable framework where the benefits of economic development are widely shared and accessible to all, allowing for prosperity that is not only measured in monetary terms but also in the improvement of quality of life.

Modern technologies, including blockchain and smart contracts, serve as practical and innovative embodiments of these age-old concepts and ideals that have fascinated thinkers for centuries. These advanced systems provide effective and cutting-edge solutions to the significant issues that early philosophers and thinkers philosophized about: centralization often leads to inefficiency and can unfortunately breed corruption, whereas decentralization promotes both innovation and the ongoing cultivation of trust among individuals and various entities. By harnessing the transformative power of these groundbreaking technologies, we have an unprecedented opportunity to build an inclusive financial ecosystem that is purposefully designed to not only satisfy the rapidly evolving demands of today's intricate global economy but also to align with the enduring and timeless principles of transparency, fairness, and the collective benefit of all stakeholders who are involved in this dynamic landscape. This evolution is essential for fostering new relationships and building a future that resonates with the ideals of equity and shared prosperity.

For policymakers, the invaluable lessons derived from an array of alternative theories of wealth present a compelling and persuasive argument that advocates for a serious rethinking and comprehensive reform of our traditional monetary systems. These insightful perspectives vividly underscore and highlight the pressing need for enhanced decentralization and markedly improved accountability in the management of money. This transformative vision, if it can be properly realized, harbors the potential to foster the development of more sustainable and innovative economic policies. Additionally, it promises a fairer and more equitable distribution of wealth among various populations, which is crucial in today's world. For investors, these alternative wealth theories provide a logical and robust framework that is essential for systematically evaluating and thoroughly assessing newly emerging financial instruments. This includes not just cryptocurrencies but also the diverse and expanding range of decentralized finance platforms that have taken root. These innovative technologies and platforms promise to substantially democratize access to wealth. In doing so, they empower individuals in ways that are unprecedented and indeed revolutionary in nature. By leveraging these advancements, they offer remarkable opportunities that could redefine financial participation and inclusivity for people across a wide array of socio-economic backgrounds, thus bridging existing gaps and fostering an environment of economic collaboration and growth.

A Vision for the Future: Ethical, Decentralized, and Resilient

As we look ahead to the future, the thoughtful and strategic integration of alternative monetary theories, along with revolutionary and cutting-edge technology, holds tremendous promise for bringing forth a financial system that is not only ethical but also remarkably efficient and equitable. The innovative ideas that have once challenged the long-established foundations of state-controlled currency are now discovering new and exciting avenues for expression and development in the dynamic digital realm. This significant transformation offers a compelling and fresh model for how money should be created, managed, and distributed in a manner that not only aligns with contemporary values but also meets the diverse and evolving needs of an increasingly aware and interconnected society. The potential of merging these progressive ideas and technologies paves the way for a new era in finance, one that prioritizes inclusivity and sustainability, while addressing the pressing challenges of our time.

This vision is not only shockingly beautiful but also profoundly inspiring—a groundbreaking world where economic power is decentralized and equitably distributed among all. In this progressive landscape, transparency becomes the new norm, fostering an environment where the manifold benefits of wealth are shared and accessible to every individual and community. It represents a transformative world where trust is intricately woven into the very fabric of all financial transactions, ensuring authenticity and reliability in every interaction. In this innovative context, the archaic limitations of centralized control are effectively replaced by dynamic, responsive systems that seamlessly adapt to the diverse and constantly evolving needs of a truly global community. Such a vision promotes genuine inclusion and fairness, ultimately creating a society that elevates every member, ensuring that opportunities are available to everyone, and establishing a future where collaboration and equity thrive in harmony.

In this rapidly evolving financial landscape, the persuasive arguments for the necessity of decentralization are undeniably clear, compelling, and increasingly vital. By liberating money from the restrictive confines of state control and intervention, we unlock its true potential as an extraordinary catalyst for innovation, sustainable growth, and far-reaching social justice for all individuals. The logical progression from the early experiments of free banking systems, alongside various local currencies that were utilized, to the remarkable and unprecedented rise of cryptocurrencies witnessed over the past few decades serves as a strong testament to the enduring power and relevance of decentralized economic thought—a far-reaching ideology that remains just as pertinent today as it was many centuries ago when the initial ideas began to take shape. This significant shift not only encourages individual empowerment and a sense of autonomy but also promotes a much more inclusive and equitable economic system where diverse opportunities are made available to a broader and more varied population. By embracing decentralization, we create an environment that fosters greater innovation, equitable access, and collaborative economic engagement among all participants in the marketplace.

A Call to Embrace Revolutionary Change

The rise of alternative theories on wealth and exchange represents one of the most profound and transformative shifts in the entire history of money and monetary practice. These revolutionary ideas have boldly challenged the previously established and tightly centralized control of currency that has dominated financial systems for centuries. In proposing instead a radically new vision of money, these emerging theories depict a form of currency that is not only dynamic and flexible in nature but also ethical and genuinely free from the constraints that have historically governed monetary practices. From the early and spirited debates of ancient philosophers, who passionately speculated about the intricate nature of value and exchange, to the pioneering and innovative experiments in free banking that sought to democratize access to essential financial tools for broader society, the evolution of monetary systems has been an ongoing journey continuously driven by a relentless pursuit of economic freedom, transparency, and groundbreaking innovation. This ongoing transformation of financial paradigms highlights how modern societies are increasingly recognizing the critical importance of decentralized finance as a powerful means of empowering individuals and communities in ways that were previously thought to be utterly impossible. Such recognition is not merely theoretical; it is an active movement that is setting the stage for an exciting and potentially transformative future of financial interaction, where individuals hold more control over their economic destinies than ever before.

As we find ourselves standing on the threshold of a truly groundbreaking new era in finance—an era that is profoundly marked by the transformative power inherent in decentralized technologies and the captivating promise of a significantly more equitable distribution of wealth among individuals—we must earnestly draw upon the invaluable lessons that history has imparted to us over the centuries. The compelling arguments that have been presented by early critics of state-controlled currency, which are firmly grounded in clear logic, a strong ethical responsibility, and a visionary understanding of human progress, serve as a powerful and inspiring blueprint for the bright and promising future that lies ahead. These critics urge us not only to rethink and reevaluate our existing financial systems but also to actively question the deeply entrenched status quo that has prevailed for so long. Furthermore, they inspire us to wholeheartedly embrace the radical and transformative potential that comes with the advent of decentralization, as we collectively strive to build a more inclusive and equitable financial landscape for everyone involved.

This section has presented a truly shocking and mind-blowing exploration of the rise of alternative theories on wealth and exchange—a remarkable and insightful journey that reveals the deep and enduring logic behind the ongoing decentralization of money in our diverse society. It argues persuasively that true economic progress is achieved not through the hoarding of immense wealth by a centralized authority, which often leads to severe disparity and disempowerment among the populace, but rather through the free and transparent exchange of value in a well-structured system that genuinely empowers individuals and uplifts entire communities across the globe. By embracing these innovative theories and practices, we can begin to understand the immense potential for a more equitable and just economic framework that not only prioritizes the well-being of all individuals but also enhances opportunities for growth, collaboration, and prosperity on a wider scale. This calls for a rethinking of traditional methods and encourages a shift toward more inclusive practices that benefit society as a whole.

Today's decentralized financial systems stand as the logical heirs to those early experiments—systems that effectively harness the transformative power of cutting-edge technology to reshape the way we view and interact with money. These systems aim to create a world where money transcends being merely a measure of economic activity and instead becomes a powerful tool for significant social transformation and empowerment, contributing positively to the fabric of society. By thoughtfully integrating these timeless economic principles with modern innovations and technological advancements, we hold the potential to build a financial future that is not only resilient but also remarkably inclusive and dynamic, reflecting the vibrant and adaptive nature of the human spirit itself in the face of changing economic landscapes. This vision of decentralization is not just about financial transactions; it is about fostering communities, encouraging creativity, and enabling everyone to have access to resources and opportunities that were once out of reach for many.

Embrace this truly revolutionary vision for the future. Let the alternative theories surrounding wealth and exchange guide you as you reimagine the essential and transformative role of money in our society. The future of finance is not just a concept; it is actively being written today by innovative thinkers and visionaries, and this is a future where true economic freedom, ethical stewardship, and decentralized power are not merely lofty ideals but fundamental principles that can reshape our world. These principles will serve as the solid foundation upon which a more just, prosperous, and transparent world will ultimately thrive. Such a world will be created for everyone involved, allowing individuals and communities to flourish collectively without the constraints imposed by traditional financial systems. By embracing these ideas, we can work together towards a more inclusive economic landscape that benefits all.

Section 5: How Denationalization Laid the Groundwork for Digital Assets

In a world where governments once maintained an unyielding, iron grip on money and financial systems, an audacious and groundbreaking revolutionary process unfolded—one that would eventually pave the way to liberate wealth from the rigid clutches of centralized control and profoundly set the stage for the unprecedented digital financial revolution we are witnessing today. The denationalization of money signifies not just any change, but a seismic and transformative shift in the fundamental and dynamic ways societies manage, perceive, value, and distribute wealth among their citizens and communities. This intricate and multifaceted process, which evolved over many centuries, not only challenged the long-standing authority and dominance of state-controlled currencies but also laid down the essential intellectual, economic, and practical groundwork for the modern emergence of decentralized digital assets that are becoming increasingly relevant and influential in today's economy. In this expansive section, we will embark on a shocking, mind-blowing, and intellectually stimulating journey through the rich annals of history, employing meticulous reasoning, sharp logic, and thorough analytical scrutiny to illustrate how the gradual liberation of money from the constraints of state control created a remarkably fertile ground that allowed cryptocurrencies and decentralized finance (DeFi) to ultimately flourish and thrive within the ever-changing contemporary economic landscape. As we traverse this pathway, we will explore key historical milestones, technological advancements, and socio-economic shifts that facilitated this monumental change, providing a comprehensive understanding of the forces at play in the emergence of a new financial era characterized by unprecedented levels of innovation and accessibility.

A World Transformed: From Centralized Authority to Economic Autonomy

For much of recorded history, the intricate and often complex processes surrounding the production and strict control of money have remained the exclusive domain of powerful rulers, influential monarchs, and authoritative governments. State-controlled currencies emerged as not merely instruments of trade but as potent symbols of power and dominance—tools that enabled kings, emperors, and complex bureaucracies to assert their authority across vast territories and maintain a meticulously structured social order. Yet, as these systems developed and matured over time, their inherent limitations became glaringly apparent and increasingly troubling for many citizens. Centralized control of money frequently led to economic manipulation, rampant and destructive inflation, and the complete suppression of individual initiative, creativity, and entrepreneurship. As the negative consequences unfolded in various communities, it was only a matter of time before the inherent inefficiencies and profound moral dilemmas of state monopolies on money prompted a wave of critics, thinkers, and innovators alike to rise up, challenge the entrenched status quo, and earnestly seek alternative solutions and systems that would promote greater economic freedom and empowerment for individuals.

The centralization of money represented an initially logical and practical step forward for nascent states that were embarking on their development journey. As various societies began the gradual transition from traditional barter systems, which relied on direct exchange of goods and services, to the more sophisticated and systematic use of standardized coinage, the direct involvement of the state became essential. This involvement was critical to ensuring consistency and reliability in the currency, as well as the provision of a regulated measure of value that everyone within the community could recognize and trust without hesitation. However, this seemingly beneficial control over currency and finance came at a steep and unfortunate price: the overwhelming power to issue and manage money was frequently abused by those in positions of authority, often leading to detrimental consequences. Rulers and leaders had the significant capability to print excessive amounts of currency at their own discretion, which could effectively result in the dilution of its value over time. This reckless action could also disrupt the delicate balance of trade and trust that holds society together, leading to widespread economic instability. The catastrophic hyperinflations that have punctuated the annals of history—from the infamous Roman debasement of coinage in ancient times to the devastating economic collapse witnessed during the Weimar Republic in the early 20th century—serve as stark and cautionary reminders. They illustrate the profound dangers that are inherent in centralized monetary authority, as well as the far-reaching ramifications it can have on a society's overall economy and its social structure. These historical events not only highlight the risks associated with monetary centralization but also underscore the necessity for prudent governance and vigilant oversight in the management of national finances.

As these systematic abuses became increasingly evident and impossible to ignore, a counter-narrative began to emerge with an intensity that grew more pronounced over time. Thoughtful intellectuals, forward-thinking progressive merchants, and even a select group of state officials, all acting with an eye on the promising future, started to question whether genuine and authentic economic freedom could ever truly be achieved under a system in which money was tightly controlled, heavily regulated, and monitored diligently by the state. They argued with compelling conviction and persuasive reasoning that true value and meaningful prosperity could only ever be realized if money was completely liberated entirely from any form of governmental interference and manipulation—a concept that was as radical in its implications as it was rational in its foundational principles. This innovative idea of the denationalization of money, although gradual in its implementation and often met with fierce resistance and pushback from established powers and traditionalists, was an essential and significant first step toward achieving an economic autonomy that resonates powerfully in today's rapidly evolving decentralized digital age, where innovation and independence are more crucially prioritized than ever before.

The Philosophical Underpinnings of Denationalization

The intellectual revolution that profoundly questioned the deeply entrenched principles of state-controlled money was, at its essence, rooted in a rich and profound philosophical inquiry.

Early thinkers, courageous and innovative, who dared to challenge the long-standing traditional notions that had governed monetary systems for ages, suggested with thoughtful conviction that money should not merely serve as a tool wielded exclusively by the state. Instead, they posited vigorously and passionately that money, at its very core, was fundamentally a measure of value—a critical and indispensable metric that ought to genuinely reflect the authentic economic activities of a society. This reflection was crucial, as it should not be clouded or obscured by merely the arbitrary whims and caprices of political power. This compelling argument extended far beyond the realms of mere economics; indeed, it delved deeply into philosophical considerations that were inherently about the essential themes of freedom, fairness, and the fundamental right of individuals to assert control over their own economic destinies. Such control is vital for individuals to pursue their aspirations without facing undue interference or coercive constraints imposed by governing forces that may not truly represent the interests of the people.

Ancient Greek philosophers, for instance, engaged in deep and profound debates regarding the merits of state control versus private control of money and financial systems, discussions that reflected their enduring quest for understanding the ideal structures of governance and society. Plato and Aristotle, two of the most influential thinkers of their time, both pondered whether a society could ever achieve true and lasting justice if the means of economic exchange and trade were monopolized by a central authority wielding unchecked power over all monetary transactions and systems. They passionately argued that money, in its essence and fundamental role, should primarily serve the people and the community as a whole, promoting equity and fairness rather than serving narrow interests. Furthermore, they believed that it should be subject to the organic forces of trade, market fluctuations, and innovation, driven by the desires and needs of individuals within that society. This natural economic dynamism should prevail, as opposed to being shackled by rigid, state-imposed regulations and controls that could ultimately stifle creativity, suppress initiative, and impede progress across various sectors. Their revolutionary ideas, although conceived in a world constrained by limited technological means and resources, were indeed far ahead of their time, highlighting their passionate advocacy for economic liberty, a belief in the potential for individual initiative to drive societal growth, and the progressive concept of decentralization in economic matters, seeking to empower citizens rather than central authorities.

These pivotal debates that took place during this transformative period not only laid the foundational conceptual groundwork for future economic theories but also significantly influenced the later development of both private banking systems and free banking mechanisms. As the medieval period emerged, local currencies alongside merchant banks were established as a direct response to these philosophical challenges and discourses. These early experiments in finance were not merely spontaneous occurrences; rather, they represented deeply logical and innovative attempts to create monetary systems that were much more responsive and adaptable to the evolving needs of commerce and trade. Furthermore, these newly developed systems aimed to be more robust and resilient, offering greater resistance to the corruptions frequently associated with centralized power structures, which had often led to serious abuses and inefficiencies within the financial realm. By providing alternatives to traditional banking models, these innovations opened the door to a myriad of possibilities in the financial landscape that would follow.

Early Experiments: Local Currencies and Free Banking

Throughout the extensive and multifaceted Middle Ages, continuing to stretch into the dynamic and transformative early modern period, a remarkable and varied series of experiments with local currencies and innovative free banking systems emerged as compelling practical applications of the broader and significant concept of denationalization. Local currencies, which were frequently issued by various towns, influential guilds, or even individual enterprising merchants, provided a compelling and vibrant alternative to the traditional state-issued coinage that dominated the economic landscape. These locally crafted currencies were specifically designed and tailored to meet the unique needs and diverse demands of local economies, facilitating transactions and commerce in ways that larger, centralized currencies could not effectively manage. They often circulated in regions where central authorities or government institutions were notably weak, ineffective, or mired in corruption. This groundbreaking innovation allowed for greater economic flexibility and sustainability in communities, fostering increased trade and interaction while diminishing reliance on distant governmental control and intervention. As a result, these local currencies contributed significantly to the development of more vibrant and self-sufficient local economies, empowering individuals and communities in their economic pursuits.

In medieval Europe, a multitude of towns developed their own unique coins or credit systems, which played a crucial and instrumental role in facilitating trade amid the rampant political fragmentation that characterized those tumultuous times. These distinctive local currencies emerged organically, evolving dynamically in direct response to the specific economic needs and varying circumstances of their individual communities. This organic growth occurred rather than being dictated, imposed, or controlled by any central authority or governing body imposing strict regulations. This fascinating practice indicated a compelling possibility: that trade and commerce could flourish successfully without the need for stringent government oversight and intervention, creating a more flexible and responsive economic environment. It suggested that the true value of money could and should be determined by the collective agreement and consensus of the people actively using it within their local markets. This revolutionary idea represented a significant departure from the traditional economic practices of the era, laying the early and important foundations for a more decentralized approach to monetary exchange. It also anticipated the eventual development of modern currency systems that we recognize today, thereby highlighting the potential for small yet vibrant communities to create and sustain their own financial ecosystems, operating independently of overarching control and influence from powerful political entities.

The free banking era of the 19th century, particularly in countries like Scotland and the United States, serves as an important illustration of this significant and transformative shift in the understanding and management of currency throughout the period. During this intriguing and economically vibrant time, private banks were permitted, often without much restriction, to issue their own unique banknotes. This effectively created a dynamic and competitive banking landscape that featured minimal government interference and regulation, fostering growth and innovation within the sector. While these banking systems certainly faced their own array of challenges—such as the occasional emergence of a so-called "wildcat bank," which was notorious for failing to maintain proper reserves and could ultimately collapse under pressure—the overall trend observed was one that indicated a growing trust and reliance on market-driven money creation processes. In a truly free banking environment, the quality, stability, and reliability of banknotes, as well as the monetary instruments used in daily transactions, were determined by the forces of the market itself, rather than being subject to arbitrary state mandates or controls designed to regulate behavior. This atmosphere of competition among banks and their issuance of currency was indeed a revolutionary development in the financial landscape of the time. It demonstrated quite clearly that a decentralized approach to the creation and distribution of money could not only exist but could actually thrive effectively in practice. The success of such systems played a pivotal and transformative role in reshaping contemporary ideas about what banking and monetary policy could ultimately look like moving forward. It showed that competition and innovation within the banking sector could lead to remarkably better outcomes for consumers and the economy as a whole, contributing significantly to advancements in financial systems that have had lasting effects.

The Rise of Digital Decentralization: A Natural Evolution

Fast forward to the present day, and the logical evolution of denationalization has reached its ultimate and most sophisticated expression: decentralized digital currencies that represent a profound shift in our financial landscape. Cryptocurrencies such as Bitcoin and Ethereum can indeed be seen as the direct and notable descendants of those early, innovative experiments that thoroughly explored the concepts of local currencies and free banking systems. These digital currencies signify a radical and transformative shift in how we perceive, utilize, and interact with money—a world where money is created, managed, and exchanged on a truly decentralized network, free from the constraints of traditional financial systems. This network operates independently of any state or central authority, thereby fundamentally changing the landscape of financial transactions and the economic systems as we know them today. Such innovations challenge the traditional notions of currency and trust, paving the way for new economic paradigms and empowering individuals with greater control over their finances.

Blockchain technology serves as a powerful and dynamic engine behind the remarkable emergence and operation of various innovative digital assets that have captured the world's attention. It embodies the fundamental principles that passionate early critics of state-controlled currency and established money systems vigorously advocated for, underscoring their desire for a more equitable and transparent financial landscape. This groundbreaking technology provides a remarkably transparent and immutable ledger, which is diligently maintained collaboratively by a distributed network of nodes, instead of relying on a single, central authority or entity. This decentralized system of trust is not only shocking in its potential to disrupt traditional financial paradigms but also elegantly designed—a mind-blowing testament to human ingenuity and creativity that strongly mirrors the pioneering free banking experiments conducted in earlier times. Through its unique and innovative structure, blockchain redefines our understanding of financial transactions and data integrity, significantly paving the way for a future where individuals retain far more control over their financial assets and personal information, ultimately fostering a more democratic financial ecosystem.

The creation of Bitcoin in the year 2009 marked an exceptional watershed moment in the ongoing evolution of currency and financial systems across the globe. Born out of a deep-seated desire to establish a revolutionary currency that is free from the heavy hand of governmental manipulation and control, Bitcoin's radically decentralized nature poses a direct challenge to every traditional notion of what money should represent and how it should function efficiently within an economy. It operates on a sophisticated system where trust is not placed in any single entity or institution, but is instead distributed across a vast and diverse network of users, each playing a vital role in the integrity of the system. The logic underlying this groundbreaking concept is undeniably powerful: if the centralized control of money frequently leads to significant problems like rampant inflation, systematic corruption, and pervasive inefficiency, then decentralization offers a far superior alternative—an alternative that is inherently more resilient, extraordinarily transparent, and fundamentally more democratic in nature. In this way, Bitcoin not only reimagines the concept of currency itself but also aims to redefine our relationship with financial systems on a global scale, encouraging a new era of financial freedom and empowerment for individuals everywhere.

Moreover, the emergence and rapid growth of decentralized finance (DeFi) platforms further reinforces this significant evolution in the financial landscape we have been observing over recent years. These innovative platforms harness the exceptional power of blockchain technology in a remarkable way to create advanced financial instruments that operate entirely without intermediaries or traditional banking systems. By doing so, they effectively reduce the risk of manipulation and fraud that has plagued conventional financial models, thereby making a wide range of financial services accessible to a much broader population than ever before. This remarkable shift in the paradigm of finance is marked by an influx of users actively seeking more control over their financial resources and decisions. The same human drive and impetus that led to the creation of local currencies, mutually beneficial aid societies, and free banking systems is now propelling the ongoing digital revolution in the realm of finance. It serves as a powerful testament to the fact that the desire for economic autonomy, equity, and self-determination is both timeless and universal, reflecting the reality that people throughout history have consistently sought ways to gain greater control over their financial destinies and futures. The current advancements in DeFi offer exciting new opportunities for individuals to engage with their economy in innovative ways, fostering a community-focused approach to financial management. As more individuals turn to these platforms, one can only imagine the profound impact this ongoing transformation will have on the broader financial ecosystem in the years to come.

Logical Implications: Why Denationalization Matters

The transition from state-controlled money to decentralized, market-driven monetary systems is not merely an ideological shift; it carries with it profound and significant practical implications that fundamentally reshape how we understand and manage wealth in our societies today. This evolution represents a crucial moment in economic history, where the traditional frameworks of monetary control are being challenged and redefined. The logical argument for denationalization is constructed upon several key pillars that underpin this transformative process: the inherent efficiency of decentralized systems, the potential for greater innovation, and the facilitation of more inclusive economic participation. Each of these pillars contributes to a rich tapestry of possibilities that redefine our relationship with finance and economic structures on a global scale.

Transparency and Trust

One of the most significant criticisms often levied against state-controlled currency is the glaring lack of transparency and openness that tends to accompany it. When money is issued and managed by a central authority, it naturally becomes susceptible to a variety of forms of political manipulation, corruption, and mismanagement, all of which can severely undermine public trust in that financial system. Conversely, the concept of denationalization, along with the various systems that support it, inherently fosters a greater level of transparency and accountability. In decentralized systems, such as those utilizing cutting-edge blockchain technology, every single transaction is meticulously recorded on a public ledger that is fully open to scrutiny by anyone regardless of their background. This robust arrangement ensures that the money supply is not vulnerable to the arbitrary whims and decisions of a single, governing entity. Instead, trust is maintained through a well-defined process of collective verification that is rooted in the principles of democracy and inclusivity, which stands in stark contrast to the arbitrary decisions made by a centralized authority. By promoting a system where verification is distributed, democratic, and accessible, the potential for malicious manipulation is significantly reduced. As a result, the public can feel more assured about the integrity of their currency, fostering a community that participates in a more secure financial system.

Efficiency and Innovation

State-controlled systems are frequently characterized by significant bureaucratic inefficiencies that can, in various ways, hinder economic progress and development. The entire elaborate process of minting coins, carefully regulating their circulation, and rigorously enforcing monetary policy tends to be inherently slow and cumbersome, which often leads to continual delays and deep frustrations for both businesses and consumers alike. In stark contrast, decentralized systems operate on principles that are effectively driven by the market, principles that not only encourage healthy competition but also stimulate ongoing innovation within the financial sector. Free banking and localized currencies, which notably served as critical precursors to the modern and ever-evolving landscape of digital assets, demonstrated convincingly that when multiple entities are granted the freedom to issue and manage their own money, the overall system becomes significantly more dynamic, adaptable, and responsive to evolving economic needs and societal shifts. This rationale flows seamlessly into the expansive digital realm, where various cryptocurrencies and decentralized finance (DeFi) platforms persistently push the boundaries of what is feasible and achievable within the world of finance, consistently offering new, creative solutions and viable alternatives that effectively challenge traditional norms and practices.

Economic Freedom

Perhaps one of the most compelling and persuasive arguments in favor of denationalization is undeniably the promise and immense potential that comes with greater economic freedom for all individuals involved in the system. Centralized control over money and financial systems significantly restricts and confines the ability of individuals to participate fully and meaningfully in the broader economy. This concentration of power in the hands of a select few often leads to increased inequality, social injustice, and prolonged economic stagnation, while severely limiting opportunities for the masses to thrive and prosper. On the contrary, decentralized monetary systems stand in stark and refreshing contrast by democratizing access to wealth and financial resources for everyone. They empower individuals to take control of their own finances and futures, enabling them to transact freely across borders and participate actively in global markets without the hindrance of intermediary interference or bureaucratic obstacles. This significant cultural and economic shift towards increased economic freedom is not only logically sound and reasonable, but also ethically imperative. It aligns seamlessly with modern values that advocate for autonomy, individual agency, and empowerment in our increasingly interconnected world, where technology continuously reshapes the financial landscape and provides new avenues for engagement and growth.

Resilience Against External Shocks

Centralized systems are inherently vulnerable to a variety of systemic risks that can arise in an increasingly complex economic environment, one that is marked by rapid changes and unexpected challenges. When a single institution or entity holds the immense power to control the money supply, it creates a precarious situation where any kind of mismanagement, poor decision-making processes, or an unforeseen external shock can lead to catastrophic consequences for the broader economy. Historical examples serve as stark reminders of this precariousness, such as the hyperinflation experienced in the Weimar Republic, where the value of currency plummeted dramatically, rendering it almost worthless, or the systematic debasement of coinage in various ancient empires, events that illustrate compellingly how centralized control can ultimately precipitate a grave economic collapse. In stark contrast, decentralized systems effectively distribute risk across a vast and interlinked network of participants, thereby making them considerately more resilient and significantly adaptable when faced with diverse shocks and stresses to the economic framework. The intrinsic design attributes of blockchain technology, for instance, effectively ensure that the entire system remains robust and fully functional, even in situations where specific parts of the network may fail or come under severe attack from malicious entities. This remarkable resilience stems as a logical outcome of denationalization—a profound and profound safeguard against the volatility, unpredictability, and uncertainty that are inevitably inherent in any complex economic system. Such innovative mechanisms work synergistically to create a more stable environment for economic activity, thereby encouraging sustainable growth while simultaneously fostering a culture of innovation that can thrive despite existing challenges.

Arguing Against the Status Quo: Critiques of State-Controlled Currency

The alternative theories that ultimately led to the denationalization of money encountered significant and fierce resistance from various quarters, with strong opposition emerging from those who favored state-controlled currency. Proponents of this centralized control put forth a multitude of strong arguments, asserting that such oversight was not only necessary but also crucial for maintaining order in the financial system and ensuring a stable, uniform medium of exchange for all transactions. They contended that, without the oversight of a central authority, the money supply could quickly spiral into chaos, rendering it altogether unreliable, inefficient, and deeply disruptive to economic activities. However, when undertaking a closer examination of the situation, one can reveal that the logical reasoning behind the concept of denationalization, supplemented by substantial historical evidence, actually suggests a different narrative entirely. Rather than leading to chaos and disorder, the decentralized approach could very well foster innovation and adaptability within the economic landscape, ultimately leading to a more robust and dynamic economic environment that could benefit a broader range of individuals and communities.

State-controlled systems have repeatedly demonstrated their inherent vulnerability to various forms of political manipulation and mismanagement, showcasing a persistent and troubling trend. The unchecked power that these governments possess to print money without any significant restraints or oversight has inevitably led to severe and damaging cycles of inflation and deflation. These disruptive economic fluctuations erode public trust considerably and contribute to destabilizing economies on multiple levels, affecting various sectors and layers of society. When governments misuse their control over monetary policy for their benefit, it becomes increasingly apparent that this is not merely an economic failure that can be brushed aside or ignored. It stands out as a serious violation of the fundamental principles of fairness and accountability that underpin a just society. The logical critique of such practices becomes increasingly evident: if money is truly intended to serve the people of a nation, it must be managed in a responsible way that embodies transparency, equity, and is completely free from any form of political interference that could compromise its integrity and effectiveness. Such an approach is essential to restore faith in economic systems and ensure that financial resources are utilized effectively for the benefit of all citizens, rather than allowing them to be manipulated by political agendas that serve only a select few.

The Philosophical and Ethical Imperative

Beyond the practical and logical arguments, there indeed exists a deeply profound philosophical and ethical dimension to the denationalization of money that merits serious and thoughtful consideration. Centralized monetary systems tend to concentrate immense power in the hands of a select few individuals and institutions, often leading to significant and troubling disparities in the distribution of wealth. This reality brings forth the potential for egregious systemic abuse and manipulation within the financial realm. Such a concentration of financial power not only undermines individual liberties and freedoms but also diminishes the overall well-being and health of society as a whole. In stark and compelling contrast, a decentralized approach to currency aligns closely with the fundamental principles of fairness, equity, and collective responsibility, which are vital for fostering a harmonious, equitable, and thriving community. The compelling idea that money should essentially serve as a public trust—a shared resource envisioned to benefit the entire community—rather than merely enriching a privileged few individuals stands as a powerful and persuasive argument in favor of reform. This vision profoundly resonates with the ideals of social justice, economic freedom, and the democratic values that underpin an equitable and just society, underscoring the urgent need to rethink and fundamentally reconsider our current monetary systems. The reimagining of money in this way embodies the aspirations for a society that values egalitarian principles and strives for comprehensive inclusiveness and collaboration among its members. It is crucial that we recognize the potential that a more decentralized currency system has to empower individuals, create equitable opportunities, and foster a financial landscape where everyone's voice can be heard and where everybody has access to the tools necessary for their economic advancement.

Early critics of state-controlled currency have long maintained the perspective that true and lasting prosperity is most effectively achieved when individuals are empowered to fully and meaningfully participate in the entire economy without unnecessary hindrances. This grand vision of economic freedom goes beyond being just a theoretical concept; it emerges as a profound moral imperative that resonates deeply with the underlying principles of personal empowerment and individual choice. When money is unshackled from the constraints imposed by centralized control, it opens up vast opportunities for a more equitable distribution of resources. Such an environment not only allows but encourages societies to flourish in diverse and innovative manners that ultimately reap benefits for everyone involved in the economic sphere. This ethical argument stands as compelling as it is logical, providing a persuasive rationale for the continued evolution of monetary systems toward ever-increasing decentralization. In this context, embracing an economic system where currency can flow freely without excessive regulation and oversight leads to a dynamic and vibrant marketplace. In this dynamic marketplace, creativity and entrepreneurship are given the necessary space to thrive, leading to a robust economy that uplifts all members of society, fostering an environment that encourages growth, promotes innovation, and cultivates collective well-being.

Bridging Past and Future: The Legacy of Denationalization

The enduring legacy of denationalization is strikingly evident in the rapidly evolving and complex modern world of digital assets. Cryptocurrencies, alongside decentralized finance (DeFi), stand as direct and innovative descendants of the early experiments that rigorously focused on free banking practices and the use of various local currencies. These digital currencies embody the same foundational principles that early critics and advocates vigorously championed—such as transparency, efficiency, and economic freedom—all while effectively leveraging cutting-edge technology to overcome the multifaceted limitations that have long been posed by traditional monetary systems. This significant shift not only highlights the profound changes in the way we perceive value and engage in exchange but also emphasizes a broader movement toward a far more inclusive and accessible financial landscape, one that empowers individuals and communities alike.

Blockchain technology, which is distinguished by its revolutionary decentralized ledger, stands as the pinnacle realization of the long-cherished vision of denationalization in modern finance. It presents a highly sophisticated system in which trust is not concentrated in a single governing authority but is instead collaboratively distributed across an expansive global network of diverse users. This remarkable architectural framework guarantees that the value of money is dictated by the inherent market forces at play, rather than being subject to arbitrary whims or decisions made by government entities that may not always align with the interests of the public. The rise of digital currencies, therefore, represents not merely a radical departure from historical financial systems that have, for decades, operated under centralized control, but rather an organic evolution stemming from centuries of experimentation, innovation, and profound philosophical discourse regarding value, trust, and governance as foundational pillars of a thriving economy. This transformative movement offers individuals greater autonomy and security, empowering them to engage in financial transactions without the need for intermediaries, which can create inefficiencies and vulnerabilities.

As we find ourselves standing firmly on the threshold of a new economic era, the invaluable lessons imparted by the process of denationalization provide us with a comprehensive roadmap for creating an economic system that is not only more equitable but also truly resilient and profoundly innovative. This financial system must be one that serves all individuals better, catering to the diverse needs and aspirations of everyone involved. These lessons actively challenge the deeply entrenched status quo of centralized control, as they advocate for a much-needed transformation in our understanding and healthy implementation of fundamental economic principles. They provide us with a clear and logical, analytically rigorous framework to better understand why decentralization is not just preferable but, in fact, is becoming inevitable in today's rapidly evolving socio-economic landscape. The modern world, which is characterized by its breakneck pace of technological advancements, unparalleled innovations, and significant global interconnectedness, demands a monetary system that is truly adaptable, transparently managed, and, above all, free from the corrosive impacts that centralized power and influence often introduce. In this particular context, the emerging financial structures we are witnessing must prioritize inclusivity and accessibility, ensuring that all individuals, regardless of their background, can participate fully in the economy without encountering barriers that are often created by traditional centralized institutions. By reconfiguring our economic systems around these principles, we can pave the way towards a more just and inclusive financial future that genuinely uplifts every member of society.

Persuading the Skeptics: The Case for Continued Innovation

Despite the compelling historical, logical, and ethical arguments that strongly advocate for the process of denationalization, skepticism continues to persist among various observers who are wary of the implications. Critics frequently point to a variety of challenges that inevitably arise during the complex transition from centralized, state-controlled systems to more decentralized alternatives that many believe could lead to increased freedom and efficiency. Concerns regarding issues of volatility in the markets, scalability of new frameworks, and the uncertainty related to regulatory measures are often cited as potential pitfalls that could significantly derail the overall effectiveness of such reforms in place. However, it is crucial to recognize that these challenges are not insurmountable obstacles; rather, they represent a fundamental part of the growing pains that accompany any significant and revolutionary shift that we witness within our economic systems. With foresight, creativity, and collective effort from all stakeholders involved, these hurdles can be addressed, transformed into opportunities for improvement, and ultimately surmounted, paving the way for a more dynamic and responsive economic landscape that could benefit society as a whole.

History teaches us that every major innovation in the realm of money, from the groundbreaking invention of coinage to the widespread adoption of paper currency, was initially met with substantial resistance and skepticism from various segments of society. This skepticism often stemmed from fears of the unknown, as people were not ready to embrace new forms of financial transactions that deviated from what they had long known and trusted. The free banking experiments of the 19th century, while fraught with numerous challenges and obstacles, eventually demonstrated that a decentralized and competitive approach to money creation could indeed succeed. These experiments highlighted the potential for greater efficiency and consumer choice in banking, even as they faced pushback from entrenched interests that favored a more centralized control over monetary systems. In a similar manner, the early days of cryptocurrencies have been marked by significant volatility and uncertainty; however, they are already proving to be considerably more resilient and innovative compared to the centralized systems they seek to replace. As time progresses, cryptocurrencies are fundamentally altering our financial landscape by introducing new paradigms of ownership and transaction security that challenge traditional banking norms. This ongoing evolution reflects a broader trend of technological advancement wherein each successive innovation builds upon the successes and failures of its predecessors, reshaping how we perceive and utilize money in everyday life.

The persuasive argument for denationalization is significantly enhanced by a multitude of logical outcomes that stem from the process of decentralization: increased transparency in transactions involving financial exchanges, reduced opportunities for corruption in various forms, and greater economic freedom for individuals and businesses alike, allowing them to operate with more autonomy. These benefits are not merely hypothetical or theoretical—they are already being realized and observed in various innovative digital financial systems across the globe, which serve diverse communities. As this technology continues to mature and evolve, and as regulatory frameworks progress to better support it, the challenges associated with decentralized systems are likely to diminish further. This progress paves the way for a more stable, equitable, and inclusive financial future that serves a broader spectrum of society, encompassing various demographics and socioeconomic classes. This ongoing evolution points to a transformative shift that can potentially empower individuals with more direct control over their financial resources, opportunities, and choices in a way that was previously unattainable.

A New Social Contract: Empowering the Individual

The denationalization of money signifies an extraordinary and profound reimagining of the very social contract that fundamentally underpins and shapes our complex economic systems and structures. It serves as a resounding and urgent call to restore control of money back to the people, empowering individuals from all walks of life to actively participate in the global economy without being subjected to the unpredictable, often arbitrary whims of centralized authorities and institutions that have traditionally held such power. This transformative shift is not merely a technical innovation in the intricate realm of finance; rather, it embodies a significant moral and philosophical revolution that challenges existing paradigms and necessitates a thorough reevaluation of our values and beliefs regarding currency and its vital role in society. Moreover, this movement emphasizes the importance of decentralization and financial independence, fostering a new environment where the principles of equality and fairness can flourish alongside the evolving landscape of digital assets.

When money is managed by a central authority, it inevitably creates a significant power imbalance—one in which an overwhelming concentration of wealth and resources becomes prevalent in the hands of only a few individuals, while the vast majority of the population are left increasingly vulnerable and at the mercy of these few powerful entities. This dynamic invariably leads to pronounced economic disparities and social injustices that can be deeply damaging and corrosive to the fabric of a society. In stark contrast, decentralized monetary systems effectively empower individuals and distribute economic power in a manner that is significantly more equitable and just. This innovative new social contract is thoughtfully built on the principles of transparency, accountability, and collective responsibility that drive the system. It represents a transformative vision of finance that champions the inherent rights of all individuals and promotes the common good for every member of society—making it a vision that is as persuasive as it is logically sound and rigorously backed by compelling arguments. By wholeheartedly embracing this approach, we work towards creating a financial environment that is not only significantly fairer but also more resilient in the face of challenges, fostering an atmosphere of cooperation and collaboration among diverse groups across the socioeconomic spectrum.

Modern digital currencies and DeFi platforms represent the embodiment of this innovative social contract in contemporary finance, a concept that is becoming increasingly essential in today's rapidly changing economic landscape. They allow individuals to seize complete control over their own finances, facilitating the freedom to transact seamlessly across borders without the cumbersome intervention of traditional banking systems. Furthermore, these cutting-edge platforms enable broader participation in a financial system that is now governed by code rather than being reliant on a centralized authority. This kind of empowerment, which many may overlook in the midst of technological advancements, is not merely a technical feature; it signifies a profound transformation in how we perceive, manage, and interact with money on a daily basis. It marks a significant shift in the financial paradigm that holds the potential to truly democratize access to wealth and promote economic justice on a global scale. This innovative approach to finance has the power to uplift communities, foster inclusive financial opportunities, and ensure that individuals from varying backgrounds can engage in economic activities that were once dominated by a select few. Therefore, the implications of such advancements are vast and far-reaching, creating a more equitable financial future for everyone involved.

The Analytical Framework: Integrating Historical Insights with Modern Innovation

To fully appreciate the extraordinary transformative potential of denationalization in the realm of finance, it is absolutely essential to integrate the invaluable lessons of history with the groundbreaking innovations and advancements of the digital age we are currently experiencing. The early and insightful experiments in free banking, local currencies, and decentralized trade offer a logical, practical, and thoughtful blueprint for the modern financial revolution that we are witnessing today across the globe. These historical examples vividly illustrate that when money is thoughtfully liberated from the constraints imposed by centralized control or authority, it evolves in remarkable and innovative ways to effectively meet the real, pressing needs of society—ultimately becoming more adaptable, transparent, and equitable than before. This ongoing evolution highlights the critical importance of fostering an environment where diverse financial systems can thrive independently, thereby allowing for greater creativity, resilience, and inclusion in economic transactions and relationships. Embracing such an approach not only empowers individuals but also redistributes opportunities, presenting a more balanced economic landscape for all stakeholders involved.

Blockchain technology represents the contemporary realization of various historical attempts to enhance economic systems in profound and meaningful ways. In a manner akin to the free banking era, a period that fostered a much more competitive and efficient monetary landscape, blockchain provides a decentralized ledger that guarantees every transaction is captured with unmatched accuracy and detail. This innovative technology is far more than just the result of modern engineering; it stands as a meaningful progression that emerges from centuries of human creativity and ingenuity dedicated to the quest for economic autonomy and freedom. It effectively links the wisdom of the past with the exciting possibilities of the future, uniting the meticulous record-keeping practices of ancient temple scribes with the rapidly unfolding digital revolution that is transforming our global society. By drawing from historical foundations and insights, blockchain not only honors the rich legacy of previous systems but also paves the way for unprecedented advancements in how we manage, record, and verify our financial interactions in an increasingly interconnected world. The path ahead is filled with the potential to redefine various aspects of transactions, ensuring transparency and accountability that were not as feasible in earlier economic paradigms.

The analytical framework provided by these historical experiments is both shocking and enlightening in a multitude of ways that are significant to understanding our social structures. It reveals compelling insights that the challenges of centralized control are not unique to any single era—they are, indeed, inherent in any system that concentrates power too heavily and exclusively in the hands of just a few individuals. The logical remedy, therefore, is to distribute that power more effectively and equitably among the many, to subsequently create a system where trust is intricately built into the very structure of the monetary network itself. This is, at its core, fundamentally the essence of decentralized finance; a concept that is as much a product of ancient wisdom and enduring principles as it is a manifestation of modern technology and innovative thought processes that continue to evolve and adapt with the times. Such an approach paves the way toward a more inclusive financial future that seeks to empower individuals and promote fairness, thereby opening avenues for participation and prosperity that were previously inaccessible to a large portion of the population.

Persuasive Reflections: Embracing the Vision of Economic Liberation

For the modern investor, the crucial lessons that denationalization imparts offer a powerful and persuasive vision for the increasingly dynamic and complex future landscape of finance. The logical and ethical arguments that favor decentralization—such as enhanced transparency, built-in trust, and elevated economic freedom—are not merely theoretical ideals or abstract concepts; they have indeed transformed into practical necessities in an ever-evolving world where traditional monetary systems have consistently failed to deliver on promises of long-term prosperity and stability. The remarkable and unparalleled rise of cryptocurrencies, along with the emerging and innovative realm of decentralized finance, serves as a compelling testament to the enduring and widespread appeal of these revolutionary concepts—a mind-blowing and eye-opening demonstration that reveals when money is liberated from the stringent control and undue influence of the state, its true potential can ultimately be unleashed and harnessed effectively for the collective benefit of all individuals and entities.

Investors today are increasingly drawn to the enticing promise of decentralized systems in the ever-evolving financial landscape. They perceive in digital currencies not merely a new asset class to diversify their portfolios, but rather a profound and revolutionary paradigm shift that fundamentally challenges the very foundations of traditional finance as we have known and understood it for generations. The argument in favor of this shift is compelling and multifaceted: a decentralized monetary system, by its very nature, is designed to be far more efficient, inherently more transparent, and significantly less susceptible to the corruption and inefficiencies that have unfortunately plagued centralized systems for countless millennia. This emerging trend is not merely an anomaly; it represents the logical and natural outcome of centuries of experimentation, debate, and evolution in economic thought—a groundbreaking leap forward that is both shocking and ultimately inevitable in its unfolding. The far-reaching implications of this transformation extend well beyond mere investment opportunities, prompting broader discussions about trust, accountability, and the very future of money itself, ultimately reshaping the financial landscape as we move forward into an increasingly digital age.

The persuasive power of this compelling vision is significantly magnified by its profound ethical implications and far-reaching consequences. When money is liberated from the constraints of centralized control and traditional financial systems, it transforms into an incredibly empowering tool for genuine economic upliftment and sustainable growth. This liberation democratizes widespread access to wealth, allowing individuals from all walks of life to participate. It promotes innovative ideas that might have otherwise remained unsupported and fosters a more equitable and fair distribution of resources across various segments of society and community structures. This extraordinary phenomenon is not merely a financial revolution—it represents a much broader social revolution that has the remarkable potential to transform entire societies. By effectively leveling the playing field, it ensures that economic opportunities are accessible to everyone, regardless of their background, circumstances, or previous barriers they may have faced. Such changes could lead to a much more inclusive economic environment, enabling everyone to contribute their unique talents and skills toward collective progress and success.

A Call to Action: The Future of Money Is Decentralized

As we stand firmly at the critical crossroads of history and the vast future, the invaluable lessons derived from the process of denationalization provide an urgent clarion call for transformative change that simply cannot be ignored any longer. The logical, analytical, and highly persuasive arguments laid out by the early pioneering experiments in decentralized monetary systems serve to demand that we seriously rethink our current financial paradigms and structures. These compelling insights challenge us to abandon not only the outdated models of centralized control that have failed us over the years, but also to actively embrace a far more innovative and inclusive system where money is managed, both collectively and collaboratively, by the populace at large, rather than by a single imposing authority that claims sole oversight. This significant evolution towards decentralization encompasses a profound shift in how we perceive the concepts of value, ownership, and trust within our economic frameworks, reshaping our interactions and ultimately influencing the very foundations of our societies.

Digital currencies and decentralized finance can be viewed as the natural successors and evolution of these ancient experiments in economic systems and trade practices. They embody the culmination of centuries filled with intellectual debates, groundbreaking innovations, and practical experiments within the financial domain. The ongoing digital revolution in finance is not simply a radical departure from the past—it represents, in fact, the logical and inevitable result of a prolonged and intricate process of evolution regarding the methods we use to manage, value, and interact with money. Thus, these contemporary financial tools have the potential to significantly reshape our understanding of currency and the concept of value, building upon the solid foundations that were laid by our ancestors who first ventured into these economic realms. The future of finance seems poised to become even more complex and exciting as these innovations continue to unfold.

This passionate call to embrace the concept of decentralization serves as both a formidable challenge and an enticing invitation to all involved. It not only challenges the deeply entrenched interests of centralized power structures that have dominated our financial landscape for far too long but also encourages a profound shift in our collective mindset. It calls for a comprehensive reimagining of our financial systems, urging us to envision frameworks that are grounded in principles that are not only timeless but also revolutionary in their innovative approach. This compelling narrative invites every investor, every entrepreneur, and every policymaker to join a dynamic movement that is actively reshaping the world around us—an economic revolution that offers the promise of democratizing wealth, enhancing transparency in transactions, and ultimately fostering a society that is more inclusive and equitable for all individuals. Through this transformative journey, together we can begin to pave the way for a future that redefines prosperity and opportunity at all levels of society, ensuring that everyone has a rightful seat at the table in this exciting new economic order that we are working to create.

The Enduring Blueprint for Economic Freedom

In this fascinating and mind-blowing exploration of how denationalization laid the essential groundwork for the emergence of digital assets, we have traversed a truly shocking and eye-opening journey from the centralized, state-controlled systems of the past to the revolutionary, groundbreaking decentralized financial systems that we witness today. The complex and ongoing process of liberating money from the clutches of stringent governmental control was not merely an economic necessity; it was, in fact, an intellectual awakening and ethical revolution that transformed our understanding of value. This transformative shift has challenged long-held beliefs about the very nature of wealth, power, and value itself, creating an atmosphere ripe for innovation and progress. It has provided a compelling and logical framework for understanding how money should function in a truly free and liberated society that respects individual autonomy, emphasizing the importance of personal freedom and self-determination. As we navigate through these uncharted waters, it becomes clear that this evolution is not simply a technological advancement, but rather a profound change in the way we perceive finance and its role in our lives.

The lessons of denationalization are as profoundly relevant and significantly impactful now as they were countless centuries ago. They serve as powerful reminders that when money is liberated from the shackles of centralized manipulation and control, it transforms into a dynamic and vibrant force that catalyzes innovation, fosters greater transparency, and enhances social empowerment within diverse communities. The emergence of digital currencies, alongside the revolutionary advancements brought by blockchain technology, can be viewed as a direct descendant of those early and groundbreaking economic experiments—a natural and inevitable evolution that is driven by the same enduring human desire for ultimate economic freedom, increased efficiency, and the relentless pursuit of autonomy in financial transactions and interactions. As we stand at the threshold of a new financial era, these lessons gained through history must guide our understanding and approach toward the ongoing transformation of the economic landscape.

Modern society confronts a compelling and urgent imperative: the necessity to create a sustainable financial future that not only respects the foundational principles of the past but also embraces the vast possibilities offered by our rapidly developing digital age. The ongoing decentralized financial revolution presents a transformative path toward cultivating a fairer and more resilient economic system. In this new paradigm, trust is shared among a broad spectrum of diverse communities, transparency is not only crucial but foundational, and the benefits of wealth are thoughtfully distributed among all participants. This significant shift actively encourages inclusivity and the meaningful participation of various groups, enriching economic interactions and simultaneously empowering individuals to take control of their own financial destinies. By fostering innovative ideas and initiatives across different sectors, we can effectively enhance collective well-being and prosperity for current and future generations, paving the way for a more equitable and thriving society.

This enduring and transformative blueprint for economic freedom presents a radical vision that boldly challenges the existing status quo in profound ways. It offers a logical, ethical, and incredibly persuasive alternative to the centralized control of money that is prevalent in our society today. This is not merely a theoretical idea; it is a powerful and urgent call to action for all those who truly value freedom, innovation, and the pursuit of social justice. Embrace the essential lessons derived from the concept of denationalization and allow them to guide you toward a future in which money transcends basic exchange functions, transforming into a dynamic force for meaningful change that empowers individuals and communities to flourish and thrive comprehensively.

The future of money is undoubtedly decentralized and this realization marks a significant turning point in our collective financial trajectory. The remarkable journey we have embarked upon, transitioning from traditional, state-controlled currency to innovative digital assets truly serves as the ultimate testament to the incredible power of human ingenuity and creativity. This transformative journey continues to unfold before our very eyes—a technological revolution that is not only as logical as it is revolutionary, but also as ethical as it is efficient in addressing the diverse needs of society. By thoughtfully integrating the invaluable lessons learned from our rich history with the groundbreaking and awe-inspiring innovations we are witnessing in the present moment, we now find ourselves at the threshold of an unprecedented opportunity. This opportunity enables us to build a financial system that genuinely serves the common good while promoting prosperity for all individuals involved, fostering an environment where everyone can thrive and succeed in their financial endeavors. As we navigate through this new landscape, it is essential to remain focused on creating inclusive solutions that empower individuals and communities alike, ensuring that no one is left behind in this exciting evolution of our monetary system.

In conclusion, the denationalization of money represents a powerful and ongoing force that profoundly shapes and influences the landscape of global finance. The innovative ideas that challenged centralized monetary control centuries ago have now found a place at the core of the digital financial revolution, which is steadily redefining our interaction with currency in unprecedented ways. These revolutionary concepts not only offer a logical and comprehensive framework for understanding this significant shift but also establish the ethical foundations necessary for ushering in a new era of economic interaction. This emerging era effectively frees money from the traditional constraints imposed by state control, enabling a diverse array of organizations within the global community to manage and utilize their financial resources in more innovative and flexible manners. This expansive vision clearly outlines a future where economic freedom, creativity, and innovation become attainable goals for everyone involved. Recognizing and wholeheartedly embracing this financial revolution is crucial; it paves the way towards a world where wealth is fairly and widely distributed, creating enhanced opportunities for growth and prosperity. Such a significant transformation allows every individual the chance to thrive and make a positive impact on the global economy, cultivating a healthier financial ecosystem that benefits all.

Chapter 3: The History of Cryptocurrencies

Section 1: Bitcoin's Mysterious Genesis and Its Digital Gold Promise

In a world where technology and finance continuously collide in complex and unpredictable ways, few stories are as shocking and mind-blowing as the extraordinary birth of Bitcoin—a groundbreaking digital currency that emerged seemingly out of nowhere, forever altering our understanding of money and the concept of value itself. This section traces the enigmatic beginnings of Bitcoin, unraveling its journey and its rise as a revolutionary store of value, often referred to as a modern "digital gold" that has captivated and inspired the imagination of investors, technologists, and policymakers alike across the globe. In what follows, we delve deeply into the logical and analytical foundations of Bitcoin, examining the compelling arguments that propelled its meteoric rise to prominence, and the philosophical debates that continue to fuel its promise and potential future impact on the global economy. As we explore these themes, we will also consider the broader implications of Bitcoin's existence—is it merely a speculative asset, or could it genuinely reshape the way we think about and use currency in a rapidly changing world?

The Enigma of Satoshi Nakamoto: The Birth of Bitcoin

In 2008, an individual or perhaps a group, cloaked in anonymity and operating under the pseudonym Satoshi Nakamoto, made a groundbreaking contribution to the financial landscape by publishing a whitepaper titled "Bitcoin: A Peer-to-Peer Electronic Cash System." This influential document, simple in its presentation yet profoundly impactful in its implications, laid out a comprehensive blueprint for a revolutionary decentralized digital currency. Such a currency would empower individuals to engage in transactions directly with one another, completely bypassing the need for intermediaries such as banks, financial institutions, or governments. The whitepaper was crafted with an exceptional clarity and logical precision, which made its arguments both persuasive and, indeed, revolutionary in nature. The mere existence of this document posed a significant and direct challenge to the traditional financial systems that are controlled by the state, systems that have dominated and regulated economic activities for centuries, establishing a framework that would ultimately change the way we think about money and transactions forever.

Satoshi's groundbreaking proposal was shocking and revolutionary because it boldly claimed that a decentralized network of numerous interconnected computers, utilizing robust cryptographic principles, could securely manage and govern a currency without the need for any central authority. The brilliance of Bitcoin lay in its elegant and innovative solution to the persistent "double spending" problem—a fundamental and significant challenge in digital transactions that had puzzled experts. By introducing a novel concept called the blockchain, Satoshi created a transformative system where every single transaction was meticulously recorded in a public ledger that was nearly impossible to alter or tamper with. This remarkable invention not only ensured the integrity and security of the currency but also established a new and unprecedented paradigm for trust in the digital age, fundamentally changing how individuals and institutions interact with money and each other.

Imagine a fascinating world where your bank account isn't held by a single, centralized institution but is instead part of a vast, decentralized network, maintained by thousands of interconnected computers spread out across the globe. This revolutionary idea is the mind-blowing reality of Bitcoin. In this innovative system, every participant in the network plays a crucial role in verifying transactions, ensuring that trust is distributed among all users, creating a unique atmosphere where security is woven into the very code itself. This development is not merely a technological innovation; it represents a profound and complete rethinking of how we conceive of money and value in today's society. The implications of such a shift extend far beyond mere currency, inviting us to consider new possibilities for financial interaction and economic relationships.

The Digital Gold Concept: More Than Just a Currency

Bitcoin's remarkable ascent from a niche and experimental digital creation to a widely acknowledged asset class is frequently summarized by its nickname, "digital gold." However, what exactly does it signify for a digital currency like Bitcoin to be likened to gold—a physical, enduring store of value that has been sought after and cherished by humanity for thousands of years? This intriguing comparison raises questions about the inherent qualities that both possess and the implications for the future of currency and value storage in our increasingly digital world.

Gold has long stood as the ultimate symbol of immense wealth and a reliable hedge against the ever-looming threat of inflation. Its remarkable scarcity, impressive durability, and broad universal acceptance have contributed significantly to its status as a trusted store of value throughout the ages. Bitcoin, despite being a purely digital innovation, was thoughtfully designed with attributes that are quite similar to those of gold. Its supply is strictly capped at 21 million coins, establishing an inherent scarcity that closely mimics gold's finite nature. This carefully controlled finite supply is a crucial factor in why many individuals see Bitcoin not just as a speculative asset, but as a genuine safeguard against inflation and potential economic instability. In an increasingly volatile era when various governments possess the ability to print money at will, Bitcoin presents a compelling counterpoint—a self-regulating asset that strives to resist devaluation through its meticulously programmed scarcity and decentralized characteristics.

The comparison to gold is not only logical but also deeply persuasive on many levels. Throughout history, gold has consistently maintained its value over thousands of years, persisting through wars, economic collapses, and significant shifts in political power across countries and continents. Similarly, Bitcoin, with its unique decentralized and immutable blockchain technology, is poised to offer an equivalent level of reliability in a modern digital format. It represents the logical evolution of the age-old quest for a stable store of value amidst the rapidly changing dynamics of the world we live in today. In times when traditional currencies falter and face instability, Bitcoin's bold promise as digital gold truly shines through—a safe haven in a landscape that is becoming increasingly uncertain and unpredictable from a financial perspective.

The Philosophical Underpinnings: A New Era of Trust and Autonomy

The creation of Bitcoin was not merely a significant technical achievement; it represented a profound philosophical revolution that would go on to influence many aspects of modern society. At its core, Bitcoin embodies and champions the belief that money should function as a powerful tool for individual freedom, rather than serve as a mechanism for control imposed by centralized institutions. By effectively eliminating the need for centralized authorities like governments and banking systems, Bitcoin successfully returns the power of money directly into the hands of the people. This fundamental shift is not just innovative; it is radically transformative—it challenges and dismantles the very long-held notion that governments or large banks should have the ultimate authority in determining what money is worth, how it is created, and how it can be utilized by individuals.

The underlying philosophy is deeply rooted in a strong skepticism towards the idea of centralized power and control over financial systems. History has demonstrated time and again that when a single entity, whether it be a government or a financial institution, has complete control over the money supply, the consequences often include widespread corruption, rampant inflation, and various forms of abuse of power that negatively impact society as a whole. Bitcoin's decentralized nature presents a revolutionary alternative—a system designed in such a way that no single person, company, or government can dictate the rules or alter the system for selfish purposes. Trust in Bitcoin is not based on the credibility or reputation of any central authority; instead, it relies on the collective consensus derived from a vast global network of participants. Every transaction made within this network is meticulously verified and recorded on a public ledger that is accessible to everyone, ensuring that the system remains completely transparent and resilient against tampering or manipulation. This innovative approach to currency and financial transactions fundamentally shifts the paradigm of trust from centralized institutions to a more democratic, user-driven system.

This philosophical shift, while both startling and liberating in its essence, challenges existing paradigms and encourages a rethinking of traditional approaches to finance. It posits that genuine financial freedom is attainable solely when money itself is democratized, enabling every individual to have the inherent power to participate fully in and control their own financial destiny. The implications of this revolutionary idea are nothing short of profound: a decentralized monetary system lays the groundwork for a more inclusive, equitable, and resilient economy—one that can adeptly adapt to the diverse needs and aspirations of a global community comprising individuals from various backgrounds and circumstances.

The Revolutionary Technology: Blockchain's Role in Reshaping Money

At the very heart of Bitcoin's astonishing rise and its recognition as digital gold lies the revolutionary and transformative technology known as the blockchain. This groundbreaking innovation serves as the essential foundation upon which Bitcoin firmly stands, and its profound impact on the financial world is nothing short of mind-blowing and revolutionary. The blockchain, in its essence, functions as a decentralized and distributed ledger that meticulously records every single Bitcoin transaction in a carefully structured series of interconnected blocks. Once a block is added to the ever-growing chain, it becomes virtually impossible to alter or tamper with the information contained within, thereby creating a secure, transparent, and highly reliable system that operates free from any central control or authority.

Blockchain technology effectively addresses one of the most essential challenges in the realm of digital finance: the establishment of trust without relying on a trusted intermediary. In the conventional financial system, entities such as banks and governments typically serve as trusted third parties responsible for verifying and processing monetary transactions. However, the blockchain achieves this critical verification and validation process through advanced cryptographic algorithms and a decentralized network of independent nodes, effectively eliminating the dependence on central authorities. This innovative approach serves as a shockingly efficient model that not only significantly enhances the overall security of transactions but also substantially reduces the costs associated with executing financial operations, ultimately leading to a more streamlined and equitable financial ecosystem for all participants involved.

The technical elegance of blockchain technology lies in its inherent simplicity and intuitive design. It operates using a consensus mechanism—most notably, the proof-of-work model—to guarantee that all participants in the network reach an agreement on the current state of the ledger. This democratic process of verification is not only logical but also exceedingly robust, effectively leveraging the collective computing power of the network to secure transactions against any unauthorized alterations. The end result is a system that is remarkably resistant to fraud and manipulation, creating a digital fortress for financial data that protects it from potential threats, ensuring integrity and trustworthiness within the digital realm. This fortification of information fosters confidence among users and stakeholders alike, solidifying blockchain's esteemed position in the evolution of technology.

Blockchain's role in the remarkable rise of Bitcoin cannot be overstated in any sense. It serves as the essential backbone that supports the entire ecosystem, providing all the critical infrastructure necessary for the functioning and expansion of decentralized finance. As technology continues to evolve at a rapid pace, blockchain is inspiring groundbreaking new applications that extend far beyond just cryptocurrencies—from enhancing supply chain management to enabling secure and transparent voting systems. Its profound impact on our understanding and management of money is truly significant, signaling a fundamental shift away from traditional, centralized systems toward a future where value is increasingly managed by sophisticated algorithms and collective consensus among users and stakeholders alike.

The Argumentative Edge: Debating the Value of Digital Assets

One of the most contentious and provocative debates taking place in modern finance revolves around the perceived value and legitimacy of digital assets, particularly Bitcoin. Critics, in their arguments, often dismiss Bitcoin as merely a speculative bubble—a sort of fleeting experiment that carries no real intrinsic value whatsoever. However, this perspective significantly fails to take into account the logical frameworks and economic foundations that thoroughly underpin Bitcoin's complex design and functionality. The narrative surrounding Bitcoin is not solely about prices or investments; it also encompasses elements such as technology, decentralization, and the innovation of monetary systems.

At its core, Bitcoin's compelling value proposition is constructed on principles of scarcity, security, and decentralization that are interwoven within its very fabric. Its finite supply of precisely 21 million coins creates an inherent rarity that drives demand among investors and users alike, much like gold has effectively done throughout human history for millennia. Additionally, the decentralized nature of Bitcoin guarantees that it is fundamentally not subject to the arbitrary inflationary policies that central banks routinely adopt and implement. In a world where various governments possess the power to print money without any real restraint or limitation, Bitcoin's programmed scarcity serves as a logical and robust long-term hedge against potential devaluation, making it an attractive alternative for those seeking financial stability.

Furthermore, Bitcoin's security, which is guaranteed by its exceptionally robust blockchain technology, provides a level of trust that is quite difficult to replicate in traditional financial systems. Every single transaction is permanently recorded on this distributed ledger, creating a transparent and immutable history of value exchange that all participants can verify. This transparency is an absolutely critical factor in establishing trust in the digital age—a trust that is not dependent on the credibility of any single institution or organization but is instead broadly distributed across a global network of users. In this way, Bitcoin empowers individuals and fosters a sense of collective assurance that is revolutionary in the finance sector.

The argumentative case for Bitcoin as a revolutionary store of value is not only compelling but also profoundly logical when examined closely. It challenges and redefines traditional notions of what constitutes intrinsic value by demonstrating effectively that, especially in an increasingly digital world, trust and security are of paramount importance. The very features that contribute to Bitcoin's volatility in the short term—its inherent decentralization and its dependence on market forces—are simultaneously the critical factors that position it as a powerful hedge against long-term economic instability. During times when traditional currencies face significant risks associated with inflation and mismanagement, Bitcoin stands tall as a beacon of stability, emerging as a digital asset whose value is meticulously preserved by its innovative design and underlying technology.

The Economic Logic: How Bitcoin Reshapes Value

The economic logic behind Bitcoin's remarkable rise as digital gold is fundamentally rooted in its unique ability to redefine the very concept of value in modern finance. Traditional money has long been viewed as a proxy for tangible assets, such as gold, silver, or government-issued fiat currency, which are widely accepted forms of value. However, Bitcoin boldly challenges this established paradigm by effectively establishing value through a decentralized network of trust and consensus among its users. Unlike traditional currencies, its value is not solely derived from a physical material composition or the backing of a central authority, but rather from the profound trust that users collectively place in its underlying technology, as well as the inherent scarcity that is meticulously built into its design. This scarcity, akin to precious metals, elevates Bitcoin's status, suggesting that it can serve as a store of value in an increasingly digital world.

This shift carries significant implications for our understanding of wealth and the mechanisms of exchange. When value is established by the shared trust of a network, instead of being dictated by a central authority, it fosters a more democratic and resilient economic system that is less vulnerable to the pitfalls of centralized control. The emergence of Bitcoin has powerfully illustrated the idea that value is not an intrinsic quality of any physical object, but rather a social construct that has the potential to evolve alongside advancements in technology and the collective beliefs of society. This is a truly mind-blowing concept, as it fundamentally challenges the very foundations of conventional economic theory and invites us to rethink how we perceive and define value in our ever-changing world.

The economic logic of Bitcoin also extends notably to its function as a hedge against significant economic uncertainty. In times of crisis, especially when trust in centralized financial institutions falters dramatically, Bitcoin emerges as a viable alternative—a decentralized store of value that is uniquely insulated from government intervention and regulation. This enduring quality has earned it the popular nickname "digital gold," as it serves a truly similar function to gold in safeguarding wealth during turbulent times and economic upheaval. The analytical reasoning behind this phenomenon is clear and compelling: in an increasingly unpredictable and volatile global economy, the decentralized, immutable, and transparent nature of Bitcoin provides a logical and robust foundation for preserving, as well as potentially growing, wealth. Individuals are increasingly recognizing this, turning to Bitcoin not just as an investment, but as a secure refuge for their financial assets in a world fraught with uncertainty.

Persuasive Implications: A New Model for Financial Freedom

For contemporary investors and policymakers, the intriguing story of Bitcoin's enigmatic origin and its remarkable ascent as a digital store of value serves as both a cautionary tale and a source of motivation. This narrative is a stark reminder highlighting the vulnerabilities that are deeply rooted in centralized monetary systems and serves as a compelling argument advocating for the adoption of decentralized alternatives. The evolution of Bitcoin challenges traditional financial norms and encourages a rethinking of the established monetary frameworks we often take for granted.

Bitcoin's creation significantly challenged the long-held assumption that only governments and traditional banks could effectively manage the money supply in our economy. By harnessing the power of cryptography along with the capabilities of distributed computing, Bitcoin provided a logical and innovative solution to the age-old problem of trust in financial transactions that has plagued humanity for centuries. This remarkable breakthrough has had profound, mind-blowing implications for the future of money and financial systems all over the globe—it has opened the door to a fascinating new world where individuals can have unprecedented control over their financial destinies and empower themselves like never before.

The persuasive force of Bitcoin lies significantly in its remarkable ability to empower individuals and people from various backgrounds. It serves as a vital tool that actively democratizes access to wealth and financial resources, breaking down and dismantling the numerous barriers that have long been imposed by traditional financial institutions. In this decentralized system, every participant has an equal opportunity to not only contribute to but also benefit from the global economy in its entirety. This truly revolutionary vision resonates deeply with the fundamental ideals of economic freedom and individual empowerment that many aspire to achieve. By leveraging Bitcoin, individuals can reclaim control of their financial destiny, transforming the way wealth is created and distributed in society.

Furthermore, Bitcoin's inherently transparent and decentralized nature serves as an exemplary model for building significantly more resilient and robust financial systems. In a modern era where corruption, inefficiency, and malfeasance plague traditional centralized institutions, the logical alternative is to effectively distribute power among a network of trusted participants who are committed to integrity. This approach is not merely a theoretical ideal; rather, it is a practical, achievable goal that has already begun to reshape and innovate the world of finance in profound ways. The rise of decentralized finance (DeFi) stands as a testament to this transformative potential, offering a range of innovative ways to manage money that are not only efficient but also equitable and fair. This shift towards decentralization represents a significant departure from conventional methodologies, leading to improved accessibility and the democratization of financial services.

Real-World Impact: Case Studies and Lessons Learned

To truly grasp the revolutionary nature of Bitcoin, it is essential to take a closer look at real-world examples that illustrate how its fundamental principles have been applied and how they continue to significantly influence modern finance today. One particularly striking example that underscores this is the 2008 global financial crisis, which sharply exposed the inherent flaws and vulnerabilities present in centralized monetary systems around the world. In the wake of the crisis, trust in traditional banks and government-issued currency plummeted to unprecedented lows, and the urgent need for a viable alternative became painfully clear to many. Bitcoin emerged in this tumultuous environment as a beacon of hope—a decentralized currency that was designed to be immune to the corruptions of centralized power and control, offering a new paradigm for financial transactions. This innovative approach to currency has sparked a global conversation about what the future of money could look like, bridging the gap between technology and finance in unprecedented ways.

The crisis provided a significant and compelling real-world validation of the numerous arguments made by early critics of state-controlled money and monetary systems. It clearly demonstrated that when a financial system is being controlled and managed by a single, centralized authority, the risk of catastrophic failure is always present, lurking just beneath the surface. In stark contrast to this, a decentralized financial system like Bitcoin, which operates with its transparent ledger and fosters distributed trust among users, offers a much more stable and resilient alternative to traditional models. This vital lesson is not merely academic in nature; it has profound and practical implications for how we approach and design financial systems that are robust and capable of withstanding economic shocks and unforeseen challenges that may arise in the future.

Another compelling case illustrating the power of digital currency is the rapid rise of Bitcoin in emerging markets, where traditional banking systems are often unreliable or completely inaccessible. In various countries that are plagued by hyperinflation and severe political instability, Bitcoin has emerged as a crucial lifeline—a digital store of value that is not subject to the unreasonable whims of corrupt governments. The economic logic behind this phenomenon is quite straightforward: when the value of a nation's currency is eroding rapidly and consistently, people instinctively turn to alternatives that offer them stability and protection from financial ruin. Bitcoin's inherently decentralized nature and its fixed supply make it an especially attractive option for individuals seeking security, effectively becoming a modern digital gold that preserves wealth even amidst the harshest economic climates. In such situations, the importance of having a reliable and inflation-resistant asset cannot be overstated.

These compelling real-world examples serve as robust, persuasive evidence that the underlying logic of Bitcoin's innovative design is fundamentally sound. They vividly illustrate that the decentralized and transparent nature of digital currencies is not merely a theoretical advancement over conventional state-controlled money—it presents itself as a practical and effective solution to some of the most urgent and pressing economic challenges we face in our contemporary society.

Analytical Reflections: The Logical Framework of Bitcoin

The rise of Bitcoin can be thoroughly understood through a rigorous and comprehensive analytical framework that draws extensively on foundational principles of economics, advanced technology, and the intricacies of human behavior. At its core, Bitcoin is fundamentally based on the essential idea that value is derived from trust. In the case of traditional currencies, they primarily depend on the trust placed in governments and central banks—a trust that can be significantly eroded by various factors such as corruption, mismanagement, and political instability. Bitcoin, by contrast and in stark contrast, derives its value from the profound trust that users have in its decentralized network, its foundational protocols, and the robust underlying technology that supports it. This distinction highlights how Bitcoin stands apart from conventional financial systems, operating independently of centralized authorities and providing an alternative method for securing value through collective consensus.

This trust is not a fragile, intangible concept; it is constructed on a foundation of robust cryptographic algorithms and an advanced network consensus mechanism that ensures that every transaction is meticulously verified and recorded in an immutable manner. The logical architecture of Bitcoin is both elegant and undeniably compelling. Its finite supply—capped firmly at 21 million coins—creates a meaningful scarcity that is fundamental to its value proposition, much like gold has been throughout history. This inherent scarcity, combined with the unparalleled security and transparency of the blockchain technology, forms the solid and reliable foundation of Bitcoin's promise as a revolutionary store of value for individuals and institutions alike in the evolving financial landscape.

Analyzing Bitcoin from this thoughtful perspective reveals a clear and rational argument for its significant long-term potential in the financial landscape. It is a unique system that is intrinsically designed to preserve wealth, completely free from the inflationary pressures and political manipulations that have historically undermined traditional currencies over time. The analytical case for Bitcoin is further strengthened and backed by the historical record, which consistently shows that centralized monetary systems have repeatedly failed to effectively protect the real value of money for individuals and communities. In this light, Bitcoin's decentralized model is not merely an innovative experiment; it represents a logical, inevitable evolution in the way we approach and manage value in our society and economy.

Persuading the Skeptics: The Unstoppable Momentum of Digital Gold

Despite the compelling logic and persuasive evidence backing Bitcoin, its remarkable rise has not come without a significant number of critics. Skeptics have pointed to its extreme volatility, ongoing regulatory uncertainties, and clearly speculative nature as compelling reasons to question its long-term viability in the financial landscape. However, these criticisms often overlook the much larger picture surrounding the cryptocurrency. The inherent volatility of a nascent technology like Bitcoin is a natural part of its evolution and growth process. Throughout history, early adopters of groundbreaking innovations have invariably faced periods of uncertainty and doubt before their ideas and technologies became widely accepted and adopted as mainstream solutions. Such patterns of skepticism are common when innovations disrupt traditional systems.

The concept of "digital gold" stands out as a powerful and persuasive counterpoint to many criticisms often directed at cryptocurrencies. Gold has long been regarded as a trusted store of value for thousands of years, a status achieved precisely because of its inherent scarcity, remarkable durability, and recognized intrinsic worth. In a similar vein, Bitcoin adeptly replicates these valuable qualities in a digital format, thereby offering a modern solution to age-old problems that have perplexed investors and societies alike for centuries. Its value is not derived solely from mere speculation in the markets; rather, it is fundamentally built upon a logical framework of trust, security, and scarcity. These principles are as sound and enduring as those underpinning any asset that has successfully withstood the rigors of time and market fluctuations, further solidifying its position in the financial landscape.

The momentum behind Bitcoin is undeniably powerful and cannot be dismissed. From its mysterious and somewhat enigmatic genesis in a cryptographic whitepaper, which laid the foundation for its existence, to its explosive and dramatic rise as a globally recognized asset, Bitcoin has successfully captured the imagination and interest of millions around the world. Its remarkable success serves as a clear testament to the power of decentralized technology and the enduring human desire for economic freedom and independence. For those who are skeptics, the challenge is to truly recognize that the evolution of money is a continuously ongoing process—one that demands us to rethink and reassess long-standing paradigms while embracing innovative and new solutions that emerge in this fast-paced financial landscape.

Integrating the Past and the Future: A Blueprint for Economic Transformation

The rise of Bitcoin is not merely an isolated phenomenon; it represents the culmination of centuries of intellectual debate, technological innovation, and profound philosophical inquiry into the very essence and nature of money itself. The myriad alternative theories and early pioneering experiments in decentralized monetary systems have laid a solid groundwork for what Bitcoin embodies today—a truly revolutionary store of value that boldly challenges the very foundations of traditional finance and its conventional practices. As we observe its evolution, we can certainly appreciate the rich tapestry of ideas and innovations that have contributed to bringing us this digital currency, altering the financial landscape in unprecedented ways.

By thoughtfully integrating valuable lessons gleaned from the past with the most advanced cutting-edge digital technology available today, Bitcoin presents a groundbreaking blueprint for the transformation of our economy. It serves as a logical and persuasive alternative to traditional state-controlled money systems, one that is firmly grounded in key principles of transparency, trust, and decentralization. This unique synthesis of ancient wisdom alongside modern innovation is not merely a radical departure from conventional financial systems; rather, it is a natural and inevitable evolution in the way we manage and perceive value in our increasingly interconnected world. As we continue to explore this transformative path, the impact of Bitcoin may redefine our economic relationships in profound ways.

The implications for modern economies are indeed profound and far-reaching. Digital currencies such as Bitcoin have the exciting potential to democratize access to wealth and financial services, empower individuals in innovative ways, and create more resilient, adaptable financial systems that can withstand various challenges. They represent a direct challenge to the monopolistic power traditionally held by governments and central banks, offering instead a decentralized model where economic freedom and individual autonomy are of the utmost importance. This vision is not only both shocking and inspiring, but it also signifies a mind-blowing shift in how we currently conceive of and interact with money and value in our everyday lives. The possibilities presented by these digital assets could reshape the very fabric of our economic interactions, leading to a future where financial inclusivity is a tangible reality for many.

Persuasive Reflections: Why Bitcoin Matters

For today's investor, policymaker, and everyday citizen, Bitcoin has transformed into much more than just a speculative asset—it has evolved into a powerful symbol of a new economic order emerging in our society. It represents the possibility of a world where money is liberated from the control of a single authority, allowing it to be shaped instead by the power of collective trust and innovative technology. The logical and analytical arguments supporting Bitcoin's inherently decentralized nature are persuasive on numerous levels. They skillfully combine historical lessons with modern technological advancements, presenting a compelling and robust case for why digital currencies are paving the way to the future of money and financial systems as we know them today. This potential transformation beckons both caution and excitement, urging us to reevaluate our understanding of money and its role in our lives.

The argument presented is both simple and profoundly impactful: centralized monetary systems are, by their very nature, inherently flawed due to the concentration of power they entail, which makes them vulnerable to various abuses and manipulations. In stark contrast, decentralized systems, which distribute power across many nodes, promote greater transparency and accountability, as well as fostering more significant innovation within the financial space. Bitcoin stands as the embodiment of this critical logic—a revolutionary digital asset that not only challenges traditional economic paradigms but also offers a much more resilient, inclusive, and efficient alternative for storing and exchanging value in a rapidly evolving digital landscape.

Its finite supply, coupled with a secure blockchain structure and a decentralized approach to governance, creates a self-regulating system that is exceptionally resistant to various forms of manipulation. These unique qualities allow Bitcoin to emerge not merely as a revolutionary store of value but also as a powerful and transformative tool for economic empowerment in various communities. In a world where governments have the ability to devalue currency through excessive printing practices, Bitcoin stands out as a beacon of financial stability and integrity—a modern form of digital gold that not only preserves wealth but also upholds the vital principles of economic freedom and autonomy that many individuals seek.

The Road Ahead: A Future Defined by Decentralized Finance

Looking to the future, the remarkable rise of Bitcoin signals a profound and fundamental shift in the global financial landscape that cannot be ignored. The revolutionary principles of denationalization and decentralization that have driven its substantial growth are likely to reshape the world of finance in transformative ways that we are only beginning to understand. As more people, institutions, and organizations recognize the immense value of a decentralized monetary system, we are witnessing the exciting birth of a new era—an era in which the power of money is truly democratized and economic freedom becomes a tangible reality for everyone everywhere. This transition holds the potential to redefine how we think about wealth, value, and the very nature of our financial interactions in everyday life.

This transformation will undoubtedly encounter a variety of challenges along the way. The journey toward achieving a fully decentralized financial system is fraught with numerous forms of volatility, complex regulatory hurdles, and the inevitable growing pains that accompany any revolutionary technology. Nevertheless, the logical and persuasive case for Bitcoin remains robust enough to surmount these significant obstacles. The very same human ingenuity that led us from the primitive systems of barter to the establishment of coinage is now propelling us forward into a future where digital currencies and the concept of decentralized finance will come to dominate the vast economic landscape. As we move forward, we must navigate these complexities with both caution and foresight, embracing the innovations that can reshape our financial interactions.

Policymakers, too, must adapt significantly to this emerging new reality. The rise of Bitcoin poses a serious challenge to the traditional roles played by central banks and governmental institutions, compelling them to critically rethink and reevaluate their approaches to monetary policy in light of this change. The future of finance may well be defined by hybrid systems that integrate the best of both worlds—combining the established stability and reliability of traditional monetary practices with the groundbreaking innovation and transparency offered by decentralized technologies. This evolution is not only logical but essential and inevitable for the progression of our financial systems.

Persuading the Skeptics: The Case for Embracing Bitcoin

Critics of Bitcoin frequently highlight its pronounced volatility, its connections to illicit activities, and its comparatively brief history as key reasons to reject it as a credible store of value. Nonetheless, these criticisms overlook the deep, fundamental principles woven into the fabric of Bitcoin's design. While volatility does indeed present significant challenges, it is, in fact, a hallmark of any disruptive innovation, especially during its nascent phases. Just as the historical shift from barter systems to coinage necessitated periods filled with uncertainty and required adjustments, the ongoing evolution of digital currencies like Bitcoin faces similar challenges as it seeks to establish itself within the financial landscape.

In addition, the inherently decentralized nature of Bitcoin directly addresses numerous ethical and economic challenges that have historically plagued centralized financial systems. By eliminating the necessity for a central authority, Bitcoin significantly mitigates the various risks associated with corruption, inflation, and arbitrary control over the money supply. This shift towards a decentralized model is a compelling argument for the pursuit of economic freedom—one that resonates profoundly with the contemporary ethos centered on transparency, independence, and accountability. The principles behind Bitcoin not only challenge existing power structures but also empower individuals, allowing them to take control of their own financial destinies without the inevitable influence of centralized institutions.

The finite supply of Bitcoin is undeniably another compelling and pivotal point to consider in the broader landscape of digital currency. In a world where central banks wield the considerable power to print money without any real restraint or limitation, the inherent scarcity of Bitcoin serves as a logical and effective safeguard against the relentless tide of inflation. Its innovative design ensures that, no matter how immense the hype or speculative fervor surrounding it becomes, there will ever only be precisely 21 million coins available for circulation. This intrinsic scarcity creates a natural and compelling value proposition, one that is not only comparable to the enduring worth of gold throughout ages, but also superior in terms of its technological sophistication and the accessibility it offers to users across the globe. Such a feature of Bitcoin reinforces its role as a potential hedge against economic uncertainties, making it an attractive option for investors and everyday users alike in today's volatile financial markets.

Integrating Historical Lessons: From Ancient Currency to Digital Revolution

The emergence of Bitcoin is not merely an isolated event; rather, it is the culmination of centuries of gradual evolution in how we conceive, perceive, and manage money itself. From the earliest days of barter systems, through the rise and expansion of commodity money, and eventually progressing to state-controlled coinage, humanity has continually sought out and pursued better and more efficient ways to facilitate trade, transfer wealth, and securely store value over time. The numerous alternative theories and innovative experiments that have historically challenged centralized monetary authority over the years have provided both the intellectual foundation and practical groundwork for Bitcoin's revolutionary model, which offers a new paradigm in the realm of finance and transactions.

The journey from the earliest primitive trade systems to the intricate and complex digital networks that we rely on today is marked by a remarkable series of logical leaps and innovative breakthroughs. Each significant stage of monetary evolution was driven by a clear and compelling rationale: to effectively overcome the inherent limitations of the previous system and to create a medium of exchange that is not only reliable and efficient but also universally accepted across diverse economies. Bitcoin represents the latest, most radical leap in this ongoing transformation—a groundbreaking digital asset that fundamentally redefines the very nature of money itself and its role in contemporary society. Its introduction has catalyzed discussions around the future of currency.

This historical perspective is both shocking and profoundly enlightening. It reveals that the myriad challenges we face today—such as the ongoing instability of fiat currencies and the inherent vulnerabilities of centralized banking systems—are not unprecedented problems; rather, they are the natural outcomes of outdated and increasingly irrelevant systems. By drawing on the invaluable lessons of the past, we can clearly see that Bitcoin's decentralized model is not only logical in its structure, but also the inevitable and necessary next step in the ongoing evolution of money itself. The importance of adapting and evolving our financial systems cannot be overstated, as doing so will address the flaws that have plagued us for decades.

A Vision for the Future: Economic Freedom and Digital Sovereignty

The promise of Bitcoin, often referred to as digital gold, is a crucial element of a much broader vision aimed at a future defined by true economic freedom and enhanced digital sovereignty for individuals. In this envisioned decentralized financial system, money transcends its traditional role as just a tool for transactions; it evolves into a powerful means of empowering individuals and communities alike, enabling them to take control of their own destinies and make autonomous choices. This transformative vision is both radical and deeply persuasive—it boldly challenges the entrenched power and dominance of centralized institutions while simultaneously offering a tangible pathway toward a more inclusive, equitable, and resilient global economy where everyone has the potential to thrive.

Digital currencies enable a significant level of financial autonomy that was previously unimaginable during the era of state-controlled money. They allow individuals to easily transact, invest, and securely store value without being subject to the various constraints imposed by traditional banks and governments. This remarkable liberation of money from the grasp of centralized control is a logical response to the clear failures of past financial systems. It promises to unlock a future where economic power is genuinely placed into the hands of the people, empowering everyone to take charge of their financial destinies and fostering a sense of independence that was long thought to be unattainable.

The integration of blockchain technology into the global financial system exemplifies this transformative shift. With blockchain, every single transaction is accurately recorded on an immutable ledger that is accessible to all, ensuring complete transparency and accountability for all involved parties. This groundbreaking technology not only safeguards against corruption and fraud but also empowers users by giving them direct control over their financial interactions and decisions. In essence, blockchain represents the realization of the ancient ideal of a trustworthy, decentralized system—a system that effectively transcends the significant limitations imposed by physical money and centralized power structures, paving the way for a more equitable economy.

Embracing a Decentralized Future

In this mind-blowing and profound exploration of how denationalization along with alternative monetary theories have laid the essential groundwork for the transformative digital asset revolution, we have meticulously traced a logical, analytical, and persuasive narrative that stretches from the very origins of money all the way to the remarkable rise of Bitcoin. The evolution of money—from primitive barter systems and various forms of commodity money to modern state-controlled coinage—was not a straightforward linear process. Rather, it has been characterized by a series of groundbreaking and revolutionary experiments that continuously challenged the established status quo. Each of these innovative experiments was driven by a deep and fundamental human desire for greater economic freedom, transparency, and superior efficiency in transactions and exchanges.

Bitcoin's enigmatic beginnings and its rise as a form of digital gold represent the most recent developments in this ever-evolving narrative. The inception of Bitcoin was not merely a groundbreaking technological advancement; it served as a significant philosophical assertion—a bold declaration emphasizing that currency should be freed from the grips of centralized powers, and placed firmly in the hands of individuals. The architecture of Bitcoin, characterized by its limited supply, decentralized management, and strong security features, stands as a logical continuation of hundreds of years of trials and thoughtful discussions surrounding the true essence of value and what it represents in society.

The implications of Bitcoin's monumental rise are truly staggering and far-reaching. It offers an innovative solution to the multitude of inherent problems associated with state-controlled currencies, which often include rampant inflation, widespread corruption, and a significant erosion of trust among users. By addressing these critical issues, Bitcoin paves the way for a fundamentally new financial paradigm—one that is decentralized, transparent, and fundamentally aligned with the core principles of economic freedom that many value today. This emerging framework represents a persuasive and rational vision for the future of money, presenting an opportunity that challenges each of us to rethink our existing systems, question traditional norms, and embrace the transformative potential that digital assets hold for the global economy. It invites us to consider how these advancements could reshape our financial interactions and empower individuals in ways previously thought impossible.

The remarkable journey from centralized control to a decentralized, digital future stands as a testament to human ingenuity and the relentless pursuit of better solutions that define our progress. It is a fascinating story of how, over the span of millennia, societies have profoundly evolved their understanding of wealth—from the simplicity of bartering systems to the more sophisticated practices of state-issued coinage, and now moving towards the revolutionary landscape of cryptocurrencies. Each step along this significant evolution was driven by logical necessity and a visionary quest for economic liberty that resonates through the ages. This transformation has not only changed the way we perceive value but also fundamentally altered the dynamics of trade and commerce in our connected world.

For modern investors, policymakers, and citizens at large, the invaluable lessons of the past are not merely historical curiosities or fleeting anecdotes—they serve as essential blueprints for shaping a sustainable future. The same foundational principles that once guided the meticulous creation of coinage and currency now underpin the revolutionary decentralized systems that are steadily reshaping the landscape of global finance. By wholeheartedly embracing these time-tested lessons and thoughtfully applying them to the innovative technologies of today, we can build a financial system that is not only significantly more efficient and secure but also remarkably more just, equitable, and inclusive for all participants involved.

As we find ourselves standing at the precipice of a groundbreaking new era in the realm of finance, the argument for embracing a decentralized future becomes not only increasingly compelling but also undeniably inevitable. The meteoric rise of Bitcoin, along with the emergence of various other digital currencies, serves as a direct and powerful response to the numerous failures that have long plagued centralized monetary systems. This remarkable revolution is driven by a potent combination of logical reasoning, pressing ethical imperatives, and a universal human desire for genuine economic freedom and autonomy. It paints a vivid picture of a future in which trust is not solely vested in a singular authority, but rather distributed among a vast and interconnected global network of individuals. In this envisioned landscape, each person is uniquely empowered to take charge of their own financial destiny and make choices that align with their values and aspirations. This shift promises to redefine our understanding of economic interactions, fostering innovation, inclusivity, and resilience in the financial system for generations to come.

This serves as the blueprint for a radically transformed financial world—a world that is as shocking as it is fundamentally logical, as revolutionary as it is deeply rooted in ancient wisdom and enduring principles. The digital revolution in finance is not just on the horizon; it is firmly here with us now, bringing forth a host of new opportunities and possibilities to reimagine and redefine money in a manner that both honors our rich past while boldly and adventurously embracing a bright future. It challenges us to come together and create systems that are transparent, accountable, and thoughtfully designed with the collective good of all in mind. This vision is not only about innovation; it's about building inclusive frameworks that lift everyone and encourage shared responsibility, fostering a sense of community among participants.

In conclusion, the extraordinary journey from the early, centralized systems of money to the revolutionary landscape of decentralized digital currency is a powerful narrative of remarkable progress. It is indeed a story that intricately combines mind-blowing innovation with profound and timeless philosophical insights. This is a tale that clearly illustrates how the liberation of money from the grasp of state control has not only been possible but also fundamentally necessary for significant human advancement. Bitcoin, representing the latest and most advanced manifestation of these ideals, stands tall as a beacon of what the future can potentially hold—a future where economic freedom is not merely an ideal to aspire to, but a palpable, living, and breathing reality for everyone.

Embrace this transformative vision. Let the valuable lessons of history guide your understanding and perspective of the future that lies ahead. The logical, analytical, and persuasive case for a decentralized monetary system is as compelling and robust as it is revolutionary in nature. The rise of digital assets is not merely a fleeting trend; rather, it represents the natural evolution of money itself, a profound transformation that holds the potential to reshape our world fundamentally and empower each and every one of us in ways we have yet to comprehend.

Section 2: The Proliferation of Altcoins and Their Unique Innovations

In a digital revolution that has already upended centuries of traditional finance, Bitcoin emerged as the first beacon of decentralized currency—a groundbreaking innovation that wonderfully challenged the long-standing status quo of state-controlled money. Yet, as mind-blowing as Bitcoin's debut was, it was only the very beginning of a remarkable journey into the realm of digital finance. Almost immediately, a floodgate of creativity opened, and thousands of alternative cryptocurrencies, widely known as altcoins, began to emerge in this new financial landscape. These altcoins, each with their own unique features, innovations, and potential applications, sought to expand on Bitcoin's visionary foundation, addressing its limitations while exploring exciting new possibilities and pushing the boundaries of what digital money could achieve in our lives. This section offers a shocking, in-depth exploration and analysis of how the proliferation of diverse altcoins has profoundly redefined our understanding of money itself, using logical, analytical, and persuasive reasoning to demonstrate that the digital revolution in finance is as natural as it is utterly inevitable. As we delve into this transformative evolution, we will uncover the myriad ways in which these new currencies are reshaping economies, enhancing financial inclusivity, and fostering innovations that could reshape our monetary systems for generations to come.

The Spark of Innovation: From Bitcoin to a Sea of Alternatives

Bitcoin's creation in 2009 by the enigmatic figure known as Satoshi Nakamoto marked a pivotal moment that forever transformed the landscape of the financial world. This groundbreaking introduction of a decentralized currency demonstrated the unprecedented possibility of operating outside the realm of state control—an idea so extraordinary that it seemed almost implausible at the time of its inception. Despite its revolutionary nature, however, Bitcoin was not without its significant limitations. The design, while brilliant in its foundational principles, encountered several challenges that hindered its broader adoption. Among these were scalability issues that made it difficult to handle a growing number of transactions efficiently, energy-intensive mining processes that raised concerns about environmental impacts, and a transaction speed that was relatively slow when compared to modern technological expectations. These inherent limitations created a compelling opportunity for innovators and developers to take inspiration from Bitcoin's original blueprint. They sought to build upon its foundation and craft alternative cryptocurrencies that not only addressed its shortcomings but also introduced improvements and entirely new features that could cater to a wider array of needs within the evolving digital economy.

Within just a few short years, the altcoin ecosystem exploded with remarkable growth and development. Developers and visionary entrepreneurs from around the world came to recognize that Bitcoin was not merely a digital currency—it was a proof of concept that presented numerous opportunities; it was a versatile platform that could be expanded, improved upon, and creatively reimagined in a multitude of ways. Altcoins began to tackle various shortcomings that Bitcoin had, venturing into new territories while exploring innovative functions that went far beyond simply being a store of value. They introduced advanced smart contracts, accelerated transaction times, improved privacy features, and engaged new consensus mechanisms, each offering a distinct and unique twist on the fundamental idea of a decentralized digital asset. This dynamic landscape encouraged continuous experimentation and the development of diverse applications that would ultimately shape the future of digital finance.

Pioneering Technologies: How Altcoins Expanded Bitcoin's Vision

Altcoins are not merely copies or imitations of Bitcoin; they represent fascinating experiments in how money can be transformed and redefined by innovative technology. For instance, take Ethereum, a groundbreaking platform that revolutionized the concept of blockchain technology by introducing smart contracts—these are self-executing agreements that automatically enforce the specific terms of a contract without the necessity for any intermediaries, such as banks or other financial institutions. Ethereum's major innovation made it possible for decentralized applications (dApps) to thrive and flourish, thereby opening up an entirely new world of possibilities and functionalities, ranging from decentralized finance (DeFi) to non-fungible tokens (NFTs) and beyond. The remarkable ability to execute complex transactions and to build decentralized platforms on top of the blockchain marked a significant and profound departure from Bitcoin's original design, which was primarily focused on serving as a form of digital gold, a store of value. Thus, the emergence of numerous altcoins has introduced a dynamic landscape where technology continues to reshape our understanding and utilization of money in diverse and transformative ways.

Other altcoins pursued various unique improvements that distinguished them from Bitcoin. Litecoin, which is frequently referred to as the "silver" to Bitcoin's prestigious "gold," optimized transaction processing times and also significantly reduced fees. This made it much more practical and accessible for everyday transactions among regular users. In contrast, Dash and Zcash concentrated primarily on enhancing privacy features, implementing advanced cryptographic techniques to effectively obfuscate transaction details and ensure robust protection of user anonymity. This feature has proven to be particularly appealing to a segment of the community that remains wary of government surveillance or financial censorship, thereby increasing trust and usage among those who prioritize privacy in their financial dealings.

Each altcoin introduced its own unique blend of technological innovations, and when these innovations are taken together, they form a fascinating mosaic of possibilities and advancements. Some altcoins have boldly experimented with various consensus algorithms specifically designed to address the significant energy consumption issues associated with Bitcoin. For instance, the Proof-of-Stake (PoS) mechanisms, as showcased in coins like Cardano and Tezos, offer a considerably less energy-intensive alternative to Bitcoin's traditional Proof-of-Work (PoW) system, thereby making them far more sustainable options for the future of digital currency. This shift not only enhances their eco-friendliness but also encourages broader adoption among users who are increasingly conscious of environmental impacts.

These innovations should not be viewed as isolated features; rather, they represent a logical and necessary extension of Bitcoin's original revolutionary idea. By thoughtfully tweaking various elements of the protocol—such as transaction speed, privacy measures, governance structures, and energy efficiency—altcoins have managed to create an entire ecosystem that caters to a wide array of diverse needs and applications. The proliferation of these digital assets is, in many ways, a natural and expected evolution of our financial systems. Just as our societies historically transitioned from simple bartering practices to the formal creation of standardized coins to effectively meet the growing complexity of trade and commerce, the digital age has dictated the need for a more adaptable, flexible, and versatile form of money. Altcoins have actively answered that evolving call, each one bringing its unique perspectives, innovations, and solutions to the table, ultimately enriching the landscape of digital currencies.

The Marketplace of Ideas: A Diverse Ecosystem of Digital Assets

The altcoin market is an incredibly vibrant, chaotic, and at times, shocking marketplace filled with diverse ideas and opportunities. It is a unique world where innovation is not only encouraged but is absolutely necessary for survival and growth.

In this dynamic ecosystem, every new altcoin exists much like a start-up in the rapidly evolving tech industry, each one promising to solve different problems or unlock exciting new opportunities. The sheer number of altcoins—totaling in the thousands—is truly mind-blowing and awe-inspiring. Each project, regardless of its ultimate success or failure, represents a fascinating experiment in rethinking how we manage and exchange value in this increasingly digital world.

Some altcoins focus specifically on various financial applications within the cryptocurrency ecosystem. One of the most notable categories is stablecoins, which are expertly designed to minimize the notorious volatility often associated with cryptocurrencies. They achieve this by pegging their value to a stable asset such as the US dollar, gold, or other commodities. These innovative digital currencies aim to combine the best aspects of both worlds: the stability of traditional money, which has been relied upon for centuries, with the efficiency, speed, and transparency offered by blockchain technology. By doing so, they serve as a crucial bridge between the old financial systems and the new digital innovations, enabling smooth transitions and exchanges in an increasingly digital economy that requires a blend of reliability and modernity.

Other altcoins delve into entirely new and innovative realms that go beyond traditional currency. For instance, platforms such as Binance Coin (BNB) and Ripple (XRP) have been specifically designed to facilitate international trade and significantly improve the overall efficiency of cross-border transactions. Their unique innovations and advancements lie in the way they seamlessly integrate with existing financial networks, thereby reducing friction and lowering costs—offering a modern solution to the age-old problems associated with trade and commerce.

Moreover, there are increasingly numerous altcoins dedicated specifically to fostering decentralized governance within their ecosystems. These projects, such as MakerDAO, empower users by allowing them to actively participate in crucial decision-making processes that pertain to the development and ongoing operation of the platform. This democratization of control represents a radical departure from the traditional top-down models typically seen in state-controlled monetary systems. It reflects a broader and significant trend towards community-driven systems, where every participant genuinely has a voice in shaping the future direction of the currency and its functionalities. The rise of these governance-focused altcoins provides a persuasive argument for the decentralization of economic power—a theme that resonates deeply with the fundamental ideals of freedom, transparency, and inclusivity in financial systems. This shift not only empowers individuals but also promotes a more equitable distribution of power among users, creating a more robust and participatory economic landscape.

Analytical Insights: The Impact of Altcoins on Modern Finance

The rapid proliferation of altcoins has had an extraordinarily profound impact on the financial landscape, one that extends far beyond mere technological innovation. Altcoins have introduced an entirely new way of thinking about money—a perspective that places a high value on decentralization, inclusivity, and adaptability over the rigid, centralized structures that characterize traditional finance. They have boldly challenged the long-held notion that money must be issued, controlled, and regulated by a central authority, instead arguing that value can be derived from decentralized and market-driven processes. This shift has not only transformed how we view currency but also how we perceive the role of financial institutions and the very nature of transactions in our increasingly digital world. With these transformations come new opportunities, as well as challenges, in understanding the dynamics of value and trust in this new financial paradigm.

One of the key analytical insights into this significant transformation is the increasingly important concept of network effects. In a decentralized system, the overall value of a digital asset is not solely determined by its intrinsic properties or technological specifications but also, and perhaps more crucially, by the sheer size and engagement level of its user base and community. Bitcoin, having established itself as the first mover in this space, has benefited immensely from the continuous growth of a robust network of users, developers, and investors who are actively involved in its ecosystem. However, the emergence of various altcoins has demonstrated that this powerful network effect can be expanded upon and diversified in significant ways. By addressing specific shortcomings of Bitcoin or by catering to particular niche markets that are underserved, altcoins have created specialized networks that effectively drive their adoption and overall value in the digital currency landscape. This dynamic has fundamentally changed how stakeholders view the importance of community and utility in the development and sustainability of digital assets.

For instance, Ethereum's expansive network effect is largely driven by its robust and ever-growing ecosystem of decentralized applications, commonly known as dApps, along with a wide array of smart contracts. This intricate web of functionality, in turn, attracts developers of all backgrounds and businesses that are actively seeking flexible and programmable forms of digital money. As a result, this creates a positive and reinforcing feedback loop where the enhanced utility of the platform not only increases the overall value of its native currency, Ether, but also invites even more innovation and creativity from various sectors. This logical progression—where increased utility leads to greater levels of adoption and, subsequently, higher overall value—forms a fundamental principle of modern economic theory. One that is vividly illustrated by the remarkable success and rise of numerous altcoins flourishing in this vibrant ecosystem.

Another analytical perspective worth considering is the diversification of value creation in today's economy. Traditional financial systems historically often rely on a narrow set of metric indicators—such as GDP, inflation rates, and interest rates—to gauge and assess overall economic health and stability. However, altcoins, in contrast, embody a much more multifaceted approach to the concept of value. Their worth is not solely determined by the whims of market speculation and trading behaviors but is also shaped by critical factors such as technological innovation, network utility, user engagement, and community governance. This multifactorial approach to value creation provides a far more nuanced understanding of wealth and economic dynamics—one that aligns closely with modern theories of digital economics, technological advancement, and the inherent value of information in the digital age.

The Argumentative Debate: Critiques and Counterpoints

The rapid proliferation of altcoins has been marked by a significant level of controversy and debate. Critics strongly argue that the sheer number of digital currencies currently available on the market dilutes overall value, creates significant market confusion, and fosters an environment that is, unfortunately, ripe for scams and speculative bubbles. These detractors contend that many altcoins are merely experimental projects that offer little to no practical utility. Additionally, they believe that the intense focus on innovation often comes at the expense of the necessary stability and long-term reliability that investors and users seek. This dynamic raises essential questions about the future direction and sustainability of the altcoin landscape.

However, these criticisms often fail to recognize the broader and much more nuanced context. The emergence of thousands of altcoins is not merely a sign of disorder within the financial landscape but rather reflects a natural and inevitable evolutionary response to the inherent limitations and constraints of traditional centralized financial systems. Just as the rich diversity of languages and various cultures significantly enriched human civilization over the ages, the wide variety of altcoins currently available serves to enrich and diversify the global financial ecosystem by providing alternative models for value creation and methods of exchange. The experimental and sometimes unconventional nature of many altcoins is precisely what drives innovation in this field—each new project represents a unique test case, a hypothesis within the vast and intricate laboratory of decentralized finance. Through continual processes of trial and error, the market effectively filters out those ideas that prove to be unworkable or impractical, while those projects possessing genuine utility, real-world application, and true value gradually rise to prominence in the eyes of the users and investors.

Moreover, the decentralized nature of altcoins inherently promotes healthy competition and transparency in the financial landscape. Unlike traditional financial markets, where information is often controlled and manipulated by a select few powerful institutions, the world of altcoins is distinctly marked by open-source innovation, collaborative efforts, and public scrutiny. This level of transparency empowers investors and developers alike, enabling them to thoroughly evaluate projects based on their individual merits and potential. Ultimately, this fosters an environment characterized by accountability and continuous improvement. In this way, the ongoing proliferation of altcoins can be understood as a dynamic, market-driven process that serves to enhance and strengthen a more robust and resilient financial system, one that is better equipped to adapt to the needs and preferences of all participants.

Persuading the Modern Investor: Opportunities and Risks

For modern investors navigating the complex landscape of cryptocurrencies, the explosion of altcoins represents both an unprecedented opportunity and a significant risk that cannot be overlooked. On one hand, the diverse and ever-expanding range of digital assets available today offers a remarkable chance to participate in a financial revolution that is still in its early stages of development. By strategically investing in altcoins that address specific market needs—such as improved transaction speed, enhanced privacy features, or innovative governance models—investors can potentially reap extraordinary returns as these promising projects mature and gain widespread adoption in the dynamic market. This burgeoning sector has sparked interest and excitement, signaling a new era of financial possibilities for those who are willing to explore it fully.

On the other hand, the altcoin market is inherently volatile and constantly changing. Many digital currencies are still in their experimental phase, which adds to the unpredictability. The rapid pace of innovation in the space means that today's promising project can quickly become tomorrow's outdated technology, leaving investors to reconsider their choices. The risks in this environment are very real, and investors must exercise rigorous due diligence to protect themselves. This entails employing both technical analysis and fundamental research to identify which projects have genuine long-term potential and are more likely to yield favorable outcomes in the future.

The logical and analytical approach to investing in altcoins requires a meticulous balance between the potential risks and the rewards that can be achieved. Diversification plays a crucial role in this strategy—by distributing investments across a variety of altcoins that possess different strengths and occupy distinct market niches, investors are better equipped to mitigate the risks that come with any individual project. In addition, having a thorough understanding of the underlying technology, the level of community support, and the real-world utility of an altcoin offers a much more rational and grounded basis for valuation. This is preferable to merely relying on transient market hype, which can often lead to misinformed investment decisions and increased exposure to volatility.

For example, the remarkable rise of Ethereum in the cryptocurrency landscape can be attributed not solely to speculation, but also to its extensive utility as a versatile platform for various decentralized applications. The intrinsic value of Ethereum is supported by a vibrant and strong developer community, a robust and reliable technological infrastructure, and a well-defined roadmap for future improvements and developments. In stark contrast, some altcoins may present flashy and attractive features that captivate investors, yet they lack the essential substance required to sustain long-term growth in an increasingly competitive market. Therefore, the key is to identify and discern those projects that effectively combine innovative ideas with practical applications—a logical and important task that necessitates both quantitative analysis and qualitative judgment, allowing investors to make informed decisions regarding their investments.

The Future Trajectory: Scaling Innovation and Impact

As we look to the future, the landscape of altcoins is not only thrilling but also filled with uncertainty. The entire digital currency ecosystem remains in its early stages, and the swift rate of technological advancements indicates that we have merely begun to explore the vast potential of what lies ahead. Altcoins are destined to undergo continual evolution, as new projects emerge, aiming to tackle the limitations faced by earlier iterations, while also introducing completely new and innovative use cases that expand the horizons of cryptocurrency.

One of the most promising areas of innovation that has garnered significant attention is the integration of decentralized finance (DeFi) protocols with traditional financial systems. DeFi platforms are already demonstrating with impressive clarity that it is indeed possible to create complex financial instruments—such as loans, derivatives, and even various forms of insurance—without the need for centralized intermediaries. This remarkable integration has the potential not only to democratize access to vital financial services but also to significantly reduce transaction costs, thereby fostering greater economic inclusion on a truly global scale. As altcoins continue to develop, evolve, and improve in functionality, they are poised to play an increasingly central and pivotal role in this ongoing transformation. These digital assets hold the promise of offering more efficient, transparent, and accessible financial solutions that cater to a wider array of users than ever before.

Another area of innovation lies in the expansive realm of interoperability, which is increasingly gaining attention. With thousands of altcoins and cryptocurrencies competing fiercely in the market, the challenge posed by fragmentation becomes significantly magnified. However, innovative technologies and advanced protocols are actively being developed and implemented to bridge these divides effectively, thus creating robust networks where different digital currencies can interact seamlessly and efficiently. This interoperability is not just an added benefit; it is crucial for realizing the full potential of decentralized finance. It empowers users and stakeholders by enabling a more cohesive, integrated, and comprehensive global financial ecosystem. The logical extension of this positive trend is a future where digital assets are no longer isolated silos, but instead, they function as interconnected components of a vibrant and dynamic network—a visionary prospect that is as logical as it is revolutionary, paving the way for unprecedented collaboration and growth in the financial sector.

The Ethical and Societal Dimensions of Altcoin Proliferation

Beyond the technological and economic arguments, the rise of altcoins carries with it profound ethical and societal implications that cannot be overlooked. By challenging the longstanding dominance of state-controlled currency, altcoins embody a fundamental and necessary rethinking of power and control in the financial realm, bringing forth a new paradigm. They represent a significant democratization of money—a transformative shift from a traditional system where wealth is concentrated in the hands of a powerful few to one where every individual, regardless of their background, has the genuine opportunity to participate fully in the global economy. This shift not only empowers individuals but also fosters innovation and inclusivity, challenging the status quo of financial access and equity among communities worldwide.

This democratization concept is not only deeply persuasive but also critically important, especially in a world where the ongoing issue of economic inequality is an increasingly growing concern. Traditional financial systems frequently exacerbate existing inequality, leaving many marginalized communities without access to the essential tools necessary for achieving true economic empowerment. Altcoins, with their unique decentralized and borderless characteristics, present a remarkable opportunity to truly level the playing field among individuals. They offer a viable means for people in underserved regions to not only access vital financial services but also engage in global trade opportunities. Furthermore, altcoins enable individuals to build wealth independently, free from excessive reliance on the state or traditional banking institutions. This ethical argument favoring altcoins is not only logical but also morally compelling—a persuasive and urgent call for a significantly more inclusive and equitable financial future for everyone, regardless of their socio-economic background.

The rapid proliferation of various altcoins challenges long-standing societal norms surrounding the very nature of money itself. Traditionally, money has always been viewed as a physical entity—whether it be a coin, a bill, or a piece of precious metal like gold or silver. However, the emergence and rise of altcoins compel us to fundamentally rethink this notion, pushing us to accept that value can exist solely in digital form, maintained and safeguarded by complex code and a collective trust rather than any tangible physical substance. This significant shift represents a truly revolutionary concept, as it completely redefines what it means to possess and hold wealth in the modern era. We are witnessing a transition from the established realm of the tangible to the intangible, from the material world to the digital universe—a profound change that is as startling as it is logical in today's increasingly interconnected and technology-driven world. This evolution also invites new interpretations and discussions regarding economic systems and monetary policies in a dynamic and rapidly changing landscape.

Persuading Stakeholders: Policy, Regulation, and the Future

For policymakers and regulators, the rapid proliferation of altcoins presents a multitude of challenges and exciting opportunities that cannot be overlooked. On one hand, the overwhelming sheer number of digital currencies available today, each boasting its own unique technological quirks and distinct market dynamics, creates an increasingly complex landscape that is exceptionally difficult to oversee using traditional regulatory frameworks, which were not designed with such innovations in mind. On the other hand, the decentralization and transparency that are inherent in many altcoin projects provide a logical and data-driven approach to oversight. This could potentially lead to more effective regulation, enabling an environment where innovation can flourish while still maintaining necessary consumer protections and market integrity.

The compelling and persuasive argument for embracing the rise of alternative cryptocurrencies, commonly referred to as altcoins, is not to completely eliminate regulation altogether, but rather to embark on a journey to reform it—shifting from a traditional model of centralized control to one that is collaborative, adaptive, and informed by the same fundamental principles that underpin decentralized systems. This transformative approach means creating regulatory environments that actively foster innovation while simultaneously protecting consumers and ensuring the overall stability of the financial system. The lessons learned from the early days of free banking and local currencies can significantly inform and shape modern policy, encouraging regulators to adopt flexible frameworks that robustly support technological advancement rather than stifle it, thereby paving the way for a more inclusive financial future.

In this light, the rapid rise of alternative cryptocurrencies, commonly known as altcoins, serves as a significant call to reimagine and rethink the current landscape of financial regulation. It challenges the traditional paradigms of monetary control that have existed for decades and advocates for a new system that truly values transparency, competition, and ethical stewardship in the financial sector. For regulators, this situation presents both a unique challenge and a remarkable opportunity—to harness the numerous benefits that come with decentralized finance while also effectively mitigating the associated risks through smart, innovative, and forward-thinking policies that can adapt to this evolving landscape.

Logical Synthesis: A Blueprint for a Decentralized Future

When we carefully integrate the myriad innovations of various altcoins with the fundamental principles that underpin economic freedom and the concept of decentralization, a remarkably clear blueprint for the future of money begins to emerge. This innovative blueprint is meticulously constructed on a foundation of logical reasoning, sound principles, and a relentless drive to overcome the various limitations and challenges posed by the past. It envisions a vibrant world in which the power and control of money are distributed equitably among a diverse global community. In this emerging landscape, trust is inherently woven into the very architecture of financial systems, ensuring transparency, security, and reliability. Additionally, this vision fosters an environment where wealth is democratized and shared, ultimately benefiting all individuals and communities throughout the world.

Digital currencies represent the logical culmination of centuries of experimentation and innovation in financial systems. They embody the same key principles that drove early societies to abandon inefficient barter systems in favor of embracing standardized coinage that facilitated trade. Just as the ancient world evolved from localized trade practices to a more unified and cohesive monetary system, the modern world is currently moving toward a decentralized financial network that transcends traditional borders and central authorities. This significant progression is both natural and inevitable—a shockingly brilliant evolution that is driven by the enduring human impulses which have always sought to create better, more efficient systems of exchange. The transition to digital currencies signifies not just a technological advancement, but also a profound shift in how we perceive and handle value in our interconnected global economy.

The analytical and logical case for decentralization is indeed compelling and noteworthy. It represents a system where every single participant, regardless of their diverse backgrounds and experiences, possesses the potential to actively contribute to and benefit from the collective economy. This model is not only effective in enhancing efficiency and transparency but also plays a crucial role in promoting social justice and fostering economic empowerment for all. The rise and proliferation of altcoins serve as a powerful testament to the enduring influence of these groundbreaking ideas—a persuasive argument that challenges us to rethink our financial systems in deeply profound and transformative ways, encouraging a shift towards a more equitable and inclusive economic landscape.

Embracing the Diversity of Digital Innovation

In this explosive and captivating exploration of the rapid proliferation of altcoins and their remarkable unique innovations, we have traced a shocking and enlightening journey from Bitcoin's revolutionary beginnings to an increasingly complex ecosystem bursting with incredible diversity and boundless creativity. Altcoins are undeniably more than just mere copies of the original—they represent bold and ambitious experiments that boldly push the boundaries of what money can truly become. These fascinating digital assets challenge the limitations imposed by state-controlled currencies, introducing innovative features such as smart contracts, faster transaction times, and enhanced privacy measures that are simply groundbreaking. Moreover, they open up exciting new avenues for decentralized governance and actively engage communities in ways that were previously unimaginable.

The logical, analytical, and persuasive case for altcoins is abundantly clear and cannot be overstated: when money is truly liberated from the often stifling confines of centralized control, it evolves into a dynamic, multifaceted asset that beautifully reflects the incredible ingenuity and adaptability of human society. The remarkable diversity of altcoins serves as a significant strength in this new financial arena, providing a rich and competitive landscape where innovation thrives and various forms of value are determined by the collective will and understanding of a diverse global community. This ongoing evolution is not merely a technological shift—it represents a profound reimagining of the very nature of money itself, which is a mind-blowing progression that continues to redefine economic possibilities and opportunities in ways that were once unimaginable.

For investors, policymakers, and everyday citizens alike, the emergence of altcoins serves as a beacon of hope, illuminating the path toward a revolutionary financial landscape—a promising vision that suggests the future of money will be free, fair, and propelled by the collective intelligence of the people. This evolution compels us to transcend outdated, centralized systems and wholeheartedly embrace a new era characterized by financial freedom and groundbreaking innovation. The compelling allure of this vision stems from a harmonious blend of ethical imperatives, logical reasoning, and unparalleled technological potential—a future in which every individual possesses the opportunity to actively participate in and reap the benefits of a genuinely decentralized economy, where autonomy and equality reign supreme, offering a level playing field for all.

As we find ourselves standing on the precipice of this remarkable financial revolution, the invaluable lessons gleaned from the rapid proliferation of altcoins urge us to rethink, reimagine, and ultimately rebuild our economic systems from the ground up. They compel us to not only embrace a future where money serves no longer as a mere tool of oppression but instead rises to become a powerful force for empowerment for everyone involved. This transformation calls for a financial framework that democratizes wealth, fosters unprecedented innovation, and ensures that the fruits of prosperity are shared equitably by all members of society, enabling a fairer and more inclusive economic landscape for future generations.

In conclusion, the remarkable rise of alternative cryptocurrencies has significantly transformed our understanding of wealth and exchange in unprecedented ways. It is a fascinating journey marked by shocking innovations, profound philosophical debates, and relentless experimentation that continually pushes the boundaries of what we once perceived as monetary systems. The incredible diversity of altcoins, along with the groundbreaking innovations they consistently bring to the table, offers a logical, persuasive, and deeply inspiring blueprint for the future of money that becomes more tangible with each passing day. This ongoing evolution, firmly grounded in centuries of human progress and driven by an unwavering quest for economic freedom, not only promises but also guarantees to reshape our global financial landscape in ways that are as revolutionary as they are inevitable. The impact of this transformation will resonate for generations to come, redefining the very nature of how we interact with money itself.

Embrace the remarkable diversity and endless possibilities of digital innovation in our modern age. Let the proliferation and increasing popularity of altcoins inspire you to rethink the very nature of value itself, encouraging you to question long-established paradigms and conventional wisdom. By doing so, you can actively participate in a future where money evolves into a dynamic, decentralized force that genuinely works for the greater good. The world of altcoins is not merely a market—it is an inspiring movement, a vibrant testament to human creativity, ingenuity, and the enduring drive that seeks to build a more equitable and prosperous society for everyone.

Section 3: Key Milestones that Cemented Crypto's Legitimacy

In the chronicles of financial history, very few innovations have sparked as much controversy, intense wonder, and profound revolutionary change as cryptocurrencies have. What began as a niche experiment that was largely shunned and dismissed by mainstream finance has, over the course of the past two decades, remarkably evolved into a globally recognized and established asset class. This dramatic transformation—from a fringe technology that few understood to a prominent and credible financial instrument embraced by many—is marked by a sequence of pivotal events and milestones. Each of these milestones serves as a testament to the ingenuity, unwavering resilience, and audacity of those pioneering individuals who dared to believe in a system free from the constraints of centralized control. The upcoming exploration will unpack these critical milestones in more detail, presenting a shocking and mind-blowing journey that combines logical reasoning, analytical insight, and persuasive arguments, all while remaining realistic and accessible in language and explanation.

The Birth of the Idea: The Bitcoin Whitepaper (2008)

The journey of cryptocurrency legitimacy began in the year 2008 with a groundbreaking document that would forever change our collective perception of money: "Bitcoin: A Peer-to-Peer Electronic Cash System." This influential whitepaper, published anonymously under the pseudonym Satoshi Nakamoto, outlined a radical and innovative new approach to currency—one that relied heavily on advanced cryptographic principles and a decentralized network of nodes rather than the traditional authority and control of governments or banks. This fundamental shift not only introduced a new form of digital currency but also sparked an entire movement towards financial independence and the exploration of blockchain technology's potential applications in various sectors.

This document represented a pivotal turning point in the financial landscape. Its logical, systematic, and clear explanation of how digital money could effectively operate without intermediaries was both remarkably shocking and strikingly innovative. Critics at that time were deeply skeptical, dismissing it as just an academic exercise with little to no practical application in the real world. Yet, the groundbreaking whitepaper laid the essential groundwork for a revolutionary system that would ultimately challenge and disrupt the very foundations of traditional finance as we know it. It introduced groundbreaking concepts such as the blockchain technology, which ensures unparalleled transparency and robust security by meticulously recording every single transaction on a public, immutable ledger that cannot be altered or tampered with.

The significance of the Bitcoin whitepaper cannot be overstated in any way. It was not merely a technical manual; rather, it was a powerful manifesto for economic freedom—a bold call to liberate money from the centralized control that had dominated human civilization for countless millennia. By proposing a decentralized form of currency, it fundamentally changed the way we think about money and its role in society. In doing so, it set the stage for a future where money could be truly global, borderless, and completely immune to the manipulations of centralized powers and institutions that have historically held sway over financial systems. This revolutionary concept has given rise to untold possibilities for individuals seeking sovereignty over their wealth and financial transactions.

The Genesis Block and Early Network Adoption (2009-2010)

In January of the year 2009, Bitcoin embarked on its initial journey into the expansive world of digital finance with the mining of its very first genesis block—a block that thoughtfully contained a message hinting at the underlying political and economic motivations that drove the creation of this revolutionary system. This block was not just a simple starting point for a new digital currency; it represented a powerful and symbolic act that truly marked the birth of a decentralized financial system, one that would challenge the traditional norms and frameworks of finance and governance.

The early days of Bitcoin were indeed marked by very modest beginnings that many would consider quite humble. A small group of dedicated enthusiasts and cryptography experts came together to begin mining and exchanging Bitcoin, as they were eager to experiment with the vast potential it presented while simultaneously testing its underlying code. In a world where digital money was an entirely novel and untested concept, these early adopters faced an array of skepticism, doubt, and numerous technical challenges that could easily have deterred less determined individuals. Yet, their unwavering persistence and commitment laid a solid and enduring foundation for what would eventually blossom into a global phenomenon that continues to evolve and influence many aspects of economic life.

The early network adoption of Bitcoin was a grassroots experiment marked by trust, cooperation, and innovation. Every miner, every node operator, and every participant played a crucial role in contributing to a robust system built on shared principles and collective verification. This decentralized model ensured that trust was not placed in any single entity but was instead distributed across the entire network. The logical and ingenious design of the blockchain, with its inherent resistance to tampering and fraud, quickly showcased how digital money could function effectively—providing a practical solution to long-standing issues like double-spending and enabling secure transactions without the need for intermediaries. The collective effort of individuals participating in this system underscored the power of community in fostering a new way of managing value.

By the year 2010, Bitcoin started to witness its first tangible and real-world transactions, exemplified by the notable and famous purchase of two pizzas for the staggering amount of 10,000 bitcoins. Although, at that point in time, these transactions were nearly trivial in terms of monetary value, they actually represented a significant and critical shift in the perception of Bitcoin. This transition transformed Bitcoin from being merely an abstract digital experiment into a practical and usable medium of exchange, effectively proving that it could be utilized to buy various goods and services. This important milestone marked the pivotal shift from theoretical concepts to practical applications and began to firmly cement Bitcoin's growing legitimacy as a viable alternative to traditional forms of money.

The Mt. Gox Era and the First Taste of Mainstream Attention (2011-2013)

The Mt. Gox exchange, which was once regarded as the largest and most influential Bitcoin trading platform, played an incredibly pivotal role in shaping Bitcoin's journey from being an obscure experiment to becoming a mainstream asset that is recognized globally. Established back in 2010, Mt. Gox initially commenced operations as a platform for trading game cards, yet it quickly evolved into the central hub for Bitcoin transactions, attracting a vast number of users and investors from around the world. Its rapid rise to prominence was experienced as both a tremendous blessing and a significant curse—ushering in remarkable and unprecedented volumes of trade while simultaneously exposing the nascent and rapidly evolving industry to a myriad of significant risks that would challenge its integrity and stability.

During this fascinating period, Bitcoin's price surged and plummeted with wild fluctuations that drew both intrigue and deep concern from the media and potential investors alike. The dramatic price swings were not only shocking but also often attributed to the highly speculative nature of the market combined with the small size of early trading volumes. However, these turbulent events also served to demonstrate the immense potential of Bitcoin as a stable store of value in an increasingly digital economy. As more individuals began to actively buy, sell, and trade Bitcoin on the exchange platform Mt. Gox, its utility as a decentralized currency became increasingly evident to everyone watching. This emerging trend of digital currency caught the attention of many, raising questions about its long-term viability and future role in the financial landscape.

Despite the later collapse of Mt. Gox, which was primarily due to severe security breaches and a significant lack of effective management, the exchange undeniably played an essential and pivotal role in the early mainstream adoption of Bitcoin and other cryptocurrencies. It provided a critical testing ground for the complex market dynamics, intensive regulatory discussions, and the numerous practical challenges of successfully running a digital currency exchange. The invaluable lessons learned during the Mt. Gox era—spanning both notable triumphs and devastating tragedies—served to markedly accelerate the evolution of crucial cryptocurrency security protocols and much-needed regulatory frameworks. In a shocking twist of fate, the very failures and shortcomings of Mt. Gox spurred an impressive wave of improvements within the industry, leading to the development of modern exchanges that are now far more secure, robust, and reliable than ever before.

The Emergence of Altcoins: Expanding the Digital Ecosystem (2012-2014)

As Bitcoin began to carve out its unique niche in the evolving digital landscape, it inevitably inspired a vibrant and diverse new generation of digital currencies—what we now refer to as altcoins. These alternative cryptocurrencies were thoughtfully designed to address various limitations that Bitcoin faced while also exploring exciting new applications of blockchain technology. Different altcoins like Litecoin, Ripple, and Peercoin emerged during this period, showcasing innovative features that set them apart from their predecessor. For instance, Litecoin introduced faster transaction times, enabling quicker transfers and enhancing the user experience. Ripple focused on improving the efficiency of cross-border transactions, making it an attractive option for financial institutions. Meanwhile, Peercoin offered a unique approach to energy usage with its alternative consensus mechanisms, aimed at creating a more sustainable cryptocurrency ecosystem. These developments marked a significant evolution in the digital currency space, paving the way for the thriving market we see today.

The rise of altcoins was not merely an event; it represented a direct and formidable challenge to the entrenched notion that Bitcoin was the sole progenitor of digital money. Instead of remaining isolated, this dramatic shift opened up a remarkably diverse ecosystem of digital assets, each contributing unique innovations and characteristics to the burgeoning field. The widespread proliferation of altcoins is a shockingly significant development—transforming what began as a single, fringe idea into a multi-faceted and complex industry that now encompasses thousands of different projects, each with its unique purpose and potential.

This remarkable explosion of alternatives served several key functions that reshaped the financial landscape. First, it validated the underlying concept of decentralized digital money by clearly showing that Bitcoin was not merely an isolated phenomenon, but rather the initial step in a much broader and more significant revolution in finance. Second, it spurred innovation across the tech landscape, as developers and visionaries alike experimented with a multitude of different ways to enhance the efficiency, security, and overall functionality of digital currencies. For instance, Ethereum's groundbreaking introduction of smart contracts not only paved the way for decentralized applications but also fundamentally changed how we view money as more than just a simple medium of exchange—it evolved into a dynamic platform for global, decentralized computing that opened up endless possibilities for future advancements in technology and finance.

The altcoin boom also had a remarkably significant impact on various market dynamics, reshaping how investors and traders engaged with the evolving digital landscape. With a wide variety of digital currencies now competing for widespread adoption and acceptance, the overall ecosystem became more resilient and notably diversified. This diversification not only helped to mitigate some of the inherent risks associated with relying on a single digital asset but also provided investors with a significantly broader array of options for meaningful participation in the ever-expanding digital economy. The logical evolution from a singular digital currency to this complex, multifaceted ecosystem truly underscores the natural and ongoing progression of human innovation in the fascinating realm of money and finance. This evolution reflects the adaptability of financial systems, as they aim to address the diverse needs and preferences of a growing number of users around the world.

Institutional Adoption and Regulatory Recognition (2014-2017)

The next major milestone in the ongoing journey toward mainstream legitimacy for cryptocurrencies was the progressive institutional adoption by various financial entities and the growing interest of regulatory bodies. Initially, Bitcoin along with its various altcoin counterparts were met with significant skepticism and doubt from established financial institutions and governmental entities. However, as the underlying technology matured and the numerous benefits of decentralization became increasingly apparent to a broader audience, a noticeable shift began to occur. This change reflected a growing recognition of cryptocurrencies as valid financial instruments, driving further exploration and acceptance within the traditional financial landscape.

In the years that followed 2014, a significant number of high-profile institutional investors began to take serious notice of Bitcoin and its burgeoning potential. Prominent hedge funds, well-established family offices, and even a select few banks started to allocate small but meaningful portions of their investment portfolios to digital assets like Bitcoin. This notable shift in investment strategy was shocking to many traditional economists and financial analysts who had long dismissed cryptocurrencies as merely a passing fad or trend. However, the increasing involvement of institutional players in the cryptocurrency market signaled a powerful message: Bitcoin's underlying technology was not only sound, but its potential as a viable store of value was also being acknowledged and recognized on a global scale by investors worldwide.

At the same time, regulators across the globe began to adopt a much more proactive stance toward cryptocurrencies. Instead of outright dismissing these digital currencies as insignificant or unworthy, many governments and regulatory bodies started to investigate and explore various regulatory frameworks that could effectively integrate digital assets into the mainstream financial system we have today. This appearance of regulatory recognition proved to be a crucial and significant milestone—it offered a much-needed sense of legitimacy and stability to an industry that had been, up until that point, operating on the fringes of the global economy, almost outside of the reach of traditional financial systems.

The establishment of various regulatory standards has played a crucial role in helping to quell some of the deep-seated fears surrounding the world of cryptocurrencies, thereby paving the way for much broader adoption across different sectors. As the regulatory environment became increasingly clearer and more defined, a growing number of institutional investors began to feel more comfortable and confident about entering the market, which in turn further fueled the remarkable growth of digital assets across the globe. This dynamic period has ultimately marked a significant turning point in the industry, as Bitcoin transitioned from being merely a niche experiment into a fully recognized asset class with considerable global significance and impact.

The Technological Breakthrough: The Advent of Blockchain 2.0 and Beyond (2017-Present)

The technology that underpins cryptocurrencies has consistently continued to evolve and mature, leading to what many enthusiasts and experts refer to as "Blockchain 2.0." While Bitcoin still remains the flagship and pioneering example of decentralized digital money, the innovations and advancements in blockchain technology that have emerged over the past few years have expanded its applications far beyond mere simple transactions. Notable projects such as Ethereum, Cardano, and Polkadot have introduced a host of new features and capabilities, including the implementation of smart contracts, enhanced scalability, and improved interoperability between various blockchain networks. These developments have not only diversified usage but have also paved the way for a future where blockchain technology can significantly impact numerous industries.

These remarkable technological breakthroughs are nothing short of mind-blowing and truly astonishing. They have significantly transformed the blockchain from being a simple ledger primarily used for recording Bitcoin transactions into a highly dynamic platform that allows for the building of decentralized applications, commonly referred to as dApps. The implications of these innovations are incredibly far-reaching and profound—they are not only improving the overall functionality and capabilities of digital currencies, but are also actively redefining how we think about contracts, governance models, and even the fundamental organizational structures of businesses and institutions today.

Section 3: Key Milestones that Cemented Crypto's Legitimacy

In a world where digital technology and finance collide with explosive force, cryptocurrencies have remarkably emerged as one of the most revolutionary and controversial innovations of our time. What started as a fringe experiment in the realms of cryptography and computer science has, over a relatively short period, metamorphosed into a widely recognized and mainstream asset class, capturing the intense attention of governments, financial institutions, and individual investors alike. This evolution is vividly marked by a series of pivotal events—shocking milestones that have profoundly reshaped not only our understanding of what money is but also the foundational elements of the entire global financial system. In this section, we delve deeper into these fundamental milestones with a reasoning-driven, logical, analytical, and highly persuasive approach. We demonstrate how each significant event has contributed to establishing the legitimacy of cryptocurrencies as a viable and invaluable asset that challenges traditional financial paradigms, offering unique advantages, and introducing new considerations for investors and regulators in the modern age.

The Genesis: Bitcoin's Birth and the Whitepaper Revolution

The story of the legitimacy of cryptocurrency truly begins in the year 2008, with the enigmatic publication of the Bitcoin whitepaper by an unknown individual, or potentially even a group of people, operating under the pseudonym Satoshi Nakamoto. This groundbreaking document, titled "Bitcoin: A Peer-to-Peer Electronic Cash System," was nothing short of revolutionary in its simplicity, yet profound in its clarity. It outlined a comprehensive blueprint for a digital currency designed to function without the need for any central authority, relying instead on sophisticated cryptographic proof and a decentralized network of interconnected computers. This innovation presented the very first significant challenge to the age-old system of money that has been controlled by states for centuries. The implications of this new form of currency reshaped discussions around finance and trust, paving the way for an entirely new approach to the concept of money in modern society, igniting the imaginations of tech enthusiasts and investors alike.

Satoshi's groundbreaking ideas were nothing short of revolutionary in the landscape of finance. They boldly rejected the long-standing, traditional notion that money must be issued, controlled, and heavily regulated by governments. Instead, Bitcoin was intricately designed to empower individuals, allowing them to transact directly, securely, and without the need for intermediaries. This radical idea struck deeply at the very heart of the financial establishment, and the existence of Bitcoin itself was a daring declaration that money could thrive and exist outside the stringent constraints of centralized control and influence. In a sense, Bitcoin's whitepaper represented not only an academic treatise but also a powerful manifesto for economic freedom and empowerment. It proposed a transformative world where trust was no longer placed in banks or governments, but rather in the robust code and the collective consensus of a decentralized network. This shift promised to redefine the fundamental principles of how value is exchanged and perceived in society.

The early days of Bitcoin were undeniably shrouded in significant mystery and intrigue, sparking a broad array of discussions and debates among early tech enthusiasts. Satoshi Nakamoto's true identity continues to remain a deeply guarded secret, and his unexpected disappearance from public discourse in the year 2010 added even more layers to the allure and fascination surrounding this groundbreaking project. The enigma that surrounds Bitcoin, when coupled with its elegant and innovative technological design, helped to effortlessly capture the imaginations of technologists, pioneering early adopters, and ardent libertarians alike who saw its potential. This initial period, rife with speculation and curiosity, set a compelling stage for what was to come next—a gradual yet definitive transition from a niche digital curiosity, which was initially dismissed by many skeptics, to a truly global phenomenon that has dramatically redefined the way we think about currency, transactions, and value in our modern world. The journey that Bitcoin has undergone is a fascinating one, full of trials, innovations, and transformative moments that have shaped its trajectory in the digital landscape.

The Mt. Gox Saga: A Crisis That Paved the Way for Change

One of the most dramatic and highly significant milestones in the evolving and intricate history of cryptocurrency was undoubtedly the meteoric rise and eventual fall of Mt. Gox, which was once regarded as the world's largest and most influential Bitcoin exchange. During its peak, Mt. Gox astonishingly handled over 70% of all Bitcoin transactions taking place on a global scale. However, its eventual and devastating collapse in 2014, which was primarily caused by massive security breaches and severe mismanagement, sent tremendous shockwaves throughout the burgeoning and rapidly emerging crypto community, leaving countless investors and users reeling from the unexpected and chaotic financial turmoil that ensued. The fallout from this incident dramatically reshaped the landscape of cryptocurrency exchanges and led to renewed calls for greater regulation and oversight in the industry.

The Mt. Gox incident marked a truly significant turning point in the ever-evolving world of cryptocurrency. It dramatically laid bare the numerous vulnerabilities that existed within the early crypto infrastructure and powerfully underscored the urgent and pressing need for the thorough implementation of better security practices as well as comprehensive regulatory oversight. The catastrophic loss of hundreds of thousands of Bitcoins—which would later be valued at staggering billions of dollars—served as a major wake-up call to everyone involved in the cryptocurrency ecosystem and those observing it from the sidelines. This shocking and unprecedented event highlighted the inherent risks associated with digital assets and brought to light the critical importance of diligently safeguarding these valuable assets. However, even with the disastrous conclusion of the Mt. Gox saga, it inadvertently played a crucial role in cementing the legitimacy of cryptocurrency as a whole and promoting its relevance in the financial world. It compelled the entire community to confront the harsh realities of digital asset management, in a serious way that hadn't fully happened in such a widespread manner before. This incident ultimately spurred a wave of significant and transformative improvements throughout the entire industry. In the aftermath, new exchanges began to emerge swiftly, all of which implemented enhanced security protocols aimed at preventing similar catastrophic failures in the future. Consequently, the entire cryptocurrency industry began to mature at an accelerated pace, introducing innovative solutions and technologies that addressed the emerging challenges in this rapidly evolving and often volatile space. The repercussions of Mt. Gox can still be felt today, with its lessons shaping the way digital assets are managed and protected.

This ongoing crisis has also brought to light an incredibly important aspect of crypto's evolution: the intricate balance that exists between risk and innovation. While the devastating collapse of Mt. Gox created turmoil for countless investors and users alike, it simultaneously demonstrated that the technology itself, at its core, was fundamentally sound and remarkably reliable. The underlying blockchain remained intact throughout the ordeal, showcasing its inherent robustness, and Bitcoin continued to function effectively, unwaveringly maintaining its integrity amidst the chaos. The market's remarkable ability to endure such a colossal failure and eventually rebound from it was a profound testament to its resilience and served as a compelling argument for the overall robustness of decentralized systems. This incident underscored the pressing necessity for the crypto space to evolve and improve continuously, while adapting to new challenges and threats that may arise. It highlighted the importance of learning from past failures and leveraging those lessons to create a more secure and innovative landscape for future developments in the blockchain domain. The evolution of crypto is not merely about technological advancements but also about fostering a culture of adaptability, investor confidence, and proactive measures to address vulnerabilities.

Institutional Adoption: The Turning Point for Mainstream Acceptance

After navigating through the tumultuous and particularly challenging early years of development, the next significant milestone arrived with the gradual and notable adoption of various cryptocurrencies by a growing number of institutional investors. This crucial phase represented a profound transition from what was once a niche technology that had previously been embraced primarily by enthusiastic hobbyists and ardent libertarians to a widely recognized mainstream asset class that is now acknowledged by Wall Street's most influential players, major central banks around the world, and numerous corporate giants looking to diversify their portfolios. This evolution marked a pivotal point in the financial landscape, as the acceptance of digital currencies began to reshape traditional investing paradigms, paving the way for broader integration and innovation within the global financial system.

In the early 2010s, as Bitcoin began to slowly but surely gain traction in the world of finance, a small yet influential group of institutional investors, along with market analysts and visionary thinkers, started to recognize its immense potential as a viable hedge against increasing economic uncertainty and instability prevalent in various sectors. The transformative and exhilarating bull run of 2017 marked a significant turning point in the perception and acceptance of Bitcoin within broader financial circles. During this remarkable period, Bitcoin's price skyrocketed dramatically from around $1,000 to an astonishing nearly $20,000, catching the attention of many who had previously been skeptical. This meteoric rise not only fueled a media frenzy that captured headlines worldwide but also ignited public interest in cryptocurrencies on an unprecedented scale, drawing enthusiasm and curiosity from a diverse audience. While this surge in value was partly driven by speculative exuberance and fervor among retail investors eager to get in on the action, it simultaneously drew the discerning attention of serious, seasoned institutional investors and financial analysts who were keen to fully understand the implications of this new, disruptive digital asset. Consequently, hedge funds, asset managers, and even family offices began to carefully allocate portions of their investment portfolios to Bitcoin and other emerging cryptocurrencies, striving to diversify their holdings and capitalize on the revolutionary and innovative potential of this cutting-edge digital currency. This shift marked the dawning of a new era in finance, as the incorporation of cryptocurrencies became an essential strategy for many investment firms looking to stay ahead of market trends.

This institutional influx was undeniably a significant game changer for the entire landscape of financial markets and investment paradigms. It introduced not just the rigorous analytical frameworks, which are essential for informed decision-making, but also advanced risk management practices that are typical of traditional finance. These elements played a crucial role in helping to stabilize the previously volatile crypto markets that had seen wild fluctuations. With the strategic entrance of well-capitalized players hailing from mainstream financial institutions, the entire narrative surrounding Bitcoin shifted dramatically. What was once perceived as a fringe experiment, relegated to the fringes of the financial world, rapidly evolved into being recognized as a legitimate asset class with considerable long-term potential and viability. The backing and endorsement from these established financial institutions provided the much-needed legitimacy that many skeptics had been demanding for years. It truly felt as though the world of high finance was finally saying, "We trust you, Bitcoin," which signaled a transformative moment in the ongoing integration of cryptocurrencies into the broader financial ecosystem. This pivotal shift holds significant implications not just for the future of digital currencies, but also for the evolution and stability of the entire global financial landscape as we move forward into this new era.

Moreover, the introduction of regulated investment vehicles, such as Bitcoin futures and, later on, Bitcoin exchange-traded funds (ETFs), played a crucial and transformative role in further cementing cryptocurrency's evolving status within the mainstream financial landscape. These innovative financial instruments offered investors an exceptional opportunity to gain exposure to digital assets without the necessity of directly holding them, effectively significantly lowering the barrier to entry and, in turn, attracting a much broader base of market participants than ever before. This noteworthy shift has allowed even those who were previously skeptical, hesitant, or uncertain to finally enter the market space. The logical progression from individual speculation, which was often driven by FOMO (fear of missing out), toward more serious institutional adoption and engagement is truly a powerful, mind-blowing testament to the maturation and evolution of the entire crypto ecosystem over time. It clearly demonstrated that, over time, even the most radical and seemingly outlandish ideas could gain widespread acceptance when they are nurtured and supported by sound technology, combined with robust, concrete market fundamentals. This ongoing evolution highlights how the financial world is becoming more inclusive and accessible, thereby allowing a diverse range of investors to engage and participate actively in shaping and experiencing the future of finance.

Technological Breakthroughs: The Advent of Smart Contracts and Ethereum

While Bitcoin laid the foundational groundwork for digital currencies, it certainly was not the conclusion of the story as many would like to believe. The journey of cryptocurrency continued forward, evolving and adapting over time, and the next significant milestone in this ever-changing narrative came with the groundbreaking creation of Ethereum in the year 2015. Ethereum introduced a revolutionary concept that fundamentally changed the landscape of digital finance and how we interact with technology: smart contracts. These smart contracts are self-executing agreements, with the precise terms and conditions of the agreement directly inscribed into code, which effectively eliminates the need for intermediaries and greatly enhances overall efficiency and trust. This remarkable innovation not only transformed the blockchain from merely serving as a straightforward ledger of transactions but redefined it as a fully programmable platform, one that is capable of supporting a wide and diverse array of decentralized applications (dApps) in various domains. With these significant advancements, Ethereum truly paved the way for new possibilities and functionalities within the realm of blockchain technology, thereby opening doors to countless opportunities in multiple industries and sectors, reshaping our digital interactions as we know them.

Smart contracts have dramatically transformed and removed the traditional need for intermediaries in the realm of complex transactions, paving the way for an extensive range of innovations from automated financial agreements to decentralized voting systems that ensure both transparency and efficiency. The remarkable ability to create and execute contracts autonomously, all without a central authority, is nothing short of astonishing—it has fundamentally redefined and reshaped the entire concept of trust in digital transactions and interactions, leading to new levels of security and reliability. Ethereum's groundbreaking innovation significantly expanded on Bitcoin's initial vision, not merely functioning as a store of value, but also emerging as a robust platform for unprecedented innovation, thereby opening the door to a myriad of applications that were previously deemed unimaginable and impossible to accomplish in the digital sphere. This shift has encouraged various sectors to explore the vast potential of blockchain technology, fostering creativity and establishing new methodologies for conducting business and governance.

The meteoric rise of Ethereum has undoubtedly spurred an unprecedented explosion of countless new projects—each one representing an individual altcoin, meticulously crafted and specifically designed to cater to a distinct purpose or effectively address a particular market need. These diverse and innovative altcoins, which are intricately built on the foundational principles of smart contracts as well as state-of-the-art decentralized protocols, have allowed for a far greater level of experimentation and groundbreaking innovation within the ever-evolving blockchain ecosystem. By doing so, they have laid the robust groundwork for the modern decentralized finance (DeFi) movement, which boldly promises to revolutionize and fundamentally reshape traditional banking systems by providing a wide array of essential financial services without any need for intermediaries. This innovative approach is helping to empower individuals all over the globe and is transforming the intricate financial landscape in ways that were previously thought to be impossible.

Ethereum's impact on the technological landscape was indeed profound, extensive, and far-reaching in multiple dimensions. It not only demonstrated with clarity that blockchain technology could be adapted and significantly enhanced, but also provided developers all around the globe with the essential tools and frameworks necessary to create entirely new and innovative forms of value. The innovative logic underpinning Ethereum's design—specifically, the ground-breaking creation of a platform that supports programmable money—was both revolutionary and extremely persuasive in its execution. It clearly illustrated and showcased that blockchain technology was not merely a static, unchanging asset but rather a dynamic and evolving platform, fully capable of supporting a vast, diverse, and vibrant ecosystem of applications. This monumental breakthrough marked a pivotal and transformative moment in the evolution of digital assets, effectively shifting the narrative from viewing Bitcoin solely as digital gold to embracing a far broader and much more ambitious vision of what decentralized technology could ultimately achieve and deliver in the future across various sectors.

Global Integration and Regulatory Recognition

Another significant milestone that greatly contributed to cementing the legitimacy of cryptocurrencies was the gradual and continuous growing recognition, along with the eventual integration of these innovative digital assets into the broader global financial system by a range of regulators and governments across various regions of the world. As cryptocurrencies gained an impressive increase in popularity and market capitalization, more and more governments began to take serious notice of their potential impact on economies and financial markets. Initially, the regulatory responses to the rise of digital currencies were mixed, and they varied significantly among different jurisdictions—ranging from outright bans in certain countries, which exhibited a fear of the unknown, to cautious acceptance and responsible monitoring in others who recognized the transformative potential of this technology. However, over time, a more balanced and thoughtful approach eventually emerged, allowing for a more conducive environment for innovation as well as addressing pressing concerns related to security, fraud, and market stability. This substantial shift in perspective has played a crucial role in fostering an atmosphere where digital currencies can thrive and attract investment, encouraging further development in blockchain technology and financial applications.

In the 2020s, various regulatory bodies across the globe began to actively and strategically develop comprehensive frameworks that are specifically designed to effectively manage the burgeoning and rapidly evolving field of cryptocurrencies. Countries such as Japan, Switzerland, and Singapore took the lead in this significant endeavor by systematically creating regulatory environments that not only supported crypto innovation and growth but also placed a strong emphasis on protecting consumers and promoting fairness in the market. The United States and the European Union soon followed suit, taking decisive action to introduce a diverse range of regulations aimed at ensuring greater transparency in cryptocurrency transactions, combating fraud effectively, and preventing money laundering activities, all while striving to avoid stifling the crucial innovation that this dynamic and transformative sector represents.

This gradual regulatory acceptance represented a momentous turning point in the ongoing evolution of financial systems worldwide. It powerfully signaled that cryptocurrencies were increasingly being recognized as not merely a passing fad but rather as a legitimate asset class deserving of the same level of careful scrutiny and considerations that traditional financial instruments typically receive in established markets. The recognition was indeed profound; the undeniable fact that governments and regulatory bodies could no longer afford to ignore the rapid growth and transformative potential of digital assets added considerable credibility to the ever-expanding and dynamic crypto market. It became a logical and undeniable conclusion: when a significant amount of economic activity and groundbreaking innovative developments occur within a new financial system, regulatory frameworks must inevitably adapt and evolve, or they risk becoming entirely obsolete and losing their relevance in a rapidly changing financial landscape. The implications of this acknowledgment extend beyond mere acceptance; they pave the way for a future where the interplay between traditional systems and emerging technologies can thrive and mature, fostering an environment where innovation is embraced rather than stifled by outdated regulations.

The integration of cryptocurrencies into the existing regulatory framework not only played a critical role in stabilizing the volatile market but also opened up numerous promising new avenues for institutional investment that had previously gone unexplored. With clearer guidelines and legal certainty now firmly in place, an increasing number of traditional investors began to allocate substantial and significant funds to digital assets. This noteworthy shift was significant, as it further reinforced the rapidly growing legitimacy of the crypto market in the eyes of the general public and investors alike. This ongoing process represented a dramatic and mind-blowing affirmation that decentralized technology could not only coexist harmoniously with established financial systems but could also potentially enhance, transform, and innovate them in truly extraordinary ways. By bridging the gap between traditional and modern digital finance, we are witnessing a remarkable transformation that is reshaping the entire investment landscape, creating unprecedented opportunities for growth and diversification that were once considered impossible and merely the stuff of dreams.

The Mainstream Moment: Corporate Adoption and Public Awareness

Perhaps one of the most striking and significant milestones in the ongoing evolution of crypto legitimacy was undeniably the widespread and continually growing corporate adoption of a variety of digital currencies. Major companies, ranging from notable technology giants to influential payment processors, began to actively and eagerly integrate cryptocurrencies into their diverse and multifaceted business models and frameworks. Notable companies such as Tesla, MicroStrategy, and Square captured headlines and the public's attention by investing billions of dollars in Bitcoin specifically, showcasing their commitment to this innovative financial landscape. These bold moves were not merely speculative gambles; rather, they represented strategic decisions made by forward-thinking executives that clearly signaled a broader acceptance and acknowledgment of digital assets not just as an investment but as a legitimate store of value and a viable medium of exchange in today's rapidly evolving economy. This growing acceptance by such high-profile corporations has greatly contributed to the increasing legitimacy and mainstream recognition of cryptocurrencies.

The corporate adoption of cryptocurrencies has brought forth an unprecedented level of public awareness and intense media scrutiny the likes of which no other significant milestone has ever achieved in the annals of history. As eye-catching headlines splashed vividly across newspapers and a plethora of online platforms about high-profile investments pouring into Bitcoin as well as various other cryptocurrencies, the general public found themselves compelled to confront the undeniable reality that digital assets were indeed here to stay for the long haul. The shock factor of this revelation was enormous and certainly could not be overstated—traditional Wall Street, with all its inherent conservatism and pronounced risk aversion, was now not only acknowledging but actively embracing a groundbreaking technology that had once been quickly dismissed as merely a fringe experiment, something that barely registered on the radar of conventional financial systems. This radical and heretofore unimaginable shift in perspective and investment patterns has signaled a transformative change that might very well redefine financial landscapes and principles in the years to come, heralding an era where cryptocurrencies could blur the previously rigid lines of financial management and investment strategy.

This widespread acceptance of digital currencies has seen significant growth and was further bolstered by the introduction of an ever-expanding array of crypto-related financial products such as futures, options, and exchange-traded funds (ETFs). These innovative instruments effectively allowed institutional investors to gain tailored exposure to the rapidly evolving landscape of digital assets without having to navigate the complexities and potential challenges that come with directly holding cryptocurrencies themselves. By offering these advanced products, the financial market provided a crucial bridge between the established world of traditional finance and the new, transformative realm of blockchain technology that has emerged in recent years. The advent of these financial products represented a logical and necessary extension of the ongoing trend toward mainstream adoption of cryptocurrencies and digital assets among various types of investors. In this way, they offered investors a broader array of essential tools to diversify their portfolios, capture new opportunities, and manage risk effectively in the changing and often unpredictable economic environment prevalent today.

The collective and substantial impact of corporate adoption, the thorough regulatory integration, and the rapid proliferation of a myriad of various financial instruments all played a vital role in contributing to the construction of a compelling and logical case for the growing legitimacy and acceptance of cryptocurrencies within the financial realm. These meaningful developments effectively proved, with convincing clarity, that digital assets could indeed be seamlessly integrated into the expansive and intricate global financial ecosystem in a manner that was not only highly efficient but also remarkably secure—a revelation that was both astonishing and, in many ways, as predictable as it was profoundly impactful on a global scale. Each of these elements worked in tandem to bolster confidence in the viability of digital currencies, paving the way for their wider adoption and higher acceptance across diverse sectors of the economy.

A New Era of Financial Innovation

The journey from the mysterious genesis of Bitcoin to its current status as a globally recognized and highly valued asset is indeed a captivating tale filled with revolutionary milestones that have consistently pushed the boundaries of what money can genuinely be. Each pivotal event—whether it be the groundbreaking creation of the Bitcoin whitepaper that laid the foundation for a decentralized currency, the dramatic collapse of early exchanges like Mt. Gox that highlighted the risks in the market, or the significant rise of institutional investment that brought a new level of legitimacy to the space—has played an essential role in this ongoing evolution. The advent of Ethereum, alongside the introduction of groundbreaking smart contracts, sparked new possibilities and fostered innovations that have further captivated the imagination of both investors and developers alike. Additionally, the gradual regulatory acceptance by governments around the globe, paired with the widespread adoption by various corporations and businesses, has significantly contributed to the impressive transformation of cryptocurrency—from what was once perceived as a fringe technology, existing on the periphery of finance, into a legitimate and mainstream asset that is now firmly established in today's complex global economy. This evolution continues to unfold, with new technologies and applications emerging regularly, ensuring that the story of Bitcoin and its companions remains an exciting and ever-developing narrative in financial history.

This logical, deeply analytical, and mind-blowing progression represents not solely a sequence of historical events; it stands as a powerful persuasive argument for the future of money and our economic interactions. The fascinating evolution of cryptocurrencies is fundamentally rooted in the same basic human drive for economic freedom, groundbreaking innovation, and the relentless pursuit of fairness that propelled the significant transition from barter systems to coinage centuries ago. The decentralized, transparent, and remarkably resilient nature of digital assets provides a vital solution to the inherent flaws and vulnerabilities of traditional, centralized financial systems that have long governed our complex economic interactions. As we delve deeper into this remarkable transformation, we begin to recognize the tremendous potential of cryptocurrencies to reshape the landscape of finance and define the way economic relationships are structured for generations to come. The implications of this evolution stretch far beyond mere transactions; they encompass a shift in power dynamics, a reimagining of trust in financial systems, and an unprecedented opportunity for individuals to reclaim control over their wealth and assets.

For modern investors, policymakers, and engaged citizens alike, these crucial milestones serve not only as a warning to heed but also as a significant source of profound inspiration. They challenge the existing status quo of state-controlled currency and power structures, providing a comprehensive blueprint for a future where economic power becomes increasingly distributed among the people. The remarkable and unprecedented rise of digital assets like Bitcoin and Ethereum signifies a fundamental shift in our economic landscape—this is a redefinition of value that is both astonishing in its vast scale and entirely logical in its evolution. It reflects changing attitudes towards money, trust, and ownership, showcasing a rapid transformation occurring within society that cannot be ignored. This evolution in economic thought and practice encourages active participation and engagement in financial systems, empowering individuals to take charge of their financial destinies.

In this transformative and exciting new era of financial innovation, the invaluable insights and lessons gleaned from the pivotal milestones achieved by crypto are undeniably unmistakable and increasingly evident. These lessons powerfully and effectively demonstrate that when individuals, communities, and organizations come together to harness the immense capabilities and potential of decentralized technology, they can indeed create a financial system that is not only significantly more efficient in operation and accessibility but also fundamentally more equitable and just in nature. The remarkable and inspiring journey of cryptocurrencies, which spans from their enigmatic and mysterious beginnings to their increasingly prevalent and mainstream acceptance in everyday life, stands as a powerful testament to the enduring power of human ingenuity, creativity, and perseverance. It serves as a poignant and powerful reminder that the future of money is not dictated or controlled by central authorities, traditional financial institutions, or existing systems of power, but rather shaped and defined by the collective will, innovative spirit, and determination of the people who actively engage with and support these innovative technologies. Furthermore, the ongoing evolution of this financial landscape has the potential to empower individuals, promote financial inclusivity, and pave the way for a more collaborative economic future.

Embrace this incredible revolution fully, and let these transformative milestones serve as your compass, guiding you into a fascinating world where financial innovation is not merely a possible scenario, but a tangible reality unfolding before your eyes. The future of money is already here, and it is decentralized—a truly shocking, mind-blowing vision that continues to reshape our global landscape remarkably, one transaction at a time. This evolution is creating countless opportunities and redefining how we perceive and interact with value in our daily lives, challenging traditional boundaries and opening doors to new possibilities we had only dreamed of before.

Section 4: Institutional Adoption and the Road to Mainstream Acceptance

In a world where digital currencies were once dismissed as nothing more than a quirky fringe experiment to be ignored by the majority in mainstream finance, the tide of perception has dramatically turned in a way that is both shocking and mind-blowing to a considerable number of observers from all walks of life. Over the past decade, a variety of major institutions, alongside a wide array of visionary investors, have not only embraced digital currencies with open arms—they have actively and enthusiastically helped to redefine what money truly means in the context of a modern, interconnected global economy. In this economy, transactions occur at unprecedented speeds, surpassing what many thought possible just a few short years ago. This section takes you on a comprehensive, detailed deep dive into the transformative journey from widespread skepticism to a state of genuine acceptance, thoroughly detailing the nuanced logical, analytical, and persuasive forces that drove institutional adoption. It also examines how these forces forged the complex, winding road that has led us to mainstream acceptance of digital currencies. This remarkable evolution reflects a significant and substantial shift in perspectives that has resonated globally across continents and reshaped financial landscapes in ways that cannot be underestimated.

The Early Days: From Rejection to Curiosity

In the very beginning, digital currencies such as Bitcoin were viewed by many as wild, speculative experiments fraught with a great deal of uncertainty. Financial pundits and traditionalists scoffed loudly and openly at the notion that money could exist in a purely digital format, especially without any backing from a government, central bank, or another authoritative entity that typically provides stability and trust to currency. Yet, even during these early and uncertain days, a small but determined group of tech enthusiasts, entrepreneurs, and libertarian idealists found themselves not only captivated but also inspired by the incredible potential of a decentralized monetary system. They perceived in Bitcoin not merely a tool for facilitating transactions but rather a radical challenge to centuries of established state-controlled currency systems. This passionate community believed fervently in a future where individuals could have far greater control over their finances, liberated from governmental oversight and interference that traditionally accompany financial transactions. They saw digital currency as an opportunity to promote financial freedom and innovation, opening doors to exciting new possibilities for economic interaction on a global scale that could transform the way people trade, save, and invest.

These early adopters were fueled by a fundamental yet remarkably potent idea: if money serves merely as a tool for exchange among people, then why should it be governed or controlled by any single authority or entity standing alone? Their revolutionary vision was truly startling because it fiercely challenged the very foundation upon which our conventional financial systems have long relied and have been built upon. While banks and governmental institutions had traditionally maintained strict control over the money supply and its flow through various mechanisms, these visionary pioneers contended that emerging technologies, particularly those rooted in decentralization, could ultimately free money from such restrictive constraints that had previously held it captive, thereby empowering individuals and fostering a new era of economic freedom, inclusivity, and personal autonomy that had never been experienced before.

This intellectual rebellion, characterized by its fervent passion and commitment, undeniably set the stage for the truly remarkable institutional revolution that was destined to unfold in the coming years with unrelenting momentum. As the technology continued to mature, evolve, and develop in increasingly sophisticated ways, a much broader and diverse audience began to take serious notice of its immense potential. What had once been considered merely a niche interest—often sidelined and underestimated—gradually evolved into an expansive and significant movement that commanded attention and respect from various sectors. This evolution ultimately caught the keen eye of institutional investors who recognized the transformative possibilities, as well as major corporations eager and enthusiastic to explore new and innovative opportunities on the horizon.

The Turning Point: A Surge in Value and Visibility

One of the most dramatic and influential turning points in the expansive history of digital currency came with the massive and unprecedented price surges that were witnessed in the mid-2010s. Bitcoin, which had been trading at comparatively modest levels for several years, began to experience explosive and remarkable growth that caught the attention of not just investors but also the general public. As the price started climbing steadily, so too did the public's awareness and understanding of digital currencies as a legitimate financial option. Major media outlets, financial analysts, and even longtime skeptics could no longer afford to ignore the burgeoning phenomenon that was cryptocurrencies. The rapid and significant appreciation in Bitcoin's value served as a tangible signal and powerful indicator that something profoundly big and transformative was indeed happening within the financial landscape.

This significant surge in value was not just a fleeting market phenomenon—it emerged as a pivotal catalyst for growing institutional interest. As large sums of money began flowing into these digital currencies, traditional investors and established financial institutions started to view them as increasingly viable assets. The volatility that had once acted as a deterrent for mainstream finance began to be reinterpreted in a more favorable light, seen as an opportunity rather than a risk to avoid. Early price spikes, although they were accompanied by dramatic swings and fluctuations, showcased that digital currencies could indeed generate outsized returns. This realization prompted hedge funds, seasoned asset managers, and even pension funds to take a closer look and reassess their stance on this evolving asset class. As this awareness spread, the landscape of investment began to shift, paving the way for a broader acceptance of cryptocurrencies within traditional finance.

The remarkable reality that Bitcoin's price could dramatically surge from just a few hundred dollars to several thousands within an impressively short span of time was, for numerous institutional investors, a clear and undeniable indication that this innovative new technology represented much more than merely a speculative bubble. It stood out as a transformative innovation that possessed the potential to fundamentally upend and reshape traditional financial paradigms in profound ways. The enticing allure of exceptionally high returns, combined with the enticing promise of a decentralized financial system that is immune to government manipulation and oversight, made digital currencies an exceptionally attractive alternative for those investors willing to look beyond the confines of conventional investment options and explore the vast possibilities of this emerging financial landscape.

Institutional Investment: The Arrival of the Big Players

As the market continued to mature, institutional investors began to make an increasingly significant presence felt. The entry of these major players into the digital currency space represented a watershed moment that firmly cemented crypto's long-term legitimacy in the eyes of the broader financial world. When established institutions such as hedge funds, prominent investment banks, and even sovereign wealth funds started to allocate substantial capital to digital assets, it sent a clear and undeniable message: cryptocurrencies were undeniably here to stay and were poised to become a crucial element of the global financial landscape.

One of the most influential and significant signs of institutional adoption in the financial landscape was undoubtedly the development of regulated investment vehicles tailored for cryptocurrencies. The introduction of Bitcoin futures and options, followed by the emergence of exchange-traded funds (ETFs), created a pathway for traditional investors to gain valuable exposure to digital currencies without necessitating direct management of the inherent technical challenges associated with owning cryptocurrency directly. This represented a logical evolution within the financial markets—by creating a diverse range of financial products that effectively bridged the gap between the conventional financial system and the evolving digital realm, these vehicles were able to provide an efficient way for institutional money to flow into the crypto markets while operating under familiar and established regulatory frameworks that they are used to navigating.

Moreover, several high-profile companies began to invest heavily in various digital currencies and assets. Companies like MicroStrategy and Tesla famously allocated significant portions of their corporate treasuries to Bitcoin and other cryptocurrencies, not merely as a speculative play intended for short-term gains, but as a strategic move designed to hedge against ongoing inflation and the risk of currency devaluation in the broader economic landscape. When a multi-billion-dollar corporation chooses to hold Bitcoin as an integral part of its long-term financial strategy, it challenges and disrupts every preconceived notion about the legitimacy, utility, and future potential of digital currencies in the global marketplace. This shift reflects a growing acceptance and recognition of the transformative power that these digital assets hold for the future of finance.

These moves were certainly not without their share of controversy and debate. Critics vocally argued that such significant investments were excessively risky and could potentially expose companies to unnecessary volatility and unforeseen financial turmoil. Nevertheless, the underlying logic behind these decisions was crystal clear. In an economic environment where governments possess the ability to print money at will, often leading to alarming inflation and subsequent devaluation of fiat currencies, holding a scarce digital asset such as Bitcoin provided a much-needed hedge against these pervasive risks. The very fact that corporate giants were willing to embrace this kind of financial risk indicated a seismic shift in the way the world at large began to view and understand the concept of money.

The Role of Technology: Blockchain and Beyond

At the heart of the institutional adoption of digital currencies lies the groundbreaking technology that makes digital currencies possible: blockchain. This innovative blockchain technology, characterized by its decentralized, transparent, and secure ledger, effectively addresses and alleviates many of the deep-seated concerns that institutional investors had regarding trust and accountability in financial transactions. Unlike traditional financial systems, which rely heavily on centralized institutions that are often vulnerable to corruption, mismanagement, and catastrophic failure, blockchain operates on a robust distributed network. In this system, no single party possesses complete control, and every transaction is meticulously recorded permanently, ensuring a high level of security and trustworthiness.

For institutional investors, this level of transparency is not only reassuring but also revolutionary in many ways. With blockchain technology, every single transaction and every movement of digital currency is verifiable by anyone with access. This open ledger system serves as a direct challenge to the opaque practices that have long characterized traditional centralized banking systems. The immutable nature of blockchain records ensures that the system remains tamper-proof, significantly reducing the risk of fraud while enhancing overall security in a dramatic fashion. This remarkable technological breakthrough has become a key factor in convincing institutional investors that digital currencies are not simply a passing fad, but rather a fundamentally sound innovation with lasting implications.

The technology within the realm of cryptocurrencies has continued to evolve significantly in ways that extend far beyond Bitcoin. Platforms such as Ethereum have greatly expanded the possibilities offered by blockchain technology by introducing innovative smart contracts. These smart contracts have the ability to automate complex financial transactions seamlessly and efficiently, eliminating the need for intermediaries. This groundbreaking innovation has given rise to an entire ecosystem of decentralized finance, commonly known as DeFi. Within this ecosystem, a wide range of financial services, including lending, borrowing, and trading, are conducted on fully decentralized platforms, transforming the landscape of finance as we know it. For institutions and enterprises, the logical progression from merely engaging with a simple digital asset to developing a comprehensive financial infrastructure is undeniably compelling. It opens up a new realm of possibilities and opportunities, whereby traditional financial products can be entirely reimagined in a decentralized, transparent manner. This shift not only enhances the efficiency and accessibility of financial services but also paves the way for a more inclusive financial system that empowers individuals and businesses alike.

Regulatory Shifts: Legitimacy Through Legal Recognition

As digital currencies grew in prominence and popularity, governments and regulatory bodies around the world were forced to confront their existence in an increasingly digital economy. Initially, the response from different nations was mixed—some countries outright banned cryptocurrencies due to concerns over security and illegal activities, while others adopted a cautious, wait-and-see approach, observing the market and its impacts. Over time, however, a discernible trend emerged: regulators began to recognize the legitimacy and potential of digital assets, prompting them to work towards integrating these currencies into the existing financial system. This shift not only influenced policy-making but also sparked discussions about how to effectively regulate and harness the benefits of cryptocurrencies for the economy.

This regulatory shift marked a pivotal milestone in the broader acceptance and recognition of cryptocurrencies in the mainstream financial landscape. When governments begin to acknowledge and impose regulations on a new asset class like crypto, it conveys a strong and compelling message to both investors and the general public. This acknowledgment signals that the innovation in question is substantial enough to merit legal oversight, demonstrating that it is not simply a passing trend or speculative bubble. The introduction of various regulatory frameworks played a significant role in stabilizing the cryptocurrency market by considerably reducing uncertainties and establishing clear and transparent guidelines for all participants involved. This important legal recognition provided the much-needed institutional green light that many cautious investors had been awaiting, effectively further cementing the position of cryptocurrencies within the complex structure of the global economy. As a result, we are witnessing an increasing trust in digital currencies that augurs well for their future development and integration into traditional financial systems.

For instance, in countries such as Japan and Switzerland, the regulatory bodies have taken significant steps to create highly favorable environments for digital currency exchanges. These measures ensure that the exchanges operate under high standards of transparency and security, which are essential for building trust among investors. Such initiatives not only serve to protect investors but also play a crucial role in encouraging and fostering further innovation within the digital currency space. As regulatory clarity continues to improve over time, institutional investors become increasingly likely to enter the market, bolstered by the confidence that the inherent risks are being managed effectively within a robust and well-structured legal framework.

Market Maturity: From Speculation to Strategic Asset Allocation

Another key factor that significantly contributed to the institutional adoption of digital currencies was the overall maturation of the crypto market over time. In the early years of this evolving landscape, the market was predominantly dominated by retail investors engaging in high-risk speculation. Price swings during this period were wild and erratic, which added a layer of uncertainty for potential investors. Furthermore, the lack of reliable infrastructure and regulatory clarity made it especially difficult for serious institutional investors to justify any substantial exposure to digital assets. As the market evolved, it gradually began to attract more sophisticated players who saw the potential for more stable investments.

Over time, however, the market began to mature significantly. With improved security measures, the development of reliable and trustworthy exchanges, along with the introduction of sophisticated financial products, the perception of crypto shifted from being a volatile playground to becoming a recognized and viable asset class. This notable evolution was primarily driven by the logic of market forces—a natural and inevitable progression from chaos to order in the financial landscape. As the market gradually stabilized and became more predictable, institutions began to see an opportunity to effectively diversify their portfolios with an asset that was largely uncorrelated with traditional investments. Digital currencies emerged as a promising hedge against inflationary pressures, a robust safeguard against increasingly prevalent geopolitical risks, and an alternative source of potential returns in an economic environment that is becoming more and more uncertain. This transformation not only attracted the interest of institutional investors but also encouraged a broader acceptance of digital currencies in mainstream finance, further solidifying their place in the investment world.

The transition from speculative trading to strategic asset allocation marked a truly pivotal moment in the evolving journey of cryptocurrencies. No longer were digital currencies merely viewed as transient tools for making a quick profit; they increasingly came to be recognized as significant long-term investments that could play a crucial and indispensable role in a well-diversified portfolio. This profound change in perception was driven by a complex combination of technological improvements, regulatory advancements that inspired confidence, and a much deeper understanding of the underlying economic principles guiding these assets. The analytical and logical framework supporting this important transition is undeniably clear: as the market continues to become more sophisticated and mature over time, the rational and strategic allocation of capital to digital assets becomes not just prudent but utterly necessary for serious investors aiming to navigate the future landscape of finance effectively.

Persuasion Through Proof: Real-World Success Stories

One of the most compelling and persuasive aspects of institutional adoption in recent times is the significant wealth of real-world success stories that have emerged with increasing visibility over the past decade. These remarkable stories are not mere isolated incidents; instead, they form a coherent and interconnected narrative that demonstrates the growing legitimacy and potential of digital currencies in various sectors. Each story contributes to a broader understanding of how these currencies can be integrated into existing financial systems and how they offer innovative solutions to longstanding challenges.

Take, for example, the fascinating story of MicroStrategy. Once a relatively small business software company, MicroStrategy underwent a remarkable transformation, evolving into one of the most prominent and influential corporate holders of Bitcoin in the modern age. By investing billions of dollars in digital assets, particularly Bitcoin, the company not only safeguarded its own value in an era marked by significant currency devaluation but also boldly signaled to the world that Bitcoin was indeed a serious and viable asset worthy of institutional interest. The company's dramatic and unprecedented rise in market capitalization served as a powerful, compelling argumentative case for the broader institutional acceptance and legitimization of cryptocurrencies, paving the way for a new era in digital finance.

In a similar manner, Tesla's significant and high-profile investment in Bitcoin sent shockwaves reverberating through the financial world and the markets at large. When a major, publicly traded company of Tesla's immense stature and influence made the bold decision to hold Bitcoin as an integral part of its treasury strategy, it fundamentally challenged conventional wisdom and typical norms. This move sparked a global conversation regarding the increasingly crucial role of digital assets in the realm of corporate finance today. These success stories presented tangible and compelling evidence that digital currencies could not only withstand the rigorous demands of institutional scrutiny but also deliver real and measurable value to investors and stakeholders alike. They were not simply theoretical constructs confined to academic discussion; they represented practical, real-world examples of how decentralization could effectively operate on a massive scale in a fast-evolving financial landscape.

The Impact on Global Finance: A New Economic Order

The institutional adoption of digital currencies carries with it a multitude of far-reaching implications for the entirety of the global financial system. This significant move represents a pivotal shift away from traditional centralized, state-controlled forms of money, paving the way towards a more decentralized and democratized model of economic exchange. Such a profound transformation is not merely a technological upgrade of the existing frameworks—it is a fundamental, comprehensive rethinking of the foundational principles behind how money is created, distributed, and ultimately valued in our economies. This evolution may significantly affect individual privacy, transaction efficiency, and overall financial inclusivity in various markets and communities.

As institutional investors gradually allocate an increasing amount of capital to digital assets, the traditional barriers that once clearly separated fiat currencies and cryptocurrencies begin to blur noticeably. Banks, which were previously wary and cautious of the disruptive potential that cryptocurrencies presented, are now actively and enthusiastically exploring the possibilities of blockchain technology in various ways, even going so far as to develop their own digital currencies that align with the evolving financial landscape. Central banks around the world are deeply investigating or even piloting a variety of central bank digital currencies (CBDCs), which are influenced in part by the decentralized ethos that underpins crypto while still retaining a significant measure of government control and oversight in their operations.

This hybridization of old concepts and new innovations is creating a truly dynamic and continuously evolving financial ecosystem. The legitimacy that arises from institutional adoption is compelling a thorough redefinition of what money truly means—a significant shift towards a system where the value of currency is determined by the collective, participatory actions of the global market rather than by the dictates of any single government or regulatory body. The implications of this transformation are staggering and profound: it means greater financial inclusion for underserved populations, increased transparency in transactions, and a far more resilient economic system that is capable of adapting effectively to the multifaceted challenges we face in the 21st century.

The Logical Imperative: Why Institutions Embraced Digital Currencies

The journey towards mainstream acceptance of digital currencies is underpinned by a clear, logical imperative that cannot be overstated. Institutions, by their very nature, tend to be risk-averse and cautious. They demand not only stability but also transparency and a clearly defined path to value preservation that they can trust. Bitcoin and its digital counterparts, with their innovative technology and decentralized design, initially appeared to be risky and unproven ventures in the eyes of many. However, over time, the logical and analytical case for these emerging assets became undeniably compelling. As more evidence surfaced regarding their potential, the perception shifted in favor of these digital alternatives to traditional financial systems.

The finite supply of Bitcoin, combined with its exceptionally robust security model, as well as its notable potential as a hedge against inflation, presented an increasingly compelling alternative to the traditional fiat currencies we have been accustomed to. Fiat currencies are often subject to the unpredictable whims of monetary policy, which can vary significantly over time and across contexts. The logic behind investing in Bitcoin was refreshingly straightforward: in an era where central banks have the ability to print money at will, this often leads to rampant inflation and currency devaluation. Therefore, holding onto a scarce, decentralized asset such as Bitcoin emerges as a rational, long-term strategy for effectively preserving and potentially growing wealth amidst such economic uncertainties.

Furthermore, the advent of groundbreaking blockchain technology has provided a highly transparent and immutable ledger that effectively addresses one of the most critical concerns facing institutional investors: trust. In a truly decentralized system, every transaction undergoes rigorous verification by a network of independent nodes, effectively eliminating the need for a trusted third party to mediate. This innovative distributed model of verification is not only logical; it serves as a compelling and powerful argument for a more secure and resilient financial system. The analytical evidence and research supporting decentralized finance are overwhelmingly robust, and this body of work has gradually won over even the most skeptical institutions, convincing them of the legitimacy and potential of this revolutionary approach.

Persuasive Lessons: Changing the Narrative of Money

The evolution of digital currencies, transitioning from a fringe experiment to a recognized and mainstream asset, represents one of the most compelling narratives of our time. It is a multifaceted story that boldly challenges conventional wisdom and compels us to reevaluate the very essence and nature of money itself. The journey of digital currencies has been marked by a remarkable series of shocking and mind-blowing milestones—each one serving as a powerful testament to the immense potential of decentralized innovation, along with the relentless and passionate pursuit of economic freedom that drives this movement forward.

For modern investors navigating the complexities of today's financial landscape, the persuasive lessons presented by digital currencies are clear and undeniable. These novel assets offer a compelling alternative to the centralized, often opaque financial systems that have long dominated and controlled the global economy. Digital currencies provide a remarkable level of transparency and security that simply cannot be matched by traditional financial institutions. They empower individuals significantly by democratizing access to wealth and financial resources, allowing more people to participate in the economy. The fact that numerous major institutions and corporations have now embraced digital currencies serves as a powerful validation of their immense potential. This trend stands as a persuasive signal that the future of money is evolving; it is not only digital but also decisively decentralized, allowing more individuals to take control of their financial destinies.

This narrative goes beyond merely discussing technology; it fundamentally addresses a significant shift in our perceptions and interactions with money. It serves as a powerful call to challenge established norms and conventions, advocating for the embrace of a new paradigm that prioritizes decentralization, transparency, and the empowerment of individuals within financial systems. The logical progression that we observe from initial skepticism to widespread mainstream acceptance is a clear and compelling indication that digital currencies have indeed arrived—not as a fleeting trend that might fade away, but as a permanent and transformative force within the global financial system, poised to redefine how we think about value, transactions, and our economic landscape in the years ahead. It invites us to rethink our relationship with traditional financial structures and encourages active participation in this evolving reality.

The Road Ahead: Embracing a New Financial Reality

As digital currencies continue to mature at a rapid pace, the implications for the global financial landscape are undeniably profound and far-reaching. Institutional adoption has strategically paved the way for a new era where the boundaries between traditional finance practices and the advancing world of decentralized digital assets are increasingly blurred and intertwined. This intersection is fostering the creation of a hybrid financial system that harmoniously leverages the strengths of both models. By effectively combining the stability and regulatory oversight that traditional finance offers with the remarkable innovation, transparency, and efficiency that blockchain technology facilitates, this transformation is reshaping how transactions, investments, and financial interactions occur on a global scale.

The road ahead is both thrilling and daunting at the same time. On one hand, the growing acceptance and embrace of digital currencies by major financial institutions, as well as regulatory bodies, clearly signals a future where these assets are set to play a central and pivotal role in the landscape of global finance. This acceptance might transform how transactions are conducted, creating new opportunities for innovation and efficiency in the market. On the other hand, the rapid pace of technological advancements and the inherent volatility that characterizes digital currencies indicate that this journey will undoubtedly not be without its share of significant obstacles and challenges. Yet, despite these hurdles, the logical, analytical, and persuasive arguments supporting the adoption and integration of digital currencies are robust and compelling enough to navigate and ultimately overcome these difficulties. The potential of digital currencies continues to inspire confidence and excitement within the financial community.

For policymakers, the rise of digital currencies presents an important warning as well as a significant opportunity. Traditional financial systems are increasingly showing their inherent limitations—inefficiencies, systemic corruption, and a high susceptibility to external economic shocks are becoming more obvious than ever before. The decentralized model inherent in digital currencies offers a rational alternative, one that promises enhanced transparency, greater accountability, and improved economic resilience. By actively embracing these technological innovations and adjusting regulatory frameworks to accommodate them appropriately, governments can create and nurture an environment that not only supports sustainable economic growth but also promotes broader financial inclusion for all citizens.

A New Paradigm for the Future of Money

The journey of digital currencies from the fringes to the mainstream is a compelling saga of relentless innovation, logical reasoning, and persuasive transformation that captivates many observers. The institutional adoption of various digital assets, illustrated by key milestones such as the introduction of well-regulated investment vehicles, strategic corporate treasury allocations, and growing global regulatory recognition, has irrevocably altered the landscape of modern finance in profound ways. This transformation encapsulates not only technological advancement but also shifts in societal perceptions and trust in these currencies.

Today, the remarkable rise of digital currencies is not merely a fleeting technological trend—it is a profound and fundamental shift in the way we conceive of money and value itself. The logical and analytical arguments that once seemed abstract and distant have now become concrete realities that we can all observe. As institutions and investors increasingly embrace the decentralized, transparent, and resilient nature of these digital assets, we witness an evolutionary process taking place. This evolution is a powerful, mind-blowing demonstration of human ingenuity and innovation—a clear and persuasive case for the future of money and financial interactions. This transformation in our financial landscape signifies not just a change, but a revolution in how we understand and interact with value in our daily lives.

As we look ahead to the future, the road toward achieving mainstream acceptance of digital currencies continues to progressively unfold before us. The convergence of various aspects such as technology, regulatory frameworks, and ever-evolving market dynamics is creating an innovative new financial ecosystem where trust is intricately woven into the very structure of the network itself. This transformative new paradigm holds the promise to not only democratize access to wealth but also enhance financial security significantly, thereby empowering individuals and communities around the globe in ways that were previously unimaginable.

In conclusion, the institutional adoption of digital currencies marks an essential and significant turning point in the long and evolving history of money. It represents not just a passing trend, but is a logical, analytical, and deeply persuasive transformation that challenges the established old guard of centralized finance. This revolutionary change paves the way for a future defined not only by economic freedom but also by unprecedented innovation. The road to mainstream acceptance has been undeniably long and tumultuous, filled with both challenges and triumphs, but the milestones that have been achieved so far serve as a powerful testament to the enduring promise and potential of digital currencies in reshaping the financial landscape.

Embrace this new and transformative reality. Allow the profound lessons learned from widespread institutional adoption to inspire you in rethinking your approach to money, encouraging you to look beyond the many limitations imposed by traditional finance. It is time to participate in a remarkable global revolution that is actively reshaping the very fabric of the world of wealth as we know it. The future of money is not just on the horizon; it is present and unfolding before us. It is decentralized, transparent, and relentlessly innovative—an extraordinary, mind-blowing vision that keeps evolving and adapting with each passing day, offering new possibilities and opportunities for all who engage with it.

Section 5: The Global Shift: Cryptocurrencies as the Future of Money

In a rapidly changing world where traditional financial systems are increasingly being called into question and often found inadequate, a new and revolutionary paradigm has emerged that is as shocking as it is profoundly transformative. Cryptocurrencies, which were once dismissed as a mere fringe experiment for tech-savvy rebels and enthusiasts, have now evolved to challenge the very foundations of our established global financial order. This section delves into the worldwide transition from traditional assets—such as gold, real estate, and various fiat currencies—to a decentralized financial system that is built upon blockchain technology and the innovative potential of digital assets. The journey we are witnessing is both mind-blowing and entirely logical, an evolution driven by our urgent necessity for change, groundbreaking technological innovations, and a profound desire for greater economic freedom and autonomy in our financial lives.

The story of this significant global shift begins with a simple yet revolutionary idea that has far-reaching implications: money, at its core, is fundamentally a social contract between individuals and societies. For centuries, governments and central banks have taken control of money, diligently managing its supply and determining its value through various policies and regulations. This centralization was originally designed to create not only stability but also a certain level of uniformity in trade practices across regions. However, over time, this centralized system has also morphed into a tool that can be used for political control and economic manipulation by those in power. As economies grew more complex, intricate, and interconnected, the drawbacks of state-controlled currency—such as rampant inflation, widespread corruption, and limited accessibility for the everyday individual—became increasingly glaring and apparent. Out of this widespread dissatisfaction among the populace arose the powerful belief that money should be liberated from these constraining frameworks and monopolistic systems, paving the way for the emergence of a decentralized financial paradigm that aims to empower individuals and create a more equitable economic landscape.

Cryptocurrencies represent a significant and radical departure from the concept of traditional money that has existed for centuries. They are built fundamentally on the innovative principle of decentralization, meaning that no single institution, entity, or government has absolute control over them at any point. Instead, cryptocurrencies are maintained and regulated by a vast global network of computers that continuously work together using complex algorithms and advanced technology. This decentralized system not only offers greater transparency but also ensures enhanced security and a degree of autonomy that traditional financial systems often struggle to match or replicate fully. In this new digital financial world, value is not dictated by central banks or government policies but rather emerges organically from the collective trust, engagement, and active participation of users from every corner of the globe. The emergence of this digital currency landscape is transforming how individuals view and use money in today's interconnected society.

One of the most compelling arguments for this significant shift toward cryptocurrency is the remarkable transparency that is inherent in blockchain technology. Each and every transaction made with any given cryptocurrency is recorded on a public ledger that anyone, anywhere, can inspect at any time. This means that there is absolutely no hidden manipulation of the money supply, no secretive printing of money behind closed doors, and no single point of failure that could potentially bring the entire system crashing down in an instant. For both investors and everyday users alike, this extraordinary level of openness helps to build a strong sense of trust—a trust that is absolutely essential for any sustainable financial system. This stands in stark contrast to traditional banking practices, where the opaque nature of operations has often led to numerous financial scandals and catastrophic crises over the years.

Moreover, the decentralized nature of cryptocurrencies allows for true global participation that is truly unprecedented. Traditional financial systems are typically tied to rigid national borders, with complex rules and regulations that vary significantly from country to country. This often leaves a substantial portion of the world's population either completely excluded from or significantly underserved by these traditional financial systems. Cryptocurrencies, on the other hand, transcend these limitations in remarkable ways. Anyone with access to an internet connection, regardless of their location or socioeconomic status, can easily access and utilize them, creating a truly expansive and global financial network. This democratization of money is not merely a compelling concept; it is a powerfully persuasive idea with far-reaching implications. It offers the potential to level the economic playing field in profound ways, enabling individuals in developing countries, or those who lack access to traditional banking services, to actively participate in and benefit from the global economy in meaningful ways.

The economic freedom offered by cryptocurrencies, as an innovative financial solution, significantly extends to how individuals store, manage, and transfer their wealth. In traditional financial systems, wealth is frequently tied up in physical assets such as real estate or precious metals, which may hold substantial value. However, these tangible assets are not always easily transferable and can be vulnerable to various risks, including theft, loss, or interference by regulatory bodies. In stark contrast, digital assets powered by cryptocurrency can be swiftly and securely transferred over vast distances, making them an appealing alternative. This remarkable ability to move money with minimal friction and barriers is especially pertinent in today's fast-paced and interconnected global economy, where transactions are conducted in real time and financial markets operate around the clock, 24 hours a day, seven days a week. The convenience and efficiency of cryptocurrencies pave the way for new financial possibilities that allow individuals to gain more control over their resources.

The global financial crisis of 2008 served as a pivotal turning point that underscored the profound vulnerabilities inherent in centralized monetary systems. When various governments and banks struggled significantly to manage the overwhelming fallout from this crisis, a growing number of individuals began to deeply question the wisdom of relying on institutions that had repeatedly failed to protect their interests. Out of this economic uncertainty and distress, Bitcoin emerged as a compelling beacon of hope—a decentralized currency that promised an innovative alternative to the flawed traditional financial systems that had contributed to the crisis. Bitcoin's remarkable subsequent rise in value captured the public's imagination and fascination, signaling the beginning of a global shift towards embracing digital money and currencies, potentially transforming the future of finance as we know it.

As institutional investors started to take considerable notice of the developments within the cryptocurrency space, the overall narrative surrounding cryptocurrencies began to undergo a significant transformation. What was initially regarded as a niche interest primarily for tech enthusiasts and early adopters morphed into a legitimate and viable asset class that was attracting the attention and involvement of major corporations, influential hedge funds, and even government entities around the world. These institutions were, at first, drawn to cryptocurrencies primarily as a safeguard against inflationary pressures and as a strategic means of diversifying their financial portfolios. However, as time progressed, the technology underpinning cryptocurrencies has matured significantly, and regulatory clarity has continued to improve, further solidifying the rationale for institutional investment in this evolving space. No longer was the global shift toward digital currencies regarded as a mere fringe phenomenon—it has now established itself as a fundamental transformation of the financial landscape that is reshaping how we perceive value, transaction methods, and the very nature of money itself. The incorporation of cryptocurrencies by these large investors signaled a new era, where innovative financial technologies play an integral role in shaping economic futures and investment strategies on an unprecedented scale.

One of the most important factors driving this remarkable transformation in the financial landscape is the finite and limited supply of many cryptocurrencies, with Bitcoin being the most notable example. Unlike fiat currencies, which can be printed endlessly and without restriction by central banks, Bitcoin has an immutable hard cap of 21 million coins. This inherent scarcity creates an intrinsic value proposition that is strikingly reminiscent of gold, which has been highly valued for thousands of years precisely because of its limited supply. In an economic environment where traditional currencies are often devalued and eroded by inflationary pressures, the scarcity of Bitcoin offers a logical, compelling, and persuasive reason for its adoption as a reliable store of value. This unique characteristic distinguishes Bitcoin in the digital currency market, positioning it as a sought-after asset that many believe can withstand the test of time and economic turbulence.

Another significant and noteworthy milestone in the ongoing global shift toward digital currencies is the substantial development of robust, well-regulated platforms designed specifically for trading and investment. In the early days of its history, the cryptocurrency market was often marked by wild price swings and a glaring lack of regulatory oversight, which made it notably difficult for traditional investors to take the market seriously or engage with it confidently. Over the years, however, a range of exchanges and innovative financial products, such as futures and exchange-traded funds (ETFs), have been developed to provide a much more stable and regulated environment for trading and investment. These critical innovations have played a crucial role in bridging the gap between the traditional financial world and the rapidly emerging realm of digital assets. As a result, the evolution of these platforms has made it significantly easier for institutions and individual investors alike to invest in cryptocurrencies with a sense of confidence and security.

The regulatory landscape has significantly evolved to actively support this transformative shift in the financial system. Initially, many governments around the world were quite hostile to cryptocurrencies, citing various concerns about issues such as fraud, money laundering, and the glaring lack of consumer protection mechanisms. However, as the cryptocurrency market matured and the potential benefits of digital currencies became increasingly apparent, regulatory bodies began to adopt more nuanced and sophisticated approaches to regulation. Countries like Japan, Switzerland, and Singapore have successfully emerged as major hubs for cryptocurrency innovation, offering clear and comprehensive guidelines that not only protect investors but also encourage ongoing technological advancement in the sector. This shift towards regulatory acceptance has proven to be a crucial factor in the process of legitimizing digital currencies on the global stage, fostering an environment where innovation can thrive while maintaining necessary safeguards for consumers and investors alike.

The global transition from traditional assets to a decentralized financial paradigm is not merely about technology or economics—it's also deeply rooted in evolving ideology. Centralized financial systems have long been synonymous with significant power imbalances and pervasive economic inequality. The concentration of money and financial control in the hands of a select few individuals and institutions has frequently resulted in economic policies that disproportionately benefit the wealthy at the expense of the larger population. Cryptocurrencies present a revolutionary alternative to this status quo. By decentralizing control over money and financial transactions, they empower individuals and provide a mechanism for a more equitable distribution of wealth across society. This transformative vision of economic democracy is both shocking to some and persuasive to many—it boldly challenges the entrenched power structures of the past and presents a new pathway toward establishing a fairer, more inclusive financial system that works for everyone, not just a privileged elite.

For many individuals, the very idea that digital currencies could evolve into the future of our monetary system was once deemed unthinkable. The notion that a decentralized network of computers could efficiently manage the global money supply without any oversight from governments or banks seemed to many like pure science fiction. However, the evidence is rapidly mounting that this vision is not only possible, but is already well underway. The meteoric rise of Bitcoin, along with the subsequent proliferation of thousands of altcoins, stands as a powerful testament to the transformative potential of decentralized technology. These remarkable developments have compelled even the most skeptical institutions and financial experts to seriously reconsider their stance on money, currency, and intrinsic value in today's digital age.

The impact of this significant global shift is indeed profound and far-reaching. In traditional financial systems, value is often measured by a variety of tangible assets, such as property, physical gold, or reliable government bonds. However, in this rapidly evolving digital age, value is increasingly determined by a combination of network effects, groundbreaking technological innovation, and the trust established among users and investors alike. Digital currencies, with their unique decentralized structures and transparent ledgers, represent a fundamentally new and transformative way of creating, managing, and preserving value in society. These assets are not subject to the same vulnerabilities and risks that often affect fiat currencies, which can be severely devalued by unpredictable political decisions and inflationary policies imposed by governments. Instead, digital assets derive their value primarily from the trust and confidence of their users, along with the inherent scarcity that is deliberately built into their design and framework. This shift presents both exciting opportunities and challenges that require careful consideration and adaptation from all stakeholders involved.

This shift towards a new financial paradigm has broad and far-reaching implications for how economies globally function. For one, it democratizes and expands access to various financial services and opportunities. In many diverse parts of the world, traditional banking systems are often inaccessible or blatantly unreliable. Cryptocurrencies, by contrast, are readily available to anyone equipped with an internet connection, regardless of their geographical location or economic status. This remarkable inclusivity has the potential to significantly transform and reshape economies by empowering individuals who have long been excluded from the financial mainstream, thereby paving the way for a more equitable economic landscape.

Furthermore, the decentralization of money significantly fosters and encourages innovation across various sectors. When value is determined by a vast, interconnected global network, rather than being dictated by a central authority, it creates much more room for creative solutions and competitive dynamics to flourish. This open landscape allows startups and entrepreneurs to experiment with diverse new financial models. By leveraging cutting-edge blockchain technology, they can create revolutionary products and services that were previously deemed unimaginable. This dynamic and ever-evolving environment continually drives improvement and adaptation, ensuring that the financial system progresses and evolves in response to the rapidly changing needs and challenges faced by society and the marketplace. The result is a more resilient and responsive financial ecosystem.

Critically, the global shift towards digital currencies represents not merely a matter of technological innovation—it embodies a fundamental rethinking of the intricate social contract that exists between individuals, institutions, and governments. For centuries, the control of money has stood as a central and influential source of power. Central banks and government treasuries have wielded this significant power to steer and influence economies, often acting in ways that are to the detriment of the general populace and the average citizen. The emergence of digital currencies boldly challenges this entrenched concentration of power, proposing instead a system in which money is managed collectively, thereby becoming transparent and accessible to all members of society. This philosophical shift, in essence, is as revolutionary as the technology that underpins it, promising to reshape the global order and existing financial landscape in ways that are both profoundly impactful and far-reaching. The implications of this transition could lead to a redefined relationship between citizens and their governments, promoting greater financial equity and empowerment for individual users around the globe.

The journey toward mainstream acceptance of digital currencies is marked by a series of pivotal milestones that collectively illustrate the logical progression from initial skepticism to widespread adoption across various segments of society. In the early days of digital currencies, Bitcoin was predominantly seen as a niche asset, largely favored by a small yet passionate group of technologists and libertarians who understood its underlying technology. Its initial price was rather modest and unremarkable, and its potential was frequently dismissed by many seasoned investors as a mere passing fad without any substantial future. However, as the technology behind Bitcoin matured and the benefits of decentralization became increasingly clear to a broader audience, more and more investors began to view Bitcoin not merely as a speculative asset but also as a viable store of value and an effective hedge against economic uncertainty and inflationary pressures. This shift in perception paved the way for greater acceptance and integration of digital currencies into the financial mainstream, allowing for their growth and increased recognition as legitimate financial instruments.

Institutional investors played a truly pivotal role in this remarkable transformation. As large-scale investors, hedge funds, along with various corporations, began to allocate significant capital to digital assets, the overall credibility of the market grew exponentially. The development of regulated investment products, including Bitcoin futures and Exchange-Traded Funds (ETFs), created a crucial bridge for traditional investors to enter the dynamic space of cryptocurrencies. This substantial influx of institutional capital not only stabilized the market but also sent a powerful and compelling signal that cryptocurrencies were indeed here to stay for the long haul. It marked the significant beginning of the global transition from traditional assets to a more decentralized and innovative financial system, altering the landscape of investment.

The emergence and rise of digital currencies can be seen as a direct response to the numerous failures that have plagued the traditional financial system for years. In the aftermath of the global financial crisis that occurred in 2008, the trust placed in banks and central authorities suffered a significant and profound erosion. People from various backgrounds witnessed firsthand how centralized control over money could lead to catastrophic consequences—massive bailouts that burdened taxpayers, soaring public debt that threatened economies, and an overall loss of individual financial autonomy. In stark contrast, the inherently decentralized nature of cryptocurrencies gives them an edge, providing an alternative that is fundamentally resistant to such systemic failures. By removing the need for a central authority, digital currencies enhance the level of transparency and security in transactions, which traditional financial systems simply cannot match or replicate. This shift towards decentralized forms of currency reflects a growing desire among individuals for more control over their financial resources and a move away from the vulnerabilities associated with conventional monetary systems.

Furthermore, the numerous technological innovations that underpin the emerging realm of digital currencies have significantly paved the way for a more dynamic and highly responsive economic system that adapts to the fluctuations of global markets. Blockchain technology, which serves as the integral backbone of cryptocurrencies, facilitates the creation of a decentralized ledger wherein every single transaction is meticulously recorded and easily verifiable by all parties involved. This inherent transparency is a key factor in building and maintaining trust—an absolutely critical element in any successful financial system. Additionally, it allows for a more efficient and highly accurate tracking of value, thereby markedly reducing the potential for fraud and mismanagement that has plagued traditional financial systems. The logical implications of these developments are nothing short of profound: with the advent of blockchain, the very concept of money is entirely reimagined, giving rise to a system that is not only more secure but also far more efficient, flexible, and readily adaptable to the diverse needs of an increasingly interconnected and globalized economy.

In addition to their unique characteristics, the digital nature of cryptocurrencies means that they are not restricted by geographical or political constraints in any manner. Unlike traditional assets such as gold and fiat currencies, which are inherently tied to specific physical locations and inevitably subject to varying national policies and regulations, cryptocurrencies operate in a boundless digital realm that effortlessly transcends borders. This allows for incredibly seamless and efficient global transactions, paving the way for a new financial landscape. The universality of cryptocurrencies and their decentralized nature represent a substantial game-changer in today's increasingly interconnected world, where trade and finance are steadily becoming more borderless than ever before. The global shift toward decentralized finance is not merely a trend; it is a natural and logical response to these new realities of the digital age—a vital and necessary evolution in a world where traditional physical limitations no longer pose significant barriers to economic activity, allowing for innovative possibilities that can be harnessed worldwide.

The economic logic driving this significant global shift is both compelling and multifaceted. Digital currencies introduce a remarkable level of decentralization that not only enhances individual autonomy but also bolsters systemic resilience across diverse financial landscapes. By decentralizing the control of monetary systems, they create an environment in which value is dynamically determined by the market's own forces, rather than being dictated by the decisions and interests of a limited number of centralized entities. This fundamental shift in control is not merely a technical innovation; it represents a profound philosophical transformation—a deliberate move toward establishing a more democratic and equitable financial system for all participants. The persuasive argument supporting this idea is quite clear and straightforward: if money is to genuinely serve the best interests of the people, it must be liberated from the restrictive confines of state control. It is essential that currency is allowed to evolve naturally in a decentralized, transparent manner, reflecting the true needs and desires of the individuals who use it.

Regulators around the world have begun to recognize and embrace this tremendous potential that cryptocurrencies offer to the global economy. Initially, many governments were quite hostile to the idea of cryptocurrencies, viewing them primarily as a significant threat to national monetary sovereignty and economic stability. Their reluctance stemmed from concerns over security, fraud, and the unregulated nature of these digital assets. However, over time, it became increasingly clear that digital currencies were not only viable alternatives to traditional financial systems but that they were also here to stay, becoming a permanent fixture in the financial landscape. Countries like Japan, Switzerland, and Singapore have taken the lead in developing comprehensive regulatory frameworks that actively support crypto innovation while simultaneously protecting investors from potential pitfalls. This evolution in regulatory attitudes is a key milestone in the global shift toward adopting and integrating digital currencies—it represents a significant convergence of advanced technology, growing market demand, and astute legal oversight that lends enduring legitimacy to the entire cryptocurrency ecosystem, fostering further development and broader acceptance of these digital assets.

Institutional adoption has undeniably emerged as a crucial driver of this significant shift in the financial landscape. When major corporations and influential financial institutions begin to invest substantial resources in digital assets, it serves as a powerful signal that this groundbreaking technology has transcended the realm of pure speculation and has entered a new phase of legitimacy. Companies like MicroStrategy, Tesla, and Square have made headlines for their massive holdings, often amounting to billions of dollars, in Bitcoin. This bold strategy demonstrates that digital currencies can function effectively as a stable store of value while also acting as a robust hedge against various traditional financial risks. Moreover, the actions taken by these forward-thinking corporations not only bolster public confidence in digital currencies but also play a significant role in accelerating the integration of these innovative financial instruments into mainstream financial practices and investment strategies. As more institutions follow suit, the landscape of finance continues to evolve, embracing the potential that digital assets hold in the modern economy.

The persuasive power of this significant global shift is strikingly evident in the sheer scale and magnitude of the profound change. In just a matter of a few short years, cryptocurrencies have moved from a state of relative obscurity to becoming an absolutely fundamental part of the global financial landscape that we all navigate today. This rapid transformation is nothing short of mind-blowing—it challenges everything we once thought and believed about money, and it highlights the incredible pace of both technological and economic evolution that we are witnessing in our times. The future of money, as clearly evidenced by the remarkable rise of various digital currencies, is increasingly decentralized, borderless, and driven by the collective power and agency of individuals rather than by centralized authorities or institutions that have traditionally governed the financial systems.

The implications of this significant shift are vast and profound. A decentralized financial system offers greater financial inclusion, enabling individuals in underbanked or unstable regions to access global markets and participate in economic activities that were previously out of reach. It fosters innovation by encouraging competition among various players in the market and rewarding creative solutions that can lead to better financial products and services. Furthermore, it enhances economic resilience by distributing risk across a wide network of participants rather than concentrating it in a single institution or entity. These benefits are not merely theoretical—they are already being practically realized in various parts of the world, from established financial centers with robust infrastructures to emerging economies that are rapidly adopting new technologies and approaches to finance. As we witness this transformation, the opportunities that arise are changing the landscape of global finance for the better.

For the modern investor, the global shift toward digital currencies is not just a mere trend but a persuasive call to embrace a whole new era of finance. The traditional financial system, with its heavy reliance on state-controlled money and centralized institutions, has unfortunately shown its vulnerabilities time and again, particularly during economic downturns and financial crises. In contrast, digital currencies and cryptocurrency technologies offer a promising future that is defined not only by transparency and efficiency but also by inclusivity for everyone. The logic behind investing in these digital assets is undeniably compelling: if the primary goal of money is to facilitate trade, store value effectively, and empower individuals across the globe, then a decentralized system that eliminates intermediaries and redistributes control among users is undoubtedly the logical next step forward. This transformation has the potential to reshape the landscape of finance, leveling the playing field and providing new opportunities for individuals and businesses alike.

The road to mainstream acceptance is still very much under construction, and numerous challenges continue to remain. Volatility in the market, regulatory uncertainty, along with various technological hurdles are indeed real issues that must be thoroughly addressed in order to move forward. However, the undeniable global momentum behind digital currencies cannot be ignored. As more and more institutions, regulators, and individuals begin to come to a greater understanding and appreciation of the many benefits that decentralization offers, the vision of a truly decentralized financial system is becoming increasingly clear and achievable. It foresees a future where the power of money is genuinely democratized, where transparency is seamlessly built into every single transaction, and where the ideals of economic freedom and opportunity are available to everyone, regardless of their background or circumstances.

In conclusion, the global shift toward cryptocurrencies represents a logical, analytical, and profoundly persuasive evolution in the way we fundamentally think about money in today's society. This transformation signifies a remarkable journey from the traditional, centralized models that have dominated the financial landscape of the past to a future that is increasingly defined by decentralization and remarkable digital innovation. The evidence supporting this shift is overwhelmingly compelling: digital currencies offer an innovative, more efficient, secure, and inclusive way to manage value in a rapidly changing world. The significant rise of institutional adoption, growing regulatory acceptance, and extraordinary technological breakthroughs have collectively cemented crypto's legitimacy in the economy, clearly signaling that the future of money, as we once knew it, is indeed here, and it is digital in every sense of the word.

This transformation is not only shocking but also incredibly inspiring—a mind-blowing testament to the remarkable ingenuity of humans and the relentless pursuit of economic freedom that drives them forward. The extraordinary journey we are witnessing, from a world dominated by state-controlled currency to one thriving on decentralized digital assets, is far from being just a simple story of technological advancement; it represents a profound and fundamental rethinking of the very essence of what money is and what it can truly become. This sweeping global shift toward the adoption of cryptocurrencies challenges each one of us to embrace a future where money is not bound by the constraints of centralized control, but rather empowered by the collective will and autonomy of individuals across the globe, illuminating the path toward a more liberated economic landscape.

As you take time to consider the future of money in the coming years, it's crucial to understand that this shift we are witnessing is not merely a passing trend that will fade away but rather an inevitable evolution of the financial landscape. The logical and persuasive arguments advocating for decentralization, when combined with the overwhelming evidence of technological advancements and significant institutional progress, make it abundantly clear that cryptocurrencies are poised to fundamentally redefine the entire global financial system we know today. While the road ahead may be fraught with numerous challenges and potential obstacles, the significant potential rewards—a more transparent, inclusive, and resilient financial ecosystem that benefits everyone—are far too important to ignore or overlook in our discussions about the future.

Embrace the global shift toward a new financial future. Recognize that the future of money is undeniably decentralized, and that digital currencies now offer an unparalleled opportunity for deep economic empowerment which many never thought possible. The traditional paradigms of finance are currently being dramatically reshaped before our very eyes in ways that we are only beginning to understand. The new era of digital money is not merely a speculative dream; it is a logical, inevitable, and truly transformative reality that is unfolding all around us. The ongoing journey from centralized control to decentralized innovation is undoubtedly one of the most profound and significant shifts in human history—a shift that promises to democratize wealth, empower individuals to take charge of their financial destinies, and build a better, more inclusive world for generations to come. As we navigate this exciting transition, we have the chance to redefine economic relationships and create systems that work for everyone. This is a moment of immense potential.

Chapter 4: The History of Cryptocurrency Wallets

Section 1: Early Wallets: From Paper to Software Solutions

In the vast and rapidly evolving world of digital currencies, one of the most fascinating and mind-blowing stories is that of early wallets—the humble beginnings of a technology that today secures billions of dollars in digital assets and influences financial transactions on a global scale. Long before our smartphones housed sophisticated wallet applications that allow for seamless transfers and payments, people relied on primitive methods to store, transfer, and secure their digital wealth, often employing rudimentary systems that reflected the limitations of the times. The evolution from simple, paper-based systems to advanced software solutions is not merely a technical upgrade; it is a remarkable journey of human ingenuity, logical reasoning, and relentless innovation that transformed how we perceive, manage, and interact with money in an increasingly digital economy. This section explores that shocking transformation in detail, unraveling the complexities with plain, natural language and a persuasive, analytical approach that invites readers to appreciate the profound impact of this technological evolution on our daily lives and the broader financial landscape.

The Humble Beginnings: Paper Wallets and Analog Methods

Imagine a time when the very notion of "digital money" was almost inconceivable—a fascinating period when people had to devise ingenious and creative methods to securely store their cryptographic keys on nothing more than paper. In those early days of Bitcoin, one of the foremost challenges every user faced was the secure storage of private keys. These keys are essentially the unique passwords that grant access to one's precious digital funds. Without a central bank to safeguard their money like traditional systems, early adopters had to rely on physical means and clever strategies to ensure that their keys—and thus their valuable coins—remained secure and safe from unauthorized access. This challenge sparked a wave of innovation in security practices among a community of passionate believers in the promise of cryptocurrency, illustrating the lengths to which individuals would go to protect their digital assets.

Paper wallets emerged as the very first widely used and popular method for securely storing cryptocurrencies and digital assets for this purpose. A paper wallet is, in its most simplistic form, essentially a physical piece of paper on which the public and private keys are meticulously printed. The concept is as straightforward as it is astonishing: by carefully printing out your immutable digital keys, you create a cold, offline record that is completely immune to hacking attempts over the internet and unauthorized access. This groundbreaking method was revolutionary in its time because it granted users the ability to take complete and absolute control of their valuable digital assets without having to rely on potentially risky third-party services or platforms.

However, paper wallets came with their own set of significant challenges and drawbacks. They were particularly vulnerable to physical damage, loss, or outright theft, making them a risky choice for storing crucial information. A single unfortunate event, such as a smudge of water, a tear in the paper, or a misplacement within a messy drawer could all too easily result in the irreversible loss of access to valuable digital funds. Despite these considerable risks associated with their use, many early Bitcoin users chose to embrace paper wallets, as they represented the best and most practical solution available at the time when digital security was still very much in its infancy and not yet well developed.

The reasoning behind the concept of the paper wallet was both astute and compelling: by ensuring that your private keys remain offline, you drastically diminish the risk of potential online attacks that could compromise your holdings. This represented a brave and bold departure from the traditional reliance on banks and various online security protocols that have been commonly embraced. It was a groundbreaking early experiment in taking back control from centralized institutions, pushing the boundaries of personal finance, and entrusting security and responsibility to the individual user. This growing ideology would ultimately evolve into a fundamental cornerstone of the decentralized financial movement that seeks to empower individuals and foster greater autonomy in managing their financial assets.

The Shift to Software Wallets: Embracing Digital Innovation

As Bitcoin and other cryptocurrencies began to gain significant traction in the financial landscape, the limitations of paper wallets became increasingly apparent to users and enthusiasts alike. While these paper wallets offered unparalleled security against various digital threats, their physical nature made them cumbersome and impractical for everyday use and transactions. Managing physical documents for digital keys proved to be a hindrance, as it was not a scalable solution in the rapidly expanding digital economy. The growing demand for a more user-friendly and efficient method of storing and accessing cryptocurrency securely led to the birth and development of software wallets, which provided a promising alternative to traditional paper wallets.

Software wallets are sophisticated applications or programs that are specifically designed to securely store digital keys, which are crucial for managing and facilitating transactions in the digital realm. They represent a significant leap forward and improvement from the outdated analog methods of the past. Unlike traditional paper wallets, software wallets provide the added advantage of being easily updated, backed up, and protected with an array of additional security measures. These can include strong passwords, two-factor authentication, and sophisticated encryption techniques. With these features, users can enjoy greater peace of mind and enhanced security in handling their digital assets.

The transition to software wallets was an entirely logical and necessary response to the steadily growing needs of an ever-expanding crypto community, which had begun to emerge in response to the rise in popularity of digital currencies. As more individuals started to hold and trade various digital assets, the increasing importance of convenience and accessibility became an undeniable factor that could no longer be ignored. Software wallets provided users with unparalleled flexibility, allowing them to seamlessly interact with their funds on a daily basis—whether they were making transactions, checking balances, or managing their diverse assets, all with just a few simple clicks. This development represented a transformative innovation that fundamentally made the use of digital currencies not only feasible but also practical and user-friendly for mainstream adoption.

Moreover, software wallets have significantly paved the way for a vast array of additional functionalities that cater to diverse user needs. They represented the very first step toward the establishment of a comprehensive ecosystem comprising digital financial services that are not only innovative but also user-friendly. With the advent of mobile wallets, users could conveniently carry their digital assets right in their pockets, thereby allowing for real-time transactions that are quick and efficient. This development facilitated the seamless integration of cryptocurrency into everyday life, transcending traditional financial barriers. The evolution from the use of paper to that of software was not merely about enhancing security protocols; it was fundamentally about improving usability, promoting innovation, and reflecting the logical progression of technological advancements in the digital financial landscape. The ongoing transformation continues to shape how individuals interact with their finances and conduct transactions in a whole new way.

The Analytical Advantages: Enhanced Security, Backup, and Recovery

One of the most compelling aspects of software wallets is the significant enhancement they have made in addressing the security and recovery issues that are often inherent in the use of paper wallets. With traditional paper wallets, the physical medium represented the sole record of your private keys. If you happened to lose the paper, or if it became damaged in any way, there was absolutely no practical way to recover your funds or access your cryptocurrency. Software wallets, on the other hand, introduced a range of sophisticated backup and recovery mechanisms that greatly mitigate this risk. They come equipped with various features designed to ensure that your assets remain secure and easily recoverable, should you ever encounter any issues.

Modern software wallets generally come equipped with a variety of important features, one of the most notable being the utilization of mnemonic phrases. These phrases consist of a series of carefully chosen words that serve as a crucial tool for recovering your wallet in the event that your device is lost or suffers any kind of damage. This straightforward yet highly effective method for securing one's digital assets has emerged as a direct response to the logical and essential need for reliability during financial transactions. The capability to easily back up and restore access to a wallet not only offers users a greater sense of peace of mind, but it also significantly diminishes the risk of experiencing a permanent loss of their valuable financial resources.

Furthermore, software wallets have the capability to integrate a variety of additional layers of security measures, such as biometric authentication techniques and multi-signature functionality options. These enhancements significantly increase the level of difficulty for unauthorized users attempting to gain access to the wallet, effectively combining cutting-edge digital innovation with practical and essential security measures. The reasoning behind the implementation of these features is straightforward and clear: as digital assets gain value and importance, the necessity for robust and comprehensive security measures increases sharply. Software wallets provide a dynamic and scalable solution that can adapt and evolve with the ever-changing threat landscape—a logical necessity in our current environment, where cyber attacks are not only frequent but also becoming increasingly sophisticated and complex in nature.

The Role of Open-Source Innovation

A critical factor contributing significantly to the rise of software wallets in the digital finance space is undoubtedly the open-source movement. In fact, many of the early software wallets were developed as open-source projects, which means that their underlying code was freely available for anyone to review, modify, and enhance in various ways. This level of transparency not only fostered a greater sense of trust among users within the crypto community but also spurred rapid and continuous innovation. Developers from diverse backgrounds and regions across the globe could actively contribute to the ongoing improvement of these wallets, identifying potential vulnerabilities and proposing meaningful enhancements. This collaborative approach ultimately led to more secure and user-friendly wallet solutions that could adapt quickly to changing needs and emerging threats in the ever-evolving landscape of cryptocurrency.

The open-source model stands as a remarkably powerful and transformative example of collective intelligence working effectively in action. It truly embodies the very essence and spirit of decentralization by ensuring that no single individual or entity has overarching control over the software—a principle that closely mirrors and aligns with the broader goals and philosophies of various cryptocurrencies. The collaborative and communal nature inherent in open-source projects significantly accelerates technological progress and advancement while providing a robust, thoroughly peer-reviewed foundation for security measures. This logical, community-driven approach to innovation has been a vital cornerstone in the ongoing development of software wallets, and it continues to drive ongoing improvements and advancements in this dynamic field.

Real-World Challenges and Adaptations

Despite the many advantages that software wallets offer in terms of convenience and accessibility, the transition from traditional paper wallets to digital formats was not without its considerable challenges. In fact, early iterations of software wallets were sometimes plagued by numerous bugs, significant security vulnerabilities, and various usability issues that made them difficult for the average user to navigate. The learning curve for new users was indeed steep, as they often struggled to understand how to operate these emerging technologies effectively. Furthermore, the technology itself was still rapidly evolving, leading to further confusion for those trying to adapt. However, these challenges were met with a logical, methodical, and analytical approach by dedicated developers: through continuous improvement, rigorous testing, and active community collaboration, developers were able to refine and enhance software wallets to the point where they became increasingly secure and remarkably user-friendly for everyone.

For instance, the development of hardware wallets—specialized devices that efficiently store private keys in a secure, offline environment—can be seen as a strategic adaptation to the inherent shortcomings of early software solutions that were prevalent in the digital asset management landscape. While hardware wallets are not purely software-based solutions, they effectively represent a hybrid approach that artfully combines the convenience of digital management with the heightened security that comes from physical isolation. This significant innovation was a direct response to the various limitations faced by software wallets and serves to clearly demonstrate the iterative nature of technological progress in the realm of cryptocurrency and digital assets. Every challenge encountered during the evolution of these technologies led to the emergence of a new solution, thereby further cementing the crucial role of software in the ongoing management of digital assets and ensuring greater safety for users engaged in transactions in a digital environment.

The Impact on User Behavior and Market Dynamics

The shift to software wallets has had a profound and lasting impact on user behavior, as well as the overall dynamics of the crypto market. As wallets have become increasingly accessible and user-friendly, a significantly wider audience has begun to actively participate in the burgeoning digital economy. No longer confined solely to tech experts, enthusiasts, and early adopters, cryptocurrencies have now become readily available to virtually anyone with a smartphone or a computer device. This broad democratization of access is undeniably one of the most persuasive and compelling arguments for the ongoing evolution of wallet technology within the rapidly changing landscape of digital currencies.

With increased participation from a diverse range of participants, the overall volume of transactions grew exponentially, driving further significant innovation in the infrastructure supporting various digital assets. Software wallets played a crucial role in this evolution, enabling a host of new applications to emerge, ranging from mobile payments and peer-to-peer transactions to more sophisticated trading platforms and decentralized finance (DeFi) applications. The logical consequence of this increased adoption was not just acceleration in market growth, but the creation of a self-reinforcing cycle where a surge in users drove the continuous development of better, more secure wallets. This ongoing improvement in technology, in turn, attracted an even larger number of users, creating a dynamic ecosystem that thrived on interaction and innovation.

The rise of software wallets has significantly changed the way people perceive and engage with the storage and management of their wealth. Once, individuals relied heavily on physical documents and tangible objects as the standard means of managing finances, but the advent of digital solutions has introduced a remarkable level of flexibility and immediacy that was previously unimaginable. Transactions that once took days or even weeks to process can now be completed in mere seconds, allowing for almost instantaneous financial exchanges. This newfound ability to manage funds in real time has revolutionized everyday financial interactions, reshaping how individuals and businesses conduct their monetary affairs. This dramatic shift in behavior and practices is a powerful testament to the relentless advancement of technological innovation and serves as a clear indicator that the future of money is not just leaning towards, but is actively becoming digital. The implications of this transformation are profound, as they signal a changing landscape in which traditional methods are increasingly being replaced by digital alternatives, fundamentally altering our relationship with money itself.

The Broader Economic and Social Implications

The evolution from traditional paper wallets to advanced software solutions is not just an isolated phenomenon—it represents a significant part of a broader transformation in the way modern societies manage and perceive the concept of money itself. As digital wallets increasingly became the norm, they effectively laid the groundwork for the development of sophisticated decentralized financial systems that extend far beyond mere storage solutions. In today's landscape, software wallets play a vital and critical role within the crypto ecosystem, serving as essential gateways to a vast world of digital assets, intricate smart contracts, and groundbreaking financial innovation. These wallets have not only changed the way we store value but have also revolutionized the entire landscape of financial transactions and interactions.

This transformation carries significant implications for global finance and society as a whole. Digital wallets truly empower individuals by providing them with direct control over their funds, allowing them to bypass the traditional need for financial intermediaries, such as banks. This notable shift can be seen as a logical and necessary response to the long-standing issues of financial exclusion and inequality that many people face today. In numerous parts of the world, individuals are unfairly denied access to basic banking services due to various geographical or economic barriers that exist around them. Software wallets, which can be accessed with minimal infrastructure, present a robust solution that is both practical and transformative, enabling greater financial accessibility for underserved populations, fostering inclusion, and enhancing economic participation across diverse communities.

Furthermore, the rapid proliferation of software wallets has significantly accelerated the pace of economic innovation across various sectors. With secure and easily accessible tools for managing digital assets, a diverse range of entrepreneurs and innovative developers are now free to experiment with groundbreaking new business models and intriguing financial products. This creative environment has led to the remarkable expansion of decentralized finance (DeFi), a dynamic sector that promises to revolutionize a wide array of financial services, from lending and borrowing to comprehensive asset management and innovative insurance solutions. The logical, evolutionary progression from primitive storage methods to sophisticated, advanced software solutions serves as a clear and compelling illustration of how cutting-edge technology can drive unprecedented economic growth and empower individuals worldwide on a global scale.

The Role of Security and Trust in Wallet Evolution

Security stands as the cornerstone of any financial system, underpinning the trust and reliability that users demand. The evolution of wallets over time reflects a relentless pursuit of enhanced security and user experience. Early paper wallets, though innovative in their concept, posed significant risks as they exposed users to a variety of challenges, including the potential for physical damage and loss. In an increasingly digital world, where a single misprint or smudge could easily render a wallet completely useless, the necessity for more robust and reliable solutions became more than just apparent; it became essential. As technology progressed, so too did the development of digital wallets, aiming to address these vulnerabilities and enhance user confidence in their financial dealings.

Software wallets effectively addressed these vulnerabilities by providing a broad range of security features that paper wallets simply could not match or replicate. They introduced various methods of encryption, robust password protection, and eventually embraced multi-factor authentication to enhance security. As the technology continued to mature and evolve, developers began incorporating additional measures such as biometric verification, which uses unique physical traits for entry, and multi-signature capabilities, which require multiple approvals for a transaction to take place. This ensured that only authorized users could access their funds, providing not just ease of use, but a significantly improved level of security against unauthorized access and potential theft.

These advancements were not merely accidental; they were the culmination of rigorous, methodical engineering meticulously designed to meet the ever-growing demands of an increasingly valuable asset class. In an ever-evolving world where cyber threats loom large and are ever-present, the remarkable ability of software wallets to evolve and adapt presents a powerful and persuasive argument for their undeniable superiority over alternative options. Each security breach that has occurred, along with every subsequent innovation in the wallet space, has contributed significantly to the development of a more resilient and trustworthy system that is now able to handle the immense scale and complexity of modern digital finance with greater efficiency and confidence. As these technologies develop further, we can expect ongoing enhancements that will fortify their foundations and build an even more secure framework for users around the globe.

The strong emphasis on security and trust in the realm of digital currencies is a natural extension of the foundational philosophies that underpin decentralized money. In a landscape where no central authority can be successfully relied upon to manage your funds and protect your financial interests, the only viable alternative is to develop a system that distributes trust across a comprehensive network of participants. By implementing software wallets, which function by ensuring that every transaction is both encrypted and thoroughly verified, we create an operational framework that is inherently transparent and profoundly resistant to tampering and external interference. This represents the ultimate realization of an essential principle: that money should indeed be managed by the people and for the people—a principle that is not only logical but profoundly persuasive to those who seek a more equitable financial system. This shift towards decentralized finance exemplifies an important movement in our approach to personal and communal wealth management, challenging traditional norms and advocating for a radically inclusive model that empowers all individuals.

The Future of Wallet Technology: Integration and Innovation

As we look to the future, the evolution of wallet technology shows no signs of slowing down, and the ongoing advancements are truly exciting. The transition from traditional paper wallets to sophisticated software solutions was a monumental leap forward, but this leap is only the beginning of a continuous journey toward more integrated, user-friendly, and innovative financial tools that cater to the diverse needs of users everywhere. Today, talented developers across the globe are tirelessly working on creating wallets that not only store digital assets securely and reliably but also interface seamlessly with a wide range of decentralized applications, enhancing user experience significantly. These next-generation wallets promise to integrate groundbreaking features like automated investment strategies tailored to individual user profiles, real-time market analytics that keep users informed and ready to act, and even social trading functionalities, where users can share insights, experiences, and learn from each other's trading strategies and investment decisions. This collaborative aspect is set to revolutionize the way individuals interact with their financial assets.

The seamless integration of wallet technology with mobile devices and the Internet of Things (IoT) represents yet another significant advancement in our technological evolution. Picture a reality where your smartwatch not only tracks your fitness but also securely interacts with your digital assets, allowing you to manage finances effortlessly right from your wrist. Envision a scenario where smart home devices, such as refrigerators or security systems, can autonomously conduct transactions without requiring any manual input. These groundbreaking innovations, while they might appear to belong to a distant future, are very much in the pipeline today. This progress is fueled by an unwavering pursuit of enhanced convenience, robust security, and unparalleled efficiency, the same driving forces that facilitated the monumental transition from traditional paper-based methods to the dynamic capabilities of modern software solutions.

Blockchain and smart contract technology significantly enhance the functionality and versatility of software wallets. They enable the concept of programmable money, where transactions can be automatically executed without manual intervention based on a set of predefined conditions. This incredible capability opens up a vast array of new possibilities, ranging from automated savings programs that help facilitate financial planning to decentralized escrow services that assure secure transactions without needing a trusted third party. All of these advancements represent the next logical evolution of wallet technology in our increasingly digital landscape. The argument is straightforward and compelling: as the digital economy continues to expand and evolve, the tools we use to manage our money must also advance to meet the ever-changing demands of our rapidly evolving world. With these innovations, users can expect a more efficient and streamlined experience when it comes to handling their finances, ultimately leading to greater financial independence and smarter investment strategies.

Persuading the Skeptics: The Case for Continued Innovation

Despite the remarkable progress that has been made in the evolution of digital wallets, the journey from simple paper wallets to increasingly sophisticated software solutions has not been without its fair share of critics. Some skeptics firmly argue that the rapid pace of technological change in the wallet space creates a certain level of uncertainty among users, and that many individuals may be overwhelmed by the sheer complexity of modern digital security measures that are required today. Others point to the vulnerabilities that still exist within some software implementations, suggesting that the current system is not yet completely foolproof, and there are still potential risks that users must navigate carefully in their digital transactions. This ongoing debate highlights the challenges that come with innovation in the financial technology sector and underscores the need for continued improvement and education.

However, these criticisms tend to overlook the broader, logical trajectory of innovation that is essential to its understanding. Every significant technological breakthrough is, without fail, accompanied by a crucial period of adjustment and learning that is vital for its success. The early days of any truly revolutionary technology are invariably marked by a phase of trial and error, and the ongoing evolution of wallet technology is no exception to this trend. The shift from paper to software was primarily driven by the urgent need to solve practical, real-world problems—problems that continue to be actively addressed and redefined as the technology matures and progresses over time.

The logical response to these challenges is to make a sustained commitment to ongoing investments in research, development, and collaboration across the various sectors involved in digital asset management. Open-source communities, where developers consistently share knowledge, ideas, and best practices, and work together collaboratively to enhance security and usability, have been instrumental in significantly advancing wallet technology. This collective and cooperative approach ensures that vulnerabilities are swiftly identified, effectively addressed, and resolved in a timely manner, leading to a system that becomes progressively more robust and reliable over time. The iterative process of continuous innovation—where each new version of a wallet builds upon the successes, incorporates feedback, and learns from the failures of its predecessors—serves as a powerful argument for the long-term viability and efficacy of digital asset storage solutions. Additionally, fostering an inclusive environment encourages diverse perspectives, which can lead to even more creative solutions in addressing emerging challenges.

The Human Element: Empowering Users Through Education

A crucial component in the ongoing evolution of wallet technology is undoubtedly the human element involved. Technology by itself cannot single-handedly create a secure financial system; it must be paired effectively with user education and empowerment to achieve that goal. In the early days of paper wallets, the initial adopters were frequently tech-savvy individuals who not only understood the technology but also the inherent risks and responsibilities tied to managing their own digital assets securely. As wallet technology has progressed and transformed, the challenge has shifted significantly. It has now become one of making these innovative tools both accessible and easy to understand for a much broader audience beyond just the tech enthusiasts.

Educational initiatives, along with user-friendly interfaces and intuitive design, have all significantly contributed to transforming software wallets from niche tools into applications that are part of our daily lives. The logical progression of this transformation is undeniably clear: as more individuals gain an understanding of how to use digital wallets securely and confidently, the adoption of cryptocurrencies will surely accelerate, leading to a substantial improvement in the overall resilience of the ecosystem. Education plays a crucial role in empowering users to take charge of their own finances, thus reducing their reliance on third parties and fostering a culture rooted in individual responsibility and collective trust, encouraging a more engaged and proactive user base that thrives in a decentralized financial environment.

This emphasis on education and empowerment is an organic continuation of the fundamental tenets of decentralization. In a landscape where each individual user bears responsibility for their own security, the acquisition of knowledge transforms into the paramount safeguard. This argument is both compelling and reasoned: a highly informed user base is not merely beneficial but indispensable for the overall success and sustainability of any decentralized system. As the technology behind wallets and digital assets continues to progress and develop, the importance of ongoing education and outreach initiatives will become increasingly critical. It is essential to ensure that the considerable benefits associated with digital currencies are made accessible and understandable to all, rather than being limited to just a privileged few. In this way, the vision of a truly inclusive financial system can be realized, fostering equal opportunities and participation for everyone involved.

The Broader Impact: How Wallets Shape the Digital Economy

The evolution of wallet technology has far-reaching implications that extend well beyond the limited realm of mere cryptocurrency storage. It is a critical component and foundational element of the broader digital economy, influencing everything from how various transactions are conducted to how value is created, managed, and subsequently distributed. As wallets have continued to evolve and improve, they have enabled a host of innovative new financial services and diverse business models that were once unimaginable, revolutionizing the way we think about money and financial interactions in the modern age.

For example, the rise of decentralized finance (DeFi) is closely connected to the rapid development and enhancement of robust, secure software wallets. DeFi platforms depend on these innovative wallets to empower users to lend, borrow, trade, and earn interest on their digital assets while eliminating the need for conventional intermediaries. This significant shift represents a fundamental rethinking of financial services as we know them, one that actively challenges the long-standing monopoly of centralized institutions and promotes a more inclusive, transparent, and efficient economic system for everyone involved.

Furthermore, digital wallets have significantly facilitated the creation of entirely new types of economic activity that were previously unimaginable. They have given rise to the fascinating phenomenon of microtransactions, where tiny, often negligible amounts of value can be exchanged instantaneously over the internet. This remarkable capability has opened up entirely new markets for digital content, gaming, online services, and much more, creating a dynamic and vibrant ecosystem where value is constantly generated, modified, and exchanged in various ways. The logical and analytical framework supporting these innovative advancements is genuinely compelling and transformative—digital wallets are not merely storage solutions; they have evolved to become the engines driving a revolutionary new economic paradigm that is reshaping commerce and interaction in profound ways.

The Enduring Legacy of Early Wallet Innovation

The journey from paper wallets to advanced software solutions is a fascinating testament to human ingenuity and the relentless drive to solve complex problems with simple yet effective solutions. Early wallet technology, despite all its imperfections and vulnerabilities, represents the very first steps in a long evolution that has now given rise to an immensely sophisticated digital financial ecosystem. These early experiments in storing digital assets, though they may seem primitive by today's advanced standards, were indeed groundbreaking in their own right. They stood as a bold attempt to reclaim control over one's wealth—a concept that resonates deeply at the core of the decentralized movement. This transformative path reveals not just a progression of technology, but also the natural evolution of ideas that aim to empower individuals and provide security in financial transactions. The continuous innovation in the digital wallet space is being driven by a community dedicated to enhancing user experience, privacy, and accessibility, marking a pivotal moment in our interaction with money. Each iteration builds upon the last, pushing the boundaries of what is possible and illustrating our desire for greater autonomy and a better understanding of our financial world.

The logical progression of wallet technology is a fascinating and mind-blowing narrative that intricately combines elements of shock, careful reasoning, and profound innovation. Starting from the fragile and vulnerable paper wallets that risked everything on a single piece of fragile paper, the journey has evolved into sophisticated software solutions that now empower seamless, secure transactions on a global scale. The dramatic evolution has been nothing short of revolutionary in every aspect. At every step of this remarkable journey, dedicated innovators have consistently applied rigorous logic and insightful analytical thinking to overcome numerous challenges, driving the continuous improvement of these complex systems and making them more accessible and efficient for users worldwide.

The persuasive argument for this significant evolution is abundantly clear: as our world continues to become increasingly digital, the urgent need for secure, efficient, and accessible methods of managing digital assets is more critical than ever before. Early innovations in wallet technology have laid the essential groundwork for a revolutionary new financial era—one in which decentralized systems grant power to individuals, foster enhanced transparency, and promote unparalleled economic freedom. This profound evolution is not merely a technological advancement; it represents a deep and transformative reimagining of how we view, utilize, and interact with money in our ever-evolving digital landscape.

For modern investors, entrepreneurs, and policymakers, the captivating story of wallet evolution provides invaluable lessons that are crucial for understanding our contemporary financial landscape. It demonstrates clearly that even the most primitive solutions can serve as a strong foundation for revolutionary systems when they are driven by a combination of logic, creativity, and a relentless commitment to improvement. The remarkable journey from simple paper wallets to sophisticated software solutions stands as a testament to the enduring power of human innovation—a transformative journey that continues to shape the digital economy and holds the promise to redefine the future of money in exciting new ways.

As we look ahead to the future, the ongoing and continuous development of wallet technology will undoubtedly continue to be a significant and critical factor in the overall success of decentralized finance. New and exciting innovations, along with greater integration with mobile technology, as well as advancements in security protocols, will work together to enhance the overall usability and safety of digital wallets. These improvements will make them truly indispensable tools in the modern financial landscape we navigate today.

In conclusion, the fascinating evolution of early wallet technology is a truly mind-blowing narrative filled with shock, deep logic, and relentless innovation. It is an incredible story that challenges our conventional understanding of money and reveals the profound transformation that digital technology has fundamentally wrought on the way we manage value and assets. From the fragile, often insecure beginnings of rudimentary paper wallets to the sophisticated, highly secure software solutions we utilize today, each step in this remarkable journey represents a essential and critical milestone in the global shift toward decentralized finance and the future of transactions.

The early experiments in wallet technology are not merely historical footnotes; rather, they serve as the very foundation upon which our modern digital economy has evolved and is built. These formative experiments illuminate the fact that even the simplest and most unassuming ideas, when synergistically combined with human ingenuity and creativity, can lead to revolutionary changes and transformative innovations in the financial landscape. This crucial lesson is as persuasive as it is logical: by wholeheartedly embracing the spirit of innovation and continually refining and enhancing our methods of managing digital assets, we can collaboratively create a financial system that is not only secure and efficient but also truly empowering and beneficial for everyone involved, especially the end-users.

Embrace and reflect upon the rich legacy of early wallet innovation as you consider its significance. Let it inspire you to delve deeper into and truly appreciate the incredible journey that has taken us from the simplicity of paper to the complex world of digital finance, from a state of vulnerability to one marked by resilience and strength. The evolution of wallet technology serves as a fascinating microcosm of the broader revolution in money—an ongoing transformation that not only promises to democratize access to wealth but also aims to fundamentally redefine the future of finance in ways that are both deeply shocking and, at the same time, profoundly logical and understandable.

Section 2: The Evolution of Hardware Wallets and Cold Storage

In a digital landscape teeming with risks and numerous cyber threats, the paramount need to effectively safeguard one's valuable digital assets has led to one of the most mind-blowing innovations in the ever-evolving world of cryptocurrency: the revolutionary introduction of hardware wallets and sophisticated cold storage solutions. This remarkable evolution—from the earlier, often risky and perilous methods of storing digital keys to the cutting-edge, highly secure offline storage devices that exist today—is nothing short of an extraordinary revolution. In this detailed exploration, we trace the fascinating journey from vulnerability to robust security, employing a logical, analytical, and persuasive approach that reveals a shocking transformation in how investments are meticulously protected in a world that is increasingly defined by the rapid advancement of digital technology and the ever-growing complexity of online threats.

The Perils of the Digital Frontier

Before the advent of hardware wallets and the establishment of cold storage as the definitive standard for securing digital assets, the crypto community found itself compelled to rely on a variety of less secure, often makeshift methods to safeguard private keys—the crucial codes that provide access to invaluable digital funds. In the early days of cryptocurrency, pioneering users stored their keys on personal computers, within digital files, or even scribbled onto sheets of paper. While these methods were creative and represented a new frontier in technology, they were nonetheless fraught with significant risks and vulnerabilities. Cybercriminals quickly learned to exploit software flaws, while phishing attacks snagged many unsuspecting users who were not aware of the dangers lurking online. Additionally, the physical risks associated with paper storage—like damage or simply misplacing these notes—could lead to dire consequences, with the potential for irrevocable financial loss hanging over those who used such insecure practices.

Imagine the reality of possessing millions of dollars' worth of valuable digital assets precariously tied to a simple text file on your personal computer—a file that could potentially be stolen with just one single malware attack or completely wiped out due to a catastrophic hardware failure. In this incredibly vulnerable digital frontier, each and every day brought with it a new, shocking story of lost fortunes and devastating financial losses. The inherent risks associated with online storage options starkly underscored the urgent need for a lasting solution that could effectively protect digital wealth from the relentless and ever-growing tide of cybercrime that threatened individuals everywhere.

The Birth of a New Era: Hardware Wallets

The evolution of hardware wallets has marked a truly seismic and transformative shift in the way people think about and approach the security of their precious digital assets. A hardware wallet is essentially a physical device that has been specifically engineered and designed to securely store cryptocurrency private keys offline, away from potential online threats. Unlike software wallets, which typically reside on a computer or mobile device and are therefore constantly connected to the internet, hardware wallets are uniquely designed to be "cold" or completely disconnected from any online access. This fundamental design choice drastically reduces the risk of suffering from online hacks or cyberattacks that can lead to the loss of valuable cryptocurrency.

The technology that underpins hardware wallets is not only elegant but also profoundly logical and well-structured. These devices incorporate a range of advanced cryptographic techniques along with secure elements, which are specialized chips designed specifically to store sensitive data within a tamper-resistant environment. When a user initiates a transaction, the hardware wallet carefully signs this transaction internally, ensuring that the private key is never exposed to the internet at any point in time. This meticulous process guarantees that even in the unfortunate event that the connected computer becomes compromised or hacked, the private key remains secure and protected, safely stored within the confines of the hardware device itself. Thus, users can engage in digital transactions with a robust sense of security and confidence.

For a significant number of individuals within the crypto community, the introduction of hardware wallets represented a startling revelation—a physical and tangible solution to a pressing problem that had threatened to completely undermine the entire promise of decentralized finance as we know it. This transformative moment occurred when the abstract risk associated with digital theft was met head-on with a concrete and reliable solution that many had desperately sought. Hardware wallets emerged as a groundbreaking innovation, offering a practical and effective way to take back control over one's digital assets. They empowered individuals to safeguard their own wealth in a manner that was previously quite unimaginable, allowing users to feel a renewed sense of security and confidence in their financial autonomy.

Cold Storage: The Ultimate Fortress for Digital Wealth

Alongside the ongoing development of hardware wallets, the concept of cold storage has emerged as another vital and innovative approach in the realm of cryptocurrency security. Cold storage specifically refers to any method or technique of keeping private keys safely offline, ensuring they remain completely disconnected from the internet and its associated vulnerabilities. This method can encompass a variety of storage solutions including hardware wallets, which are specifically designed for secure key management, as well as paper wallets that provide a physical representation of keys. Moreover, there are even more exotic techniques such as storing keys on encrypted USB drives that are then placed in highly secure physical locations such as safety deposit boxes or even safes. This multifaceted approach to cold storage significantly enhances the security of cryptocurrency holdings by minimizing exposure to online threats and hacking attempts.

The appeal of cold storage is fundamentally rooted in its remarkable simplicity and impressive effectiveness. By keeping private keys completely off the internet, cold storage not only enhances security but also eliminates the primary attack vector that hackers commonly exploit. Without an internet connection, malicious actors are rendered helpless as they cannot remotely access the keys, which consequently renders many common cyber attacks—such as phishing, keylogging, or remote malware infections—completely and utterly ineffective. In a more profound sense, cold storage effectively transforms the digital asset into a form that resembles a physical one, which is protected by the same tried-and-true logic that secures precious gold held safely in a vault. This concept illustrates the importance of safeguarding digital assets with the utmost care, akin to how one would protect tangible treasures.

The practical benefits of cold storage are as straightforward as they are profoundly significant. It provides an almost ironclad guarantee that if this method is executed with due diligence and care, your digital assets remain effectively out of reach from cybercriminals and other malicious actors. This level of security is vital for investors who hold significant sums in cryptocurrencies, as even a small breach can translate into catastrophic financial loss and irrevocable damage to one's investment portfolio. The shift to cold storage solutions represents a logical and necessary response to a clear and present danger: the ever-increasing vulnerability of digital assets in an interconnected and often perilous world. As the technology landscape continues to evolve, safeguarding one's investments through cold storage has become not just a recommendation but a critical strategy for ensuring the integrity and safety of financial assets in the cryptocurrency market.

The Logical Evolution: From Paper to Hardware

The journey from paper wallets to hardware wallets represents a captivating case study in human creativity and technological advancement. In the beginning, early adopters turned to paper wallets—an elementary technique that involved writing down or printing private keys and storing these securely. While paper wallets initially provided a quick solution by keeping keys offline and away from prying eyes, they were fundamentally fragile and vulnerable. Paper can be easily damaged by water, exposed to fire, or simply lost through carelessness. Additionally, managing these paper wallets proved to be cumbersome; each transaction necessitated creating a new paper copy, making the entire process not particularly user-friendly for those unfamiliar with the technology. As the landscape of cryptocurrency evolved, the need for more robust solutions became clear, paving the way for the development of hardware wallets.

Recognizing these significant limitations, developers increasingly sought out a more durable, efficient, and secure method for managing digital assets. The innovative solution emerged in the form of dedicated hardware wallets—these are compact, specialized devices meticulously designed specifically for the purpose of effectively safeguarding digital keys. This pivotal transition was both surprising in its immediacy and yet entirely logical upon reflection. It represented a clear and deliberate response to the critical, fundamental need for security in an era when the threat of digital theft was not merely a theoretical risk, but rather a daily and pervasive reality faced by countless individuals.

Hardware wallets provide a wide array of distinct advantages compared to their paper counterparts. Primarily, they are constructed from very robust materials, ensuring durability and longevity, unlike paper, which can wear out or be easily damaged. Furthermore, these wallets frequently come equipped with built-in screens that allow users to verify transactions directly on the device itself, adding an essential layer of security and convenience. In addition to these features, hardware wallets often include advanced security measures such as PIN protection and recovery phrases, making them a far more secure option for managing digital assets. This significant evolution from traditional paper wallets to advanced hardware counterparts exemplifies the natural progression of technology over time: as the stakes involved in digital finance continue to rise, so too does the sophistication and complexity of the available solutions. It serves as a truly mind-blowing demonstration of how logical thinking, coupled with persistent innovation, can effectively overcome challenges that may have previously seemed insurmountable.

Security by Design: The Engineering Behind Hardware Wallets

At the very heart of hardware wallets lies an intricate and sophisticated blend of advanced engineering and cutting-edge cryptography. These specialized devices are meticulously designed with security as their paramount function, incorporating multiple robust layers of defense to effectively protect against a wide range of both physical and digital threats that can jeopardize user assets. The secure element—a highly specialized microprocessor utilized in various hardware wallets—stands out as one of the most critical components. It functions like a mini fortress, providing a fortified barrier for sensitive information and ensuring that even if the device is subjected to physical tampering attempts, the private keys remain completely inaccessible and secure from malicious actors and unauthorized access.

The design of these wallets is governed by strict security protocols, often including:

- **Isolation of the Private Key:** The private key is stored in a secure element that is completely isolated from the internet. This isolation is the primary defense against hacking.

- **Multi-Factor Authentication:** Users are required to set up PIN codes and, in some cases, biometric authentication, adding additional layers of security.

- **Backup and Recovery Mechanisms:** Most hardware wallets generate a recovery phrase—a set of words that can be used to restore the wallet if the device is lost or damaged. This feature addresses one of the major vulnerabilities of early storage methods.

- **Tamper-Resistance:** The physical construction of hardware wallets is designed to detect and prevent unauthorized access. Some devices will erase the private key if they detect signs of tampering, ensuring that the data never falls into the wrong hands.

These design principles are not merely shockingly effective; they represent a logical culmination of countless years spent in trial, error, and a relentless pursuit of security. The transition to hardware wallets stands as a testament to the power of rigorous analytical thinking: by meticulously and systematically addressing each vulnerability inherent in earlier methods and practices, engineers were able to create a device that is not only as secure as possible but also as convenient as one could hope for in this modern age of technology.

The Impact on Investor Confidence and Market Maturity

The advent of hardware wallets and cold storage solutions has truly had a transformative and profound impact on the ever-evolving cryptocurrency market landscape. For a great number of investors, the previously overwhelming inability to securely store their valuable digital assets was a significant barrier to entry and participation. The persistent fear of hacks, theft, and the irreversible loss of funds prevented even the most enthusiastic and hopeful participants from fully committing to the thrilling crypto revolution that was taking place. These innovations have opened up new avenues for safety and security, enabling more individuals to confidently engage in this exciting financial frontier.

The introduction of hardware wallets dramatically altered this prevailing dynamic in the cryptocurrency space. By offering a highly secure and user-friendly method to manage private keys, hardware wallets instilled a fresh and unprecedented level of confidence among investors in digital assets. Suddenly, these digital assets were transformed from mere theoretical constructs into tangible, manageable entities that, most importantly, boasted enhanced security. This newfound sense of security attracted not only a wave of institutional investment but also a significant surge in public interest in cryptocurrencies. The logical and inevitable result of this development was a more mature and stable market capable of withstanding the inherent volatility that accompanies any emerging technology, creating a safer environment for both seasoned investors and newcomers alike.

This increased confidence has had far-reaching implications across various sectors. With robust and secure storage solutions in place, an increasing number of investors began to view cryptocurrencies as legitimate, long-term investments rather than merely as speculative instruments that could result in volatility. The evolution of wallet technology provided the crucial missing piece in the complex puzzle of crypto adoption—without it, the rapid growth and mainstream acceptance of digital currencies might never have materialized in the way we see today. The persuasive power of these secure wallets lies in their remarkable ability to transform deep-seated fear into unwavering trust, and prevailing uncertainty into steadfast confidence—a logical progression that has effectively fueled the phenomenal rise of the crypto market over time.

The Social and Economic Implications of Secure Storage

Beyond the technical and financial benefits, the evolution and development of hardware wallets has broader social and economic implications that cannot be overlooked. These secure storage solutions empower individuals significantly by giving them direct control over their digital assets, thereby bypassing the often cumbersome and potentially risky need for intermediaries like banks. This democratization of financial control is a powerful and persuasive idea that challenges the traditional, centralized financial system that has long maintained its hold over individuals. In a world increasingly characterized by skepticism, where trust in banks and governments has been severely eroded by numerous scandals, mismanagement, and widespread corruption, this shift towards personal responsibility becomes even more critical. The ability to securely manage one's own wealth without relying on institutions that may not have the individual's best interests at heart is both liberating and transformative, offering a new path toward financial independence and security for everyone involved.

Moreover, secure wallets play a significant role in enhancing the overall stability and resilience of the cryptocurrency ecosystem. When investors feel assured that their valuable assets are secure, they are significantly more likely to hold onto and actively use them, rather than succumbing to panic selling or engaging in irrational speculative behavior. This kind of stability is absolutely crucial for the maturation and development of the market, and it fosters broader acceptance of digital currencies as a legitimate asset class in the eyes of both the public and regulators. The transition from traditional paper forms of currency to modern hardware solutions is not merely a technological upgrade; it represents a profound and fundamental change in the way society interacts with money, one that holds the promise to truly reshape the future of finance in a digital age.

The impact of secure storage extends not only to individuals but also significantly to the dynamic realm of decentralized finance (DeFi) as well. DeFi platforms fundamentally rely on users being able to securely access, manage, and oversee their funds to participate effectively and confidently in various financial activities such as lending, borrowing, and trading endeavors. Without reliable and robust wallet technology, the entire DeFi ecosystem would face serious vulnerabilities, exposing it to potential breaches, hacking attempts, and various forms of fraudulent activities. By ensuring that digital assets are stored safely and securely, hardware wallets effectively form the backbone of a new, decentralized financial system. This innovative system has the tremendous potential to revolutionize traditional banking and conventional financial services, offering users a more secure and efficient way to engage with their wealth and assets.

Challenges and Ongoing Evolution

Although hardware wallets and cold storage solutions have significantly enhanced the security of digital assets, this technology does come with its own set of challenges. The initial development of hardware wallets, despite being groundbreaking, occasionally experienced problems related to usability and technical glitches that hindered user experience. For many new users, the learning curve could be quite steep, making it difficult for them to navigate the complexities involved. Additionally, the ever-present risk of human error—like misplacing or incorrectly writing down a recovery phrase—continues to be a critical concern for users looking to safeguard their investments.

However, the evolution of wallet technology is an ongoing story of continuous improvement and advancement. Developers have taken these challenges head-on, refining existing designs, enhancing security protocols, and making user interfaces much more user-friendly for a broader audience. The iterative nature of innovation means that each new generation of hardware wallets builds upon the learned lessons of its predecessors, systematically addressing vulnerabilities and streamlining overall functionality.

As a result, the user experience is constantly being optimized, ensuring that wallets become increasingly reliable and secure over time.

The ongoing shift towards seamlessly integrating hardware wallets with mobile and web applications is another significant trend that is emerging in the cryptocurrency landscape. As the crypto market expands and reaches new heights, there is an increasing demand for innovative, user-friendly solutions that allow individuals to manage their digital assets effortlessly across various devices. This convergence of hardware security features with powerful software solutions not only enhances usability but also ensures that security protocols can keep pace with the evolving needs of users. This exciting merging of hardware and software signifies a groundbreaking, mind-blowing fusion of physical security elements and digital convenience. It reflects the next logical and essential step in the evolution of wallet technology, catering to a diverse user base eager for efficiency and enhanced safety in their transactions.

Furthermore, the surge of open-source initiatives within the wallet sector has significantly accelerated the pace of innovation in this field. By opting to make their code accessible to the public, developers have successfully cultivated a collaborative atmosphere where security vulnerabilities can be efficiently located and promptly rectified. This community-centric methodology not only bolsters the overall strength and reliability of the technology but also fosters a sense of trust among users. Trust, as we know, is an essential element for the broad acceptance and adoption of any technology in today's digital landscape.

The Future Landscape: Next-Generation Wallets and Beyond

Looking ahead, the evolution of hardware wallets is set to continue, propelled by ongoing technological advancements and the ever-increasing importance of security in our increasingly digital world. Next-generation wallets are expected to incorporate even more sophisticated security features that enhance user protection, such as biometric authentication processes, advanced encryption methods designed to safeguard sensitive information, and improved tamper-resistance measures that will physically secure the devices. These advancements in security technology will further reduce the risks associated with digital asset storage, making it substantially safer for users. Ultimately, these innovations will not only fortify the defenses around digital assets but also streamline the user experience, making it even easier for everyday users to manage their wealth in a secure and efficient manner. As these technologies continue to evolve, they promise to substantially improve user confidence in digital currencies and encourage wider adoption among the general public.

Moreover, as decentralized finance (DeFi) continues to expand and gain traction in the financial landscape, the growing demand for integrated and multifunctional wallets will inevitably increase. Future wallets are expected to offer an extensive suite of advanced financial services—such as real-time trading capabilities, automated portfolio management features, and seamless integration with numerous DeFi platforms—all while maintaining the highest possible standards of security to protect users' assets. This holistic and comprehensive approach to managing digital assets represents the logical evolution of wallet technology in the modern era—a true convergence of convenience, security, and enhanced functionality that promises to fundamentally redefine the way we interact with money and conduct transactions in our daily lives.

The broader economic implications of these significant advancements are truly profound and far-reaching. As secure storage solutions become more accessible and more reliable, they are poised to play a critical role in the mainstream adoption of various cryptocurrencies. This increased adoption and acceptance will, in turn, drive even further innovation within the crypto space, ultimately resulting in the creation of a more robust and inclusive financial ecosystem. The logical progression from here is abundantly clear: secure wallets, which are essential tools for safeguarding digital assets, are the very foundation upon which the future of decentralized finance will be built and expanded.

Persuading the Masses: Transforming Fear into Trust

One of the most compelling and significant outcomes of the evolution and transition from traditional paper wallets to more advanced hardware wallets is the profound transformation of investor sentiment regarding digital assets. In the early days of Bitcoin, when the cryptocurrency market was still in its infancy, the intense fear of hacking, theft, and irreversible loss was a major deterrent for potential investors who were contemplating entry into this new financial ecosystem. The persistent idea that millions of dollars' worth of valuable digital assets could be lost in an instant due to security breaches or technical failures was a constant source of anxiety and apprehension for many individuals. However, the development and introduction of hardware wallets fundamentally changed that narrative entirely, instilling greater confidence in investors.

With the advent of highly secure, offline storage solutions, the risk of digital theft has been dramatically reduced, significantly altering the landscape of financial security. Investors began to realize that their valuable assets could be safeguarded with a level of security that was previously unimaginable and truly groundbreaking. This pivotal shift in perception—from deep-rooted fear to newfound confidence—has been nothing short of revolutionary in the digital finance world. It creates a persuasive argument for the bright future of digital finance: when innovative technology can offer such robust protection and reassuring security measures, the potential for widespread adoption becomes nearly inevitable and overwhelmingly likely.

The transformation that is taking place within the financial landscape is both logical and deeply grounded in common sense principles that everyone can understand. In any effective financial system, trust is truly paramount. If individuals and investors do not possess confidence that their money is being kept safe, they will certainly refrain from making investments, and inevitably, markets will fail to thrive. Hardware wallets and cold storage methods provide that essential trust by ensuring that private keys remain secure and protected, regardless of the numerous and escalating threats posed by an increasingly interconnected and complex digital world. This vital reassurance is the key to unlocking a whole new era of digital asset management, one that is not only empowering for users but also transformative in nature, paving the way for new possibilities and innovative financial solutions for everyone involved.

The Enduring Impact of Wallet Innovation

The remarkable evolution from simple paper wallets to highly advanced hardware wallets stands as a powerful testament to the incredible capacity for human innovation, especially when faced with unprecedented challenges and difficulties. This journey reflects not only the technological advancements but also the resilience and adaptability of the crypto community. It is a compelling story of how, driven by logical reasoning, relentless experimentation, and a steadfast commitment to continuous improvement, the crypto community has worked tirelessly to transform what once was a vulnerable and insecure system into a robust and secure groundwork for managing digital wealth. Through collaborative efforts, innovative designs, and the application of cutting-edge technology, they have built a framework that instills confidence in users looking to protect their valuable assets in the digital realm.

This transformative journey is not solely about the advancements in technology—it is fundamentally about reclaiming control over one's financial destiny, particularly in a world where centralized systems have persistently failed to meet the needs of the people. The significant shift toward hardware wallets and cold storage solutions has not merely enhanced security measures; it has also established a solid groundwork for the more widespread adoption of digital currencies among various demographics. This movement signifies a logical and inevitable progression in the evolution of money, acting as a remarkably brilliant and timely response to the myriad challenges presented by the digital age. In this context, individual empowerment through financial sovereignty becomes paramount, paving the way for innovative solutions that reflect the values of transparency and freedom.

For investors in the ever-changing digital landscape, the lessons are unmistakably clear: the security of your digital assets is absolutely paramount and of utmost importance; thus, investing in reliable technology is essential. Moreover, the continuous evolution of wallet technology stands out as a critical factor that plays a vital role in ensuring that your investments remain secure and protected from various threats. For the broader market, the ongoing development of robust, user-friendly wallet solutions is paving the way for a promising future where digital currencies are accessible to everyone, democratizing financial opportunities and transforming the global financial landscape into one that is significantly more transparent, inclusive, and resilient for all participants involved.

As we look towards the future, the promise and potential of next-generation wallet technology is not only inspiring but also fundamentally logical. With ongoing and continuous advancements in security, seamless integration, and enhanced usability, the tools available to manage and protect digital wealth will continue to improve remarkably, thereby further solidifying the role of cryptocurrencies as a foundational cornerstone of modern finance in our increasingly digital world. The evolution of wallets stands as a microcosm of the broader transformation occurring in the financial landscape—a journey that shifts from vulnerability to robust security, and from chaotic systems to organized frameworks, all driven by the relentless and unyielding pursuit of innovation and excellence in technological advancement.

In this shocking and profoundly mind-blowing narrative, we deeply explore how the evolution of hardware wallets and cold storage solutions has not only effectively solved the critical and pressing problem of digital asset security but has also played a pivotal and transformative role in legitimizing the entire crypto ecosystem, which is becoming increasingly influential in our digital age. It is a compelling story of how even the simplest of ideas, when combined with logical, analytical, and relentless innovation and creativity, can substantially change the world for the better. The secure storage of digital assets is no longer merely a luxury option—it is an absolute necessity in an era where every transaction, every investment, and every digital dollar must be meticulously protected from an ever-present and diverse array of threats that lurk online daily.

Embrace this profound evolution. Recognize that the journey from traditional paper-based wallets to sophisticated hardware wallets is a clear and logical progression that has fundamentally transformed digital asset security from what was once viewed as a speculative risk into a foundational and indispensable pillar of modern finance. The future of money in our increasingly digital world depends significantly on these groundbreaking innovations. As we continue to push the boundaries of what is possible within this realm, the invaluable lessons derived from this evolution will persist as a guiding light—a powerful testament to the strength of human ingenuity and the relentless pursuit of economic freedom that underpins our financial systems.

The global shift towards digital assets is profoundly underpinned by the secure and reliable technology that both hardware wallets and cold storage solutions provide. These devices are not merely tools; they are the vigilant guardians of a thrilling new financial frontier—one where the promise of decentralized, secure, and easily accessible wealth is rapidly becoming a tantalizing reality for millions of individuals around the world. This is the truly mind-blowing future of money—a future meticulously built on the robust and solid, logical foundations laid by the remarkable evolution of wallet technology over the years. With every innovation, the landscape of finance transforms, cementing the role of these advanced technologies at the forefront.

Section 3: Custodial vs. Non-Custodial: Balancing Convenience and Control

In the wild, ever-changing landscape of digital money, one of the most critical choices for anyone holding cryptocurrencies is deciding how to store them safely and effectively. This important decision—custodial versus non-custodial wallets—is not just a technical matter; it strikes at the very heart of personal financial control and security for users and investors alike. The contrast between third-party managed wallets and self-managed solutions reveals a shocking world filled with numerous trade-offs. On one side, custodial wallets offer significant convenience and ease-of-use; users can quickly access their funds and perform transactions without much hassle. On the other hand, non-custodial wallets provide unparalleled control and security, allowing individuals to retain full ownership of their assets, which can be a powerful advantage. Understanding this essential balance is crucial in a world where a mere few seconds of inattention can lead to catastrophic financial consequences, including the potential loss of millions of dollars in assets and investments. As the cryptocurrency landscape continues to evolve, it is increasingly vital for users to carefully weigh their options and make informed decisions about how best to protect their wealth in the digital realm.

This section delves deeply into the reasoning that informs these two distinct approaches, the underlying logic that motivates their design decisions, and the tangible real-world implications for both individual users and various institutions alike. We will conduct a thorough investigation into the numerous advantages and potential pitfalls associated with both custodial and non-custodial wallets. Our examination will be conducted in a plain, natural style that is designed to be as analytical as it is persuasive, ensuring clear communication of the complexities involved.

The Basics: What Are Custodial and Non-Custodial Wallets?

Before we delve into the various complexities involved, let's take a moment to clearly define our terms. In the most straightforward terms possible, a custodial wallet refers to a type of digital wallet in which a third party—typically an exchange platform or a financial service provider—retains control over your private keys and oversees the management of your funds on your behalf. You can think of it in a similar way to how a traditional bank account operates: you place your trust in the bank to safeguard your funds, and in return, they take care of the security, management, and various other aspects related to your money for you. Consequently, the responsibility of protecting your assets is effectively transferred to this organization.

Non-custodial wallets, on the other hand, are wallets where you are the only guardian of your own private keys. In this particular model, you are solely responsible for every aspect of the security concerning your wallet. If by any chance you lose your keys, you effectively lose your money, and there is no way around that, period. This approach can be likened to being your own bank, which entails a considerable amount of freedom but also all the responsibility that comes along with it. You must exercise diligence and care to ensure that your assets remain safe and secure at all times.

The choice between these two options is undeniably more than just a technical preference—it significantly represents a fundamental decision about the level of control you desire over your financial assets versus the degree of convenience you are willing to sacrifice in the process. It reflects your individual priorities and how you balance the need for autonomy in managing your investments with the ease of a system that might take care of things for you.

The Case for Custodial Wallets: Convenience and User Experience

For numerous individuals who are just stepping into the captivating world of cryptocurrencies, the attraction of custodial wallets is quite compelling and hard to overlook. These wallets are remarkably user-friendly, designed to require minimal technical expertise, and they provide an experience that closely mirrors that of conventional online banking services. When you opt to use a custodial wallet, you are essentially delegating the intricate, often anxiety-inducing task of securing your assets to a dedicated service provider. This provider assumes the significant responsibility of managing your private keys, protecting your holdings against potential hacks, and ensuring that your funds are readily accessible whenever you require them. In essence, custodial wallets offer peace of mind for those who may find the technicalities of cryptocurrency security overwhelming.

Picture the experience of setting up your very own online bank account. You take the time to fill in a few easy forms, undergo a simple identity verification process, and before you know it, you have a secure and reliable place to store your hard-earned money. This is essentially how custodial wallets operate as well. You simply log in, and immediately, your digital assets are conveniently right there at your fingertips, easily accessible whenever you need them. There's absolutely no need to stress over complicated backup procedures or the complicated cryptographic details—everything is diligently managed on your behalf, allowing you to enjoy peace of mind while you handle your financial transactions.

This convenience, however, comes with a significant caveat: trust must be established. When you choose to opt for a custodial wallet, you're essentially putting your confidence in a third party tasked with the safeguarding of your most valuable asset, which in this case is your digital currency. That trust is fundamentally built upon the reputation of the provider and their proven track record in the realm of cybersecurity. While many custodial services are indeed highly secure and operate in a professional manner, it is important to recognize that history has demonstrated time and again that even the most reputable providers can find themselves falling victim to security breaches.

For instance, there have been alarming cases where exchanges were hacked and millions—possibly even billions—of dollars' worth of cryptocurrencies were stolen from unsuspecting users. These unfortunate incidents serve as a stark and sobering reminder that when you hand over control of your cryptographic keys, you are also ceding significant control of your financial future and your economic autonomy. Being aware of these risks is crucial in making informed decisions about asset storage.

Yet, for numerous individuals, the convenience and benefits offered by custodial wallets significantly outweigh the inherent risks involved. Custodial wallets make it possible for people to actively participate in the ever-evolving digital economy without needing to grasp every intricate technical detail associated with cryptocurrencies. They effectively lower the barrier to entry, thereby inviting a larger demographic of people into the crypto space. From a logical standpoint, if you are not ready or willing to take the responsibility of managing your own cryptographic keys securely, then a reputable custodial wallet stands out as a practical and sensible solution. It's a choice made based on a trade-off between ease-of-use and self-sovereignty—a delicate balance that many individuals find acceptable, particularly when they are just starting their journey into the world of cryptocurrencies. By choosing this option, newcomers can mitigate the overwhelming nature of the crypto landscape while they gain experience and knowledge.

The Case for Non-Custodial Wallets: Security and Personal Control

On the flip side, non-custodial wallets embody the purest essence of financial independence and autonomy. In a non-custodial setup, you retain and hold your private keys, which means you possess complete control over your funds and their management. This newfound autonomy is a double-edged sword: with great power indeed comes great responsibility. There is no reliable third party to fall back on if you happen to lose your keys, which can pose significant risks, and the entire onus is squarely on you to maintain security and safeguard your assets effectively.

This approach strongly appeals to individuals who place a high value on personal sovereignty over mere convenience. Non-custodial wallets are frequently preferred by experienced users as well as institutional investors who possess a comprehensive and deep understanding of the intricacies of digital security. They represent a remarkably bold and significant move away from the conventional frameworks of traditional banking, essentially placing the individual firmly at the helm of their financial destiny and journey. The underlying logic behind non-custodial wallets is quite simple yet profound: if you genuinely believe in the principles of decentralization and the essence of financial freedom, then you must take full control and responsibility for your own keys, thereby ensuring a greater degree of security and autonomy in your financial dealings.

The security benefits are undeniably clear and compelling. By keeping your keys offline—often employing various methods like hardware wallets or air-gapped computers—you significantly reduce the risk posed by cyber attacks and unauthorized access. Non-custodial wallets can incorporate a range of advanced security features, such as multi-signature authentication, biometric verification, and encrypted backups, all of which enhance your protection. These robust measures make it extremely challenging for hackers to gain access to your funds or digital assets. The reasoning here is sound and solid: the fewer intermediaries there are between you and your money, the lower the risk of exploitation and the potential for financial loss due to malicious intent. As such, ensuring that your assets are shielded from online threats should be a top priority for any investor or cryptocurrency user.

However, the flip side of this newfound autonomy in the financial landscape is that it demands a considerable level of technical know-how and diligence, which many individuals find quite daunting and intimidating. If you lose your private keys, there is no convenient "forgot password" button to rescue you—your funds will be lost forever, leaving you with a profound sense of regret. This potential for catastrophic loss serves as a significant risk and a stark reminder of the immense responsibilities that come with achieving true financial freedom in a decentralized world. For those individuals who are willing to invest the time and effort necessary to thoroughly understand these complex systems and navigate their intricacies, the rewards can be incredibly immense and fulfilling. However, the stakes in this arena are unavoidably high, and one must tread carefully to avoid financial ruin.

Balancing Convenience and Control: The Trade-Off

At the very heart of the ongoing debate between custodial wallets and non-custodial wallets lies a fundamental trade-off that many users must consider: the balance between convenience and control over one's assets. Custodial wallets are designed to provide ease-of-use and quick accessibility, allowing users to manage their funds without much hassle. However, this convenience comes at a significant cost, as it requires users to place their trust in a third party to safeguard their valuable assets. In contrast, non-custodial wallets offer users complete control over their funds and inherently superior security features. Nonetheless, these wallets demand a much higher level of personal responsibility and diligence from the user. Ultimately, the choice between these two types of wallets involves weighing the benefits of ease and access against the critical importance of personal control and security over one's financial resources.

This trade-off is not merely technical in nature—it is profoundly personal and philosophical in character. It raises essential questions about what it truly means to be in control of your own financial destiny. In a world where centralized institutions have historically held the reins of money and financial power, the idea of managing your own assets, investments, and savings is both liberating and terrifying at the same time. It challenges long-held beliefs about trust in financial systems and the nature of power itself. Furthermore, it compels individuals to confront their own willingness to take full responsibility for their financial security and well-being, examining the depths of their understanding and engagement with their personal finances in ways that were previously unimagined.

For many individuals, the answer to this dilemma lies in finding a suitable middle ground that balances convenience and security. Some users opt for a hybrid approach, which involves using custodial wallets for smaller, everyday transactions while strategically storing the bulk of their digital assets in non-custodial solutions. This balanced approach allows them to enjoy the convenience and ease of managed services for routine expenditures while still maintaining ultimate control over the majority of their wealth in a more secure environment. It is indeed a practical compromise that reflects a deep understanding of the intricate risks and benefits associated with both systems. By adopting this strategy, users are able to navigate the complexities of digital asset management effectively.

Real-World Examples: Lessons from the Field

To fully grasp the practical implications that arise when choosing between custodial and non-custodial wallets, it is essential to delve into illustrative real-world examples. Take, for instance, the infamous hack of Mt. Gox, which was once recognized as the largest Bitcoin exchange in the world. Mt. Gox functioned as a custodial wallet, meaning that it managed and safeguarded private keys on behalf of its users and clients. However, when this exchange was unfortunately compromised, an astounding sum of millions of dollars' worth of Bitcoin suddenly vanished into thin air, leaving many investors grappling with catastrophic and devastating financial losses. This shocking and alarming event underscored the significant risks that are inherently associated with entrusting your valuable digital assets to a single institution—regardless of how reputable or trustworthy it may seem on the surface.

Conversely, numerous high-profile investors and various institutions have increasingly turned to non-custodial solutions, especially hardware wallets, as a means to effectively secure their significant holdings. For instance, well-known cryptocurrency investors frequently choose to store the vast majority of their digital wealth within the confines of hardware wallets, fully relying on the robust and sophisticated security measures that these devices are equipped with. These hardware wallets, which are fundamentally non-custodial by design and operation, have proven to be instrumental in safeguarding millions of dollars in assets from various cyber attacks and potential threats. The logical takeaway from this trend is abundantly clear: for individuals and entities who prioritize control over their investments and security above all else, the use of non-custodial wallets emerges as the superior choice. This remains true despite the fact that managing these wallets involves a certain level of added complexity and responsibility, which can initially seem daunting.

The Evolution of Wallet Technology: Continuous Innovation

The ongoing debate surrounding custodial and non-custodial wallets is not a static matter; rather, it represents an evolving conversation that is driven by continuous innovation and advancements in technology. In the early days of cryptocurrency, software wallets, regardless of whether they were custodial or non-custodial, tended to be relatively rudimentary in design and were often prone to various security vulnerabilities that could compromise users' assets. However, as the cryptocurrency space matured and expanded, wallet technology began to advance at an astonishing rate. With the emergence of new protocols, the introduction of significantly improved encryption methods, and the development of more user-friendly interfaces, there has been a marked enhancement in both the security and functionality of custodial and non-custodial wallets alike. This evolution continues to shape how users interact with their digital currencies and the broader ecosystem.

For custodial wallets, recent advancements have concentrated on developing robust and highly secure platforms that can efficiently manage vast amounts of digital assets with minimal risk involved. Reputable exchanges within the industry have invested significantly in sophisticated cybersecurity measures, implementing multi-factor authentication, rigorous regulatory compliance, and other protective strategies to safeguard user assets. The ultimate goal of these efforts is to offer a safe and convenient experience that rivals traditional banking options while fully leveraging the numerous benefits that modern digital technology has to offer, ensuring users feel confident in their transactions and investments.

Non-custodial wallets have undergone even more dramatic evolution in recent years. What initially began as simple software applications has now transformed into exceptionally sophisticated systems that incorporate advanced hardware components, enhanced biometric security measures, and innovative solutions for backup. Today's non-custodial wallets provide an unparalleled level of security and control that was once considered unimaginable, all while maintaining a significant degree of convenience through seamless integration with mobile applications and reliable cloud backup services. This continuous improvement in design and functionality serves as a testament to the logical, analytical approach that propels innovation within the cryptocurrency space—a relentless pursuit to surmount the persistent challenges associated with securing digital assets against potential threats and vulnerabilities. As the landscape of digital finance continues to evolve, non-custodial wallets remain at the forefront, ensuring that users can confidently manage and protect their holdings.

Analytical Insights: Trust, Control, and the Future of Finance

At its core, the ongoing and evolving debate over custodial versus non-custodial wallets fundamentally centers around the concepts of trust and control. Trust is indeed the cornerstone of any financial system, serving as the foundation upon which financial transactions and relationships are built. In traditional banking systems, that trust is typically placed in large institutions that have long-standing histories and established reputations, bolstered by regulatory frameworks and government guarantees. However, in the rapidly changing world of cryptocurrencies, trust must be constructed and nurtured in an entirely different manner—primarily through technology, rigorous transparency, and active community consensus. This shift demands a rethinking of how individuals perceive and engage with their financial assets.

Custodial wallets build trust by effectively leveraging the reputation and security measures of well-established financial institutions. They provide a familiar and streamlined experience for users who are accustomed to engaging with traditional financial services. This ease of use is appealing, as it allows individuals to navigate their assets without needing to understand the complexities of blockchain technology. However, it is crucial to recognize that this trust is a double-edged sword. When you place your assets in a custodial wallet, you are inherently trusting that institution not only to safeguard your hard-earned funds but also to act in your best interest at all times. History has shown that even the most trusted and reputable institutions can falter under pressure, leaving their users vulnerable to theft, mismanagement, or outright collapse. Such instances serve as reminders of the risks associated with reliance on third-party custodians and the importance of thoroughly researching and evaluating institutions before putting one's trust in their hands.

Non-custodial wallets, by contrast, require users to build and cultivate a strong sense of trust in themselves. The responsibility for ensuring security rests entirely on the individual user, and while this can certainly feel daunting and overwhelming at times, it also provides unparalleled control over one's assets and finances. The decentralized nature of non-custodial solutions means that trust is distributed widely among a network of participants rather than being concentrated in a single centralized entity or institution. This approach aligns perfectly with the fundamental principles of decentralization and self-sovereignty that underpin the entire cryptocurrency movement, empowering individuals to take charge of their own financial destinies. This empowerment comes with both challenges and immense possibilities, and it encourages users to educate themselves further in managing their digital assets responsibly.

The logical analysis being presented here is crystal clear: the more control and authority you possess over your own assets, the less vulnerable you are to the potential failures, mishaps, or mismanagement that may arise from third parties. However, it is important to remember that with great power comes significant responsibility. The primary challenge that users face is to effectively strike a balance—leveraging the convenience of custodial services for routine transactions and day-to-day operations while maintaining a robust and secure non-custodial storage solution for the bulk of their valuable holdings. This approach allows users to enjoy safety and liquidity without exposing themselves excessively to the risks associated with entrusting all their assets to external entities.

The Persuasive Argument: Empowering Individuals in a Decentralized Economy

The ongoing debate between custodial and non-custodial wallets is not merely a technical issue—it carries profound implications for individual empowerment and the broader concept of economic freedom. In a centralized financial system, power is concentrated within the hands of a select few institutions, which can result in significant systemic vulnerabilities, exploitation, and a lack of transparency for users. This centralization can lead to abuses of power and a diminished sense of trust among individuals relying on these entities for their financial transactions. In stark contrast, decentralization distributes power more equitably among the people, fostering a financial ecosystem that is more resilient, inclusive, and just. By allowing individuals to maintain control over their own assets, non-custodial wallets prioritize personal agency and ensure that users are less susceptible to the failures or misconduct of centralized authorities.

Non-custodial wallets epitomize this vital principle of individual empowerment and autonomy in the financial realm. They allow you to take complete control of your financial destiny, without having to depend on banks or exchanges, which can often be restrictive. This empowerment is not only logical but also inherently persuasive: if you genuinely believe in the core ideals of decentralization and financial freedom, then you must be prepared to take full responsibility for your own security and the safeguarding of your assets. Embracing this responsibility is essential in a world that increasingly values personal agency and independence in managing one's finances.

For a significant number of people within the crypto community, this pivotal shift towards adopting non-custodial solutions represents a strong declaration of independence—a courageous statement asserting that they refuse to allow traditional financial institutions to dictate the direction of their wealth and financial future. This argument holds true as much on a philosophical level as it does from a practical standpoint. It serves as a rallying call to reclaim control over one's own assets and to decisively reject the pervasive notion that money must be managed and overseen by centralized authorities. In an era where financial systems have frequently failed to fulfill their promises of security, integrity, and fairness, non-custodial wallets provide an empowering and liberating alternative that puts the user back in control.

Real-World Impact: How Wallet Choice Influences Market Behavior

The choice between custodial and non-custodial wallets plays a crucial role in influencing the dynamics of the market for digital assets. When investors demonstrate a high level of confidence in the security and safety of their digital assets, they are far more inclined to hold their investments and engage in long-term strategies. This behavior, often referred to as "HODLing" within the crypto community, serves to enhance market stability while simultaneously fostering growth. On the other hand, if users harbor concerns regarding the security of their assets, they may feel compelled to sell off their holdings quickly, which inevitably results in increased volatility and uncertainty in the market. Consequently, understanding these wallet types is paramount for investors who wish to navigate the ever-changing landscape of cryptocurrency.

Hardware wallets, alongside various non-custodial solutions, have become an essential component in stabilizing the market by offering a highly secure and offline method for storing valuable digital assets. This enhanced security not only protects against potential hacks and breaches but also encourages long-term holding among investors, further decreasing the frequency of panic selling—an important factor in the maturation and evolution of the crypto market as a whole. The analytical logic behind this phenomenon is quite straightforward: when security measures are robust and well-regarded, they lead to heightened investor confidence. This increased confidence naturally drives market stability and consistent growth over time.

Moreover, as institutional investors begin to adopt increasingly secure and innovative, non-custodial solutions, the overall credibility and trustworthiness of the crypto market is significantly enhanced. When major financial institutions and large corporations are seen actively using robust security measures to protect their valuable digital assets, it sends a strong and persuasive message to the rest of the market. This institutional involvement suggests that the technology is maturing and evolving, and that the potential risks associated with it are manageable—a crucial factor in effectively convincing more conservative and risk-averse investors to participate in the expansive digital economy and explore the opportunities it offers.

The Future of Wallets: Innovation and Integration

As the cryptocurrency market continues to evolve and expand, the technology that underpins digital wallets is also advancing significantly. The next generation of wallet solutions is set to integrate even more seamlessly with the broader digital ecosystem that encompasses various platforms and currencies. Future wallets may indeed combine the convenience of custodial services—where third parties manage user funds—with the enhanced security of non-custodial control, which allows users to maintain direct authority over their assets. This innovative hybrid solution has the potential to offer users the best of both worlds, capitalizing on the benefits and strengths of each approach. As this evolution unfolds, users can expect smarter, more secure, and user-friendly wallet experiences that cater to their diverse needs and preferences in the digital finance landscape.

For instance, a variety of innovative projects are currently focused on developing advanced multi-signature wallets, which require multiple keys to successfully authorize any transaction. This setup effectively introduces an additional layer of security by ensuring that even if one key were to be compromised, the funds would still remain secure and safe from unauthorized access. Furthermore, other significant advancements are also being made, such as the seamless integration of sophisticated biometric authentication methods alongside secure enclave technologies in modern mobile devices. These cutting-edge innovations bring high-level security and protection literally right into your pocket, enhancing user confidence and overall safety in digital transactions.

Moreover, the continuous and rapid advancement of decentralized finance, commonly referred to as DeFi, has significantly intensified the demand for digital wallets that possess not just security, but also remarkable versatility. In today's financial landscape, modern software wallets are being meticulously crafted to seamlessly interact with a diverse range of DeFi protocols. This functionality empowers users to not only manage their digital assets with ease but also to invest wisely and potentially earn attractive interest on their holdings, all without the need to navigate away from the wallet interface. This trend towards integration epitomizes a logical progression in wallet technology, where the crucial elements of convenience and control are masterfully balanced within a user-friendly interface, thus enhancing the overall user experience, enabling individuals to make informed financial decisions on their own terms.

The continuous and rapid innovation in wallet technology serves as a powerful testament to the relentless pursuit of enhanced security and improved usability in our ever-evolving digital age. As skilled developers diligently refine and enhance these advanced tools, the intricate trade-offs that exist between convenience and control have begun to blur and become less stark. Looking ahead, the future may well witness an exciting convergence of custodial and non-custodial features—a sophisticated system in which users can seamlessly enjoy the numerous benefits of both types without any significant compromise on security or usability. This promising evolution could transform the landscape of digital wallets, making them more accessible and secure for everyone.

Persuading the Skeptics: The Case for Personal Responsibility

Despite the clear advantages that non-custodial solutions offer, many individuals still opt for custodial wallets primarily due to their simplicity and ease of use. However, the argument for taking personal responsibility for your digital assets is not only logical but also incredibly compelling. By managing your own keys, you can effectively eliminate the significant risk associated with a third party mismanaging or potentially losing your funds in the process. The profound freedom that comes with self-custody truly embodies the very essence of decentralization—it is a clear, bold statement that you gain full control over your own financial destiny and future. This choice empowers you to make decisions that align with your values and financial goals, enabling a more secure and autonomous approach to handling your assets in an ever-evolving digital landscape. Ultimately, embracing self-custody represents a deeper understanding of the responsibilities and rewards that come with the ownership of digital wealth.

The persuasive argument presented here is twofold. First, when we examine it from a purely technical perspective, non-custodial wallets deliver a significantly higher level of security that custodial solutions simply cannot match. They stand immune to the myriad risks associated with centralized failures and, as such, offer a transparency that is truly unparalleled in the digital financial realm because the ultimate control resides solely in your hands, which is crucial for ensuring your assets remain safe from external threats. Second, when viewed from a philosophical standpoint, opting for self-custody is a bold declaration of independence in the modern digital age. It represents a conscious refusal to rely on institutions that have, time and again, proven themselves all too capable of failing their users, often with devastating consequences for those who put their trust in them. In this way, choosing non-custodial wallets reflects a deeper commitment to personal privacy and autonomy in an increasingly interconnected world.

This perspective has gained significant traction among a growing number of serious investors and dedicated crypto enthusiasts, who fully recognize that the true promise of decentralized finance lies in the profound sense of personal empowerment it offers. The logical conclusion to draw from this understanding is straightforward: if you genuinely value your financial freedom and aspirations and want to ensure that your valuable assets are secure and protected, you must be willing to shoulder the full responsibility that inevitably comes with adopting non-custodial solutions. While this concept may initially seem daunting or overwhelming to some, the multitude of benefits far outweighs the potential risks involved—creating a compelling and persuasive argument for the long-term security and stability of digital assets in our ever-evolving financial landscape.

The Economic Impact: How Wallet Security Influences the Market

The debate over custodial versus non-custodial wallets carries significant economic implications that cannot be underestimated. When investors feel confident that their valuable digital assets are secure and protected, they are much more likely to invest and hold onto those assets for the long term. This favorable "HODLing" behavior encourages market stability and gradually drives sustainable growth that benefits all participants. Conversely, if there is widespread concern and fear regarding wallet security among investors, it can lead to panic selling and increased market volatility. Such fluctuations can create a sense of uncertainty, deterring potential investors from engaging in the market and adversely affecting its overall health and stability.

The evolution of wallet security—from the fragile paper wallets used in Bitcoin's early days to the advanced and sophisticated hardware and software solutions we see today—has been a crucial factor in the maturation and overall growth of the crypto market. Improved security measures have significantly reduced the risk of hacks and thefts, which has, in turn, increased public trust in digital currencies. This enhanced trust among users has, in essence, attracted a much broader base of investors, including institutional players who now demand rigorous and high security standards before engaging in any transactions. As a result, the landscape of cryptocurrency investment has shifted dramatically, leading to a greater overall stability in the market.

The impact of secure wallets is also clearly evident in the significant rise of decentralized finance (DeFi) applications. As secure, non-custodial wallets become increasingly prevalent within the cryptocurrency landscape, they enable the development of more complex and innovative financial applications that rely heavily on the safe and effective management of digital assets. DeFi platforms, which allow users to lend, borrow, trade, and engage in various financial activities involving cryptocurrencies without the need for traditional intermediaries, depend fundamentally on robust wallet technology. The stability, security, and user-friendliness provided by modern wallets are thus a cornerstone of the broader crypto ecosystem, underscoring the logical necessity of consistently investing in and continuously improving wallet solutions to ensure user confidence and facilitate the growth of the decentralized finance sector. Overall, secure wallets are vital to the future success and evolution of digital finance.

User Experience and Accessibility: The Driving Force of Adoption

While security remains paramount in the realm of digital finance, it is crucial to recognize that the user experience holds an equally significant role in the widespread adoption and utilization of wallet technology. Custodial wallets, which are known for their ease of use, particularly appeal to beginners and those individuals who prefer a more hands-off and straightforward approach to managing their digital assets. However, as users gain more experience and familiarity with the technology, many begin to appreciate the valuable benefits offered by non-custodial solutions that provide increased control and enhanced security over their funds. This shift in user preference is important as it highlights the evolving landscape of digital wallets and the varying needs of users at different stages of their journey.

The evolution from traditional paper wallets to advanced software options, and eventually to the increasingly popular hardware wallets, has been primarily driven by the pressing need to effectively balance security with usability. The most successful wallet solutions available today are those that effectively manage to combine robust and powerful security measures with a user-friendly and accessible interface. The persuasive argument here is abundantly clear: if digital wallets are to gain widespread mainstream acceptance across various demographics, they must be made accessible to everyone—regardless of individual technical expertise or background knowledge.

Recent advancements in wallet technology have notably focused on significantly enhancing the overall user experience, which greatly simplifies the process for people when it comes to navigating the often complex landscape of digital asset management. Mobile wallets, for instance, have effectively brought secure and reliable crypto storage directly into the palms of millions of individuals across the globe, making it incredibly simple to send, receive, and efficiently manage funds while on the go. This unparalleled accessibility stands as a key factor in driving the ongoing global shift towards adopting digital currencies, as it effectively removes barriers to entry and empowers a larger number of individuals to actively participate in and engage with the decentralized financial ecosystem. Through these innovations, the world of finance is becoming more inclusive and user-friendly.

Bridging the Gap: Hybrid Approaches and Future Innovations

As the ongoing debate between custodial and non-custodial wallets continues to gain traction, many users and experts are actively exploring various hybrid approaches that aim to merge the best of both worlds into a singular solution. These innovative and versatile solutions offer users the undeniable convenience of custodial services while still allowing them a significant level of autonomy to maintain control over their private keys. For instance, some of the more advanced and modern wallet providers today offer multi-signature solutions, whereby multiple parties must authorize a transaction to facilitate its completion. This approach not only enhances the overall user experience but can also provide several additional layers of security, thereby minimizing risks, without completely relinquishing control from the user. By striking a balance between ease of use and security, hybrid wallets are positioning themselves as an increasingly popular choice for both new and experienced cryptocurrency users alike.

The evolution of hybrid wallets represents a logical and necessary progression in the ongoing quest for achieving balance in digital asset management. These wallets acknowledge the undeniable reality that different users have diverse and varying needs—some individuals may prioritize ease-of-use and seamless transactions, while others insist on maintaining full control over their assets and security. By offering highly customizable solutions that can adapt to individual preferences, hybrid wallets effectively cater to a much broader audience and pave the way for a more inclusive and accessible crypto ecosystem. This adaptability not only enhances user experience but also encourages broader participation in the digital economy.

Looking ahead into the future, the realm of wallet technology is likely to be defined by ongoing and continuous innovation as well as seamless integration. With remarkable advances in fields such as artificial intelligence, biometrics, and cloud computing, we can certainly expect even more sophisticated and robust solutions that will make managing digital assets not only simpler but also significantly safer and far more efficient. The logical trajectory is unmistakable and clear: as technology evolves and progresses, the tools and systems we use to secure our wealth and assets must evolve in tandem with these advancements as well. In this dynamic landscape, adaptability will be paramount for both users and service providers alike.

Persuading the Skeptics: The Importance of Self-Custody

Despite the undeniable convenience that custodial wallets offer, the argument for choosing non-custodial, self-managed solutions remains exceptionally powerful and compelling. The very essence of the decentralized financial revolution is rooted deeply in the principle of self-sovereignty—the profound idea that individuals should possess complete, unwavering control over their own money and financial assets. This concept is particularly persuasive and resonates strongly in a world where centralized financial institutions have frequently failed their users, leaving them vulnerable and exposed. It highlights the importance of personal ownership and autonomy in financial matters, advocating for a system where individuals can trust in their ability to manage their own funds without relying on potentially unreliable third parties.

Self-custody is not without its various challenges and complexities, but it is also the ultimate and most profound expression of true financial independence. When you take the initiative to manage your own private keys, you are assuming full responsibility for your financial future in the most direct and personal way that is possible. This responsibility may initially sound daunting, intimidating, or overwhelming, but it is also incredibly empowering and liberating. The logical argument is straightforward and simple: if you truly value your freedom and autonomy, and you want to ensure that your hard-earned assets are secure and safe, then you must be willing to take complete control of them yourself, without relying on external parties or institutions.

The benefits of self-custody extend far beyond just enhanced security measures. They foster a culture of increased responsibility and deeper awareness among users, encouraging individuals to educate themselves about the various intricacies involved in digital asset management. By engaging in this educational journey, they contribute significantly to creating a more knowledgeable, resilient, and empowered community of users—one that is much better equipped to navigate the myriad complexities of the ever-evolving digital economy. This presents a compelling and persuasive case for wholeheartedly embracing self-custody as a core principle that should underpin the decentralized financial future we aspire to create. Ultimately, it is through self-custody that users can truly take charge of their financial destinies.

The Economic Impact: How Wallet Choices Shape the Market

The decision-making process regarding custodial versus non-custodial wallets carries significant economic implications. When a greater number of users decide to utilize secure and self-managed wallets, the overall security and resilience of the cryptocurrency ecosystem experiences a notable enhancement. Such changes bolster investor confidence, which acts as a catalyst for increasing market stability and growth. Conversely, an over-reliance on custodial solutions tends to concentrate risks within a few large institutions, potentially making the entire financial system susceptible to centralized failures or malfunctions. This dynamic can create an environment of uncertainty that affects all participants in the market.

The evolution of wallet technology has already had a significant and tangible impact on market dynamics, reshaping the landscape in numerous ways. As secure, non-custodial solutions become more prevalent, they inherently encourage a more cautious, thoughtful, and long-term investment mindset among participants in the market. Investors who actively manage their own keys are much less likely to engage in panic selling and are significantly more inclined to hold their assets through various market fluctuations. This behavior, in turn, contributes positively to overall market resilience and stability. The logical progression of this trend is evident: when the tools for securely managing digital assets are both secure and reliable, the market as a whole benefits tremendously from increased stability and a reduction in volatility.

Furthermore, the enhanced transparency provided by non-custodial wallets significantly boosts accountability within the cryptocurrency realm. With every single transaction meticulously recorded on a public ledger, it becomes increasingly difficult for malicious actors to manipulate the system or engage in any form of fraudulent activities. This heightened level of trust not only benefits individual users who seek security and reliability, but it also attracts substantial institutional investment. As a result, this influx of investment plays a critical role in further solidifying the legitimacy and long-term viability of digital currencies in the global financial market.

Social and Cultural Dimensions: Empowering the Masses

Beyond the technical and economic aspects, the evolution of wallet technology carries profound social and cultural implications that cannot be overlooked. In traditional financial systems, control over money is predominantly concentrated in the hands of a few centralized institutions, which results in significant barriers for countless individuals who seek access to their resources. The advent of non-custodial wallets marks a radical and transformational departure from this conventional model—it effectively democratizes access to essential financial tools and empowers individuals to take charge of their own economic destinies, paving the way for a more inclusive and equitable financial landscape. This shift enables individuals to manage their assets directly, fostering financial independence and encouraging new forms of economic participation that were previously unattainable.

This shift represents a pivotal component of the broader decentralized finance movement, which earnestly seeks to level the playing field and create a more inclusive and accessible financial system for everyone. When individuals have direct and complete control over their digital assets, they become significantly less dependent on traditional intermediaries, making them much more capable of actively participating in the global economy. This newfound empowerment has the incredible potential to transform societies in profound ways by enabling greater financial inclusion for all, significantly reducing inequality, and fostering innovation across various sectors. In turn, such transformations can lead to a more equitable and balanced financial landscape, where everyone has the opportunity to thrive and succeed.

The evolution from traditional paper wallets to sophisticated hardware and software solutions is not merely a significant technological achievement; rather, it is a profound social revolution. This progression represents a fundamental and essential rethinking of the relationship that individuals have with their own money—a transformative shift from a passive reliance on established financial institutions to an active, self-determined, and empowered management of personal wealth. This cultural transformation, which encompasses a wide array of perspectives and practices, is both shocking and immensely inspiring. It offers a bold new vision of financial freedom that is as logical as it is revolutionary, inviting individuals to reclaim control over their financial futures and navigate their own paths toward economic independence. This newfound approach challenges traditional notions and opens doors to a more equitable and inclusive financial landscape.

Future Directions: The Ongoing Evolution of Wallet Technology

As we look to the future, the ongoing evolution of wallet technology is far from complete and is expected to progress even further. The journey from simple paper wallets to today's sophisticated and complex non-custodial solutions has been marked by continuous and remarkable innovation. As we gaze ahead, we can confidently expect even further advancements that will make the management of digital assets not only more secure but also vastly more convenient and seamlessly integrated into our daily lives.

Emerging trends in the cryptocurrency landscape point to an exciting development of hybrid wallet solutions, which seamlessly combine the convenience and efficiency of custodial services with the enhanced security and control associated with non-custodial wallets. These innovative approaches may feature advanced multi-signature configurations, robust biometric security measures, and seamless integration with a variety of decentralized applications (dApps). The main goal is to create a unified and versatile system that effectively caters to a diverse range of users, which includes everyone from novice investors who are just starting out to experienced traders who require more sophisticated features, all without compromising on vital security protocols or user-friendly accessibility.

Furthermore, the integration of cutting-edge artificial intelligence and sophisticated machine learning into the realm of wallet technology has the potential to completely transform how users interact with and manage their valuable digital assets. Picture a wallet that isn't just a static storage solution for your keys, but rather an intelligent system that actively learns from your individual behavior patterns. This smart wallet could optimize your security settings in real time and even offer customized investment advice tailored specifically to your financial goals and preferences—all of this while upholding the highest possible standards of privacy and user control. Such advancements, although still in their infancy, hold great promise in bridging the existing gap between unparalleled convenience and complete control, thereby making the process of digital asset management significantly more intuitive, versatile, and robust.

The future of wallet technology serves as a remarkable testament to the extraordinary power of human ingenuity—a mind-blowing convergence of security, cutting-edge innovation, and everyday practicality. It represents a logical evolution that not only builds on the valuable lessons learned from the past but also addresses the diverse needs of an increasingly digital and interconnected world we live in today. As the tools and methods for managing digital assets continue to become more sophisticated and advanced, the benefits will extend far beyond merely enhancing individual security. Instead, they will play a crucial role in stabilizing markets, empowering users with greater autonomy, and overall shaping the broader ecosystem of decentralized finance in significant and transformative ways.

Persuading the Skeptics: Embracing the Next Generation of Security

Despite the remarkable and significant progress that has been made in the realm of wallet technology, skepticism still remains firmly entrenched among some circles of users and critics. Detractors frequently point to the learning curve that is often associated with non-custodial solutions and the substantial potential for human error that can arise in their use. However, the ongoing and continuous evolution of wallet technology is steadily and progressively addressing these concerns that critics raise. Open-source development initiatives, rigorous security audits, and the introduction of user-friendly interfaces are collectively and constantly improving the overall reliability and accessibility of non-custodial wallets in today's digital landscape.

The persuasive argument for these significant advancements is very much rooted in clear and compelling logic: as technology continues to mature and evolve, the systems we rely on necessarily must adapt and transform to effectively meet the challenges presented by a rapidly changing and increasingly complex digital environment. The thoughtful integration of advanced security features—such as robust hardware isolation, highly effective biometric authentication, and sophisticated multi-signature functionality—demonstrates that the industry is definitely not standing still. Rather, it is engaging in a constant state of improvement, innovation, and evolution, driven by the same analytical and forward-thinking spirit that originally brought us the first paper wallets, which were groundbreaking in their own right.

For users, the remarkable evolution of wallet technology has fundamentally transformed the once-daunting task of managing private keys into an accessible and secure process that can be easily navigated. It empowers individuals from all walks of life to take full control over their digital assets, ensuring that they can do so without sacrificing the convenience that is necessary for everyday use and interactions. This delicate balance of security and usability is the logical and impressive culmination of decades of technological progress—a profound transformation that is both shocking in its rapid pace and mind-blowing in terms of its wide-reaching impact on how we handle digital ownership. The implications of this advancement ripple throughout the entire digital landscape, providing users not only with enhanced security but also with unprecedented ease of access.

The Broader Impact: Wallet Technology as a Foundation for Decentralized Finance

The evolution of wallet technology possesses far-reaching implications that extend well beyond merely the security of individual assets and holdings. It forms the crucial bedrock upon which the entire decentralized finance (DeFi) ecosystem is firmly built. Secure and efficient wallets not only protect users' funds but also enable individuals to actively participate in a wide array of financial activities. These activities include lending, borrowing, trading, and even earning interest on various digital assets—all without the need for traditional financial intermediaries that often create barriers and additional costs. This technological advancement empowers users to take control of their financial destinies in ways previously thought impossible.

This new and innovative financial paradigm has the tremendous potential to revolutionize the entire global economy in significant ways. By effectively removing the numerous barriers that are often imposed by traditional centralized institutions, decentralized finance offers a much more inclusive, transparent, and efficient system for managing wealth and resources. The logical foundation for this major shift is abundantly clear: when individuals possess direct control over their own assets, the entire financial system becomes far more resilient and responsive to the ever-evolving needs of a diverse and varied population. In this way, we can build a stronger and more equitable economic future for all.

The advancements in wallet technology have indeed emerged as a crucial driver in this evolving process. As digital wallets continue to become more secure, reliable, and user-friendly, they significantly facilitate the broader adoption of a wide range of decentralized financial services. This increased accessibility and usability, in turn, attracts a larger number of users, which enhances market stability and drives ongoing innovation throughout the entire crypto ecosystem. The continuous evolution and improvement of wallets is, therefore, not merely an isolated technological development but rather a key and integral component of the broader movement towards a more decentralized, equitable, and dynamic financial future that benefits all participants.

Persuasive Reflections: The Logical Path to Digital Empowerment

For individuals who remain skeptical about the numerous merits that non-custodial wallet technology offers, the logical argument presented in favor of it is indeed compelling and hard to ignore. The remarkable journey from basic paper wallets to increasingly sophisticated hardware and software solutions serves as a clear and impressive demonstration of human ingenuity, creativity, and the relentless pursuit of security in an ever-evolving digital landscape. Each significant innovation developed along the way has been driven by a simple, yet profoundly important, need: to effectively protect digital assets from a world that is full of unpredictable and often treacherous threats. This evolution illustrates not just a technological advancement, but also the growing awareness and necessity for robust security measures in the management of digital property.

The analytical case for non-custodial wallets is quite straightforward and compelling: when you have full control over your own keys, you essentially have full control over your own money. This fundamental principle is placed at the very heart of the concept of decentralization and serves as a powerful antidote to the various vulnerabilities found in centralized systems. It makes for a logical and persuasive argument tailored for anyone who deeply values both financial freedom and security in their transactions. By retaining control of your keys, you mitigate the risks associated with trusting third parties, allowing for greater peace of mind when managing your assets.

In a world that is becoming increasingly dominated by sophisticated cyber threats and where centralized institutions have repeatedly demonstrated their vulnerability to corruption and mismanagement, the vital shift toward non-custodial solutions represents a logical and rational response to these challenges. This evolution is one that builds upon the critical lessons learned from past experiences and is further reinforced by the clear and analytical evidence that showcases significantly improved security, increased transparency, and enhanced user empowerment in various digital landscapes. As we observe the unfolding complexities of modern technology, it becomes apparent that non-custodial approaches not only address existing vulnerabilities but also pave the way for a more decentralized future where individuals maintain greater control over their assets and data.

The Enduring Importance of Wallet Innovation

The evolution of wallet technology—from the fragile and easily damaged paper wallets that early adopters utilized to the cutting-edge, advanced hardware and software solutions we rely on today—presents a truly mind-blowing narrative that vividly embodies the astounding power of human innovation in the face of overwhelming challenges. This remarkable journey is distinctly marked by logical reasoning, thorough and rigorous analysis, and an unwavering, relentless drive to secure digital wealth in a world that is becoming increasingly volatile and unpredictable. As technology advances, the necessity for security and convenience has propelled the development of wallets that not only safeguard our assets but also provide unparalleled accessibility, reflecting both the ingenuity and resilience of the human spirit.

This evolution represents more than just a simple technical upgrade; it signifies a profound and transformative process that has reshaped the entire landscape of digital finance in unprecedented ways. By offering a highly secure and reliable means of managing private keys, hardware wallets and cold storage solutions have successfully instilled a remarkable level of trust and stability that has empowered cryptocurrencies to transition from the fringes of the financial world to an accepted and established mainstream presence. They have effectively transformed what was once perceived as a risky, uncharted frontier into a viable, robust, and accessible financial system that countless individuals can confidently engage with. This change has opened up new opportunities and broadened financial inclusivity for many, marking a significant milestone in the evolution of modern finance.

For individuals navigating the complex landscape of digital finance, the evolution of wallet technology presents a remarkable and powerful choice between convenience and control over their assets. While custodial wallets provide notable ease of use and accessibility, non-custodial solutions grant users complete sovereignty and governance over their cherished digital assets. This critical balance strikes at the heart of a fundamental tenet of the decentralized financial revolution—a truly mind-blowing shift in our collective perceptions and management of money as we know it. The implications for users in this ever-evolving financial ecosystem are profound and transformative.

The persuasive power of these remarkable innovations undoubtedly lies in their logical and methodical progression. Each advancement, whether it be the traditional paper wallets or the latest cutting-edge hardware, signifies a significant step forward within the ongoing quest for enhanced security and improved efficiency. The meticulous and precise engineering behind modern wallets, when combined with open-source collaboration and relentless continuous improvement, has culminated in the creation of a system that is not only accessible to the masses but also incredibly secure. This is indeed a shockingly clear demonstration that, even in a world as unpredictable and chaotic as the ever-evolving digital realm, human ingenuity possesses the remarkable ability to create order, reliability, and unwavering trust in systems that we employ.

As we gaze into the horizon of possibilities, the promise of further groundbreaking innovation in wallet technology is not only exciting but also seems inevitable. The seamless integration of advanced biometrics, sophisticated artificial intelligence, and cutting-edge encryption methods will undoubtedly enhance the overall security and user experience of digital wallets. These significant advancements will greatly democratize access to digital assets, fostering financial inclusion and enabling a larger number of individuals than ever before to actively participate in the global economy. This evolution in technology could reshape how we engage with our finances, ensuring safety while opening doors to newfound opportunities for all.

In conclusion, the evolution of wallet technology marks a pivotal chapter in the ongoing narrative of digital currencies—a narrative that is as logical, analytical, and systematic as it is groundbreaking and revolutionary in nature. The remarkable journey from basic paper wallets to advanced, secure, and sophisticated solutions serves as a powerful testament to the relentless pursuit of financial freedom and security in an increasingly complex world that is rapidly embracing the principles of decentralization. For investors, everyday users, and creative innovators alike, the future of money will ultimately depend on the continuous and dynamic evolution of these financial tools. This future envisions a space where the balance between convenience and control is not only maintained but is actively and continually improved upon, addressing the needs of a diverse and growing user base while fostering trust and innovation in the financial ecosystem.

Embrace the ongoing evolution of wallet technology, and do so with excitement and anticipation. Recognize fully that every innovation, every groundbreaking breakthrough in security and usability, represents a significant step towards creating a more secure, resilient, and empowering financial system for everyone involved. In this fast-paced digital age, where the stakes are higher than they have ever been, the ability to manage, protect, and grow your digital assets is absolutely paramount. The journey of wallet innovation is not merely a tale of technological progress; it is, in truth, a profound, logical, and persuasive argument for the very future of money itself—a future where decentralization and personal empowerment become the standard, and where the totality of your financial freedom lies entirely within your own hands and decision-making power.

Section 4: User Empowerment Through Enhanced Security Protocols

In today's rapidly evolving digital economy, where vast millions of dollars worth of assets can be conveniently stored on a single device, the stakes have reached unprecedented heights. The startling and sobering reality is that even a small, seemingly minor lapse in security protocols can ultimately lead to catastrophic financial loss, affecting individuals and businesses alike. Yet, amid this high-risk environment for digital transactions and data storage, a significant revolution in security technology is quietly unfolding—a profound revolution that is empowering users to take control of their digital wealth and assets like never before. This section delves deeply into the technological advancements and innovations that have dramatically transformed the landscape of digital asset security. It offers a logical, analytical, and persuasive look into how these enhanced security protocols not only protect individuals but also empower them to safeguard their hard-earned money against theft and fraud in an ever-changing digital world.

A New Frontier in Digital Security

Imagine a world where your financial future isn't at the mercy of centralized institutions that are often prone to hacks and mismanagement, but is instead secured by cutting-edge technology that truly puts you in full control. This is the empowering reality for millions of cryptocurrency users across the globe today. In the early days of digital currencies, security was often an afterthought for many individuals navigating this new financial landscape. People stored private keys carelessly in simple text files, handwritten on paper, or even in unencrypted digital wallets. These rudimentary methods left users embarrassingly vulnerable to cyber-attacks, phishing scams, and horrifying hardware failures. The shocking aftermath of losing an entire fortune due to a single devastating hack drove home the absolute necessity of innovation in security protocols. The evolution of more robust security measures has transformed the crypto space, making it safer and more reliable for users who are seeking to protect their valuable assets.

Over time, the vibrant and ever-evolving crypto community came to a startling realization: to genuinely empower users and ensure their peace of mind, security must undergo significant evolution. No longer could the digital wealth of individuals be left exposed and vulnerable in a digital landscape that is constantly teeming with potential threats and dangers. Thus began a remarkable journey filled with mind-blowing innovations—each one meticulously crafted and designed to provide users with unparalleled control, protection, and unwavering confidence over their precious digital assets.

The Evolution from Basic Storage to Advanced Protocols

The journey of security technology in the crypto space can be traced back to the initial, primitive storage methods that were available at the time. Early adopters took the plunge and began using paper wallets—a simple yet remarkably effective method for securely storing private keys offline. Paper wallets were revolutionary in their own way because they provided a reliable cold storage solution that was immune to the threats of online hacking and cyber theft. However, despite their logical advantages, paper wallets came with serious drawbacks that could not be ignored. They were often very fragile, could be easily lost, and, most importantly, offered no built-in backup mechanism to ensure recovery. A single tear or an accidental spilled drink could devastate and wipe out a person's entire digital fortune, leaving them with nothing in the blink of an eye. As the landscape of digital currency and technology continues to evolve, it became evident that more robust solutions needed to be implemented to address these vulnerabilities.

Recognizing these vulnerabilities in the realm of digital security, developers began diligently creating software-based wallets specifically designed to safely store private keys on various digital devices. These innovative wallets incorporated essential features such as encryption and password protection to enhance security measures. This development represented a significant step forward in safeguarding digital assets—by effectively encrypting the private keys, users were now able to protect their sensitive data from unauthorized access and potential theft. However, as the digital landscape expanded and evolved into a more complex environment, it soon became clear that further enhancements and improvements were needed to ensure the continued safety of users' information and assets.

The evolution of digital currency management continued decisively with the innovative introduction of hardware wallets, which have proven to be a true game changer in the realm of online financial security. Hardware wallets are specialized physical devices, which often resemble standard USB drives, that store private keys in an exceptionally secure and isolated environment. Unlike traditional software wallets that reside on an internet-connected device, hardware wallets maintain the keys securely offline, which drastically reduces the risk of potential online attacks and hacking attempts. This advanced technology is founded on robust cryptographic techniques and secure elements—these are specialized chips that have been meticulously designed to resist various forms of tampering and unauthorized access. When a transaction is initiated, the hardware wallet performs the signature process internally, without ever exposing the private key to the connected device, thereby ensuring that even in the unfortunate event that the connected computer is compromised or compromised, the funds and sensitive information held on the hardware wallet remain completely safe and secure. By implementing hardware wallets, users can enjoy increased peace of mind knowing they have taken substantial precautions to protect their digital assets from the myriad threats present in today's digital landscape.

The shift to hardware wallets has undeniably marked a significant turning point in the realm of digital asset security for users and investors alike. It provided these individuals with a level of protection that was once thought to be unimaginable in this rapidly evolving landscape, effectively turning what was once considered a vulnerable and risky venture into a secure and manageable process. This remarkable transformation is both logical and quite persuasive: when the potential loss of millions of dollars is at stake in the digital asset world, it is only rational to make a substantial investment in the most robust and advanced security measures available to safeguard one's financial interests and future.

Enhanced Security Protocols: Multi-Factor and Beyond

Modern hardware and software wallets do not simply rely on a single layer of security; rather, they are fortified by multiple, overlapping, and complementary defenses that work together to provide enhanced protection. One of the most significant advancements in this vital area of security is the integration of multi-factor authentication (MFA). MFA requires users to verify their identity through several different channels, which can include entering a password, inputting a code that has been sent to a mobile device, or even utilizing biometric data, such as a fingerprint or facial recognition. This extra layer of security dramatically increases the difficulty for hackers trying to gain unauthorized access to sensitive information, as they would need to successfully bypass several independent security measures simultaneously. This comprehensive approach greatly diminishes the likelihood of breaches and helps ensure that personal and financial data remain secure from potential threats. By combining multiple verification methods, users can feel more confident that they are protected against a wide range of attack vectors, making it essential for anyone seeking to safeguard their digital assets.

Consider this scenario: even if a malicious actor were to successfully obtain your password through some means, they would still face the significant challenge of needing the second or third factor—something that is typically unique to you as an individual, such as a fingerprint, facial recognition, or a one-time code that is generated securely on your phone. This logical enhancement in security protocols significantly improves overall security measures, not only providing a much higher degree of protection but also helping to build lasting user confidence in the system. The argument is straightforward and quite clear: the more factors that are employed to protect your valuable assets and sensitive information, the lower the risk of unauthorized access becomes, effectively acting as a strong deterrent against potential cyber threats.

Advanced encryption algorithms undoubtedly play an absolutely crucial role in the security landscape. In contemporary digital wallets, state-of-the-art encryption methods are employed rigorously to ensure that private keys are securely stored in a format that is entirely unreadable without the appropriate decryption key. This level of encryption serves as the digital equivalent of a sophisticated lock on a safe—functioning as an essential protective barrier that effectively prevents any unauthorized outsider from gaining access to your valuable assets. The ongoing and continuous improvement of encryption protocols, spurred on by both extensive academic research and relentless industry innovation, has rendered it practically impossible for cybercriminals to crack these advanced systems without possessing the proper keys. The logic behind this is undeniably clear: as cyber threats grow increasingly sophisticated and complex, our security measures must likewise evolve in response to these challenges accordingly. Today's encryption standards are, without a doubt, among the strongest in the world, showcasing the advancements we have made in protecting sensitive information.

The Role of Open-Source Technology in Security Innovation

One of the most compelling and persuasive aspects of enhanced security protocols in the ever-evolving crypto space is undoubtedly the significant impact of the open-source movement. A large number of the leading wallet solutions are developed as open-source projects, which means that their underlying code is readily available for anyone to inspect, modify, and improve upon as they see fit. This level of transparency fosters and builds trust within the community, as users can be assured that there are no hidden backdoors or malicious components lurking within the software. Furthermore, open-source projects benefit immensely from a vast and diverse global community of developers who continuously scrutinize the code, tirelessly work to identify vulnerabilities, and swiftly implement necessary improvements and enhancements. This collaborative approach not only enhances security but also encourages innovation in the crypto space.

This collaborative approach to security is not only logical but also remarkably effective in practice. When thousands of keen eyes are diligently examining the intricate code, flaws and vulnerabilities are significantly more likely to be caught and rectified before they ever have a chance to be exploited by malicious entities. The open-source model fundamentally democratizes the concept of security—ensuring that the finest and most innovative ideas can flourish and thrive, leading to an overall system that becomes increasingly stronger and more resilient over time. This represents a mind-blowing demonstration of collective intelligence in action—a fundamental and transformative shift from the traditional model, where security measures are developed behind closed doors by a limited number of centralized entities, often lacking the necessary transparency and outside input that can enhance their efficacy.

Real-World Examples: Successes and Lessons Learned

The impact of enhanced security protocols is perhaps best illustrated by a variety of compelling real-world examples that demonstrate their effectiveness and necessity. Consider the remarkable story of Ledger, a leading and highly respected provider of hardware wallets in the digital security landscape. Ledger's devices are now utilized by millions of individuals around the globe to securely safeguard their precious digital assets, and they have truly become synonymous with state-of-the-art security measures in the fast-evolving crypto space. The rigorous and meticulous design principles behind

Ledger's hardware—featuring advanced secure elements, comprehensive multi-factor authentication processes, and robust encryption techniques—have effectively withstood numerous hacking attempts over time, proving that a well-engineered security solution can successfully protect even the most valuable and sensitive assets in an increasingly threatening cyber environment.

On the other hand, the early failures encountered in the domain of wallet security have provided invaluable lessons that have significantly influenced the ongoing evolution of these technologies. In the initial stages of development, numerous software wallets suffered greatly due to poor user interface design and inadequate encryption practices. This led to unfortunate instances where many users lost their funds due to vulnerabilities. These failures, which were shocking and alarming at the time, ultimately served as key catalysts for improvement in wallet security. The vulnerabilities that were exposed by these early missteps not only highlighted serious issues but also led to a more comprehensive and robust understanding of the challenges involved in effectively securing digital assets in a rapidly changing environment. Today, the lessons learned from those past mistakes are meticulously integrated into each new iteration of wallet technology. As a direct result, the current generation of wallets is now far more secure, reliable, and user-friendly than ever before, providing enhanced features that protect users from similar risks.

The Psychological Impact: Transforming Fear into Confidence

Beyond the technical and logical aspects, enhanced security protocols play a crucial role in shaping the psychological landscape for users. In the ever-volatile world of digital currencies, the fear of loss—often referred to as "FUD" (fear, uncertainty, and doubt)—has emerged as a significant barrier to the widespread adoption of these technologies. When users are gripped by the terrifying thought that a single security breach could potentially wipe out their hard-earned savings, they are understandably less likely to invest in or even hold onto their digital assets with any degree of confidence. Enhanced security protocols, by effectively and significantly reducing the risk of theft or loss, serve to transform that pervasive fear into a newfound sense of confidence and assurance for users. This shift not only encourages users to participate more actively in the market but also fosters a more supportive environment for the growth and evolution of digital financial systems.

The reassurance provided by robust and comprehensive security measures greatly empowers users to fully participate in the ever-evolving digital economy with a sense of peace and confidence in their safety. Knowing that their valuable assets are securely protected by multi-factor authentication systems, advanced encryption techniques, and hardware-based security solutions, users can focus on effectively using and strategically investing in digital currencies rather than constantly worrying about potential breaches or vulnerabilities that could jeopardize their investments. This significant psychological shift represents a crucial and persuasive factor in the widespread mainstream adoption of cryptocurrencies. When individuals feel secure and confident in the protection of their assets, they are much more likely to invest, seamlessly transact, and even actively advocate for broader adoption, further promoting a thriving digital financial ecosystem.

The Broader Economic and Social Implications

The advancements in security protocols extend far beyond the mere protection of individual users; they have a profound and multifaceted impact on the overall stability and growth of the entire crypto ecosystem. Enhanced security measures substantially increase investor confidence, which in turn attracts a much larger pool of institutional investment. As more capital continues to flow into the burgeoning market, the legitimacy and stability of digital currencies are profoundly reinforced. This creates a positive feedback loop where enhanced security leads to greater adoption across the board, which subsequently drives further innovation as well as refinement of security measures that are critical in this evolving landscape. The interconnectedness of these factors underscores the importance of robust security in fostering a thriving crypto environment that can be trusted by users and investors alike.

Furthermore, as digital asset management continues to evolve and enhance security measures, the obstacles to achieving financial inclusion are increasingly diminished. In conventional financial systems, a significant number of individuals across the globe are often left out and marginalized due to the lack of access to reliable and secure banking solutions. By implementing robust and advanced security protocols, digital wallets emerge as a feasible and accessible alternative, enabling people in underserved and economically challenged regions to effectively engage and participate in the broader global economy. This significant shift towards the democratization of finance is not only a logical development stemming from technological advancements but also serves as a compelling argument for the transformative potential inherent in digital currencies and assets. The capacity to securely manage, store, and transact digital wealth is recognized as a fundamental human right in today's digital age—a profound truth that the introduction and continuous improvement of enhanced security protocols strive to actualize and uphold each and every day.

The Future: Innovations on the Horizon

As we look to the future with anticipation, the evolution of security protocols is indeed far from over and continues to develop at a rapid pace. The field of digital asset security remains in a constant state of flux, driven by the relentless ingenuity of developers who are continually innovating to meet new challenges, and the ever-present threat of cyber attacks that looms large. New and advanced technologies, such as quantum-resistant cryptography, are already being actively explored and tested in order to effectively future-proof wallets against the potential threats posed by quantum computing that could compromise existing security measures. Furthermore, the integration of artificial intelligence and machine learning into security systems holds great promise to significantly enhance threat detection and response times, ultimately creating an even more secure and robust environment for digital transactions. This convergence of cutting-edge technology will likely result in security solutions that are not only faster but also smarter, adapting in real time to the changing landscape of cyber threats. The road ahead is complex, yet filled with possibilities that can lead to a safer digital future.

Furthermore, the next generation of hardware wallets is anticipated to incorporate even more advanced and sophisticated features that will revolutionize how users interact with their digital assets. Innovations like biometric authentication, which adds an extra layer of security by using unique user traits, and ultra-secure multi-signature solutions, which require multiple approvals for transactions, will significantly enhance user protection. Additionally, the seamless integration with decentralized applications (dApps) will empower users, allowing them to access a wide array of services directly from their wallets. These exciting advancements will not only enhance security measures considerably but will also improve the overall user experience, ultimately making it much easier for individuals to manage and control their valuable digital assets without compromising their ability to maintain autonomy over their financial decisions.

The future of wallet technology is an impressive testament to the incredible power of continuous innovation. Each breakthrough in security measures and every new protocol that emerges is meticulously built upon the valuable lessons learned from our past experiences—transforming previous vulnerabilities into newfound strengths and overcoming fear with unwavering confidence. The logical evolution of these groundbreaking technologies serves as a clear indicator that as long as human ingenuity continues to thrive and push boundaries, the tools we rely on to protect our wealth will only become increasingly robust, more reliable, and undeniably accessible to a wider audience.

Persuading the Skeptics: A Rational and Empowering Choice

Despite the significant advancements and improvements made in security, some skeptics continue to remain cautious about the decentralized management of digital assets. Critics argue that the responsibility placed on individuals to effectively manage their own keys is too burdensome for many users. They believe that the risks, although diminished through these advancements, are still too high for the average person to handle safely without external support. However, the continual evolution of enhanced security protocols provides a compelling counterargument to their concerns. These protocols are designed specifically to reduce risks and offer users a greater sense of security, making the management of digital assets much more accessible and effective.

The logical stance is that increased personal responsibility is indeed a small price to pay for the substantial empowerment that comes with true ownership. When you actively manage your own keys, you are not left at the mercy of a central institution that could potentially fail or become compromised at any moment. Instead, you gain direct and unrivaled control over your assets—a notion that is both liberating and entirely logically sound. The additional security measures put in place, ranging from multi-factor authentication to cutting-edge advanced encryption, significantly mitigate the various risks associated with self-custody. This means that every individual can take charge of their financial well-being, making informed decisions that safeguard their wealth and future.

For those individuals who prefer a balance between control and convenience, hybrid solutions that thoughtfully combine aspects of custodial and non-custodial models are emerging and gaining popularity. These innovative solutions provide users with the ability to maintain a degree of personal control over their assets while still benefiting from the undeniable convenience of third-party services. The logical conclusion we can draw is that, as technology continues to advance at a rapid pace, the gap between convenience and security will persist in narrowing, ultimately making it increasingly easier for everyone to securely manage their digital wealth with confidence and ease.

Empowering the Future of Finance

The remarkable evolution of security protocols in digital wallets is a shockingly brilliant story that illustrates continuous innovation, logical progression, and relentless improvement in the face of ever-growing challenges. From the initially fragile paper wallets utilized by early adopters who were navigating the uncharted territory of digital finance, to today's sophisticated hardware and software solutions, every significant step in this transformative journey stands as a logical response to the pressing need for secure, reliable digital asset management in an increasingly digitized world. Enhanced security protocols serve to empower users by giving them greater and more direct control over their wealth, significantly reducing the reliance on traditional centralized financial institutions, while simultaneously transforming what once was fear and uncertainty into newfound confidence and assurance for individuals managing their digital assets.

In a world where digital assets are rapidly becoming a crucial cornerstone of the global economy, the significance of secure and user-empowering solutions cannot be overstated or minimized. The ongoing advancements in multi-factor authentication, sophisticated encryption techniques, open-source development efforts, and comprehensive integrated security features have fundamentally redefined what it means to securely store and effectively manage money in the digital landscape. These innovations offer an unprecedented level of protection that not only safeguards individual investments but also crucially underpins the overall stability and growth potential of the entire crypto ecosystem, allowing for a more robust and reliable financial future.

The broader implications of these groundbreaking innovations are, in fact, profoundly significant. By giving power to users to take full control over their own financial destinies, these enhanced security protocols truly democratize the digital economy. They foster an environment characterized by trust, transparency, and inclusivity, which is essential in today's interconnected world. As an increasing number of individuals gain access to the advanced tools necessary to manage their digital wealth securely and effectively, the immense potential for decentralized finance to fundamentally reshape the global financial system grows ever stronger and more promising. This evolution can potentially lead to a future where financial services are more accessible to diverse populations, breaking down barriers that have historically excluded many.

The future of finance is being constructed on the robust foundation of these remarkable advancements. With a relentless focus on continued innovation, the diverse tools designed to protect our precious digital assets will evolve to become even more sophisticated, increasingly accessible, and ultimately integral to our everyday economic lives. The evolution of wallet security is not merely a technical achievement; rather, it represents a significant paradigm shift that is actively transforming how we perceive and interact with our money in the modern world. This progression we are witnessing is a clear, logical journey from vulnerability to empowerment, paving the way from chaos to a new sense of control that individuals can embrace wholeheartedly.

For the modern investor navigating today's complex financial landscape, the choice between custodial and non-custodial solutions represents much more than just a simple preference. It embodies a profound philosophical debate about essential concepts such as trust, control, and personal freedom. With cutting-edge enhanced security protocols now in place, the balance of power increasingly tips in favor of individual empowerment. This advancement presents a transformative future where your digital wealth is not only secure but also highly accessible, enabling you to maintain control over your assets in a way that was previously unimaginable. This shift is not merely an upgrade in financial security; it constitutes a revolutionary change in the very nature of how we protect and secure our financial futures. As an investor, embracing this evolution means embracing innovation that prioritizes your autonomy and peace of mind in an ever-changing market.

In conclusion, the ongoing evolution of security protocols in digital wallets serves as a powerful testament to human ingenuity and the relentless drive we all possess to overcome various challenges. It is a remarkable journey that is marked by shock, logical reasoning, and undeniable progress—an ongoing journey that has transformed what was once a risky, vulnerable process into a robust, user-empowering system. This system now stands proudly as a pillar of modern decentralized finance, providing users with a sense of safety and confidence in engaging with their financial assets.

Embrace the thriving future of wallet security, for it is indeed the key to unlocking the vast potential of digital assets. With every significant advancement in encryption technology, paired with every improvement in multi-factor authentication methods, we are moving ever closer to a world where your wealth is undeniably your own—a world where financial freedom is not merely an aspiration but a tangible reality. This ongoing evolution represents a powerful, mind-blowing, and ultimately empowering narrative that will not only continue to shape but will revolutionize the future of money for generations yet to come. The promise of secure digital transactions fosters an environment where individuals can safeguard their assets with confidence, creating a stronger economy rooted in trust and innovation.

Section 5: Future Trends in Wallet Technology and Digital Sovereignty

In a world where digital currencies have significantly grown in importance and become a central part of our everyday financial interactions, the methods we employ to store and diligently protect these valuable assets are undergoing continuous and dynamic evolution. This transformation in wallet technology and the overarching concept of digital sovereignty are far more than just abstract ideas or mere technical enhancements—they are actively reshaping the financial landscape we know today in ways that are both astonishing and profoundly transformative. In this section, we will take an in-depth look at the future trends that promise to revolutionize the very foundations of how digital assets are securely stored and protected. We will explore a range of innovations that extend well beyond simple storage solutions, venturing into the realm of cutting-edge technology and novel approaches that empower every user to not only own but also gain complete control over their money with an unprecedented level of security and autonomy that was previously thought unattainable.

A Brave New World of Digital Security

Imagine a remarkable world where your digital wallet is so incredibly secure that even the most sophisticated hackers are left scratching their heads in confusion and disbelief. A world where your precious private keys are vigilantly guarded by multiple layers of state-of-the-art security protocols that not only protect your information but also adapt in real time to emerging threats and vulnerabilities. This is not merely a fantasy—it is the exciting direction in which wallet technology is headed as we speak. In recent years, we have witnessed a rapid and astounding evolution from simple software-based solutions to advanced hardware wallets that store your keys securely offline, away from prying eyes. Now, experts predict that future wallets will ingeniously combine the best features of both worlds, offering seamless access with unmatched, ironclad security that gives users peace of mind in their digital transactions.

One of the most exciting and innovative future trends that is rapidly gaining momentum is the integration of biometric authentication into various digital systems. In the near future, your digital wallet might unlock not by merely entering a password, but through advanced methods such as your fingerprint, cutting-edge facial recognition technology, or even your unique voice signature. This leap in technology is not only surprising in its simplicity but also mind-blowing in its ability to seamlessly merge the digital and physical worlds in ways previously unimaginable. Biometric security offers a level of customization and ease-of-use that is simply unparalleled in the realm of personal authentication. It ensures that even if your device accidentally falls into the wrong hands, the chances of unauthorized access remain virtually nil, providing peace of mind. The implications of such advancements in security are profound, as they promise to revolutionize the way we interact with our devices and safeguard our personal information.

However, biometric security is just one piece of the larger puzzle. The future of wallet technology is expected to witness the emergence of innovative multi-layered security architectures that seamlessly combine hardware isolation, various biometric data, and advanced encryption protocols. These sophisticated systems will be specifically designed to adapt dynamically to a wide range of threats, learning from each attack and continually improving their defenses in real time. This adaptive security model represents a logical and essential next step in the overall evolution of digital asset protection—an approach that is not only responsive but also remarkably robust, ensuring greater safety and security for users in an increasingly digital world.

Quantum-Resistant Cryptography: Preparing for the Next Frontier

As powerful as current cryptographic methods are in protecting our sensitive information, the dawn of quantum computing brings with it a potential threat to existing digital security frameworks. Quantum computers, equipped with their extraordinary and unparalleled processing power, could theoretically and practically break the cryptographic codes that underpin and secure our current wallet technologies and digital transactions. This looming threat has spurred significant research into developing quantum-resistant cryptography, which is becoming an area of intense interest and innovative advancements among researchers and industry experts alike. The urgency to adapt to this emerging technology is crucial for maintaining the integrity of our digital ecosystems.

Quantum-resistant algorithms are specifically designed to be secure, even with the advanced capabilities of quantum computers, which could potentially compromise current security measures. In the not-so-distant future, wallet technology will likely incorporate these cutting-edge algorithms to ensure that private keys remain secure and confidential long into the future, safeguarding them against any possible threats posed by quantum computing. This transition to quantum-resistant security is an absolutely critical and necessary step for the long-term viability and sustainability of digital currencies in a rapidly evolving technological landscape. It represents a mind-blowing shift that guarantees our digital assets remain protected and secure in an era marked by exponential technological growth and innovation.

The ongoing development of quantum-resistant cryptography represents a logical and proactive measure—a crucial adaptation to the unavoidable advances in computing power that we are witnessing today. Researchers from various corners of the globe are tirelessly engaged in the task of developing and implementing these cutting-edge cryptographic standards. As this technology reaches its full potential, quantum-resistant wallets will play a pivotal role, not only offering protection against future threats posed by quantum computing but also significantly enhancing the overall integrity of the blockchain. This enhancement will be vital in ensuring that the foundational trust and transparency that define digital currencies remain intact and unbroken in an era of rapidly evolving technology and potential vulnerabilities.

Decentralized Identity and Self-Sovereign Solutions

One of the most revolutionary trends in modern wallet technology is the remarkable emergence of decentralized identity solutions. In traditional identity verification systems, this task is often managed by centralized authorities, which typically include institutions such as governments or banks. These entities store vast amounts of sensitive personal data, making them highly attractive and vulnerable targets for malicious hackers. However, with the rise of decentralized identity solutions, individuals now have the empowering ability to regain control over their own digital identities without the need to rely on a central repository that could potentially compromise their information. This transformation represents a significant shift towards enhancing privacy and security in digital identity management.

Self-sovereign identity (SSI) platforms empower users to take control of their personal information and manage their credentials securely, often leveraging the benefits of blockchain technology. In a not-so-distant future, your digital wallet will not only be a place to store your cryptocurrency and other digital assets but will also act as a centralized and secure hub for managing your complete personal identity. This significant integration marks a revolutionary change in how we perceive privacy and security in our online lives. By ensuring that you remain the sole owner of your identity data, SSI platforms effectively diminish the risk of data breaches and identity theft, thereby creating a far more secure and autonomous digital ecosystem for all users involved. This new paradigm empowers individuals and instills a heightened sense of trust in their online interactions.

This trend undeniably represents a logical progression in the ongoing journey towards achieving digital sovereignty and autonomy. When you take control of your own identity, along with your assets and resources, you ultimately achieve true self-sovereignty—a powerful state where you are not at the mercy or beholden to centralized institutions for your financial security or the safeguarding of your personal data. The persuasive nature of this idea cannot be overstated: in a decentralized world, trust and control must fundamentally reside with the individual rather than any overarching systems. This empowerment and agency are core tenets of the digital revolution, which is promising to democratize not only money and finance but also personal identity and data privacy, ultimately reshaping the way we interact with technology and society at large.

Integration with the Internet of Things (IoT) and Beyond

The future of wallet technology will undoubtedly be shaped significantly by its seamless integration with the ever-expanding realm of the Internet of Things (IoT). In a world that is becoming increasingly interconnected, everyday devices—such as smartphones, wearable technology, and even common household appliances—are evolving to become integral parts of a vast, intricate, and interconnected network. This remarkable convergence of various technologies not only enhances functionality but also presents unprecedented opportunities for innovative advancements in wallet technology. As we move forward, the possibilities for wallet enhancement and user experience are virtually limitless, paving the way for a new era of digital transactions and convenience.

Envision a near future where your advanced digital wallet is perfectly integrated with your sophisticated smartwatch, allowing for effortless and seamless transactions while you are on the move. Imagine a scenario in which your intelligent smart refrigerator can automatically detect when you are running low on essential groceries and can reorder them for you without you lifting a finger. Furthermore, it can handle payment for those items using your crypto funds, all while ensuring that your transaction details remain secure, private, and completely confidential. These scenarios are not distant fantasies from science fiction; rather, they represent logical and practical extensions of the exciting current trends in the rapidly evolving realms of IoT and digital payments. The future of convenience and efficiency is rapidly approaching, transforming everyday experiences.

The integration of IoT technology into wallet systems will significantly enhance the user-friendliness and accessibility of these financial tools. It will enable real-time transactions, allowing users to make purchases and transfer funds instantly without unnecessary delays. Furthermore, this integration will automate various routine financial tasks, which can save users time and streamline their financial management processes. Consequently, it will create a highly seamless experience that effectively bridges the gap between the digital and physical realms of financial transactions. This tech advancement will also contribute to the emergence of innovative business models and diverse financial services, ultimately solidifying the crucial role of digital currencies in the everyday activities and transactions of individuals and businesses alike.

Moreover, as IoT devices continue to grow in prevalence across various sectors, the pressing need for secure communication between these devices will become even more pronounced. Wallet technology that is capable of effectively interfacing with IoT networks must incorporate a range of advanced security protocols to guarantee that transactions remain private, secure, and tamper-proof against potential threats. The logical outcome of these developments is an increasingly interconnected, efficient, and secure financial ecosystem that adeptly leverages the best of both digital innovation and physical connectivity, ensuring that users can conduct their transactions with confidence and ease while reaping the benefits of the vast opportunities presented by IoT advancements.

The Rise of Hybrid Wallets: Merging Convenience with Control

While the ongoing debate between custodial and non-custodial wallets is likely to continue for quite some time, future trends are strongly indicating the rise of hybrid solutions that effectively blend the best features of both approaches. Hybrid wallets strive to provide the ultimate convenience of custodial services—such as straightforward recovery options and user-friendly interfaces that appeal to a wide range of users—while still allowing individuals to retain significant control over their private keys. These innovative wallets may become essential for both newcomers and seasoned users looking for a balance between security and convenience in their cryptocurrency management.

These innovative hybrid solutions are specifically designed to be flexible, catering to a diverse range of users with varying needs and preferences. For those individuals who place a high value on convenience but are simultaneously concerned about security, a hybrid wallet can provide an appealing compromise: you get to enjoy the benefits of professional management while not having to completely surrender control over your assets. Innovations in this area may include advanced features like multi-signature arrangements, where a greater number of multiple keys are required to authorize a transaction, making it more secure. Additionally, there are split-key systems that effectively distribute risk across different devices or geographical locations, further enhancing security and peace of mind for the users.

The evolution of hybrid wallets represents a natural progression in the ongoing quest for an optimal balance between ease-of-use and self-sovereignty. These innovative wallets serve to provide customizable levels of control, thus empowering users to effectively tailor their security measures to align with their unique personal needs and preferences. This multifaceted approach is not only practical but also highly persuasive, as it acknowledges the varied and diverse requirements that exist within the global crypto community. Furthermore, it offers a thoughtful solution that adeptly adapts to the differing individual risk profiles presented by users, ensuring that everyone can find a level of security that fits their specific situation and comfort. The rise of these hybrid wallets marks an important milestone in the evolution of cryptocurrency management and usage, providing a perfect blend of autonomy and user-friendly features that cater to a wide array of expectations from users around the world.

The Impact of Artificial Intelligence on Wallet Security

Artificial intelligence (AI) is set to assume a crucial and increasingly significant role in the evolving future of wallet technology. AI-driven security protocols are capable of analyzing intricate patterns in user behavior, detecting anomalies effectively, and responding to potential threats at a speed that far surpasses the capabilities of any human response. By seamlessly integrating advanced AI with cutting-edge wallet technology, future systems will be empowered to anticipate and neutralize sophisticated cyber attacks in real time, adapting to new threats as they emerge and ensuring a safer user experience. This evolution promises to enhance security measures, making digital wallets not only more user-friendly but also significantly more secure against emerging threats.

For example, envision a digital wallet that employs sophisticated machine learning algorithms to persistently observe and monitor for any signs of potentially suspicious activity or behavior. If the system identifies an unusual pattern—for instance, a login attempt originating from an unrecognized or unfamiliar location, or an unexpected large transaction suddenly appearing—it could automatically lock the wallet for safety and promptly alert the user. This innovative and proactive approach to security represents a remarkable leap forward in technological advancement, effectively combining the comprehensive analytical power of artificial intelligence with the robust protections that modern wallet technology has to offer. This method not only enhances user safety but also builds trust in the digital transaction environment.

AI has the incredible capability to assist significantly in optimizing backup and recovery procedures. By thoroughly analyzing historical data alongside user behavior, AI-driven systems can accurately suggest the most effective methods for securely managing recovery phrases and handling encryption keys, thereby substantially reducing the risk of human error. This integration of advanced technologies is not merely mind-blowing in its vast potential; it is also a logical necessity in a modern era where the speed and complexity of cyber threats continue to escalate at an alarming rate. AI's contribution to this field represents a vital advancement in our approach to cybersecurity.

Regulatory and Privacy Considerations in Future Wallets

As wallet technology continues to evolve and advance, so too will the regulatory landscape that governs it. The future of digital wallets must not only prioritize security and robust protection but also ensure compliance with a wide array of global regulations that are designed to protect user privacy and prevent any potential illicit activity. The challenge that developers face is significant; they must design innovative systems that effectively balance these sometimes conflicting demands. This complex task requires not only analytical rigor and attention to detail but also creative problem-solving abilities to navigate the intricate web of regulations while enhancing user experience.

Innovations in wallet technology are increasingly leveraging advanced privacy-preserving techniques, including zero-knowledge proofs and complex cryptographic methods, which enable users to verify their transactions without exposing any sensitive personal information. These sophisticated technologies empower users to effectively maintain their privacy while still complying with necessary regulatory requirements. This careful balance is absolutely critical in today's world, where digital transactions face relentless scrutiny from governments as well as various regulatory bodies. As the digital economy expands and evolves, the need for robust privacy measures that can withstand external pressures becomes more important than ever, ensuring that users can engage in transactions confidently and securely.

The development of innovative wallets that prioritize user privacy as well as regulatory compliance stands as a compelling argument for the future trajectory of decentralized finance. By ensuring that digital assets are secured in a manner that also preserves user privacy, these groundbreaking innovations help to build trust and confidence among users and regulators alike. The logical conclusion one can draw from this is that as technological advancements continue to unfold, the tools we use to manage our wealth will evolve to become not only significantly more secure but will also be increasingly respectful of our individual personal freedoms—a remarkably mind-blowing prospect in the rapidly advancing digital age we live in today.

The Role of Community and Open-Source Collaboration

One of the most striking and noteworthy aspects of the ongoing evolution and transformation of wallet technology is the significantly vital role of community-driven innovation. The open-source movement has played an instrumental and critical role in advancing the overall security of wallets in the digital landscape. By making their code publicly available and accessible to all, developers enable a global community of experts and enthusiasts to scrutinize, test, and continuously improve the software. This collaborative and collective approach ensures that any potential vulnerabilities are identified and patched swiftly, leading to a more resilient and robust system overall, which benefits users around the world.

The power of open-source collaboration is not only logical but also deeply inspiring. When thousands of passionate developers come together to share their skills and ideas, the vast pool of collective knowledge and specialized expertise achieved far surpasses what any single organization could accomplish in isolation. This collaborative and distributed model of innovation is a fundamental principle of the decentralized philosophy, and it plays an essential role in the ongoing enhancement and improvement of wallet security protocols. As contributors from diverse backgrounds unite, their combined efforts lead to more robust, secure, and efficient technologies that benefit everyone involved in this thriving ecosystem.

The community-driven approach has remarkably led to rapid advancements in the realm of wallet technology, encompassing everything from the ongoing refinement and improvement of encryption techniques to the seamless integration of user-friendly interfaces that cater to a diverse range of users. This phenomenon serves as a powerful testament to the immense potential of collective intelligence—a truly mind-blowing demonstration that when individuals come together to unite in solving common problems and addressing shared challenges, the results can indeed be transformative and far-reaching. This collaborative model not only greatly enhances the security and functionality of digital wallets but also actively empowers users by involving them directly in the dynamic process of innovation, allowing their feedback and ideas to shape the future of this vital technology.

The Persuasive Case for Continued Innovation

Despite the remarkable progress that has been made in securing digital assets through various means, the evolution of wallet technology is far from being complete or settled. The landscape of digital security is still evolving, and new challenges continue to emerge as the digital economy continues to expand and grow at an unprecedented rate. However, the case for continued innovation in this sector is both logical and deeply compelling. The inherent risks associated with a digital world and its increasingly complex nature demand that we constantly seek to improve and enhance our security measures. The rapid pace of technological advancement we are witnessing ensures that there is always ample room for further improvement and innovation in securing digital assets effectively.

Future trends indicate a significant convergence of numerous advanced technologies—specifically including artificial intelligence, quantum-resistant cryptography, and Internet of Things integration—all of which are directly tied to the enhancement of wallet security. These groundbreaking innovations are set to not only bolster the safety of our digital assets but also make wallet technology considerably more accessible and intuitive for everyday users who may not be tech-savvy. The logical progression is undoubtedly evident: as threats evolve and become more sophisticated, so too must our defenses adapt and improve. The dynamic and ever-changing nature of the digital world necessitates a proactive and forward-thinking approach to security—one that is continuously refined, updated, and optimized to effectively counteract emerging challenges and risks associated with digital transactions.

For investors and users alike, the promise of future innovations in wallet technology serves as a compelling call to action that cannot be ignored. It effectively reassures them that the digital assets they currently hold are not merely static entities; rather, they are integral components of an evolving ecosystem that is wholeheartedly committed to protecting their wealth in an increasingly dynamic and unpredictable environment. This unwavering commitment to continuous improvement is not just a technical detail to be brushed aside—it represents a fundamental pillar of the decentralized financial future we are moving towards. This is a future where the ideals of security, usability, and personal empowerment resonate harmoniously, working together seamlessly to create a robust and resilient financial landscape.

The Broader Impact on Global Finance

The evolution of wallet technology, particularly the significant advancements in security protocols, has far-reaching implications for the global financial system as a whole. As digital wallets become increasingly secure and user-friendly, they are playing a critical role in contributing to the overall stability and growth of the cryptocurrency market. Secure wallets serve to reduce the risk of high-profile hacks and thefts, which consequentially builds trust among not only individual investors but also institutions in the financial sector. This increased sense of trust leads to higher adoption rates for digital currencies, fosters more robust market liquidity, and ultimately results in a more mature and stable financial ecosystem that can adapt to the changing demands of users and regulatory frameworks. The interplay between technology and security is pivotal in shaping the future of financial transactions.

The implications of these trends extend well beyond the immediate realm of cryptocurrencies. The principles of decentralized security—such as enhanced transparency, distributed trust, and community-driven innovation—are beginning to influence traditional financial systems in profound ways as well. Banks, financial institutions, and other entities are actively exploring blockchain technology and secure wallet solutions in order to enhance and improve their own operations. This cross-pollination of innovative ideas is helping to drive a broader transformation within the landscape of global finance, one that is characterized by increased efficiency, heightened transparency, and greater resilience in response to market challenges and changes. As these traditional institutions adopt decentralized principles, they are opening new avenues for collaboration and fostering a more inclusive financial ecosystem.

As digital asset management continues to evolve and become significantly more secure, it paves a vital path for wider financial inclusion across the globe. Millions of people around the world, especially in regions where banking infrastructure is underdeveloped or lacking, now have the opportunity to access essential financial services through innovative digital wallets. This democratization of finance represents a crucial turning point, with the potential to address and reduce economic inequality dramatically, empowering individuals who were previously marginalized and excluded from the global economy. The persuasive power of this transformative vision is utterly undeniable—a secure and accessible financial system, built upon advanced wallet technology, is not only logical and practical but also a pressing moral imperative for the 21st century, offering the promise of economic empowerment and sustainability for everyone involved.

The Future Landscape: What Lies Ahead

Looking to the future, the ongoing evolution of wallet technology is undoubtedly poised to continue at an impressive and rapid pace. Emerging trends within the industry indicate that we will witness further integration of enhanced security features with everyday usability that caters to the needs of an evolving digital landscape. Next-generation wallets are likely to incorporate even more sophisticated biometric authentication methods, including cutting-edge techniques such as iris scanning or voice recognition, which will serve to complement existing multi-factor authentication systems. These exciting advancements will make it significantly easier for users to safely and securely access their digital assets, providing them with peace of mind and alleviating the fear of unauthorized access to their valuable information and funds.

Additionally, the advent of quantum computing presents both a significant challenge and an exciting opportunity for the future of technology. As quantum technology continues to evolve rapidly, the existing cryptographic methods that we rely on could eventually become vulnerable and less secure. In response to this looming threat, researchers and experts in the field are diligently developing quantum-resistant algorithms that aim to ensure that wallet security remains robust and reliable in the face of this new and formidable risk. The integration of quantum-resistant cryptography into wallet technology is not only a logical step but also a mind-blowing advancement to future-proof our digital assets against potential vulnerabilities that quantum computing may introduce. This proactive approach will be essential in safeguarding our information and maintaining trust in digital currencies.

Another exciting trend that is rapidly emerging in the world of finance is the potential for digital wallets to evolve into comprehensive all-in-one financial hubs. Future wallet solutions may evolve to not only store and secure digital assets with advanced encryption but also integrate seamlessly with various decentralized finance platforms, cutting-edge payment systems, and even traditional banking services. This kind of convergence would empower users by allowing them to manage and oversee all aspects of their personal financial lives from a single, intuitive interface that prioritizes convenience. Imagine a wallet that offers the ability to monitor your investments in real time, easily pay for goods and services with just a few taps, access loans with swift approvals, and even earn interest on your holdings—all while ensuring that your funds remain secure and protected against potential threats. This compelling vision of a unified financial ecosystem is becoming increasingly persuasive and appears inevitable as technology continues to advance and reshape the landscape of how we handle money. The future of wallet technology is indeed bright and filled with limitless possibilities, capturing the imagination of users everywhere.

Furthermore, the integration of artificial intelligence (AI) into wallet technology promises to not only enhance but also revolutionize the entire way we interact with our digital assets. This transformation is foundational to creating a more secure and user-friendly experience. AI-driven security protocols have the capacity to analyze patterns of user behavior, detect anomalies with precision, and provide real-time alerts in the event of any suspicious activity or potential threats. This proactive and vigilant approach to security, combined with advanced adaptive learning algorithms, will make future digital wallets even more resilient and robust against the ever-evolving cyber threats that loom in today's digital landscape. The analytical reasoning behind these significant advancements is abundantly clear: as cyber threats continue to become more sophisticated and complex, our defenses must similarly evolve and strengthen in tandem to ensure that our digital wealth remains well-protected and secure in this dynamic environment. In conclusion, the future of wallet technology, fortified by AI, holds immense potential for enhancing the safety and management of our digital assets in unprecedented ways.

The Human Element: Education, Awareness, and Empowerment

No discussion of wallet technology can truly be considered complete without a thorough exploration of the human element involved. Ultimately, even the most advanced and sophisticated security protocols are only as effective as the individuals who use them and how well they understand them. User education and awareness emerge as critical components in ensuring that our digital assets remain secure and protected from potential threats. The evolution from basic paper wallets to increasingly sophisticated hardware and software solutions has been accompanied by a parallel evolution in user interfaces and educational tools specifically designed to help individuals grasp the complexities of managing and safeguarding their digital wealth effectively. This shift underscores the necessity of empowering users with knowledge and skills to navigate the rapidly changing landscape of cryptocurrency and digital finance.

Modern wallet providers are increasingly focusing on creating intuitive and user-friendly interfaces that greatly simplify the complex world of digital asset management for not just the seasoned investors but also for beginners who are just entering the space. These comprehensive efforts include thorough tutorials that guide users through every step of the process, responsive customer support that addresses questions and concerns as they arise, and vibrant community forums where users can freely share best practices, insights, and learn valuable lessons from one another. By empowering users with the knowledge they need along with practical tools that enhance their experience, these initiatives play a crucial role in helping to mitigate the risks that are often associated with self-custody. Furthermore, they ensure that individuals from various backgrounds are well-equipped with the skills necessary to confidently take control of their own financial security and make informed decisions about their digital assets.

The human aspect of wallet technology serves as a compelling argument in its own right. It is insufficient merely to create advanced security measures; these instruments must also be user-friendly and comprehensible to the everyday individual.

When users feel confident and capable in managing their digital assets, they are increasingly inclined to adopt the advantages of decentralization, thus fostering a more secure and resilient financial ecosystem. This shift not only empowers individuals but also strengthens the overall infrastructure, creating a more inclusive environment where everyone can participate effectively in the evolving financial landscape.

Persuading the Masses: The Broader Implications of Secure Wallets

The impact of enhanced wallet security goes far beyond just individual user protection and personal safety. It has the potential to transform entire financial systems fundamentally by fostering greater trust among users, reducing risks associated with digital transactions, and encouraging a wider adoption of digital currencies within both casual and institutional markets. As these wallets become increasingly secure and more user-friendly for everyday consumers, the overall stability of the cryptocurrency market improves significantly. This increase in stability, in turn, attracts a greater volume of institutional investment, which further legitimizes the digital asset ecosystem and stimulates ongoing innovation across the entire financial spectrum.

From a logical standpoint, the relationship between secure wallet technology and market stability cannot be overlooked or dismissed. When investors possess a high level of confidence that their valuable assets are being protected by cutting-edge security measures and technologies, they are significantly more likely to maintain their holdings and make additional investments in digital currencies for the long term. This confidence inherently reduces the likelihood of panic selling and, in turn, market volatility, which creates a more predictable and sustainable financial environment for everyone involved. The persuasive power of secure wallets lies deeply in their remarkable ability to build and strengthen a foundation of trust—a critical and essential component for any successful and thriving financial system in the modern age.

Furthermore, the broader economic implications of secure and accessible wallet technology are not only significant but also transformative. This technology can play a crucial role in driving financial inclusion by equipping individuals around the globe with essential tools necessary to participate effectively in the burgeoning digital economy. In areas where traditional banking services remain either limited or widely considered unreliable, secure digital wallets serve as a vital lifeline—providing a much-needed means to store, manage, and transfer wealth seamlessly and efficiently without relying on costly and often inaccessible centralized financial institutions. This democratization of financial services represents not just a logical progression stemming from rapid technological innovation but also embodies a pressing moral imperative in our increasingly interconnected global landscape. It is imperative that we strive to ensure that everyone, regardless of their geographical location or socio-economic status, has fair access to these essential financial tools.

The Unstoppable Evolution of Wallet Technology

The future of wallet technology is truly a fascinating story of relentless innovation, logical progression, and transformative impact. From the humble beginnings of simple paper wallets, which once seemed revolutionary in their time, to today's highly advanced hardware and software solutions that we have at our disposal, every step along the way in the evolution of digital asset storage has been driven by a fundamental need that is becoming ever more apparent: the urgent need to protect and empower individuals within an increasingly digital and interconnected world. Enhanced security protocols have not only effectively addressed the vulnerabilities and weaknesses of earlier systems but have also paved the way for the creation of a more inclusive, resilient, and dynamic financial ecosystem that benefits everyone. This constant evolution reflects our collective drive to innovate and adapt in a fast-paced technological landscape.

As we find ourselves poised on the edge of an exciting new era in the realm of digital finance, the advancements we see in wallet security have evolved into something far more significant than merely technological achievements—they represent the very foundation upon which the entire future of money is now being constructed. The seamless integration of advanced encryption techniques, robust multi-factor authentication systems, open-source collaboration among software developers, and innovative hardware design collectively represents an exceptionally logical, highly analytical, and incredibly persuasive response to the pressing challenges we face in safeguarding our digital wealth. Each of these elements works together harmoniously to create a secure environment where individuals can confidently engage in financial transactions without fear, paving the way for a more secure digital economy.

For investors, users, and policymakers alike, the remarkable evolution of wallet technology presents a clear and compelling vision of the future: a future in which financial freedom transcends mere aspiration, becoming a tangible reality for everyone. Secure digital wallets empower individuals to confidently take control of their own financial destinies, creating and fostering a robust global ecosystem where trust is genuinely distributed among participants. In this promising landscape, transparency is paramount, ensuring that information is accessible and clear to all stakeholders. Ultimately, this innovative approach to finance paves the way for profound economic empowerment that is available to individuals from all walks of life, encouraging participation and inclusivity in the financial arena.

In conclusion, the remarkable evolution of hardware and software wallets represents a shockingly brilliant narrative of human ingenuity and the incredible advancement of technology. It is a fascinating journey that transforms the way we secure and manage our digital assets and, by extension, the manner in which we interact with money itself on an everyday basis. The future of digital asset management is being shaped and influenced by innovations that are not only mind-blowing in their complexity but also logically sound in their implementation—a future where every transaction is meticulously protected by multiple layers of advanced security protocols. In this emerging landscape, individual empowerment is not an occasional privilege but rather the norm and standard practice, ensuring that everyone has the tools and resources they need to take control of their financial interactions effectively and securely. As we move forward, we can anticipate even more exciting developments that will further enhance our relationship with digital currency.

Embrace this promising future that lies ahead. It is essential to recognize that the ongoing evolution of wallet technology goes beyond merely protecting digital wealth. It is fundamentally about redefining what financial freedom means in the ever-expanding digital age we find ourselves in. As we continue to push the boundaries of what is possible in this dynamic landscape, secure wallets will undoubtedly stay at the very heart of the decentralized financial revolution. These innovative solutions are designed to empower individuals, giving them control over their finances while simultaneously transforming the global economy. We are witnessing a significant change, one secure transaction at a time, as more people realize the potential and the benefits of these remarkable advancements.

Chapter 5: The History of Cryptocurrency Exchange Platforms

Section 1: The Birth of Crypto Trading: Early, Unregulated Platforms

In the early days of cryptocurrency, the world of digital trading was a wild, chaotic frontier—a digital Wild West where rules were few, and fortunes were made and lost in the blink of an eye, often leaving traders reeling. The birth of crypto trading was not a smooth, orderly evolution; rather, it was a shocking, mind-blowing transformation driven by unprecedented innovation that emerged from an environment rich in uncertainty, risky experimentation, and even outright failure. This section delves deep into the tumultuous and often unpredictable beginnings of crypto trading, detailing the unregulated platforms that set the stage for the global phenomenon we see today. It explores how early exchange failures taught invaluable lessons, shaping a landscape that eventually cemented the legitimacy and acceptance of digital currencies in the broader financial world. The journey from chaos to order was filled with challenges, but it laid the groundwork for the vibrant ecosystem we experience now.

The Chaotic Origins: A Digital Frontier with No Law

Before the rise of professional exchanges and the establishment of robust regulatory oversight, early crypto trading was characterized by an absolute lack of formal structure and order. Picture a world where there existed no market makers, no dedicated regulatory bodies, and no standardized protocols to govern transactions whatsoever—a world where every single trader was essentially on their own, navigating a highly volatile and unpredictable market landscape. In this chaotic and often bewildering digital frontier, anyone with just a computer and an internet connection could engage in trading cryptocurrencies. However, with that newfound freedom came immense risk and uncertainty. The absence of oversight meant that traders had to rely on their own judgment, often leading to devastating losses or exploitative situations. Each transaction was a leap of faith into the unknown, where profit and loss hung in a precarious balance.

Throughout this transformative period, various trading platforms began to emerge, created by enthusiastic developers, opportunistic entrepreneurs, or tech-savvy individuals who recognized the vast potential of this exciting new asset class. These pioneering exchanges often operated on a shoestring budget, frequently constructed on hastily written code that lacked the critical security features necessary for safeguarding investments. Many of these platforms were managed by individuals who had little prior experience in dealing with substantial amounts of money or in navigating the complex regulatory requirements typically imposed on financial institutions. The significant absence of regulatory oversight meant that these trading platforms were primarily experimental in nature—existing within an environment where innovation thrived but recklessness was equally prevalent. This unique combination fostered both groundbreaking advancements and notable vulnerabilities in the emerging market.

This era was truly shocking for its sheer unpredictability and constant upheaval. Without any proper safeguards in place, early traders found themselves having to contend with wild price fluctuations that could swing dramatically within moments, slippage that compromised their expected gains, and situations involving outright scams that preyed upon unsuspecting individuals. The complete absence of any kind of standardized system meant that even the simplest of transactions could easily be marred by an array of technical glitches or worse, malicious activity designed to deceive the unwary. In such a precarious landscape, trust was exceedingly hard to come by, and every trade made was an act of bravery, or perhaps, it was more akin to desperate hope against a backdrop of uncertainty and risk.

The Early Exchanges: A Mix of Innovation and Insecurity

Some of the earliest crypto trading platforms emerged with the significant rise in popularity of Bitcoin and its initial success in the financial landscape. These platforms were developed quickly, often by small, enthusiastic teams who were more captivated by the revolutionary idea of decentralization than by the pressing need for robust security measures and protocols. A particularly notorious example of this is Mt. Gox, which quickly came to dominate the market during its height before ultimately experiencing a catastrophic collapse. Mt. Gox began its journey as a modest and unassuming trading platform but rapidly expanded in a remarkably short time, managing to handle a significant majority of Bitcoin transactions around the world. At its peak, the platform astonishingly processed over 70% of the global Bitcoin trade volume, showcasing both the rapid growth of cryptocurrency trading and the vulnerabilities inherent in such a fast-evolving industry.

Yet, the very features that allowed Mt. Gox and similar platforms to grow and flourish also sowed the seeds of their inevitable downfall and destruction. In the absence of proper regulatory oversight and sufficient security protocols, these exchanges became breeding grounds for numerous technical failures and rampant fraud. Mt. Gox, for instance, suffered from multiple security breaches that went undetected for alarmingly long periods of time. In one particularly catastrophic incident, hackers cunningly exploited serious vulnerabilities in the exchange's system to steal hundreds of thousands of Bitcoins, leading to an enormous loss of trust from users and a devastating collapse that sent shockwaves throughout the entire crypto community and beyond. The repercussions of that incident reverberated, influencing regulations and security practices across the entire industry in the years that followed.

Other early exchanges also fared poorly, showing little improvement over their predecessors. Many of these platforms were riddled with software bugs, suffered from insufficient customer support, and operated under management practices that were often shrouded in a veil of opacity. Users frequently found themselves completely at the mercy of administrators who wielded significant power—power that included freezing accounts at will, altering prices without notice, or even disappearing entirely with users' hard-earned funds. The chaotic and unpredictable nature of these early platforms was mind-blowing and distressing— it was a precarious world where entire fortunes could vanish without a trace overnight, leaving users in utter disbelief, while the stakes remained incredibly high for everyone involved.

The logical reasoning behind the significant growth of these innovative platforms is fairly straightforward: when an entirely new asset class emerges in the financial landscape, early adopters eagerly rush to capitalize on its immense potential and opportunities. The notable absence of regulation and the lack of standardized practices within the industry meant that these pioneering platforms could innovate rapidly and effectively, enabling them to capture substantial market share by being the first movers to market. However, this rapid and aggressive growth came with a considerable cost. The very lack of organizational structure that allowed for such dynamic innovation also meant that the platforms were inherently fragile and unstable, leaving them vulnerable to both internal mismanagement issues and external attacks or threats from various competitors and regulatory bodies.

Lessons from Early Failures: The Evolution of Security and Regulation

The chaotic and tumultuous beginnings of crypto trading were undoubtedly not without their very important lessons. Every single failure, every hack that compromised security, and every exchange collapse that shook investor confidence provided valuable insights that gradually led to significant improvements in security protocols, regulatory oversight, and the overall market structure. Notable early failures like the collapse of Mt. Gox, while utterly devastating at the time for many investors, served as a crucial wake-up call to the entire crypto community. They emphasized and brought to the forefront the urgent need for robust security measures that could safeguard user assets, transparent operational practices that would build trust, and comprehensive regulatory frameworks that could protect both users and the integrity of the market as a whole.

One of the most important lessons learned was that trust must be actively earned and carefully maintained through a commitment to transparency and open communication. The staggering loss of millions of dollars in hacked funds served as a stark reminder of the critical importance of having rigorous security protocols in place. In response, developers began to adopt more advanced encryption methods, improve existing system architectures, and implement comprehensive continuous security audits to safeguard against future breaches. These significant changes, driven by a logical and thorough analysis of past mistakes, gradually transformed the entire landscape. Nowadays, exchanges and trading platforms employ highly sophisticated multi-factor authentication mechanisms, advanced cold storage solutions for funds, and cutting-edge real-time monitoring systems that were truly unimaginable in the early days of digital trading. Such measures reflect a deep understanding of security needs, prioritizing the safety of customer assets above all else.

In parallel, the regulatory environment began to gradually catch up with the rapid pace of innovation observed in the cryptocurrency space. Initially, many governments around the world viewed cryptocurrencies with a great deal of suspicion and skepticism, often opting to ban or severely restrict their use across various sectors. However, as the market continued to mature and the distinct benefits of digital currencies became increasingly apparent to a broader audience, regulators began to adopt a more balanced and thoughtful approach. Regulatory frameworks were developed meticulously to ensure robust consumer protection, prevent potential money laundering activities, and promote overall market stability without stifling the innovation that was driving this burgeoning sector. This evolution in regulation proved to be a critical turning point for the industry—it effectively legitimized crypto trading in the eyes of traditional finance institutions and attracted institutional investors who had previously been wary and cautious of the unregulated market landscape. As a result, this shift fostered a new level of confidence and encouraged further investment in the cryptocurrency ecosystem.

The Institutional Impact: Mainstreaming Crypto Trading

One of the most persuasive and compelling arguments advocating for the evolution and maturation of crypto trading came with the significant entrance of institutional investors into the market landscape. When well-established financial institutions, prestigious hedge funds, and even governmental entities began to allocate substantial amounts of capital to various digital currencies, it signaled a definitive turning point, indicating that the era of unregulated, chaotic trading was coming to an undeniable end. The growing institutional adoption of crypto trading represented a powerful and undeniable validation of the underlying technology. In addition, it served as a clear and telling sign that cryptocurrencies were shifting and transitioning from being fringe, speculative assets to fully-fledged mainstream financial instruments in the global economy.

Institutions brought with them a significant level of discipline, comprehensive due diligence, and advanced risk management practices that were markedly lacking in the early days of market development. They demanded not only robust security measures but also reliable and accurate market data, along with a clear understanding of regulations. In response to these pressing needs, exchanges began to improve their operational standards in various ways. New trading platforms were developed from the ground up with security and regulatory compliance as central priorities. It became abundantly clear that the logical evolution of the market was necessary: as more substantial amounts of money entered the investing landscape from institutional investors, the existing infrastructure needed to undergo a transformation to adequately support that heightened level of participation and investment activity.

The introduction of regulated investment products such as Bitcoin futures, options, and exchange-traded funds (ETFs) has played a significant role in further cementing the legitimacy of cryptocurrencies within the investment landscape. These innovative financial instruments have enabled traditional investors to gain exposure to digital currencies without having to navigate the complexities of directly holding and managing them on their own. By providing a structured way to invest, they have alleviated some of the apprehensions that many potential investors may have had regarding the security and volatility associated with direct cryptocurrency investments. Furthermore, these products have introduced a much-needed mechanism for price discovery and effective risk management, which was previously absent from the crypto market. This convergence of traditional finance with digital currencies represents a logical and evolutionary step in the financial sector, one that successfully bridges the gap between the established old guard and the rapidly evolving new age of digital assets. As a result, this development has made the entire market more accessible and robust for a broader range of investors.

Persuasive, Real-World Examples: Transformations that Shook the Industry

Real-world examples stand as the most persuasive and compelling evidence showcasing the significant evolution from early, chaotic platforms to a sophisticated and mature, institutionalized market. A notable case is the collapse of Mt. Gox, which represented a watershed moment that compelled the entire industry to confront its many vulnerabilities. The devastating and shocking loss of funds not only affected numerous investors but also highlighted the critical need for enhanced security measures and improved transparency. This incident led to an urgent call for widespread reforms across the entire crypto ecosystem, prompting stakeholders to prioritize safeguarding assets and fostering a more robust regulatory framework.

Another striking example of success in the cryptocurrency landscape is represented by exchanges like Coinbase and Binance. These platforms emerged successfully in the wake of early failures, learning invaluable lessons from the past mistakes of others and building robust, resilient systems designed specifically to handle the ever-increasing demands of a global market. Coinbase, in particular, has grown remarkably, establishing itself as a trusted name in the industry. This trust is bolstered by its unwavering commitment to regulatory compliance, rigorous security standards, and exceptionally user-friendly interfaces that make navigating the complex world of cryptocurrencies easier for everyone. Its impressive success story serves as a powerful testament to the fact that when critical lessons are learned and meaningful improvements are made, even the most volatile market can be transformed into a stable and reliable asset class that attracts a diverse range of investors.

Furthermore, institutional investments in prominent companies such as MicroStrategy and Tesla—both of which gained widespread attention by allocating substantial portions of their treasuries specifically to Bitcoin—furnished compelling evidence that crypto trading had advanced well beyond the realm of mere speculation. These high-profile decisions not only caught the eye of the public but also attracted even greater interest from both retail and institutional investors alike, effectively creating a virtuous cycle of adoption and ongoing innovation in the cryptocurrency space. As more institutions began to recognize the intrinsic potential of digital currencies, the logical case for their use as a long-term store of value became increasingly persuasive. This recognition was fueled by the growing consensus on the capacity of cryptocurrencies to hedge against inflationary pressures and economic instability, further solidifying their place in the financial landscape.

The Logical, Analytical Framework: Why This Evolution Matters

At its very core, the remarkable evolution of crypto trading from its early, chaotic, and largely unregulated platforms to a far more structured, secure, and institutionally-recognized market today is a logical and necessary response to the considerable inherent challenges associated with managing and navigating digital assets. The initial chaos and disorder that characterized this landscape was a natural byproduct of an entirely new and groundbreaking technology—one that emerged seemingly out of nowhere, without any precedent and lacking established rules and guidelines. It was only through a continuous process of trial, error, and relentless innovation that the market began to mature and develop into the sophisticated environment we see now.

This progression is deeply rooted in the fundamental principles of economics. In any trading system characterized by free trade, initial conditions tend to be chaotic and unpredictable until certain standards and norms begin to solidify and take shape. The early days of crypto trading were a prime example of this phenomenon. What started as a wild and somewhat reckless experiment has gradually been refined and structured by individuals and organizations that recognized the urgent need for order, transparency, and enhanced security protocols. The notable improvements in wallet technology, the increased adoption of various regulatory frameworks, and the substantial influx of institutional capital flowing into the market are all logical, essential steps in the natural evolution of any financial system. These developments signify a substantial shift away from a trading environment driven primarily by speculation and vulnerability, evolving into one that is built on foundations of trust, stability, and a focus on long-term value creation for all stakeholders involved.

Analytically, the evolution of crypto trading can indeed be seen as a dynamic process of self-correction and continuous improvement. The early failures, although catastrophic, provided critical feedback that allowed developers and regulators alike to refine the technology and create much more robust systems. The collapse of prominent exchanges like Mt. Gox, for instance, drastically exposed the significant weaknesses in existing security protocols and highlighted the inherent dangers of unregulated trading platforms. In direct response to such crises, the entire industry rallied together to develop and adopt much better security measures, implement rigorous compliance standards that were sorely needed, and establish a set of best practices that have since become the essential foundation of the modern crypto market. This collective response has paved the way for increased trust and greater stability within the ever-evolving landscape of cryptocurrency trading.

The logical progression from chaos to a state of stability serves as a robust and persuasive argument for the remarkable resilience of digital currencies in the financial landscape. It compellingly demonstrates that while the early days of cryptocurrency were fraught with significant risk and uncertainty, the underlying technology itself was fundamentally sound, and the potential for growth and expansion was indeed enormous. The market's inherent ability to learn from its mistakes, adapt, and evolve over time stands as a testament to the power of human ingenuity, resilience, and the natural progression of technological innovation that drives industries forward. This evolution highlights not only the maturity of the market but also the ongoing demand for innovative solutions to traditional financial challenges.

The Persuasive Case for Decentralization and Transparency

One of the most compelling outcomes of this ongoing evolution is the increased emphasis on both decentralization and transparency in various systems and markets. In the early days of these developments, the notable lack of regulation and oversight allowed for a high degree of centralization to take root, where a limited number of individuals or platforms had the ability to control large portions of the market landscape. This concentration of power created a situation that made the system vulnerable to a variety of manipulative practices and fraudulent activities. As the market began to mature and grow in complexity, the push towards decentralization became significantly more pronounced—a logical solution to the numerous problems that were inherent in centralized control structures. The shift towards decentralization not only promotes a fairer distribution of power but also enhances the overall security and reliability of systems by reducing the risks associated with having too much control concentrated in the hands of a few.

Decentralized exchanges (DEXs) are among the most promising and innovative developments in the realm of digital finance. Unlike traditional, centralized exchanges that rely on a single governing authority, DEXs operate in a completely different manner—without the need for any central authority to manage trades. This unique structure allows users to trade directly from their wallets, which in turn enables them to maintain control of their assets throughout the entire trading process. This significant shift toward decentralization not only reduces the inherent risks of hacking and fraud but also aligns seamlessly with the broader ethos of cryptocurrencies. The overarching goal is to create a financial system that is open, transparent, and readily accessible to everyone, regardless of their background or location. The logical argument in favor of decentralization is not only compelling but also persuasive: when power is distributed among many participants, rather than concentrated in a few hands, the system becomes inherently more robust and resilient, making it less prone to abuse or exploitation by malicious entities. This transformation fundamentally changes the landscape of finance and trading, empowering individuals and fostering a community-driven approach to economic interaction.

Transparency is undeniably another key pillar that underpins the modern crypto ecosystem and its continued evolution. The innovative use of blockchain technology ensures that every single transaction is methodically recorded on a public ledger, which can be audited and accessed by anyone interested. This unprecedented level of transparency was unthinkable in traditional finance systems, where opaque practices often shrouded monetary policy and complicated financial transactions. In the dynamic world of cryptocurrency, transparency is crucial as it builds trust among users and allows for greater accountability—this is a critical factor in attracting substantial institutional investment and fostering long-term stability within the market. The implications of such transparency extend far beyond mere reassurance; they create an environment conducive to the growth and maturation of the entire crypto landscape.

Social and Cultural Shifts: Changing Perceptions of Money

The transformation of crypto trading from chaotic, unregulated platforms to a well-recognized and widely accepted mainstream asset class is not merely a technical or economic evolution—it represents a significant and profound social and cultural shift. In earlier times, digital currencies were primarily the exclusive domain of niche communities consisting of tech enthusiasts, libertarians, and early adopters. Many in the mainstream viewed these currencies as radical, speculative endeavors, and sometimes even dangerous trends that were best avoided. However, as the market continued to mature and the various benefits and opportunities presented by digital currencies became increasingly apparent, public perceptions began to change in a dramatic and positive way. The journey of cryptocurrency has transformed the way we think about money, investing, and the future of financial transactions, leading to a broader acceptance that was once unimaginable.

Today, cryptocurrencies are increasingly acknowledged as legitimate and valuable assets that possess the significant potential to transform the landscape of global finance. This notable change in perception is driven by a variety of technological advancements, innovations, and the tangible successes seen in the burgeoning market. The fact that major corporations, institutional investors, and even governments are now actively investing in these digital assets serves as a clear and compelling indication that the narrative surrounding cryptocurrencies has evolved dramatically. What was once considered a fringe experiment has now emerged as a powerful driving force behind a new and dynamic economic paradigm—a paradigm that inherently values principles such as decentralization, enhanced transparency, and relentless innovation. As more stakeholders come to recognize their importance, the impact of cryptocurrencies on worldwide financial systems is expected to grow even further, reshaping not just how transactions are conducted, but also how value is perceived and exchanged in the future.

This significant cultural shift is having a profoundly persuasive impact on the future of finance. As an increasing number of people begin to understand and trust in the capabilities of digital currencies, the global market initiates a trajectory toward becoming more robust and resilient, and the potential for further innovation in the financial sector grows exponentially. The evolution of cryptocurrency trading is not merely a matter of technical improvement or advancement; it represents a fundamental transformation in how society perceives and views the nature of money and the essential role it plays in our daily lives. The logical and analytical case for advocating digital currencies is considerably strengthened by this growing cultural acceptance, as it clearly demonstrates that even the most radical and unconventional ideas can seamlessly transition into the mainstream when they convincingly prove their worth and utility over time. This change in perception can significantly shape economic landscapes and influence future financial practices around the globe.

A New Era of Financial Freedom

The extraordinary journey of crypto trading, which originated from early, unregulated platforms, has evolved dramatically into a sophisticated and institutionalized market. This evolution stands as a powerful testament to the resilience, adaptability, and immense transformative potential that digital currencies possess in the modern financial landscape. Each pivotal milestone along this path—whether it be the groundbreaking publication of the Bitcoin whitepaper, the eventual collapse of various early exchanges, the significant surge of institutional investment into the crypto sector, or the ongoing development of both decentralized and regulated trading platforms—has played a critical role in shaping a compelling narrative. This narrative clearly posits that cryptocurrencies are not merely a passing fad, but instead represent the undeniable future of money and finance. As time progresses, this narrative continues to be reinforced, underscoring the necessity for all stakeholders to engage with the evolving world of digital assets.

The logical progression of these significant and impactful events is undeniably clear and compelling. The early chaos surrounding crypto trading vividly exposed the numerous vulnerabilities inherent in unregulated markets, a situation that forced the entire industry to evolve at an astonishing pace. As a result, the subsequent improvements made in technology, security, and regulation have contributed to the creation of a robust framework that now effectively supports billions in various digital assets. This remarkable evolution from an unruly, highly speculative market to a stable, transparent, and inclusive financial ecosystem stands as a shockingly brilliant demonstration of how human ingenuity and creativity can overcome even the most formidable challenges and obstacles. This transformation reflects not just technological advances but also a deepening understanding of the complexities and needs of modern economic systems.

For investors, policymakers, and everyday users, the lessons derived from the ongoing evolution are undeniably clear. The transformative power of crypto trading presents a compelling argument for what the future of finance holds—a future where money exists in a decentralized manner, promoting transparency and placing it truly in the hands of the people at large. It represents a future that not only promises greater financial freedom but also enhances security measures, thereby fostering a more equitable distribution of wealth among individuals. The remarkable journey from the early days of unregulated platforms to their current mainstream acceptance is not merely a tale of technological progress; it embodies a profound revolution in how we conceptualize and engage with money itself, altering our relationships and interactions with financial systems in significant ways.

In conclusion, the key milestones that have undeniably cemented the legitimacy of cryptocurrency are not isolated events occurring in a vacuum; rather, they are interconnected steps in the ongoing evolution of a groundbreaking new financial paradigm. The logical, analytical, and persuasive arguments presented by these pivotal milestones collectively form the backbone of a future in which digital currencies will unequivocally redefine and reshape global finance as we know it today. We must embrace the reality that we are currently witnessing a historical transformation—a truly mind-blowing shift that challenges conventional wisdom and provides a remarkable glimpse into a decentralized, transparent, and inclusive future for money and financial systems worldwide.

The global transition from traditional, centralized finance to a decentralized digital economy represents a remarkable testament to the power of innovative technology and the relentless pursuit of true economic freedom. As the ongoing journey of crypto trading continues to unfold day by day, every significant step forward reinforces the enduring promise of digital currencies, positioning them as the ultimate store of value and a viable medium of exchange in our increasingly digital world. The future of money is not just on the horizon; it is actively unfolding before us, and it is a future that is defined by decentralization, enhanced transparency, and the empowerment of every individual to take full control of their own financial destiny in ways that were previously unimaginable.

This is not just a technological revolution—it is an extraordinary paradigm shift that will completely reshape societies, economies, and alter the way we think about wealth forever. It is a future that is as logical as it is revolutionary, as persuasive as it is inevitable. The story of crypto trading, which has evolved from its chaotic and tumultuous beginnings to its current status as a recognized mainstream asset, is a powerful narrative of progress—a narrative that continues to evolve and inspire significantly as we move toward a world where financial freedom is not merely an ideal but a living, breathing reality that countless individuals can experience firsthand.

Section 2: Centralized vs. Decentralized Exchanges: A Comparative Evolution

In the early days of cryptocurrency, the dazzling world of digital trading was nothing short of a chaotic frontier—a wild, unpredictable realm where cutting-edge technology, unrelenting ambition, and significant risk converged in an almost shocking display of innovation and creativity. As this fast-paced environment matured, what once was a raw, untamed marketplace evolved into a more structured and organized ecosystem marked by two distinct trading models: centralized exchanges (CEXs) and decentralized exchanges (DEXs). The evolution and development of these platforms, each possessing their own distinctive advantages, merits, and challenges, has fundamentally influenced how investors engage in buying, selling, and trading digital assets. This transformation has also redefined the very notion of trust and control in an increasingly complex digital economy. In this thorough exploration, we will delve deeply into the comparative evolution of centralized versus decentralized exchanges, closely examining how each approach has uniquely addressed the diverse needs of investors. Additionally, we will investigate why the ongoing tension between convenience and autonomy remains one of the most compelling debates in modern finance, prompting critical questions about the future of trading and investment in the cryptocurrency space.

The Genesis of Digital Trading: A Chaotic Beginning

The birth of cryptocurrency trading was anything but orderly, marked by a tumultuous and unpredictable landscape. In the early days, digital asset trading was conducted on various platforms that were as much experimental playgrounds as they were functional markets. There were no robust regulations overseeing these trades, few security protocols in place to protect users, and little to no standardization across different exchanges. Early exchanges were often built by enthusiastic individuals, pioneers in their own right, who eagerly recognized the immense potential of a decentralized financial system. However, they typically lacked the necessary resources, experience, or expertise to create secure and reliable trading infrastructures that would eventually be essential for the industry's growth. This chaotic environment fostered both innovation and a range of risks, laying the groundwork for the future of trading in digital currencies.

These pioneering platforms emerged in a wild and unregulated environment where trust was scarce, and every transaction carried with it the burden of being a leap of faith. Investors had to navigate a digital frontier without the safety nets that were traditionally provided by established financial institutions, which made the landscape even more treacherous. Every trade was fraught with the potential hazards of hacking, fraud, or outright technical failure that could disrupt the trading process. It was a shocking and tumultuous world filled with high risks, where fortunes could be made in a matter of minutes yet lost in the blink of an eye. The raw and unrefined nature of early crypto trading laid the groundwork for a series of important evolutionary milestones, each one striving to address the shortcomings and vulnerabilities of its predecessors. This dynamic and rapidly changing arena encouraged innovation and adaptation, pushing developers and investors alike to find better solutions that could enhance security, improve user experience, and foster trust.

Centralized Exchanges: The Rise of Order Amid Chaos

Centralized exchanges rapidly emerged as the first significant response to the chaotic trading environment that characterized the early days of the cryptocurrency market. These platforms, which operate in a manner quite similar to traditional stock exchanges, are managed by companies that serve as intermediaries between buyers and sellers. By centralizing the trading process, these exchanges offered much-needed structure and liquidity, effectively transforming the wild and unpredictable digital frontier into a far more manageable and organized marketplace. In doing so, they facilitated smoother transactions and fostered greater confidence among participants in this evolving financial landscape.

Advantages of Centralized Exchanges

1. **Liquidity and Speed:**
   Centralized exchanges are known for providing high liquidity levels. This is primarily because they effectively aggregate orders from a substantial pool of traders and investors. Such a significant influx of orders creates a vibrant marketplace. This liquidity translates to the ability for investors to buy or sell various digital assets promptly and at competitive prices. This characteristic is crucial in a dynamic market environment where timing can significantly impact potential gains or losses for traders and investors alike.

1. **Ease of Use:**
   For a large number of newcomers, centralized platforms tend to be considerably more intuitive and user-friendly. With familiar interfaces, readily available customer support, and seamless processes for both deposits and withdrawals, these exchanges play a vital role in lowering the barrier to entry for investors who might be feeling intimidated by the technical complexities and nuances of cryptocurrencies. This welcoming approach allows those new to the crypto

world to engage more confidently and effectively in trading activities without being overwhelmed.

1. **Regulatory Oversight and Trust:**
As digital currencies started to gain substantial mainstream attention and awareness, various regulatory bodies began to take serious notice. Consequently, many centralized exchanges have since implemented a wide array of strict compliance and security measures, which have significantly enhanced investor trust across the board. This increased regulatory oversight has provided a greater sense of legitimacy in the market, thus attracting a diverse range of institutional investors and fostering large-scale trading volumes that were previously unseen.

1. **Comprehensive Features:**
Centralized exchanges typically provide a wide range of services, including margin trading, futures contracts, staking, lending, and more. This extensive array of offerings enables investors to diversify their trading strategies and manage risk in a more effective manner, all within the confines of a single platform. By utilizing these services, users can take advantage of different market conditions and optimize their investment opportunities accordingly.

Drawbacks and Risks of Centralized Exchanges

However, centralization comes at a cost. The very factors that make these exchanges appealing also introduce significant risks:

1. **Custodial Control:**

When you decide to use a centralized exchange, you are essentially handing over complete control of your digital assets to a third party entity. This custodial model inherently means that if the exchange experiences a hack or mismanages funds in any way, investors can potentially suffer significant and massive financial losses. The infamous collapse of Mt. Gox serves as a prime and cautionary example—a once-dominant exchange that lost hundreds of thousands of Bitcoins due to serious security failures and vulnerabilities. Such incidents highlight the risks of entrusting your assets to centralized platforms.

1. **Single Points of Failure:**
Centralized exchanges inherently embody a concentrated risk that affects the entire trading ecosystem. Their infrastructure, security systems, and management practices often become single points of failure, which can have detrimental effects on millions of users all at once. A single major security breach or a technical outage can significantly disrupt the entire market, leading to widespread panic among traders and a potential collapse of confidence, which in turn can cause a ripple effect leading to financial instability across various sectors of the economy.

1. **Limited Transparency:**
While regulatory measures have indeed led to significant improvements in transparency in financial markets, centralized exchanges frequently utilize proprietary systems and maintain opaque internal processes that are not fully visible to the public. This existing lack of complete transparency can occasionally

obscure crucial information regarding fund management practices, which in turn could potentially undermine investor confidence in these platforms. It is essential for investors to be informed about the practices and processes that govern their investments, as this clarity plays a vital role in building trust and ensuring market stability.

1. **Regulatory and Geopolitical Risks:**
   Being centralized, these exchanges are inherently subject to the regulatory environment of the jurisdictions in which they operate. This means that any changes in regulations or government crackdowns can have a significant and often immediate impact on their operations. This has been observed in various countries around the world, where crypto trading has faced heavy restrictions or has even been outright banned. Such developments can lead to uncertainty and fluctuations in the market, affecting traders and investors alike. The responses to such regulatory challenges vary widely, with some exchanges adapting quickly to new rules, while others struggle to comply with shifting legal landscapes.

Decentralized Exchanges: The Emergence of a New Paradigm

In sharp contrast to traditional centralized exchanges, decentralized exchanges (DEXs) represent a radically different and innovative approach to digital trading. Rather than relying on a central authority to oversee and manage trades, DEXs leverage blockchain technology, enabling efficient and seamless peer-to-peer transactions without the need for intermediaries. This significant shift towards decentralization is as revolutionary as it is logical, embodying and reinforcing the core principles of cryptocurrencies: autonomy, transparency, and a complete trustlessness that empowers users. As users engage with DEXs, they can fully control their assets and trades, minimizing the risks commonly associated with centralization.

Advantages of Decentralized Exchanges

1. **User Sovereignty and Control:**
   One of the most compelling and significant advantages of decentralized exchanges lies in their ability to allow users to retain full and complete control over their funds and assets. In these exchanges, transactions occur directly between users, facilitating peer-to-peer trading without the need for a central authority to hold custody of assets or funds. This emphasis on self-custody aligns perfectly with the decentralized ethos and foundational principles of cryptocurrencies, empowering individuals and reducing the risk associated with centralized failures, hacks, or outages. Overall, this model fosters trust and independence among users, providing them with a greater sense of security.

1. **Enhanced Security and Reduced Risk of Hacks:**
   Because decentralized exchanges do not hold users' funds in a single location, they are inherently less vulnerable to the threats posed by large-scale hacks. Instead of relying on one central vault that could be compromised, funds are instead dispersed across a multitude of individual wallets. This strategic distribution of risk serves as a logical response to the various vulnerabilities that are often inherent in centralized systems, ensuring that potential losses can

be minimized and security is significantly enhanced. Such a model not only protects users' assets more effectively but also fosters greater confidence in the trading process overall.

1. **Transparency and Trustlessness:**
Every single transaction that occurs on a decentralized exchange is meticulously recorded on a public blockchain, which ensures a level of complete transparency that users can rely on. This means that users do not necessarily need to place their trust in a central authority; rather, they have the ability to verify the transactions for themselves at any time they choose. This trustless model serves as a compelling argument for the concept of decentralization, as it effectively minimizes the need for intermediaries who could otherwise complicate the process. Additionally, it significantly reduces the potential for fraud and wrongdoing within the system.

1. **Resilience and Censorship Resistance:**
Decentralized exchanges are inherently resistant to various forms of censorship. Since they operate on a distributed network, no single entity possesses the power to shut down the entire platform or control its operations and functionality. This remarkable resilience is particularly appealing in regions where regulatory pressures, combined with political instability, can lead to disruptions of centralized financial systems and their services. As such platforms continue to gain traction, they become a vital alternative for users seeking greater freedom and security in their transactions and trades.

Drawbacks and Challenges of Decentralized Exchanges

Despite their many advantages, decentralized exchanges are not without their challenges:

1. **Lower Liquidity and Slower Transaction Speeds:** In their early stages, decentralized exchanges, commonly referred to as DEXs, often suffered significantly from lower liquidity when compared to traditional centralized exchanges. With fewer users participating in trading activities and a limited number of orders being placed, it could prove quite difficult to execute trades quickly or at the desired prices specified by traders. This issue has been gradually addressed over time as the overall market continues to grow and mature, providing more opportunities for users to engage. However, it remains a significant challenge for some decentralized platforms, leading to continued efforts aimed at enhancing their liquidity to meet the demands of users effectively.

1. **Complexity and User Experience:** Decentralized exchanges can often be even more difficult for beginners to navigate effectively. The entire process of connecting a wallet, understanding gas fees, and managing various transactions on a blockchain can be quite intimidating for those who are new to the crypto space. Although user interfaces are steadily improving over time, the learning curve remains significantly steeper compared to that of centralized platforms. Thus, many newcomers may feel overwhelmed and unsure about how to proceed with their trading activities.

1. **Fragmentation and Interoperability Issues:**
The rapid proliferation of a diverse array of DEX platforms has resulted in a fragmented ecosystem that is becoming increasingly complex. Different decentralized exchanges may operate on varying blockchains, which poses significant challenges for users seeking to transfer their assets between multiple platforms in a seamless manner. This inherent lack of interoperability can greatly hinder the overall efficiency and effectiveness of the decentralized trading environment. Users may find themselves facing numerous obstacles, making it difficult to navigate the different exchanges and depleting the intended benefits of decentralized trading solutions.

1. **Potential for Exploits and Smart Contract Vulnerabilities:**
While decentralized exchanges certainly benefit from the enhanced security provided by blockchain technology, it is important to acknowledge that they are not entirely immune to various vulnerabilities. Bugs within smart contracts or flaws present in the underlying code can be readily exploited by malicious actors, which can lead to significant financial losses for users and investors alike. As this technology continues to mature and evolve, many of these issues are being systematically addressed through rigorous audits and ongoing development efforts. However, despite these advancements, such vulnerabilities continue to pose a considerable concern within the ecosystem of decentralized exchanges. It is crucial for users to remain vigilant and informed about these potential

risks while participating in this rapidly changing landscape.

Comparative Analysis: Meeting Investor Needs

The ongoing debate between centralized and decentralized exchanges focuses on a crucial trade-off: convenience versus control in the trading landscape. For a significant number of investors, the ease-of-use, high liquidity, and regulatory oversight provided by centralized exchanges are essential elements that greatly facilitate quick, efficient trading experiences. These platforms offer a familiar and accessible environment, complete with user-friendly interfaces and reliable customer support that closely resembles traditional banking services. For individuals who prioritize simplicity, efficiency, and rapid execution, centralized exchanges continue to remain an attractive and compelling option in the realm of cryptocurrency trading. They provide the assurance of a regulated framework that can appeal to both new and seasoned traders alike seeking a dependable trading venue.

However, for investors who highly value security, transparency, and personal control over their financial assets, decentralized exchanges provide a compellingly attractive alternative. The trustless nature of decentralized exchanges (DEXs), paired with their strong resistance to censorship and the significant empowerment of self-custody, greatly appeals to individuals who firmly believe that true financial freedom can only be achieved when individuals are placed in complete control of their assets. The logical argument supporting decentralized exchanges is robustly built on the basic principle that when you effectively remove intermediaries from financial transactions, you inherently reduce the risk of a single point of failure. This is a critical consideration in an industry where the stakes are incredibly high, and the potential for loss can be significant. By utilizing DEXs, investors can navigate the financial landscape with greater confidence, knowing that their investments are safeguarded by technology that prioritizes decentralization and autonomy.

The Security Trade-Off

One of the most significant differences that can be observed between centralized and decentralized exchanges lies in the way they handle the crucial aspect of security. Centralized exchanges, despite offering a level of convenience that attracts many users, hold custody of user funds. This practice inherently creates a concentrated target for hackers and malicious actors looking to exploit vulnerabilities. The history of cryptocurrency trading is indeed littered with numerous examples of centralized platforms suffering from massive security breaches, with the infamous Mt. Gox case being the most notorious and widely discussed in the community. Such incidents have served as stark reminders that even the most sophisticated and advanced security measures can ultimately fail when trust is placed in a single entity, highlighting the potential dangers associated with centralized systems in the world of crypto trading.

Decentralized exchanges significantly mitigate this inherent risk by allowing users to maintain direct control over their funds at all times. By keeping their assets securely held within personal wallets instead of on a centralized server, the risk is distributed across a much wider network rather than being concentrated in a single, potentially vulnerable location. This not only enhances security for the users but also aligns perfectly with the broader and more empowering philosophy of decentralization that underpins blockchain technology. However, the flip side to this arrangement is that non-custodial management does necessitate a markedly higher degree of personal responsibility from each user. It is imperative that users become diligent in managing their private keys, as any mistake or oversight can result in irreversible loss of their assets—a risk that many individuals find quite daunting and overwhelming. The trade-off here is evident: centralized platforms offer a level of simplicity and convenience that many users appreciate, but this convenience comes at the cost of reducing overall security. On the other hand, decentralized platforms provide enhanced control and a greater level of protection for the users, albeit with a steeper learning curve and the necessity for increased caution and awareness.

Liquidity and Market Efficiency

Another critical factor that plays a significant role in trading and investment dynamics is liquidity—the ease and efficiency with which assets can be bought or sold without causing significant fluctuations or changes in their prices. Centralized exchanges typically boast higher liquidity due to their ability to effectively aggregate orders from a vast number of traders and market participants. This high level of liquidity ensures that transactions can be executed swiftly, often with minimal delay, and at competitive prices. Such conditions are essential for investors who are looking to trade large volumes of assets, as they can enter and exit positions more freely and with greater certainty. A highly liquid market not only facilitates smoother transactions but also attracts more participants, further enhancing the trading environment.

Decentralized exchanges, particularly in their early iterations, often struggled with significantly lower liquidity levels. With fewer participants engaging and smaller order books available, executing trades on a decentralized exchange (DEX) could often lead to substantial slippage, which in turn reduced the overall efficiency of the market for all users involved. However, as the cryptocurrency market has matured and evolved over time, the liquidity available on these decentralized platforms has improved dramatically and considerably. Remarkable innovations such as automated market makers (AMMs) and liquidity pools have enabled DEXs to offer liquidity levels that now rival those of their centralized counterparts. The logical progression here is quite clear: as technology continues to advance and user adoption increases, the gap in liquidity and efficiency between centralized and decentralized exchanges will undoubtedly continue to narrow. This development is particularly promising, as it ultimately offers investors the best of both worlds, providing them with enhanced trading options and greater overall market efficiency.

Regulatory Considerations

Regulation plays an essential and pivotal role in shaping investor trust and ensuring market stability over time. Centralized exchanges, in particular, are subject to extensive regulatory oversight, which effectively provides a necessary layer of protection for investors. This oversight promotes and enforces transparency, accountability, and strict compliance with legal standards that are in place to protect stakeholders. While this regulatory framework can sometimes be seen as restrictive or burdensome, it has proven to be a key factor in attracting institutional investors and facilitating the integration of crypto trading into the broader financial system, which ultimately benefits all market participants.

Decentralized exchanges, often abbreviated as DEXs, operate without the oversight of a central authority, which makes them inherently more resistant to traditional regulatory approaches that typically govern centralized platforms. This attractive feature, while appealing from a standpoint of personal freedom and autonomy, brings with it certain challenges, particularly concerning the fundamental issue of investor protection. Due to their unregulated nature, DEXs can unfortunately leave users exposed to various risks and uncertainties, such as vulnerabilities present in smart contracts and potential market manipulation by unscrupulous players. However, it is important to note that the rise of decentralized governance models, alongside community-driven oversight initiatives, is starting to effectively address these pressing concerns. As these innovative frameworks evolve and mature, the regulatory landscape for decentralized platforms is undergoing constant transformation. This ongoing process of developing more suitable regulatory frameworks for DEXs is essential, and as it progresses, the logical case advocating for the use of decentralized exchanges will be further solidified and strengthened in the broader financial ecosystem.

The Future of Crypto Trading: Hybrid Models and Convergence

As the crypto market continues to rapidly evolve and change, the previously clear dichotomy between centralized and decentralized exchanges is beginning to steadily blur and overlap. Hybrid models are now emerging that aim to successfully combine the best and most advantageous features of both systems—offering the liquidity and user-friendly experience typically associated with centralized exchanges, along with the enhanced security and decentralization offered by non-custodial solutions. These innovative hybrid platforms represent the next logical step in the ongoing evolution of digital asset trading and investment, more effectively catering to the diverse needs and preferences of users in this dynamic marketplace.

Hybrid exchanges empower users to maintain control over their private keys while simultaneously taking advantage of the significant liquidity and user-friendly nature of centralized infrastructure. These platforms typically integrate a variety of features, including multi-signature wallets, decentralized order books, and advanced security protocols, all designed to foster a more balanced and secure trading environment. The convergence of these elements presents a persuasive argument for the future of trading, as it effectively addresses the primary concerns that have emerged from both sides of the ongoing debate about centralized versus decentralized trading. The logical synthesis of these varying approaches indicates that the optimal solution resides not in exclusively choosing one model over another but rather in effectively integrating the distinctive strengths of both to create a robust and versatile trading ecosystem that can adapt to the needs of all users. In this innovative landscape, traders can enjoy the best of both worlds, ensuring that security is prioritized while also benefiting from the efficiencies offered by centralized systems.

Persuading Investors: The Benefits of a Diversified Approach

For modern investors navigating the complex landscape of finance, the choice between centralized and decentralized exchanges is not merely an either-or proposition. Rather, it is essential to adopt a diversified approach that effectively leverages the unique strengths of both systems, thereby creating a more balanced, adaptable, and resilient investment strategy. A significant number of experienced investors prefer to utilize centralized platforms primarily due to their high liquidity levels and user-friendly interfaces, particularly when executing large or frequent trades. At the same time, they also make it a priority to store the bulk of their digital assets in secure, non-custodial wallets. This responsible strategy helps to substantially mitigate the risks associated with potential failures within centralized exchanges, providing an additional layer of security for their holdings.

This strategy is not only logical but also very pragmatic in nature. By diversifying the methods of asset storage along with trading approaches, investors can effectively protect themselves against the inherent risks that are associated with relying on any single system. It is a shockingly straightforward yet remarkably effective way to navigate through the complexities of the ever-changing digital asset market—a carefully balanced approach that aims to maximize both the security of assets and the convenience of transactions. The argument supporting this approach is persuasive: in a marketplace that is both volatile and rapidly evolving, flexibility and adaptability prove to be vital keys to achieving long-term success and sustainability. Investors who embrace this diversified strategy are better equipped to weather the storms of market fluctuations.

The Role of Technology and Innovation in Shaping the Future

The evolution of exchange platforms is profoundly driven by a continuous wave of technological innovation that never seems to stop progressing. Advances in areas such as blockchain technology, cryptography, and network architecture are constantly pushing the boundaries and limits of what is possible in the ever-growing field of digital trading. These ongoing innovations not only enhance the overall performance and security of various exchanges but also significantly expand the wide range of services they can offer to users and traders alike. The landscape of digital trading is being reshaped by these developments, allowing for a more robust and versatile trading experience.

For example, the advent of automated market makers (AMMs) on decentralized exchanges has significantly revolutionized the provision of liquidity in the financial ecosystem. By utilizing advanced algorithms to accurately determine prices and facilitate seamless trades, AMMs create a more efficient and user-friendly trading experience that effectively rivals that of traditional centralized trading platforms. This groundbreaking innovation has served as a key driving factor in bridging the gap between the two distinct trading models, ensuring that decentralized trading becomes a genuinely viable option for a much broader audience, including those who may have been hesitant to engage in this new system of exchanging assets.

Moreover, the integration of artificial intelligence (AI) into exchange platforms is poised to further transform the landscape in ways we are only beginning to comprehend. AI-driven analytics can optimize trading strategies by utilizing vast amounts of data to identify patterns, detect anomalies, and enhance security measures, ensuring that exchanges operate smoothly even in the face of extreme volatility. These advancements are not only logical but also deeply persuasive—they clearly demonstrate that technology can effectively address the challenges that have long plagued the crypto trading space. By streamlining operations and improving decision-making processes, AI enhances the user experience and paves the way for a more robust and resilient market overall. As this technology continues to evolve, it promises to usher in an era of unparalleled innovation and trust in digital finance, providing traders with tools that can significantly improve their performance and manage risk more effectively.

Regulatory Evolution: The Influence on Market Legitimacy

The gradual regulatory acceptance of cryptocurrencies has played a truly pivotal role in the significant evolution of exchange platforms within the financial landscape. Initially, the completely unregulated nature of early exchanges contributed to widespread chaos, volatility, and a notable lack of investor confidence. However, as the market matured and the value of digital assets became undeniably apparent and recognized, regulators began to establish structured frameworks and regulatory guidelines to effectively oversee these emerging financial instruments and protect investors. This shift has fostered a more stable environment, ultimately leading to increased trust and participation in the cryptocurrency market.

The significant shift towards regulation in the financial sector has had a dual effect that is noteworthy. On one hand, it has played a crucial role in helping to effectively weed out fraudulent and poorly managed platforms, thereby significantly increasing overall market stability in a variety of digital assets. On the other hand, it has provided the legitimacy that institutional investors urgently require to confidently enter the market. As regulatory frameworks continue to evolve and adapt, both centralized and decentralized exchanges are making adjustments, creating an increasingly favorable environment where digital asset trading is becoming more fully integrated with the traditional financial system. This integration is vital for bridging the gap between these two worlds, fostering greater trust and participation among investors.

This regulatory evolution marks a compelling testament to the reasonable and logical progression within the ever-evolving landscape of the crypto market. When an asset class grows to a significant size and achieves substantial influence in the financial world, it inevitably captures the attention of regulators and policymakers. The fact that digital currencies are now being actively discussed in terms of clear legal guidelines and robust consumer protections serves as a powerful and persuasive signal that they have moved beyond the fringes and firmly into the mainstream financial ecosystem. This shift in focus indicates a growing recognition of the importance of these assets in the broader economic framework. It is indeed a mind-blowing evolution that underscores the truly transformative impact of cryptocurrency on global finance, reshaping how we think about money, value exchange, and financial transactions on an international scale. This transformation is not just a passing trend; it represents a fundamental change in how financial systems operate and interact with emerging technologies.

Comparative Analysis: Meeting Diverse Investor Needs

When comparing centralized and decentralized exchanges, it becomes abundantly clear that both types of platforms possess distinct advantages that effectively cater to different types of investor needs and preferences. Centralized exchanges excel in providing remarkable high liquidity levels, user-friendly interfaces that are easy to navigate, and fast execution speeds that enhance the trading experience. They are particularly well-suited for active traders who require the efficiency and reliability of a system that closely mimics the traditional financial markets they are accustomed to. Institutional investors as well as large-scale traders often favor centralized platforms because they offer a familiar, regulated environment and the essential ability to execute large trades without experiencing significant slippage or price impact, which can be a huge concern for those trading substantial volumes.

Decentralized exchanges, on the other hand, provide an unparalleled level of security, transparency, and control that is difficult to find elsewhere. These platforms function on a trustless model, allowing transactions to be executed directly and seamlessly between users without the need for intermediaries. This model aligns exceptionally well with the ethos of decentralization and the principle of financial sovereignty. For investors who strongly prioritize security and control over mere convenience, DEXs truly represent the ultimate solution in the world of digital finance. They effectively eliminate the risks that are commonly associated with custodial services, ensuring that users maintain their position as the sole guardians of their valuable assets, free from the vulnerabilities that intermediaries often introduce. By empowering users to manage their investments directly, DEXs foster a more robust financial landscape where users can trade with peace of mind, knowing that they retain complete ownership of their cryptocurrencies at all times.

The choice between these two distinct models ultimately boils down to personal preference and individual risk tolerance when it comes to investing. Some investors are willing to sacrifice a degree of control over their assets for the sake of convenience and ease of use, while others are determined to maintain full sovereignty over their digital wealth. This decision highlights the varying approaches that individuals take in their financial journeys. The evolution of various exchange platforms effectively reflects this diversity of needs and desires among investors, offering a wider range of options that can be tailored to fit different investment strategies and personal financial goals.

The Persuasive Argument for a Hybrid Future

Looking ahead, it is clear that the future of crypto trading is likely to be characterized by an intriguing convergence of centralized and decentralized models—a hybrid approach that seamlessly leverages the distinct strengths of both systems. Hybrid exchanges are designed to offer the much-desired liquidity and user-friendly ease-of-use found in centralized platforms while simultaneously maintaining the critical security and enhanced control offered by decentralized solutions. This logical synthesis of the two contrasting philosophies creates a powerful and persuasive argument for what lies ahead in the world of digital trading. As we navigate this evolving landscape, the combination of these approaches may very well define the future trajectory of cryptocurrency markets.

Hybrid solutions could, for instance, enable users to execute trades seamlessly on a centralized interface while still maintaining custody of their funds in secure, non-custodial wallets. This innovative approach would effectively provide the best of both worlds—allowing for quick and efficient transactions while not compromising on the crucial security and decentralization that underpin the rapidly evolving crypto revolution. The ongoing development of hybrid models is already taking place in various projects, showcasing their potential and promise. These hybrid solutions represent the natural progression and evolution of a market that is continually adapting and transforming to meet the ever-changing needs of its diverse participants and users.

The concept of a hybrid future is not merely theoretical; instead, it is actively being pursued by a wide array of developers, investors, and regulators alike. These stakeholders recognize that the stark binary choice between centralized and decentralized exchanges poses too restrictive a framework for today's dynamic and rapidly evolving market landscape. By skillfully combining the advantages offered by both models, hybrid exchanges have the potential to create a trading ecosystem that is not only more resilient but also significantly more efficient and inclusive. Such an ecosystem can cater to the diverse and varied needs of all types of market participants, ensuring that everyone has access to innovative trading solutions and opportunities aligned with the future of financial systems.

The Broader Economic and Social Implications

The evolution of crypto trading platforms has far-reaching implications that extend well beyond the confines of the digital currency market. As cryptocurrencies increasingly become an integral part of the global financial system, the design and functionality of exchanges will undeniably play a critical role in shaping the future of money. The shift towards decentralized trading represents not only a significant technological innovation but also a fundamental rethinking of how financial systems should operate—one that prioritizes critical aspects such as transparency, efficiency, and individual empowerment. This transformation is shaping a new landscape in which each participant can engage more freely and with greater trust. Moreover, as these platforms advance, they have the potential to disrupt traditional financial institutions, challenging their roles and encouraging a more competitive environment that could lead to better services for consumers and businesses alike.

Centralized exchanges have long held a dominant position in the financial landscape, exercising control over the flow of capital and exerting considerable influence on market dynamics and participants. However, the rise of decentralized platforms has begun to challenge this traditional dominance by effectively redistributing power away from centralized institutions and moving it towards the individual investor or user. This significant shift has the potential to truly democratize finance, significantly reduce economic inequality, and foster greater financial inclusion for a greater number of people. For societies around the globe, this profound transformation represents not only a logical necessity but also a compelling argument for actively embracing a new and decentralized economic order. Such a shift could lead to enhanced opportunities for all, ensuring that financial systems are more equitable and accessible to everyone involved.

The global transition towards digital assets is dramatically reshaping the way we think about wealth and value in contemporary society. Traditional financial systems, with their centralized control mechanisms and opaque practices, have long been criticized for failing to adequately serve the diverse needs of the many. In contrast, decentralized exchanges provide a compelling vision of finance that is not only open and transparent but also accessible to everyone. This fundamental paradigm shift has the potential to create a more just and equitable global economy—a future where the benefits of financial innovation are shared broadly among the population, rather than being concentrated solely in the hands of a select few elites. It creates opportunities for increased financial inclusion, empowering individuals and communities who have historically been marginalized or excluded from the financial system.

Persuading the Skeptics: The Case for Continued Evolution

Despite the remarkable and significant progress made in the ongoing evolution of crypto trading platforms, skepticism still remains among certain observers and commentators. Critics often point to persistent issues such as market volatility, ongoing regulatory uncertainty, and the inherent challenges associated with effectively managing decentralized systems. However, the logical and analytical progression of events—ranging from the early chaotic and unregulated platforms to the highly sophisticated and streamlined systems that are in widespread use today—provides a compelling and strong counterargument that cannot be overlooked.

Every significant technological revolution invariably faces substantial resistance. For instance, the formative periods of the internet were marked by widespread skepticism and deep-seated doubt, yet in the present day, it stands as the indispensable backbone of global communication and international commerce. In a similar vein, the ongoing evolution of crypto trading represents a continuous journey of improvement, adaptation, and learning from previous mistakes. The early failures experienced in this domain, such as the dramatic collapse of Mt. Gox, imparted vital lessons that hastened the development of more secure, reliable, and robust platforms for trading. The logical trajectory from a state of unregulated chaos towards structured, institutionalized markets is not merely persuasive—it has become an inevitable reality on the path forward.

The increasing integration of regulatory frameworks coupled with the widespread adoption of hybrid exchange models significantly bolsters the case for the promising future of crypto trading. These crucial developments represent a natural response to the complex challenges posed by a rapidly evolving market, ensuring that the entire system remains robust, efficient, and secure in the face of change. The argument is abundantly clear: if the ultimate goal is to create a financial ecosystem that is not only transparent but also equitable and resilient, then the ongoing evolution of crypto trading platforms must continue to steadfastly advance along the innovative path of decentralization. It's essential for stakeholders to recognize that innovation is not simply an option; it is a necessity that will define the success and sustainability of the entire market in the coming years.

The Future Landscape: Innovations on the Horizon

As we look ahead into the future, the world of crypto trading promises to bring forth even more thrilling innovations and advancements. One of the most intriguing developments is the rise of hybrid exchanges, which uniquely combine the liquidity and convenience typically associated with centralized platforms alongside the robust security and autonomy of decentralized systems. These pioneering platforms are already on the horizon and are set to revolutionize the trading landscape. They aim to offer a seamless and highly integrated trading experience that effectively addresses the diverse needs and expectations of both retail and institutional investors, fostering a more inclusive trading environment for all participants.

Moreover, recent advancements in blockchain technology, artificial intelligence, and machine learning are undoubtedly poised to revolutionize the very way digital asset exchanges operate. For instance, AI-driven trading algorithms possess the remarkable ability to analyze vast amounts of data in real time, which significantly assists investors in making much more informed decisions and thereby reducing the overall impact of market volatility. Additionally, enhanced security protocols, including cutting-edge quantum-resistant cryptography, will further serve to protect digital assets against emerging threats, safeguarding them more effectively than ever before. These groundbreaking innovations, which are firmly grounded in logical reasoning and rigorous analysis, are set to push the boundaries of what is realistically possible in the evolving landscape of digital finance. As this technology continues to evolve, it will create new opportunities and challenges that market participants must navigate carefully, ensuring that they remain at the forefront of this exciting and rapidly changing field.

The ongoing evolution of crypto trading platforms is not merely a matter of technical improvement alone; it signifies a profound rethinking of the mechanisms through which money is traded, stored, and valued within the financial landscape. This transformation represents a mind-blowing convergence of groundbreaking technology, thoughtful regulation, and ever-shifting market dynamics that are fundamentally reshaping the entire global financial system. As hybrid models gain traction and regulatory clarity continues to improve significantly, the gap that currently exists between centralized and decentralized platforms will inevitably keep narrowing. This gradual convergence will pave the way for a unified ecosystem that ingeniously leverages the inherent strengths of both centralized and decentralized approaches, creating new opportunities and challenges that will redefine the crypto trading experience for users across the globe.

Social and Cultural Implications: Shaping the Future of Money

The evolution of crypto trading has profound social and cultural implications that are increasingly important in today's financial landscape. The transformation from chaotic, unregulated platforms to mature, institutionalized markets not only reflects a broader shift in societal attitudes towards money but also signifies a growing awareness of financial freedom and autonomy. In a world where traditional financial institutions have often failed to adequately serve the diverse needs of the many, the rise of decentralized trading platforms stands as a bold and persuasive call for a more democratic and inclusive financial system. This new paradigm fundamentally challenges existing norms, enabling individuals to take control of their financial destinies and participate in a system that prioritizes accessibility and equity.

This shift is not solely about the advancement of technology; it is fundamentally about empowering individuals and communities. The decentralization of crypto trading facilitates a more equitable distribution of financial power and resources, enabling people from all walks of life, regardless of their socioeconomic status, to actively participate in the global economy. This movement challenges long-standing power structures that have historically favored the few over the many and offers a compelling vision of a future where wealth is not concentrated solely in the hands of a select few, but is made accessible to all who seek it. This cultural transformation is not only profound but also both shocking and inspiring—a powerful testament to the enduring human desire for freedom and autonomy, especially in an increasingly interconnected world that constantly evolves and changes.

The Future Is Now

The evolution of crypto trading platforms—from their wild, unregulated beginnings characterized by volatility and a lack of oversight, to the innovative, sophisticated hybrid models we see today—is truly a remarkable story of resilience, creativity, and transformative change. Each significant milestone along this journey has been marked by a logical progression from chaos to order, from uncertainty to a growing sense of trust. The advancements in technology that drive these platforms, coupled with the ongoing integration of regulatory frameworks and fluctuating market dynamics, have collectively forged a clear path towards a future where digital currencies are not merely viewed as speculative assets, but rather as a fundamental cornerstone of global finance. This transformation is ongoing, presenting both opportunities and challenges for investors and regulators alike.

For investors, the journey of crypto trading represents a powerful and persuasive argument for the future of money as we know it today. This evolution showcases the logical and analytical progression we have witnessed, transitioning from early platforms that were fraught with risks and uncertainties to a mature and institutionalized ecosystem that is now well-established in the financial landscape. This transformation serves as a clear indication that digital currencies have not only arrived on the scene but that their potential is only just beginning to be realized and explored. The future of crypto trading promises to usher in a world where financial systems are not only more transparent and secure but also significantly more accessible than they have ever been before. This evolving landscape paves the way for a world where the power of money is genuinely and authentically placed into the hands of the people, empowering them with the freedom to make financial decisions that affect their lives.

In this astonishing and thought-provoking narrative, we witness the remarkable and transformative power of technology and innovation at work, reshaping our society. The evolution of crypto trading platforms is not just a technical achievement; it represents a groundbreaking revolution in how we perceive and think about money, trust, and the very notion of economic freedom. This evolution challenges the traditional paradigms of centralized finance and presents us with a compelling glimpse into a future where digital assets can be managed by a decentralized and interconnected, global network of participants, significantly altering the dynamics of financial transactions and interactions.

As we progress into the future, the journey of crypto trading is poised to evolve continually, propelled by groundbreaking innovations, significant regulatory advancements, and the united determination of a very diverse global community. The milestones that we have achieved up to this point are not merely historical markers; rather, they serve as the essential building blocks of a transformative new financial reality. This reality is not only logical and rational but also revolutionary in its potential; it is as persuasive in its impact as it is inevitable in its progression. The collective efforts of individuals and groups striving for progress will undoubtedly shape the landscape of finance in ways that we are only beginning to comprehend.

Embrace this bright and transformative future. Recognize that the continuing evolution of crypto trading is a remarkable testament to human ingenuity and the relentless pursuit of true financial freedom. The dynamic world of digital finance is being reshaped right before our very eyes, and the path that leads from chaos to order, from risk to resilience, is a powerful and inspiring narrative of progress that presents immense opportunities for those willing to fully embrace it. In this rapidly changing landscape, innovators and investors alike are carving new pathways, pushing boundaries, and redefining what it means to engage with finance in today's world.

The future is indeed now, and the global shift toward decentralized trading is not merely a distant dream or fantasy but rather an ongoing and transformative revolution that promises to profoundly redefine the very nature of money as we know it. In this brave new world, the unprecedented power to trade, invest, and securely manage digital assets is firmly in your hands—an empowering and mind-blowing reality that boldly challenges conventional wisdom. This shift paves the way for a more inclusive, transparent, and resilient financial system, offering individuals the opportunity to engage more freely and directly in economic activities that were once controlled by centralized entities, thus transforming the landscape of finance for everyone involved.

Section 3: Lessons Learned from Past Failures and Security Breaches

In the rapidly evolving and ever-changing world of cryptocurrencies, the immense potential for innovation is matched only by the substantial risks involved. The early days of digital asset trading were undeniably marred by catastrophic security breaches and various exchange failures that sent profound shockwaves throughout the fledgling industry. These events are not merely cautionary tales to reflect upon; they serve as powerful and mind-blowing lessons that have fundamentally reshaped our thinking and approach to the critical issue of digital security. In this insightful section, we will delve deep into the historical breaches that have occurred, thoroughly analyze what went wrong during these unfortunate events, and argue persuasively for the necessity of implementing robust security measures in the modern landscape of cryptocurrency exchanges. Through well-structured logical reasoning and comprehensive analytical insight, we will explore how past failures have, in fact, paved the way for a more secure and resilient digital financial ecosystem that better protects users and their assets.

The Early Days of Crypto Trading: A Wild Frontier

In the early 2010s, a time when Bitcoin and various other cryptocurrencies were just beginning to emerge, the entire concept of trading digital assets was essentially uncharted and had not yet been properly explored. At that moment in history, numerous exchanges were created by enthusiastic pioneers who were primarily focused on the immense potential of decentralized money rather than putting considerable energy into establishing thorough and comprehensive security protocols. These initial platforms resembled the digital equivalent of the Wild West—a lawless, chaotic environment where trust was extremely scarce and technical know-how among users was minimal at best. The sense of adventure was palpable, but so too were the risks that came with navigating this unregulated landscape.

It was an incredibly shocking and unpredictable world where just a single hack could wipe out millions of dollars worth of digital assets in an instant, and every single transaction carried with it a considerable and often devastating risk. Traders, navigating this treacherous terrain, relied heavily on rudimentary software tools and primitive security measures that were immensely inadequate in protecting their investments. Paper wallets, which were one of the basic digital storage methods available at the time, and the early, clunky exchange platforms were far from secure, leaving users highly vulnerable to a wide array of cyber attacks from malicious hackers. The risks were exceptionally high, and the consequences of these breaches were often catastrophic beyond imagination. These persistent vulnerabilities not only led to significant losses of funds but also severely tarnished the reputation of cryptocurrency trading and investment as a whole, instilling fear and hesitance among potential investors and traders alike.

Mt. Gox: The Cautionary Tale

No discussion of crypto security failures can be considered complete without a thorough examination of the infamous Mt. Gox incident, which remains a cautionary tale in the industry. Once hailed as the world's largest Bitcoin exchange, Mt. Gox was responsible for handling an astonishing 70% of all Bitcoin transactions at its peak performance. However, beneath its rapid growth, impressive user base, and popularity, there lurked a system that was deeply plagued with serious vulnerabilities and weaknesses. In 2014, the Mt. Gox exchange ultimately collapsed amid widespread allegations of massive theft and blatant mismanagement—an event that sent shockwaves through the entire cryptocurrency community and left countless investors stranded, bewildered, and disillusioned.

Mt. Gox's downfall marked a significant turning point in the world of cryptocurrency. The exchange faced numerous security breaches throughout its operational history, but a particularly catastrophic hack in early 2014 resulted in the unprecedented loss of around 850,000 Bitcoins. For countless investors, this incident proved to be a devastating blow that reverberated through the entire crypto community. The collapse of Mt. Gox unequivocally exposed critical flaws that were pervasive within the system: inadequate security protocols, insufficient regulatory oversight, and a glaring lack of transparency in operations. This unfortunate event served as a stark wake-up call to the entire industry, underscoring the reality that without implementing robust security measures, the once-promising vision of digital currencies could swiftly devolve into an absolute nightmare for users and investors alike.

The lessons derived from the Mt. Gox incident are both logical and painfully evident for all involved. First and foremost, it starkly illustrated that placing large sums of digital assets in the hands of a single, centralized platform inherently creates a single point of failure. When an exchange like Mt. Gox suffers a compromise or security breach, the consequences can be utterly catastrophic for investors and stakeholders alike. Secondly, it emphasized the crucial importance of maintaining independent, verifiable records of transactions—a principle that the innovative blockchain technology later fulfilled in a more robust manner. Thirdly, it brought to light the pressing need for comprehensive regulatory oversight and the implementation of best practices designed to protect investors from potential losses. These critical insights have since propelled the evolution of security measures within crypto exchanges, driving them to become far more resilient, secure, and trustworthy for users navigating the complex world of digital assets.

The Bitfinex Hack: A Lesson in Multi-Signature Security

Another significant security breach that left a lasting impact on the industry was the notorious Bitfinex hack that occurred in 2016. Bitfinex, a prominent and major cryptocurrency exchange, suffered the catastrophic loss of approximately 120,000 Bitcoins—an amount valued at around $72 million at that time—due to a severe vulnerability found within its multi-signature wallet system. Multi-signature wallets, often referred to as multi-sig, are designed to require the use of multiple keys to authorize a transaction, making them a remarkable breakthrough in terms of security when compared to traditional single-key systems. The issues that arose from the Bitfinex hack starkly revealed that even the most sophisticated systems could still be vulnerable to attacks if they were not implemented correctly and meticulously. This event not only shocked the cryptocurrency community but also served as a wake-up call for exchanges to reconsider and enhance their security protocols going forward.

The hack at Bitfinex served as a stark and unsettling reminder that security measures are only as strong as their weakest link. Despite the advanced and sophisticated design of multi-signature wallets, the attackers managed to exploit a specific flaw in the implementation, pointing to the alarming reality that even the most innovative and cutting-edge security measures must be rigorously and thoroughly tested, and continuously improved over time. This incident has prompted developers and security experts alike to re-examine the fundamental principles of multi-signature protocols, improve their overall code quality, and adopt far more stringent security standards across the entire board. The analytical takeaway from this unfortunate incident is abundantly clear: advanced security features, no matter how impressive they may seem on paper, must always be complemented by robust and disciplined implementation practices, regular security audits, and a proactive willingness to adapt as new vulnerabilities and threats are discovered in the rapidly evolving digital landscape.

Lessons from Smaller Breaches: The Cumulative Impact of Insecurity

While Mt. Gox and Bitfinex are widely recognized as some of the most notorious examples of security breaches in the cryptocurrency world, it is essential to acknowledge that there have been numerous smaller-scale breaches and incidents that have collectively shaped and influenced the overall landscape of crypto security. Furthermore, exchanges such as Bithumb, Poloniex, and Cryptopia have all faced significant financial losses at various points in time due to various vulnerabilities and attacks. Each of these incidents has reinforced the critical need for implementing robust and effective security measures in the ever-evolving world of cryptocurrency.

These breaches frequently arose due to a confluence of several critical factors: outdated software systems, inadequate key management practices, insufficient access controls, and a lack of effective monitoring systems. In numerous instances, the attacks took advantage of known vulnerabilities that could have been effectively mitigated with the implementation of better security practices. The cumulative effect of these significant failures led to a substantial loss of confidence among many investors and a heightened level of awareness regarding the risks that are inherently present within the crypto space.

What makes these incidents so compelling and noteworthy is the logical argument they present: if multiple platforms can be compromised due to similar weaknesses, then the entire cryptocurrency industry must take a hard look at and reassess its security protocols. The pattern was unmistakable—without a concerted effort and united initiative to improve security across the board, the crypto market would continue to remain vulnerable to catastrophic failures that could threaten the stability of the entire ecosystem. These significant failures served as a persuasive catalyst for the industry to adopt best practices in security, implement rigorous and comprehensive security measures, and embrace innovative technologies and strategies that could safeguard digital assets more effectively and robustly in the long run.

The Evolution of Security Measures: From Reactive to Proactive

One of the most mind-blowing and fascinating aspects of the evolution of the crypto industry is undeniably how drastically it transformed its overall approach to security over the years. In the early days of this revolutionary technology, security was often treated as an afterthought—essentially an area that was more reactive than proactive. The very first generation of exchanges and digital wallets were built hastily to meet the rapidly growing demand among users, and unfortunately, security vulnerabilities were only properly addressed in a substantial way after a significant breach occurred, often resulting in devastating losses for users.

However, as the number of breaches continued to mount and increase at an alarming rate, the industry inevitably shifted its mindset significantly. Security emerged as a core focus of the entire development process, with a proactive approach gradually replacing the earlier, more reactive strategies that had been commonplace. Developers began to invest heavily in robust encryption techniques, multi-factor authentication measures, cold storage solutions, and advanced monitoring systems to provide a far greater level of protection. The realization was simple yet profoundly logical: in a complex system where digital assets are stored, traded, and exchanged, security is not merely optional—it is absolutely essential for the integrity and trustworthiness of the system.

This evolution was not something that happened all at once; it was a gradual process, a slow and deliberate journey driven by the cumulative lessons learned from past failures and missteps. Every hack that occurred, every loss experienced, and every vulnerability discovered led to significant improvements in code, protocol, and overall security. Over the years, the industry managed to move from a chaotic state of disarray to one characterized by continuous, proactive innovation aimed at combating emerging threats. Today, many exchanges engage in regular, comprehensive security audits to ensure that their systems are robust. They employ dedicated cybersecurity teams whose sole focus is to safeguard digital assets, and they implement cutting-edge measures designed specifically to protect user funds from potential breaches. This transformation is as shocking as it is logical—demonstrating clearly that even the most vulnerable systems can be fortified through a combination of determination, innovative thinking, and an unwavering commitment to learning from past mistakes and failures.

The Role of Regulation: Establishing Standards and Accountability

Another critical development that emerged from the early days of unregulated crypto trading was the gradual introduction of regulatory oversight, which became increasingly essential. Initially, the glaring lack of regulation paved the way for rampant security breaches and fraudulent activities that plagued early exchanges, leading to significant losses for many participants. However, as the market matured and the stakes grew higher with larger investments pouring in, governments and regulatory bodies around the world began to take notice and recognized the pressing need to intervene more decisively and effectively.

The introduction of comprehensive regulations was a logical and necessary response to the growing need for stability and enhanced accountability in the increasingly complex crypto market. As the market matured, regulatory frameworks have since been developed to effectively enforce best practices across various sectors, mandate greater transparency in financial transactions, and protect investors from the myriad risks associated with centralized control systems. This ongoing regulatory evolution has not only helped to significantly reduce the incidence of security breaches and fraudulent activities but has also played a pivotal role in legitimizing cryptocurrencies as a recognized and valued mainstream asset class in the financial landscape. In doing so, these regulations have created a safer environment for investors and have fostered greater confidence in the market's integrity.

The impact of regulation can be clearly observed in the significant rise of reputable exchanges that diligently adhere to strict security as well as operational standards. These platforms, which are now operating under the vigilant and watchful eye of regulators, offer a notable level of accountability that effectively reassures investors in a sometimes uncertain market. While there are some critics who argue that regulation might stifle innovation and diminish the entrepreneurial spirit, the logical counterargument is that a well-regulated market is much more sustainable in the long term. Regulation, when implemented effectively and thoughtfully, does not hinder progress; rather, it ensures that progress is made in a manner that is not only secure but also transparent and ultimately beneficial to all participants involved in the economic landscape. In this way, regulation can foster a healthier environment for investment and development.

The Human Element: Education and Community Collaboration

One of the most persuasive lessons derived from a multitude of past failures is the undeniable importance of education and community collaboration in effectively enhancing security measures. Early breaches in various systems often occurred not solely because of existing technical vulnerabilities, but also due to a significant lack of user awareness regarding vital security best practices. Many users found themselves unprepared to adequately manage the complexities involved in digital asset storage, which ultimately led to mistakes that resulted in devastating financial consequences. To combat these issues, it is essential to prioritize comprehensive education and promote strong collaboration within communities to foster a safer digital environment.

As the years have progressed, the crypto community has increasingly placed a significant emphasis on educating users about the pivotal importance of security measures and practices. Various initiatives, including detailed tutorials, engaging community forums, and thorough, comprehensive documentation, have significantly empowered individuals to take proactive control of their own security. This united and collective effort has fostered the development of a more informed and aware user base that is far better equipped to safeguard and protect their valuable assets. The logical argument is evident and irrefutable: when users become well-informed about the inherent risks and the various steps they can implement to effectively mitigate them, the overall security of the entire ecosystem improves dramatically and substantially.

Moreover, the open-source nature of many crypto projects has significantly fostered a vibrant culture of collaboration and thorough peer review. Developers, security experts, and contributors from diverse parts of the world come together to work on and improve the continuous development of wallet and exchange software. This collaborative environment serves as a key factor in identifying vulnerabilities early on and ensuring that robust, state-of-the-art security measures are meticulously implemented. The community-driven approach not only brings together resources and talent from various backgrounds but also enhances the overall reliability of the software. This shared responsibility strengthens the platform's integrity and resilience. It also serves as a logical and persuasive argument for the long-term sustainability and resilience of the ever-evolving crypto ecosystem.

Persuasive Reflections: Turning Tragedy into Triumph

The security breaches and failures of early crypto exchanges serve as painful reminders of what can go wrong in an unregulated, vulnerable system that lacks proper safeguards. However, these tragic events have also been catalysts for significant change, forcing the entire industry to evolve, adapt, and improve its practices. Every hack, every incident of fraud, and every unfortunate exchange collapse has contributed to a collective learning process that has dramatically strengthened the overall security of digital asset management and trading platforms. As a result, today's exchanges are much more robust and better equipped to handle potential threats, ensuring a safer environment for all users.

The compelling and persuasive narrative that emerges from these invaluable lessons is one of profound transformation and empowerment. The initial days of crypto trading, which were marked by uncertainty, chaos, and notable vulnerability, have now given way to a more stable and secure era characterized by reliability and trust. The evolution of security protocols—from basic software wallets that initially offered minimal protection to the sophisticated hardware wallets and advanced multi-factor authentication systems prevailing today—represents a logical and inevitable progression within this dynamic space. This development stands as a powerful testament to the resilience of blockchain technology and the unwavering commitment of the community to safeguard digital wealth at all costs. The journey from fragility to fortitude highlights not just a shift in tools but a change in mindset, instilling confidence in users and encouraging broader adoption of digital currencies.

For both investors and users, the essential takeaway is undeniably clear: robust security is not merely a luxury item to consider—it is an absolute necessity of utmost importance. In a rapidly advancing digital world where every single transaction can potentially fall prey to the inevitable threat of cyber attacks, the overall security of your invaluable digital assets relies heavily on the continuous evolution and improvement of technology and the adherence to best practices. The captivating history of crypto trading stands as a compelling, mind-blowing narrative that illustrates how critical lessons learned from previous failures have effectively paved the way for a far more secure and promising future in this ever-changing landscape.

A Logical Framework for the Future: Building on Past Lessons

Looking ahead, the future of digital asset security is set to be thoroughly influenced by the valuable lessons learned from our past experiences. The logical framework that has developed over years of both trial and error is not only clear but also compellingly persuasive in its implications. The fundamental principles that underpin this framework—decentralization, transparency, user education, and continuous innovation—serve as the critical cornerstones of a secure and resilient crypto ecosystem that can adapt and thrive in an ever-evolving landscape.

Future developments in security protocols will likely focus on several critical areas that are essential for enhancing data protection and maintaining user trust. First and foremost, advancements in encryption and cryptographic techniques will play a pivotal role in further protecting sensitive private keys from unauthorized access and potential breaches. Additionally, researchers are actively working on quantum-resistant algorithms, which are being rigorously explored to effectively safeguard against the potential threats posed by the rapid advancement of quantum computing technologies. By proactively addressing these challenges, we can ensure that the security of digital assets and information remains robust and reliable in the long term, adapting to the evolving landscape of cybersecurity.

Second, the integration of advanced artificial intelligence and sophisticated machine learning into security systems holds immense promise for the future. These cutting-edge technologies have the capability to analyze intricate patterns in user behavior, detect unusual anomalies in real time, and dynamically adapt security measures as needed. Such intelligent systems will provide an additional layer of robust defense, making it significantly more challenging for hackers to exploit existing vulnerabilities. With ongoing advancements in these fields, we can expect a stronger, more resilient approach to safeguarding sensitive information and critical systems against cyber threats.

Third, user interfaces and user experience will continue to improve significantly, which will make it easier for individuals to effectively manage their security without sacrificing any degree of control. The ongoing development of increasingly intuitive and user-friendly applications will play a key role in bridging the gap between the inherent technical complexity and the everyday usability that most users require. This evolution is absolutely crucial for fostering broader adoption, as a well-informed and empowered user base is the foundation of an effectively secure digital financial system that can thrive in today's fast-paced technological landscape.

The Broader Economic and Social Implications

The persistent drive to enhance security in the realm of digital asset management extends far beyond mere individual protection—it possesses profound implications that resonate throughout the entire global financial system. A secure and resilient crypto ecosystem plays a crucial role in building trust among investors, fostering assurance, and encouraging broader adoption among participants in the market. Ultimately, this collective effort contributes significantly to the overall stability and sustainable growth of the entire market landscape. When the number of security breaches is minimized and managed effectively, the risk of market manipulation, fraudulent activities, and catastrophic financial losses is substantially reduced. Consequently, this creates a more reliable and trustworthy environment for digital trading, ensuring that all market players, whether they are individual investors or large institutions, can engage with confidence.

This increased stability is particularly crucial and significant as cryptocurrencies begin to embed themselves more firmly into mainstream finance. As the financial landscape evolves, we see the rise of institutional investors, the establishment of regulated exchanges, and the introduction of global regulatory frameworks that are all coming into play. In this dynamic environment, the security of digital assets is paramount and absolutely essential. The lessons learned from early failures in the industry serve as a constant and poignant reminder that without robust and comprehensive security protocols in place, the promising potential of digital currencies could be swiftly undermined. Therefore, the continuous evolution of security technology is not merely a technical issue—it is a foundational and critical element that underpins the very future of money and the global financial system.

On a societal level, enhanced security in digital wallets and exchanges greatly empowers individuals and actively promotes financial inclusion across diverse demographics. In regions where traditional banking systems are not reliable, ineffective, or difficult to access, secure and user-friendly digital asset management can provide a vital lifeline. By ensuring that every user has access to comprehensive and robust security measures, the crypto ecosystem is in a position to effectively democratize wealth, enabling even the most marginalized and economically disadvantaged communities to actively participate in the larger global economy. This social empowerment, driven by innovation, is a logical and direct outcome of a decentralized, secure financial system—a compelling and persuasive argument for the transformative potential of technology and its ongoing evolution in our modern world.

A Persuasive Call for Continuous Improvement

The journey of digital asset security is far from over and definitely not complete. While significant strides have been made since the early days of unsecured and unregulated platforms that posed numerous risks, the landscape of digital security is constantly evolving and changing. New threats continuously emerge as technology advances at a rapid pace, and the need for continuous improvement is an essential and logical imperative that cannot be ignored. The valuable lessons learned from past failures and mistakes have laid a strong foundation for ongoing innovation, and the industry must remain consistently vigilant in order to protect the considerable gains that have been made thus far.

The persuasive case for continuous improvement is deeply rooted in the ever-evolving and dynamic nature of the digital world we inhabit. Cyber threats are not static entities; rather, they evolve and transform rapidly, necessitating a proactive and adaptive approach to security measures. The integration of cutting-edge technologies such as artificial intelligence, quantum-resistant cryptography, and decentralized security protocols stands as the next logical and necessary step in this ongoing evolution. By wholeheartedly embracing a mindset characterized by constant innovation and by diligently learning from past mistakes and experiences, the crypto community can ensure that digital asset management practices remain secure, resilient, and ultimately trustworthy for all stakeholders involved. This commitment to improvement not only protects individual assets but also fortifies the entire ecosystem against emerging threats.

This unwavering commitment to improvement is not merely a technical necessity; rather, it constitutes a fundamental and essential part of the decentralized ethos that underpins our digital landscape. In a dynamic system where each and every participant has a crucial role to play in the ongoing maintenance of security, the collective effort to stay ahead of emerging threats fosters a self-reinforcing cycle of innovation and trust that benefits all involved. This collaborative approach is not only logical but also deeply persuasive—a compelling argument that the future of digital asset security will undoubtedly be built upon the solid foundation of continuous, community-driven progress and shared responsibility.

Persuading the Skeptics: The Logic of Resilience

Despite the undeniable progress made in enhancing security protocols across various platforms, skepticism persists among a notable group of critics who continue to point to past failures and ongoing vulnerabilities that remain a concern. However, a careful and logical analysis of these situations reveals that every single security breach has imparted valuable lessons that have ultimately strengthened the overall system we rely on today. The early failures experienced by prominent exchanges, such as Mt. Gox and Bitfinex, while tragic and unfortunate, were instrumental in driving the entire industry towards more robust and effective solutions. Each incident highlighted specific weaknesses that were subsequently identified and addressed through improved design practices, better encryption standards, and the implementation of more rigorous oversight mechanisms. This cycle of challenges has led to a more resilient framework that now underpins the systems we use.

The logical progression from vulnerability to resilience is undeniably clear and increasingly evident: as technology evolves, so too does our growing ability to effectively defend against emerging threats. The adaptive nature of modern security protocols, which diligently learn from each attempted breach and continuously improve upon their defenses, is a compelling argument for the long-term viability and sustainability of digital asset management practices. This dynamic evolution not only ensures that the crypto ecosystem is not stagnant but also is continuously moving forward towards a more secure and resilient state, adapting to challenges as they arise and reinforcing itself against potential future risks.

For skeptics, it is essential to understand that the crucial takeaway is that the valuable lessons of the past have not only been acknowledged but have also been meticulously integrated into the new systems that now predominantly control the market landscape. The logical and analytical evidence clearly demonstrates that while no system can ever be declared as 100% secure, the measures and protocols currently in place today represent a significant advancement and improvement over those that were utilized during the early days of digital asset management and security. This argument, deeply rooted in both rational thought and persuasive reasoning, highlights the importance of continual learning. If we are willing to learn from our past mistakes and remain committed to the process of ongoing innovation, then the future of digital asset security appears to be exceedingly bright and promising.

The Future Impact: Empowering a Global Financial Ecosystem

The evolution of security protocols in the rapidly developing crypto space has far-reaching implications that significantly impact the global financial ecosystem as a whole. Secure digital asset management stands as a cornerstone of decentralized finance (DeFi), a revolutionary movement that promises to fundamentally transform traditional financial services by eliminating the need for potentially risky intermediaries. As exchanges and wallets become increasingly secure, they foster greater trust among users, which in turn attracts a larger pool of investors and drives overall market stability. This virtuous cycle not only benefits individual users, enhancing their confidence and encouraging participation, but it also contributes to the overall health of the financial system, creating a more robust and resilient financial landscape for everyone involved.

The broader impact on society and the economy is truly profound. Enhanced security protocols play a crucial role in democratizing access to essential financial services by ensuring that even users in regions with underdeveloped banking infrastructure can safely and effectively participate in the burgeoning digital economy. By providing robust, user-friendly security measures, the crypto ecosystem empowers individuals to take greater control of their wealth and financial decisions, while simultaneously reducing their dependence on centralized institutions. This empowers them to engage in a more inclusive, accessible, and transparent financial system, ultimately leading to greater economic participation and opportunities for individuals who have previously faced barriers.

The societal implications of this shift are indeed significant and far-reaching. In a world that has witnessed numerous financial crises and systemic failures, these events have repeatedly illustrated the vulnerabilities inherent in centralized systems. The rise of secure, decentralized digital asset management therefore offers a compelling alternative that many are beginning to explore and adopt. This movement represents not just a reaction to past failures, but also a logical, evolutionary step towards creating a more resilient, equitable, and empowered global economy. It envisions a future where the benefits of financial innovation are increasingly shared by everyone, rather than being concentrated in the hands of a few. By embracing this change, we could foster a more inclusive financial landscape that values participation and security for all individuals.

A Journey of Continuous Innovation and Empowerment

The evolution of security protocols in the realm of digital asset management stands as a remarkably brilliant narrative that highlights human ingenuity and relentless progress. It traces the journey from the rudimentary paper wallets utilized by the early crypto pioneers, who bravely ventured into uncharted territories, to the highly advanced hardware and sophisticated software solutions we see today. Each crucial step taken in this journey has consistently been fueled by a fundamental and pressing need to protect digital wealth amid an increasingly hostile and unpredictable digital environment. As the landscape of technology continues to evolve, so too does the complexity and necessity of these security measures, ensuring that users can confidently navigate the digital realm.

The lessons learned from numerous past failures and security breaches have absolutely not been in vain. These experiences have cultivated a clear and logical roadmap for constructing a secure, resilient, and trustworthy system that not only empowers users but also fosters true economic freedom. The evolution from vulnerability to resilience stands as a persuasive argument for the future of digital asset security. This is a future where enhanced security protocols and innovative measures profoundly transform the way we effectively manage and protect our money, bringing about a new era of trust and reliability in financial transactions.

For investors, users, and policymakers alike, the ongoing journey of digital asset security offers invaluable lessons that are crucial for navigating this complex landscape. It vividly demonstrates that while the risks are very real and ever-present, the remarkable power of continuous innovation and genuine collaboration can effectively overcome even the most daunting challenges that arise. The logical progression from unregulated, insecure platforms to robust, adaptive security systems stands as a testament to the transformative potential of technology, particularly when this potential is combined with an unwavering commitment to learning from past mistakes and experiences. Through careful examination and proactive measures, stakeholders can create safer environments that foster confidence and growth in the evolving world of digital assets.

As we cast our eyes toward the future, the immense promise of groundbreaking innovation in wallet technology and decentralized security is not only mind-blowing but also fully realistic. The landscape of digital transactions is set to transform dramatically. With the integration of advanced encryption techniques, AI-driven security systems, quantum-resistant protocols, and seamless user interfaces, the tools designed to safeguard digital assets will undergo continuous evolution, paving the way for even greater protection and empowerment for users around the globe. This technological progress will empower individuals, ensuring that their sensitive information remains secure while enhancing the overall user experience in the digital realm.

The future of digital asset security is a dynamic, ever-evolving landscape that continually adapts to new challenges and opportunities—a future where the significant lessons of the past profoundly inform the innovations and advancements of tomorrow. It is a world where your financial freedom is not only safeguarded but also protected by multiple layers of cutting-edge technology designed to prevent unauthorized access and ensure integrity. In this promising landscape, trust is intricately built into the very fabric of the decentralized ecosystem, fostering confidence and collaboration among users, and enabling a safe environment for all participants.

Embrace this future with utmost confidence and assurance. Recognize that every significant advancement in security protocols, every remarkable improvement in technology, represents a crucial step towards establishing a safer, more resilient digital economy. The ongoing evolution of security measures is not merely a technical achievement; it signifies a profound transformation that empowers you to take full control of your wealth. In a world where digital assets are becoming an increasingly integral part of our daily lives, this evolution is essential for ensuring that your investments are protected and your transactions secure. Embrace these innovations and stay ahead in this rapidly changing landscape.

In conclusion, the remarkable journey from early, insecure storage methods to the highly sophisticated, adaptive security systems that we utilize today is a truly extraordinary testament to the immense power of innovation. It presents a mind-blowing narrative of progress, driven not only by logical reasoning but also by a consistent commitment to continuous learning, and an unwavering dedication to protecting what is most valuable—your digital wealth and assets. The invaluable lessons learned from past failures serve as a stark reminder of the significant risks and challenges that are at stake, and they provide a persuasive, analytical foundation for the promising future of secure, decentralized finance. As we look ahead, it is crucial that we harness the advancements made while keeping the lessons of history at the forefront of our development efforts.

The global shift towards enhanced security is not just about protecting money—it is about empowering individuals in a significant way, building trust among users, and creating a comprehensive financial ecosystem that is resilient and strong in the face of ever-changing threats and challenges. As you navigate this complex digital frontier, remember that the evolution of security protocols is indeed a critical pillar of the decentralized revolution—an ongoing transformation that is as logical, vital, and necessary as it is revolutionary in nature. Embracing these changes can lead to a more secure and trustworthy environment for everyone involved.

This is the promising future of digital asset management: envision a world where your wealth is not only protected but safeguarded by cutting-edge technology that continually evolves, enhancing your financial security. The lessons learned from past failures in financial systems have paved an innovative path toward a secure and empowered financial future for all individuals. In this new landscape, the power to control and manage your money effectively lies firmly in your hands. Embrace this transformative journey, learn from the invaluable lessons of the past, and step confidently into a new world where digital security is not merely a luxury but a fundamental right. This right is essential for the prosperity and robust functionality of a truly decentralized economy that empowers every person equally.

Section 4: Regulatory Overhauls and Market Maturation

In the ever-evolving world of cryptocurrencies, where technology continually races ahead and innovation boldly disrupts centuries-old financial norms, one of the most transformative forces that have emerged is regulation. What once was a wild, unregulated frontier—akin to the digital Wild West—has gradually, yet profoundly, become a much more structured, secure, and mature market environment. This remarkable evolution is nothing short of mind-blowing. It represents a compelling journey from chaos and uncertainty to order and legitimacy, driven by a series of regulatory overhauls that have significantly reshaped the entire crypto trading landscape. This section will explore in depth how the evolving regulations have dramatically transformed crypto trading practices, offering a logical, analytical, and persuasive look into a world where rules and oversight have now become the fundamental backbone of the rapidly growing digital finance sector.

The Early Days: An Unregulated Frontier

In the earliest days of cryptocurrency, there were virtually no rules in place—no formal oversight mechanisms, no consumer protection laws, no standardized protocols whatsoever. The crypto market existed as a chaotic arena where anyone possessing a computer and an internet connection could engage in trading digital assets freely. Exchanges sprung up almost overnight, rapidly built by enthusiastic pioneers who were more focused on experimenting with innovative technology than on implementing strict security measures or complying with existing regulations. This glaring lack of regulation ultimately led to a multitude of rampant issues: numerous hacking incidents, significant fraud cases, blatant market manipulation, and even outright exchange failures that left many investors reeling.

Imagine a world where transactions were executed in a lawless environment, a chaotic landscape—where there existed no central authority to mediate disputes or safeguard funds effectively. This was the harsh and unforgiving reality for early traders who faced risks that were both unpredictable and often catastrophic. When an exchange could simply vanish overnight with millions of dollars' worth of digital assets, investors found themselves trapped in a state of perpetual uncertainty and anxiety. The unregulated nature of the market fashioned a shockingly volatile atmosphere where fortunes could be made or lost in a matter of mere minutes, leaving emotions running high and prospects dim. As traders engaged in this high-stakes game, the fear of loss loomed large, instilling a sense of dread that could paralyze decision-making. Choices had to be made quickly, with little time to weigh the risks, often leading to hasty, impulsive actions that could prove disastrous.

The Wake-Up Call: High-Profile Breaches and Market Crashes

The unregulated crypto market did not remain chaotic forever, as its tumultuous nature eventually gave way to a more structured approach. A series of significant high-profile breaches and catastrophic market crashes acted as a wake-up call for the entire industry, compelling it to confront its inherent vulnerabilities and weaknesses. One of the most infamous and widely discussed examples was the dramatic collapse of Mt. Gox in 2014. Once heralded as the largest Bitcoin exchange in the world, Mt. Gox handled an overwhelming 70% of all Bitcoin transactions at its peak. However, due to severe security flaws coupled with mismanagement on multiple levels, it ultimately suffered catastrophic losses, resulting in the disappearance of hundreds of thousands of Bitcoins from its holdings—an incident that reverberated through the crypto community, sending shockwaves that led to massive financial losses for countless users and investors alike.

This disaster was not simply a technical failure; it became a pivotal moment that highlighted the pressing need for stringent regulation and comprehensive security measures. The collapse of Mt. Gox served as a stark reminder that without adequate oversight, even the most promising and innovative technologies could easily be undermined by human error and the malicious intentions of bad actors. It compelled investors, developers, and regulators alike to confront critical questions: How can we effectively protect digital assets in a complex and rapidly evolving world where there is no central authority to turn to for guidance? And even more importantly, how can we devise and establish a sustainable market environment where trust is built upon sound, responsible practices rather than on mere blind faith and optimism?

In the aftermath of the Mt. Gox incident, other significant events, including the notorious Bitfinex hack that occurred in 2016, along with several smaller security breaches across a variety of cryptocurrency exchanges, clearly revealed the inherent vulnerabilities and dangers present in the unregulated landscape of early crypto trading. These alarming failures collectively forged a compelling and logical case for the urgent need for robust regulatory frameworks that would establish baseline standards, enforce best practices, and ultimately safeguard investors from systemic risks that could jeopardize their financial security and the integrity of the entire market.

The Regulatory Response: From Dismissal to Embrace

In the immediate aftermath of these significant and high-profile incidents, governments and various regulatory bodies around the globe began to take substantial notice. Initially, many regulators expressed skepticism towards cryptocurrencies, viewing them predominantly as potential tools for facilitating money laundering, enabling tax evasion, and other forms of illicit and fraudulent activities. Some regulators, in a bid to preemptively address these concerns, even went as far as to impose outright bans on cryptocurrency trading. They feared that the inherent lack of oversight could lead to widespread financial instability and uncertainty in the markets, prompting a wave of caution among traditional financial institutions and investors.

However, as the technology continued to mature and the economic potential of digital currencies became increasingly undeniable, regulators began to shift their stance significantly. They came to recognize that, rather than stifling innovation and progress, smart and thoughtful regulation could actually foster a secure and vibrant market environment. This regulatory transformation has been both gradual and transformative in nature. Over the past decade, governments around the world have transitioned from dismissing cryptocurrencies as merely a passing fad or trend to actively engaging with the rapidly evolving industry. They are now developing comprehensive frameworks that effectively balance the needs for innovation with essential consumer protection measures.

For example, countries like Japan and Switzerland have emerged as highly attractive and crypto-friendly jurisdictions by establishing clear and supportive regulatory environments that foster innovation and security. Japan's Financial Services Agency (FSA) has set exceptionally high standards for cryptocurrency exchanges, mandating rigorous security protocols and regular audits to ensure consumer protection and market integrity. At the same time, Switzerland's "Crypto Valley" has quickly transformed into a global hub for blockchain innovation and development, supported by flexible regulations that actively encourage entrepreneurship and investment in the digital currency space. These significant regulatory overhauls have not only legitimized the evolving crypto market but have also attracted a wave of institutional investors who had long been wary and cautious of the unregulated Wild West of early trading practices, leading to increased confidence in the sustainability and viability of crypto assets.

A New Era of Investor Confidence

The shift towards regulation has undeniably had a profound impact on investor confidence across the financial landscape. With clear and comprehensive rules and standards now firmly in place, both retail and institutional investors can enjoy a greater sense of assurance that their funds are being managed in a secure, transparent manner that prioritizes their best interests. The introduction of a variety of regulated investment products, including Bitcoin futures, options, and exchange-traded funds (ETFs), has significantly bridged the gap between traditional finance and the rapidly evolving crypto market. These innovative products not only offer investors an effective way to gain exposure to digital currencies, but they also alleviate the burden of having to navigate the complex intricacies of direct custody. Additionally, they mitigate the inherent risks associated with potential exchange failures, allowing for a smoother and more reliable investment experience in the digital asset space.

Institutional adoption is arguably the most compelling proof that regulatory success has been achieved. Major financial institutions and corporations, which were previously skeptical and critical of cryptocurrency's legitimacy and potential, have now begun to allocate significant portions of their investment portfolios to digital assets. Notable companies such as MicroStrategy, Tesla, and Square have made headlines by investing billions of dollars in Bitcoin. Their substantial involvement in the crypto market signals a significant shift, indicating that cryptocurrencies have evolved from being regarded merely as a speculative niche into a robust and valuable asset class with considerable long-term potential. The logical reasoning behind this phenomenon is quite simple yet powerful: if government regulators can successfully develop effective and comprehensive standards for digital currencies, then institutional investors—who rely heavily on predictable, stable, and transparent systems—will naturally feel much more confident in their investments. Moreover, this convergence of enhanced regulatory clarity alongside growing institutional adoption marks a truly mind-blowing milestone in the ongoing evolution of the cryptocurrency market, further solidifying its position as a legitimate player in the global financial ecosystem.

The Impact on Market Structure and Maturation

Regulatory overhauls have significantly improved security and bolstered investor confidence in the cryptocurrency sector; they have also fundamentally reshaped and transformed the very market structure of cryptocurrency trading itself. In the early days, cryptocurrency exchanges were often characterized by a glaring lack of transparency, poor security measures, and minimal, if any, consumer protections in place for traders. However, the advent of robust and comprehensive regulation has forced these online trading platforms to undergo a process of professionalization, compelling them to adopt best practices that align closely with those observed in traditional financial institutions. Consequently, as a direct result of these changes, the market for cryptocurrencies has become far more organized, notably more efficient, and remarkably more resilient in the face of challenges.

Modern exchanges have now reached an impressive level of sophistication that was completely unimaginable during the early days of their establishment. These platforms have implemented comprehensive and robust risk management systems alongside standardized reporting practices, as well as secure custody solutions that are specifically designed to protect investors' funds from potential threats. This significant transformation has contributed to greater market liquidity and considerably reduced volatility, ultimately making digital currencies a much more viable option for long-term investment strategies. The evolution of the market structure is a logical and anticipated outcome of regulatory intervention—a noteworthy shift from what was once a chaotic and speculative arena to a mature and stable financial market that is truly capable of supporting substantial capital inflows over time. This progress highlights the ongoing development in the industry, signifying a promising future for investors and traders alike.

Furthermore, various regulatory frameworks have significantly encouraged the development of innovative financial instruments that facilitate the increasingly popular realm of digital asset trading. The creation and application of derivatives, such as futures and options, have provided much-needed mechanisms for effective price discovery and comprehensive risk management. These sophisticated instruments not only allow investors to hedge against price volatility and uncertainties but also empower them to manage their exposure effectively, ultimately participating in the market with a much greater sense of confidence and security. The logical progression from unregulated trading practices to a more structured and organized market, enriched with these advanced financial products, stands as a powerful testament to the influence and importance of regulation in driving the maturation and evolution of the market. As such, this transformation has opened up new avenues for market participants, allowing for enhanced trading strategies and expanded opportunities for investment growth.

The Logical and Ethical Case for Regulation

The push for regulatory overhauls in the rapidly evolving crypto space is not solely about exerting control over the industry—it is fundamentally about creating a system that is fair, transparent, and sustainable for all participants involved. The ethical imperative is abundantly clear: if digital currencies are to truly become a fundamental part of the global economy, they must be subject to well-defined rules that are designed to protect consumers and ensure market integrity across various platforms. The chaos and insecurity that characterized the early trading environment negatively impacted not only individual investors but also severely damaged the reputation of the entire industry as a whole. By implementing robust and comprehensive regulatory standards, governments can significantly mitigate these risks associated with volatility and fraud, thus paving the way for broader adoption and acceptance of cryptocurrencies in everyday transactions. In doing so, they foster a climate of trust and confidence that is essential for sustainable growth in this innovative financial sector.

Critics of regulation often argue that an excessive amount of oversight could stifle innovation and significantly limit the decentralized nature of cryptocurrencies, creating an environment that may deter creativity and progress. However, the logical counterargument to this perspective is that smart, well-designed regulation can indeed coexist harmoniously with innovation. The ultimate goal of such regulation is not to impose rigid controls and constraints but to establish a thoughtful framework that effectively promotes transparency, accountability, and responsible behavior among all participants in the cryptocurrency marketplace. This balanced and nuanced approach allows the industry to both grow and innovate simultaneously, while also protecting the interests of all participants involved. The persuasive power of this argument lies in its inherent fairness: it ensures that the benefits of digital currencies are fully realized and enjoyed without exposing users to undue risk or potential pitfalls that may arise in an unregulated environment. Through thoughtful regulation, we can create an ecosystem where innovation thrives, yet safeguards are in place to protect users and foster sustainable growth.

Regulation also plays an absolutely crucial role in effectively bridging the significant gap between traditional finance and the rapidly evolving crypto world. As digital currencies increasingly become more seamlessly integrated into the expansive global financial system, clear and comprehensive regulatory guidelines are truly essential for ensuring that these innovative assets are treated with the same level of rigor and credibility as traditional investments. The ongoing transition from largely unregulated trading to a well-structured and regulated market has been a transformative and pivotal milestone, one that has fundamentally reshaped investor perceptions, expectations, and market dynamics in ways that were previously unimaginable.

Real-World Successes: How Regulation Has Fostered Growth

The impact of regulatory overhauls is strikingly evident in the numerous success stories that are now emerging from crypto markets across the globe. Reputable exchanges such as Coinbase and Binance, for instance, have not just survived but thrived in regulatory environments that enforce strict standards for both security and transparency. Their remarkable success is not merely a matter of good fortune or luck—it is the result of rigorous adherence to comprehensive regulatory guidelines designed to protect investors and promote overall market stability. By prioritizing compliance, these exchanges build trust and foster a safer trading environment, ultimately paving the way for further innovation and growth in the cryptocurrency ecosystem.

Moreover, the increasing interest shown by institutional investors serves as a strong and compelling sign that regulatory measures have indeed exerted a beneficial influence on the market. When substantial financial institutions, which often have extensive resources and expertise, choose to allocate significant amounts of capital toward digital assets, it sends a definitive message that they have faith in the integrity of the system and a belief in the potential it holds for the future. This growing confidence from institutions has played a critical role in stabilizing the market landscape, enhancing liquidity, and drawing in additional investments from various sources. The reasoning behind this trend is both logical and convincing: as the clarity surrounding regulations continues to improve and evolve, the entire ecosystem surrounding digital assets becomes increasingly resilient and appealing to a broader spectrum of investors, including those who may have been hesitant in the past.

Moreover, regulatory acceptance has significantly spurred innovation within the industry, creating a dynamic landscape for both existing and emerging players. The development of compliant financial products, such as Bitcoin ETFs and futures contracts, has opened new and exciting avenues for capital inflows and increased market participation. These innovative products provide a vital bridge between the old and the new, allowing traditional investors to gain valuable exposure to digital assets while benefiting from the safety, structure, and oversight of regulated markets. This convergence represents a logical outcome of a mature, well-regulated market and is a clear sign that cryptocurrencies are transitioning from the fringes of the financial world to becoming a mainstream investment option. As more investors recognize the potential of digital currencies, the integration of such products will likely accelerate, leading to greater acceptance and an increased variety of offerings in the marketplace.

The Challenges of Regulation: Striking the Right Balance

Despite the numerous benefits that regulation can bring to the crypto space, it is also fraught with a host of challenges that cannot be ignored. One of the most contentious and debated issues is finding the right balance between effective oversight and encouraging innovation. If there is too little regulation in place, it can leave the market vulnerable to a variety of risks, including fraud, hacks, and manipulation by malicious actors. Conversely, imposing too much regulation can stifle creativity and force innovative ideas and practices underground, away from the light of scrutiny and development. Striking this delicate balance is a complex and dynamic process that necessitates continuous and open dialogue among regulators, industry participants, and the broader community of stakeholders. Only through ongoing communication can a framework be established that ensures safety while fostering the growth of new ideas and technologies.

The evolution of regulatory frameworks has consistently been marked by a significant process of trial and error. In the beginning, early attempts at regulation were often seen as heavy-handed and clumsy, frequently failing to take into account the unique characteristics and complexities of digital currencies. However, as time passed and regulators gained a deeper understanding of the underlying technology and its potential implications, they began to adopt more nuanced and sophisticated approaches that better reflect the realities of the digital landscape. Today, modern regulatory models strive to achieve a delicate balance by aiming to protect consumers, ensuring market stability, and fostering environments that encourage innovation and healthy competition among market participants.

This balance is absolutely critical for the long-term success and viability of the crypto market. A well-regulated environment not only safeguards the interests of investors but also fosters a sense of trust and credibility—both of which are essential elements for attracting meaningful institutional investment. The logical and analytical case for balanced regulation is profoundly persuasive: it is indeed the only way to ensure that digital currencies can evolve and transform into a sustainable, mature asset class without sacrificing their revolutionary potential or innovative spirit. In an ever-changing financial landscape, such regulation serves as the bedrock upon which future growth can be built, providing stability to an industry that thrives on volatility and change.

The Future of Crypto Regulation: Trends and Predictions

As we look ahead into the future, the regulatory landscape for digital currencies is likely to continue evolving at a remarkably rapid pace. As the cryptocurrency industry matures and develops further, regulators across the globe are anticipated to create more sophisticated and harmonized frameworks that effectively address the unique challenges presented by the dynamic crypto market. Several notable trends are emerging that strongly indicate a future where regulation and innovation can coexist harmoniously and productively, leading to an environment where both can thrive together while ensuring consumer protection and market stability.

One key trend we are observing today is the increasing adoption of regulatory technology, commonly referred to as RegTech, solutions across various sectors. RegTech leverages advanced data analytics, machine learning, and innovative blockchain technology to effectively streamline regulatory compliance, actively monitor market activity, and promptly detect potential instances of fraud. By automating a significant number of processes involved in the regulatory landscape, RegTech has the capability to greatly reduce the overall burden on both regulators and market participants. This shift not only simplifies the complex compliance activities but also makes it notably easier to enforce rules without stifling innovation within the industry. Such advancements are paving the way for a more efficient regulatory environment that encourages growth and safeguards against risks.

One notable trend that is increasingly gaining traction is the growing emphasis on international regulatory cooperation in the realm of cryptocurrencies. The phenomenon of cryptocurrencies is inherently global in nature, and as such, their regulation cannot be effectively confined to the limits of national borders. Significant efforts are currently underway to develop and establish international standards and comprehensive guidelines that can be adopted and utilized by regulators in various countries around the world. This initiative aims to ensure a consistent, coherent, and predictable environment for the trading of digital assets across different jurisdictions. Such a collaborative approach is not only reasonable and logical but is also essential for the effective management of a market that operates on a vast and interconnected global scale, where the actions of one nation can have far-reaching implications on others.

Additionally, as digital currencies continue to gain traction and become more mainstream in our daily transactions, we can expect to see an even greater level of integration with traditional financial systems in the near future. Central banks around the world are increasingly exploring the potential of issuing their own digital currencies, commonly known as Central Bank Digital Currencies (CBDCs). These currencies could serve as a vital bridge between conventional fiat money and the emerging realm of decentralized cryptocurrencies. The ongoing development of CBDCs represents a significant evolution in the approach to monetary policy and has the potential to fundamentally reshape the financial landscape by merging and blending the best features of both centralized and decentralized systems. This could lead to a more efficient, secure, and inclusive financial environment for individuals, businesses, and governments alike.

Persuading the Skeptics: The Irresistible Logic of Evolving Regulation

For a considerable number of skeptics, the notion of imposing regulation on a decentralized system appears to be fundamentally contradictory. They contend that regulation can undermine the core principles of decentralization and financial freedom that cryptocurrencies strongly advocate. However, a more thorough and logical examination reveals that the evolution of regulation is not only an inevitable outcome but also essential for fostering the long-term health and sustainability of the market. Regulation offers the necessary structure and oversight required to prevent various abuses and maintain essential trust—both of which are critical elements for any financial system, whether decentralized or traditional. By establishing clear guidelines, regulation can help mitigate risks and enhance transparency, which in turn can attract more participants to the cryptocurrency space.

The evolution of crypto regulation has clearly demonstrated that it is indeed possible to thoughtfully design frameworks that effectively protect investors without hindering and stifling innovation in the rapidly changing landscape of digital finance. The key to achieving this balance is to focus on core principles—such as transparency, accountability, and fairness—rather than relying solely on rigid and inflexible rules that ultimately fail to adapt to the constant and ongoing technological changes in the industry. This flexible, principles-based approach serves as a logical and insightful response to the unique and complex challenges posed by digital currencies, and it has already proven to be effective in various jurisdictions that have proactively embraced crypto-friendly policies and a more open regulatory mindset.

Moreover, as the market continues to grow and mature over time, the numerous benefits of regulation become even more apparent and pronounced. With comprehensive and clear guidelines firmly in place, financial institutions are significantly more willing to invest their resources, as they can see the long-term potential. Developers, too, are more confident in building new applications that can thrive in such an environment, knowing there are standards to adhere to. Additionally, users can have much greater peace of mind, trusting that their assets are well protected from potential threats and mishaps. This cycle of growth, innovation, and trust serves as a compelling and persuasive argument for the ongoing evolution and enhancement of regulatory frameworks in the ever-changing crypto space.

The Broader Implications: Regulation as a Catalyst for Market Maturation

The impact of regulatory overhauls extends far beyond the immediate confines of individual exchanges or trading platforms alone. These crucial changes have a transformative effect on the entire cryptocurrency ecosystem, effectively catalyzing market maturation and fostering deeper integration with the broader global financial system. When regulators take the important step of setting clear and definitive standards for security, transparency, and consumer protection across the board, it compels all market participants to adhere to these higher standards with greater diligence. This mandatory compliance, in turn, significantly reduces the risks of fraud and technical failures that have plagued the industry in the past, ultimately leading to a more stable, reliable, and resilient market that benefits all stakeholders involved.

The maturation of the crypto market, significantly driven by increasing regulatory clarity, has attracted an impressive wave of institutional investment that continues to grow. Major financial institutions, which were once wary and hesitant due to the unregulated and uncertain nature of digital currencies, are now confidently entering the market with a renewed sense of purpose and optimism. The recent development of a variety of regulated financial products—such as futures, options, and exchange-traded funds (ETFs)—further solidifies and cements the legitimacy of cryptocurrencies as mainstream financial assets. This evolution represents a logical and persuasive progression for both the market and its participants: as the market becomes safer, more regulated, and increasingly predictable, even more capital flows in, thereby driving further innovation, growth, and overall stability within this fascinating and dynamic sector.

Furthermore, robust regulation has the potential to significantly promote financial inclusion on a global scale, benefiting a multitude of communities. In many developing countries, where traditional banking systems often prove to be unreliable or completely inaccessible to the masses, digital currencies can provide a vital lifeline. By establishing clear, supportive regulatory frameworks, these regions can finally be empowered to participate actively in the global economy, which in turn fosters economic growth while helping to reduce inequality. The ethical and economic implications of such developments are profoundly significant—an effectively decentralized financial system that is well-regulated could have the remarkable capability to democratize access to wealth for individuals across various demographics, an outcome that is as desirable as it is logically sound. This evolution can change lives, offering new opportunities for countless people and communities previously left out of the financial system, thereby creating a more inclusive world.

Challenges and Future Directions

Despite the significant progress that has been made in the evolving regulatory landscape, various challenges still remain. One of the primary concerns continues to be striking the right balance between necessary oversight and fostering innovation. Overly restrictive regulations can stifle creativity and effectively push innovation underground, making it difficult for new ideas to flourish. Conversely, having too little oversight can leave the market vulnerable to fraud and instability, creating an environment where unethical practices can thrive. The key is to develop flexible, adaptive regulatory frameworks that can evolve alongside the rapidly changing technology they are meant to govern. By doing so, regulators can ensure that innovation is encouraged while simultaneously protecting consumers and maintaining market stability.

Another significant challenge that arises in the realm of digital currencies is undoubtedly the international nature of cryptocurrencies themselves. Unlike traditional currencies, cryptocurrencies do not adhere to national borders, which complicates regulatory efforts. However, regulatory frameworks are often crafted to be country-specific and may not account for the global nature of digital assets. This fragmentation, where rules can vary greatly from one jurisdiction to another, can lead to regulatory arbitrage. In such scenarios, exchanges and investors can easily relocate to jurisdictions that offer more favorable regulations, allowing them to bypass stricter rules in their home countries. To effectively address this growing issue, there is an increasing call for international cooperation and standardization in the field of crypto regulation. The most logical path forward is to establish a collaborative effort where regulators from different countries come together to create a harmonious, cohesive global framework. Such a framework should be designed to protect consumers while simultaneously encouraging innovation in this rapidly evolving sector.

. Looking to the future, several significant trends are likely to shape the ongoing regulatory evolution of the crypto market. First, the integration of advanced regulatory technology (RegTech) will play a crucial role in streamlining compliance and monitoring processes, significantly simplifying and facilitating interactions for both regulators and market participants alike as they adapt to new, complex rules and guidelines. This innovation will not only help reduce the burden of compliance but also enhance the overall efficiency of regulatory frameworks. Second, as the crypto market matures and becomes more established, we can expect to observe a greater convergence between traditional finance systems and innovative decentralized financial systems. This intersection will pave the way for the emergence of hybrid financial models that successfully combine the best features of both worlds, ultimately providing consumers with enhanced services and choices. Finally, the ongoing development and introduction of central bank digital currencies (CBDCs) across various jurisdictions will significantly further influence the regulatory landscape. As governments explore and seek to harness the myriad benefits associated with digital currencies, they will also strive to maintain a strong control over monetary policy and financial stability through these new digital instruments.

Persuading the Market: The Road to a Secure and Inclusive Future

The ongoing evolution of regulation in the crypto market presents a compelling argument for the promising future of digital finance. It illustrates that, despite the initial tumult and unregulated perils that plagued the landscape, the industry has the innate ability to self-correct and pursue continuous improvement with vigor. Each regulatory overhaul, each newly established standard, and every enforcement action taken represents a significant stride towards cultivating a more secure, transparent, and inclusive financial ecosystem for all participants. As we move forward, the growing framework of regulations not only aims to protect investors but also fosters innovation and trust within the market, ultimately leading to a more robust financial environment that can adapt and thrive amidst the ever-changing technological advancements.

For investors, the significant transformation brought about by the ongoing evolution of regulations is a powerful and clear signal that cryptocurrencies are in the process of maturing. This transition from what was once considered a lawless digital frontier to a much more structured, regulated market signifies not just a theoretical evolution—it is indeed happening in real time, and it carries profound implications for the overall stability and legitimacy of digital assets in modern finance. With well-defined regulatory frameworks now in place, investors are afforded greater confidence in the long-term viability of cryptocurrencies, which ultimately paves the way for broader adoption, increased acceptance, and sustained growth in this burgeoning financial ecosystem. The ongoing development of regulatory measures will continue to shape the landscape, providing a foundation for more secure and reliable investment opportunities.

For developers and entrepreneurs in today's fast-paced environment, the ongoing regulatory evolution presents a unique mix of both significant challenges and promising opportunities. Although the need for compliance may demand additional resources, time, and effort from businesses, it also paves the way for exploration into untapped markets. Furthermore, it establishes a level playing field where innovation and creativity can truly thrive. The natural outcome of this evolution is a much more robust ecosystem, wherein technological advancements are developed in harmony with sound regulatory practices. This synergy ensures that the industry experiences growth in a manner that ultimately benefits everyone involved, fostering a new era of advancement that aligns with societal needs and values.

A Logical Synthesis: From Chaos to Maturity

The journey of crypto trading, transitioning from a state of unregulated chaos to a more mature and regulated market, represents a logical and analytical progression that highlights the resilience and adaptability of human innovation and creativity. The early failures encountered, along with numerous security breaches, provided a stark and powerful lesson: without proper oversight and regulation, the potential for exploitation and instability within this new financial landscape is indeed enormous and can lead to significant losses. Consequently, the resulting regulatory overhauls that followed these issues have not only addressed these serious vulnerabilities but have also paved the way for a more structured, stable, and reliable market. This evolution demonstrates the capacity for growth and improvement inherent in the industry, affirming that with thoughtful regulation, the future of crypto trading can indeed thrive and develop in a more secure environment.

This logical progression can be summarized in three key points:

1. **Security and Transparency:**
   Regulatory measures and guidelines have compelled various exchanges to adopt and implement significantly higher security standards, as well as to establish transparent operational practices. This transformation in protocols not only serves to protect investors and their assets but also plays a crucial role in building and enhancing trust in the market—a fundamental factor that is essential for sustainable long-term growth and stability.

1. **Market Stability and Institutional Confidence:**
   The introduction of regulated financial products, along with significant improvements in market infrastructure, has successfully attracted a diverse range of institutional investors. Their active participation has greatly contributed to an increase in liquidity and a noticeable reduction in market volatility. This enhanced stability is absolutely essential for the

broader mainstream acceptance and integration of digital currencies into the financial ecosystem.

1. **Global Integration and Financial Inclusion:** As regulatory frameworks continue to evolve and develop, they actively promote international cooperation and the standardization of practices, thereby creating a more cohesive and unified global market. This significant transformation opens up numerous opportunities for financial inclusion for many. It enables individuals in underbanked regions and communities to gain access to essential financial services and actively participate in the burgeoning digital economy. This shift is vital for integrating diverse populations into the financial system.

Each of these points significantly represents a logical response to the various challenges that the crypto market has encountered over the years. They clearly illustrate how regulation, when implemented effectively, has the potential to transform a volatile, often unregulated space into a secure, reliable, and inclusive financial ecosystem that can benefit a wider range of participants. This evolution not only enhances safety and trust among users but also fosters innovation and growth within the industry.

Persuasive Reflections: The Moral Imperative of Regulation

The evolution of crypto regulation is a significant moral imperative that cannot be overlooked. Traditional financial systems are plagued by systemic inequality, corruption, and a lack of transparency, affecting millions. The initial idea of decentralizing money was to democratize finance and enhance accessibility for everyone, irrespective of their background.

However, without appropriate oversight and regulation, this innovation risks becoming a breeding ground for exploitation and malpractice that harms those it aims to assist. Comprehensive and nuanced regulations are essential to ensure that digital currencies benefit society while protecting individual rights in the digital age. This goal aligns with the principles of fairness, equity, and justice foundational to a democratic financial system. Regulators must balance innovation encouragement with necessary protections to create a sustainable environment for digital assets that serves all citizens' interests. Careful consideration of these regulations is crucial due to their profound impact on future global financial interactions.

The ethical case for regulation is highly persuasive and compelling because it addresses the fundamental and crucial question of how wealth should effectively be managed in a society that values both innovation and social responsibility. The establishment of regulations that promote transparency, accountability, and consumer protection is not intended to stifle innovation in any way; rather, these regulations provide the essential foundation upon which a robust, equitable, and fair financial system can be constructed. This moral imperative strongly drives the continuous and dynamic evolution of the crypto market, ensuring that meaningful progress is made in a manner that ultimately benefits all participants involved in the system. Thus, the regulatory framework plays a vital role in fostering an environment where creativity thrives while also safeguarding the interests of all stakeholders.

The Broader Picture: Impact on Global Finance and Society

The ongoing regulatory transformation of the crypto market presents implications that extend much further than just the confines of digital asset trading. It signifies a fundamental rethinking of the various ways money is managed, stored, and exchanged—a significant shift that carries the potential to influence the entirety of the global financial system. As digital currencies become increasingly integrated with traditional finance systems, the regulatory frameworks that are developed within the crypto space can serve as influential models for a variety of other sectors in finance and commerce. These frameworks provide a profound glimpse into a future where financial systems are not only more transparent but also significantly more efficient and inclusive for all participants in the economy.

Furthermore, the shift towards a more regulated crypto market carries profound social implications that cannot be overlooked. By ensuring that digital assets are both managed securely and handled with transparency, these regulations play a pivotal role in building and fostering public trust—an absolutely crucial factor that can lead to widespread adoption in the marketplace. This enhanced trust, as a consequence, opens the door to greater financial inclusion, effectively empowering individuals from various backgrounds and regions across the globe to actively participate in the burgeoning digital economy. In areas where traditional banking services are either unreliable or completely inaccessible, the emergence of a regulated crypto market presents a vital lifeline—serving as a reliable means to access essential financial services, paving the way for individuals to build their wealth independently, free from the constraints imposed by centralized financial institutions.

The cultural impact of this significant shift in perception and understanding is equally profound and far-reaching. As more and more people begin to understand and place their trust in digital currencies, the stigma that was once firmly associated with crypto trading is gradually fading away. What was once dismissed as a risky, speculative endeavor, fraught with uncertainty, is now being increasingly recognized as a legitimate, transformative force in the landscape of global finance. This change in perception, which is both substantial and critical, serves as a powerful, persuasive argument for the future of money—a potential future where regulation and innovation can coexist harmoniously, working together to create a more resilient and equitable financial system that benefits a broader range of participants.

The Road Ahead: Challenges and Opportunities

Despite the significant progress made, numerous challenges remain on the road to achieving a fully regulated crypto market that can function effectively. The inherently dynamic nature of digital currencies means that regulators must continuously adapt and evolve in response to new technologies, changing market behaviors, and various emerging threats that could impact the stability and security of the financial system. Striking the right balance between necessary oversight and fostering innovation is an ongoing and complex challenge—implementing too much regulation could inadvertently stifle creativity and deter new ideas from developing, while too little regulatory oversight could leave the market vulnerable to manipulation and abuse by malicious actors. Thus, finding the appropriate framework that supports both regulation and creativity is essential for a sustainable future.

However, while these challenges may seem daunting, they also present unique and significant opportunities. The ongoing and continuous dialogue among regulators, industry participants, and the wider community is actively driving a more informed and adaptable regulatory environment. This collaborative approach is not just logical, but is also absolutely essential for ensuring that the evolving crypto market maximizes its many potential benefits while minimizing possible risks. By fostering this partnership, all stakeholders can contribute to a more sustainable and innovative future for the industry.

Looking forward, we can confidently expect to see an increasing convergence between traditional finance and the emerging realm of decentralized digital assets. The development of central bank digital currencies (CBDCs) is a significant step in this direction, and it is poised to reshape how we view money and transactions. Moreover, the ongoing increased international regulatory cooperation among nations will play a crucial role in ensuring that the financial landscape is consistent and fair across borders. Another key aspect of this evolution is the integration of regulatory technology (RegTech) into the oversight of the crypto market. These trends collectively point towards a more harmonized global financial system that accommodates both traditional financial institutions and innovative digital platforms. As these advancements continue to unfold, they will help create a level playing field in which innovation can thrive, allowing for new business models and opportunities to emerge. Additionally, ensuring consumer protection remains paramount in this evolving landscape, guaranteeing that individuals can engage with these modern financial tools with confidence and security.

A New Era of Secure, Regulated Digital Finance

The evolution of crypto regulation has undergone a remarkable transformation from a state of complete anarchy to a structured, secure, and mature market, and this story is a narrative filled with shock, innovation, and undeniable progress. The significant key milestones that have emerged and reshaped the crypto trading landscape—including high-profile breaches, dramatic regulatory overhauls, widespread institutional adoption, and the continuous development of sophisticated financial products—form a compelling and persuasive argument for the promising future of digital currencies. Each of these elements has played a crucial role in establishing a more organized framework, thereby influencing investor confidence and market stability in the long run.

The logical progression is clear and undeniable: as the cryptocurrency market continues to mature over time, robust and effective regulatory frameworks become essential to ensure that the entire ecosystem remains secure, transparent, and inclusive for all participants. These regulations have not only served to protect investors but have also significantly reduced the risks associated with fraud and abuse that were once rampant. Furthermore, these well-designed regulatory measures have paved the way for widespread mainstream acceptance as well as institutional investment, which is crucial for the growth and stability of the market. The evolution from a period of unregulated chaos to a structured, well-regulated market is a remarkable testament to the power of human ingenuity, creativity, and the relentless pursuit of economic freedom that many strive to achieve.

For investors, regulators, and everyday users alike, the ongoing transformation of the crypto market through evolving regulations serves as a persuasive reminder that the future of money is not simply about technological innovation. It is equally about building a financial system that is fair, secure, and fully capable of adapting to the myriad challenges posed by a rapidly globalized world. The valuable lessons gleaned from past failures have led to the development of a more resilient and robust system—one that effectively balances the crucial need for oversight with the imperative of fostering innovation. This balance is essential as stakeholders navigate the complexities inherent in a dynamic financial landscape while striving to maintain integrity and trust.

As we stand on the cusp of an exciting new era in the realm of digital finance, the significant regulatory overhauls and the maturation of markets that we have witnessed in recent years provide a robust and clear blueprint for what the future may hold. These developments demonstrate compellingly that when the appropriate safeguards and regulations are firmly in place, digital currencies can offer unprecedented benefits. These benefits encompass a wide array of advantages—ranging from enhanced security and greater transparency to improved financial inclusion and increased economic stability, which can positively impact societies as a whole.

Embrace this new era of financial evolution. Recognize that the global shift towards regulated and secure digital finance is not merely a temporary trend but represents a significant and fundamental transformation. This transformation promises to dramatically redefine the ways in which we interact with money on a daily basis. The future of finance has indeed arrived, bringing with it a reality where regulation and innovation are not opposing forces but instead work harmoniously in tandem to create a more resilient, trustworthy, and equitable financial ecosystem for everyone. The ongoing evolution of crypto trading—from its chaotic and unregulated beginnings to a mature, organized market—serves as a compelling, logical, and persuasive argument that the future of money is both decentralized and secure. This future is built solidly upon the foundation of robust regulatory standards combined with technological excellence and innovation, shaping a new landscape for financial transactions across the globe.

Section 5: Building a Robust Ecosystem for Global Crypto Trading

In today's financial world, digital currencies have remarkably transitioned from the fringes of technology to the very center stage of global commerce and economic activity. Behind this monumental transformation lies an increasingly robust ecosystem that has been meticulously built on integrated and secure networks, which enable seamless and effective global crypto trading with unprecedented ease. This fascinating evolution is both shocking and mind-blowing in its extensive scope and profound impact—a true testament to human ingenuity and the relentless drive for financial freedom that many individuals crave. In this section, we delve deep into how modern infrastructure, innovative technology, and coordinated global efforts across various sectors have combined harmoniously to create a secure trading environment that not only aims to protect valuable assets but also significantly fosters transparency, efficiency, and inclusivity for all participants engaged in this evolving financial landscape.

The Early Chaos: A Landscape Without Boundaries

Imagine a world where, in the early days of crypto, trading resembled navigating the wild, uncharted territories of a vast digital frontier. There were no centralized institutions established to standardize trading practices, no robust security protocols to effectively protect funds, and absolutely no integrated systems to adequately support global trade. In this bewildering and chaotic environment, every exchange operated as a makeshift experiment, and every transaction felt like a giant leap of faith into the unknown. The early platforms were riddled with vulnerabilities, leaving users exposed to a multitude of risks, and the glaring lack of regulation meant that anyone with a bit of technical knowledge could set up a trading website with little more than a few lines of code and a vague understanding of the technology involved.

In those early days, investors found themselves compelled to rely heavily on isolated systems that offered extremely limited liquidity options, and the act of trading across international borders was often as unpredictable as it was inherently risky. Lacking a cohesive, well-designed infrastructure, traders faced the daunting challenge of dealing with wildly varying standards that often led to confusion and inefficiency, as well as poor security measures that left them at risk, and the constant threat of fraud looming over every transaction. The absence of interoperability between different trading platforms added to the complexity, making the transfer of assets from one exchange to another a process fraught with numerous obstacles and difficulties, often involving cumbersome manual processes and a very high degree of risk. During this tumultuous period, the immense potential of digital currencies was indeed recognized by a select few, but the overall ecosystem was still in its infancy—vulnerable, fragmented, disorganized, and chaotic in nature.

The Emergence of Integrated, Secure Networks

Fast forward to today, and the landscape of crypto trading has undergone a truly dramatic transformation unlike anything we've seen before. The once fragmented world of digital asset trading has remarkably evolved into a globally integrated network where transactions happen seamlessly and securely across borders and platforms. This significant evolution is driven by a combination of rapid technological advancements, progressive regulatory efforts, and a profound commitment from the crypto community to build robust systems that work effectively for everyone involved. As a result, opportunities abound, and the future of trading appears brighter than ever.

One of the most significant and foundational breakthroughs in this remarkable evolution was undoubtedly the advent of blockchain technology. This groundbreaking innovation provided a transparent and immutable ledger that underpins nearly every modern crypto trading platform we see today. Blockchain technology allowed for the recording of transactions in a manner that is verifiable by anyone with access, thereby ensuring that trust is not overly concentrated in a single entity but is instead distributed across a vast global network of participants. This radical trustless model of trading was a revolutionary and transformative idea that fundamentally changed how value is stored, managed, and exchanged in our increasingly digital economy.

As blockchain technology continued to mature and evolve over time, developers increasingly began to explore and build upon it through the creation of layer 2 solutions and various interoperability protocols. These groundbreaking innovations were specifically designed to address some of the most pressing and significant challenges that had plagued the early days of blockchain technology—especially issues related to scalability, transaction speed, and cross-chain compatibility. Today's increasingly integrated networks are no longer limited or hindered by the constraints and obstacles that once negatively impacted the growth of global crypto trading across different platforms and systems. Advanced technologies like the Lightning Network, along with a variety of interoperability protocols, now enable rapid transactions at impressively low fees while still maintaining the security and decentralization that are widely recognized as the essential hallmarks of blockchain technology.

Security: The Cornerstone of a Robust Ecosystem

At the very heart of this robust and resilient ecosystem lies an unwavering commitment to security. In a contemporary era where even the smallest minor breach can lead to catastrophic financial losses that could cripple businesses, establishing secure trading networks is not merely an option— it has become an absolute necessity that cannot be ignored. Over the years, the industry has faced numerous challenges and learned painful lessons from its early failures and missteps. In response to these experiences, the sector has adopted significant innovations and breakthroughs that dramatically enhance and improve overall security measures.

Modern exchanges and wallets incorporate various layers of security measures, which are essential in today's digital landscape. They utilize advanced encryption algorithms, multi-factor authentication, and secure hardware modules to provide robust protection for private keys. Additionally, many platforms now employ cold storage solutions, which ensure that the bulk of user funds remain offline and thus are immune to potential online hacking attempts. The rigorous and comprehensive security protocols that govern today's exchanges are a direct response to the numerous vulnerabilities observed in the early unregulated days of cryptocurrency trading. As the industry develops, the importance of these security features only continues to grow, further safeguarding investors from potential threats.

For instance, the infamous and widely publicized Mt. Gox collapse served as a significant wake-up call that drove the entire industry to take crucial steps and develop best practices aimed at ensuring greater security and transparency. Today's various platforms undergo regular and thorough security audits and adhere strictly to stringent regulatory standards that are enforced to protect users. This necessary shift from a reactive, crisis-driven approach to a proactive, preventive model of security is both logical and undoubtedly necessary for the ongoing evolution of the industry. It reassures investors and instills a deep sense of confidence in the entire ecosystem—helping to attract invaluable institutional capital and broaden market participation in a meaningful way.

The Role of Regulation in Building Trust

Alongside significant technological innovation, widespread regulatory overhauls have played a critical and essential role in maturing the ever-evolving crypto trading landscape. Initially, the glaring lack of regulatory oversight contributed to the wild, chaotic, and unstructured nature of early trading platforms. However, as the market continued to grow and the stakes became increasingly higher, regulators started to step in and enforce necessary guidelines to ensure a safer and more stable trading environment.

The establishment of clear and comprehensive regulatory frameworks in countries such as Japan, Switzerland, and Singapore has significantly bolstered overall market confidence among participants. These regulations now mandate transparency, enforce proper risk management protocols, and impose stringent security practices across exchanges and various trading platforms. This regulatory clarity has played a crucial role in reducing the incidence of fraud and market manipulation in the financial landscape. Furthermore, it has paved the way for institutional investors to enter the market with increased confidence and assurance. The confidence instilled by these regulations fosters a healthier marketplace and encourages greater participation from both retail and institutional investors alike, ultimately contributing to a more robust financial system.

By implementing and enforcing comprehensive standards designed to protect consumers, regulators have significantly contributed to the transformation of crypto trading from what was once an anarchic experiment into a fully legitimate and widely recognized asset class. This impressive transition stands as a powerful and persuasive argument supporting the promising future of digital finance. When potential investors observe that there are strong and robust legal and regulatory frameworks in place, their perception of risk diminishes considerably. This shift in perception leads to enhanced market stability and increased liquidity. Furthermore, the intricate interplay between regulation and technology serves as a key driver behind the modern integrated, secure networks that we encounter today in the landscape of digital finance.

Technological Innovations: Enhancing Interoperability and Efficiency

As the crypto trading ecosystem continued to mature and evolve, the emergence of various technological innovations became increasingly essential for overcoming the many limitations faced by early platforms. One of the most significant challenges experienced during the early days of cryptocurrency trading was the pronounced lack of interoperability—the crucial capability for different systems to communicate effectively and work together seamlessly. In a market that was fragmented, transferring assets between various platforms proved to be cumbersome, notably slow, and fraught with considerable risk. This inefficiency not only hampered global trading but also significantly limited the overall potential of the market to grow and develop. The need for improved integration solutions became glaringly apparent as traders sought more fluid and secure ways to navigate the complexities of this rapidly changing landscape.

The development of standardized protocols and interoperability solutions has truly been a game changer in the world of cryptocurrency. Innovations such as atomic swaps and cross-chain bridges now allow users to seamlessly trade assets across different blockchains without the need for any centralized intermediaries. These groundbreaking technologies ensure that the global crypto trading network is not fragmented into isolated pockets but instead functions as part of a cohesive and integrated system. The result of this evolution is a vibrant marketplace where liquidity is significantly enhanced, trading becomes remarkably more efficient, and users can easily take advantage of lucrative opportunities regardless of the specific platform they choose to utilize. This interconnectedness fosters a more inclusive trading environment, ultimately benefiting all participants in the ecosystem.

Furthermore, the advancements in user interface design have significantly enhanced the accessibility of trading for a diverse range of individuals. Today's modern exchanges and trading platforms present intuitive and easy-to-navigate interfaces, which effectively lower the barrier to entry for novice investors eager to participate. This harmonious blend of interoperability along with user-friendly design represents a critical progression—it effectively transforms the intricate and often overwhelming world of cryptocurrency trading into a more manageable, secure, and efficient marketplace for everyone involved.

Institutional Adoption: Bridging the Gap Between Old and New

One of the most shocking yet perfectly logical developments in the ongoing evolution of crypto trading has undeniably been the gradual yet decisive acceptance and enthusiastic integration of various digital assets by institutional investors. In the early days of cryptocurrency, the market was predominantly dominated by retail investors and passionate tech enthusiasts, with minimal interest or involvement from traditional financial institutions. However, as the entire crypto ecosystem has matured over time, the numerous benefits and potential advantages of digital currencies have become far too significant to ignore any longer. The shift in perception among institutional players marks a crucial turning point in the landscape of cryptocurrency.

Institutional investors arrived with a significant level of discipline, robust risk management practices, and stringent regulatory compliance that greatly contributed to stabilizing the market. Their entry into crypto trading represented a crucial milestone that transformed the entire landscape, effectively creating a bridge between the previously decentralized world of digital currencies and the more conventional financial system that many are accustomed to. With the introduction of various regulated financial products, including Bitcoin futures, options, and exchange-traded funds (ETFs), institutional capital began to flow into the market in unprecedented amounts. This influx of institutional money not only lent much-needed legitimacy to the market but also fostered considerable growth and development within the digital currency space, paving the way for further integration with traditional finance.

This significant shift is persuasive on multiple levels and carries profound implications. It clearly demonstrates that digital assets have evolved beyond being mere speculative instruments; they are now widely recognized as viable investment vehicles that possess the potential to hedge against inflation and effectively diversify portfolios. The logical argument presented here is quite compelling: when major financial institutions begin to invest in and actively trade digital currencies, the entire ecosystem stands to benefit from the resulting increased liquidity, enhanced stability, and greater overall credibility. This evolution marks a pivotal moment in the financial landscape.

Real-World Impact: Market Maturation and Global Integration

The evolution of crypto trading platforms has been significantly driven by enhanced security measures, improved interoperability between different systems, greater regulatory oversight, and an increase in institutional adoption. This maturation process has led to the establishment of a much more integrated and robust market environment. Today's exchanges are not merely the wild, unregulated entities of the past; rather, they have transformed into sophisticated, professional platforms that effectively operate on a global scale. They seamlessly connect buyers and sellers across multiple continents, thereby enabling transactions that are not only efficient but also secure and executed in real time. This transformation highlights the vast progress within the crypto trading ecosystem, fostering a sense of trust among users and instilling confidence in a rapidly evolving financial landscape.

This global integration has numerous and far-reaching implications that cannot be overlooked. It fundamentally means that digital currencies can now effectively function as true global assets—assets that are accessible to anyone, from any location, at any time. The benefits of this significant integration are manifold and diverse: increased market liquidity, substantially lower transaction costs, and the unparalleled ability to actively participate in a global economy without the numerous barriers that are typically imposed by traditional financial systems. Such advancements have the potential to revolutionize the way we perceive and engage with economic activities across borders.

Furthermore, the maturation of the market has led to a significant and notable reduction in volatility across the board. As more and more investors, both retail and institutional alike, participate actively in the market, the overall risk profile improves considerably, and price swings become substantially less extreme and less dramatic. This increased stability is crucial and fundamentally important for the long-term adoption and acceptance of digital currencies, as it reassures a wide range of investors that the market is steadily moving toward a state of maturity and reliability that can be depended upon.

The Ethical and Social Dimensions: Democratizing Finance

The transition from chaotic, unregulated trading environments to a more mature, integrated ecosystem is not just a technical or economic development—it carries with it profound ethical and social implications that cannot be overlooked. For decades, traditional financial systems have faced significant criticism for their tendency to concentrate wealth and power in the hands of a limited number of individuals and institutions, effectively leaving millions of people without access to the essential tools that are necessary for meaningful economic participation. In stark contrast, the decentralized nature inherent in cryptocurrencies, when combined with the robust infrastructure of modern exchanges, presents an opportunity for a more democratized financial system. This evolution promises to empower individuals from various backgrounds, ensuring broader participation and inclusivity in economic activities, thereby transforming the financial landscape into one that is more equitable and accessible for all.

This democratization is undoubtedly one of the most persuasive and compelling arguments for the promising future of digital finance. Secure and integrated networks ensure that anyone with a stable internet connection can participate actively in global trading activities, regardless of geographic or socioeconomic barriers that may have previously limited their access. This remarkable inclusivity has the potential to significantly transform lives—by providing access to crucial financial services, empowering individuals to take control of their own wealth, making informed decisions, and ultimately fostering a more equitable distribution of economic power within society. As more people become engaged in the financial ecosystem, the gaps between different communities can start to close, paving the way for innovative solutions that benefit not just individuals but also the global economy as a whole.

The ethical case for a decentralized financial system is indeed compelling and worthy of deeper exploration. When power is carefully distributed across a global network rather than being concentrated in a single institution or without oversight, the inherent risks associated with corruption, fraud, and systemic failure are significantly reduced. This crucial shift aligns perfectly with the broader goals of transparency and accountability within financial systems, ensuring that digital currencies can effectively serve the collective good of the global population rather than the narrow interests of a select few individuals or organizations. It represents a mind-blowing transformation in how we approach finance and economic interaction. This new paradigm promises not only to enhance economic efficiency and responsiveness but also to promote social justice on a truly global scale, potentially redefining our understanding of fairness and equity in economic systems worldwide.

Persuading the Skeptics: A Logical Necessity for the Future

Even with the distinct benefits that an integrated and regulated crypto trading ecosystem can offer, there is still a notable amount of skepticism found among various observers in the field. Many critics maintain that the swift and often unpredictable evolution of the cryptocurrency market, coupled with the continuous regulatory hurdles that arise, contributes to an overall sense of uncertainty and risk. These individuals highlight past failures and significant incidents, such as multiple exchange hacks and dramatic market crashes, as crucial evidence suggesting that digital currencies remain excessively volatile and largely untested for any serious long-term investment strategies.

However, a careful and logical analysis reveals that these criticisms unfortunately overlook the broader picture of the entire situation. The chaotic and unregulated days of early crypto trading were, in fact, a necessary phase in the evolution of digital finance—a period that was markedly marked by rapid experimentation, numerous failures, and subsequent improvements that were essential for progress. Each failure, rather than being merely a setback, served as a valuable learning opportunity, prompting the development of more secure, efficient, and resilient systems that could better withstand future challenges. The logical trajectory is quite clear: the market has matured significantly over time, security protocols have improved markedly, and regulatory frameworks have evolved in ways that make today's ecosystem far more stable and reliable than it was just a few short years ago.

The convergence of technology, regulation, and institutional investment presents a compelling argument for the long-term viability and sustainable growth of digital currencies in today's financial ecosystem. The robust and integrated networks that now underpin global crypto trading are not simply a fleeting, temporary fix; rather, they represent the vital foundation of a new financial paradigm that is both logical and, ultimately, inevitable. As more and more investors, including institutional players, enthusiastically embrace this promising future, the skeptical voices that once dominated discussions about cryptocurrency and digital finance grow quieter over time, replaced steadily by a growing and undeniable recognition that the digital financial revolution is indeed here to stay for the foreseeable future. This evolution in perception underscores a significant shift towards acceptance and integration within mainstream financial markets.

The Road Ahead: Future Trends in Global Crypto Trading

Looking ahead, the future of crypto trading is poised to be defined by a remarkable degree of integration, innovation, and enhanced security. What we see in the current ecosystem is merely the beginning phase. Emerging trends indicate that upcoming platforms will provide significantly more seamless and efficient global trading experiences, skillfully combining the optimal features of both centralized and decentralized models to create a more user-friendly environment.

Technological advancements, including enhanced protocols for interoperability, will enable various blockchain networks to effectively communicate and transact with one another, breaking down existing silos and helping to create a genuinely unified global market environment. This increased integration will not only improve overall liquidity but also significantly reduce the friction and various inefficiencies that currently plague transactions across different chains. Additionally, with better interoperability, users will experience a seamless transfer of assets and information, leading to a more streamlined process and greater user satisfaction in the burgeoning world of decentralized finance.

Moreover, the continued and ongoing development of advanced security protocols—driven by sophisticated artificial intelligence, innovative machine learning techniques, and cutting-edge quantum-resistant cryptography—will further solidify and enhance the trustworthiness of digital exchanges. These groundbreaking innovations will provide additional layers of protection, thereby ensuring that the entire ecosystem remains robust and resilient in the face of evolving and increasingly complex cyber threats. The logical progression of these trends is clear: as technology continues to advance at an unprecedented pace, the systems that support global cryptocurrency trading will inevitably become even more secure, highly efficient, and accessible to a much broader audience of users and investors alike.

Regulatory evolution will also play an incredibly critical role in shaping the dynamic and multifaceted future of the market. As governments and regulatory bodies around the world continue to harmonize their diverse approaches to digital currencies, a more cohesive, transparent, and predictable global regulatory environment will undoubtedly emerge. This evolution will not only enhance investor confidence but also facilitate and bolster the continued integration of digital assets into the mainstream financial system, paving the way for the acceptance and adoption of these innovative financial instruments across various sectors.

The Broader Economic and Social Impact

The transformation of crypto trading into an integrated, secure global ecosystem has profound implications that extend far beyond the realm of finance alone. It signifies a significant shift towards a more democratized economic system—one where access to wealth and financial opportunities is no longer restricted by geographic location or socioeconomic status. The robust and innovative networks that enable seamless global trading possess the transformative potential to empower individuals and communities all around the world. By facilitating easier access to financial resources, these systems can play a critical role in driving economic inclusion, fostering entrepreneurship, and ultimately reducing inequality in various forms. This evolution not only opens up new avenues for investment and participation but also promotes a sense of shared economic prosperity on a global scale.

This democratization is not just a theoretical benefit; it represents a significant, practical, mind-blowing shift that is already being actively witnessed in real time. In numerous regions across the globe, individuals who were previously excluded from traditional banking systems are now engaging in global trade and investment, all thanks to the advent of digital currencies. The underlying logic behind this transformative movement is quite simple yet profoundly impactful: when financial systems are secure, easily accessible, and inherently transparent, they can serve as incredibly powerful tools for both social and economic empowerment. This compelling narrative stands as a persuasive argument for the broader and more widespread adoption of digital assets—a visionary outlook of the future where financial freedom is not just a privilege for some, but is made accessible to all individuals, regardless of their background or circumstances.

A Logical, Analytical Perspective: The Journey from Chaos to Order

When we take a closer look at the evolution of crypto trading through a logical and analytical lens, the progression from the early days of unregulated platforms to the highly integrated and secure networks we see today is truly breathtaking. This remarkable journey is characterized by continuous improvement—a relentless process where each setback encountered has sparked innovation, each failure experienced has provided a valuable lesson, and each challenge faced has led to significant breakthroughs. Each stage of development has contributed uniquely to the robustness of the system we now enjoy.

The early days of crypto trading were marked by a profound sense of disorder, noticeable vulnerability, and rampant risk at every turn. Yet, in the face of such chaos, this period served as the crucial crucible in which robust and efficient systems were forged and refined. The logical and essential response to these numerous challenges was to implement stringent security protocols, develop comprehensive regulatory frameworks, and build resilient infrastructure that could adequately support the rapid and often unpredictable growth of digital assets. The end result is a market that stands as far more stable, secure, and resilient than it was just a few short years ago—this transformation is not only logical but also undeniably revolutionary in its impact on the financial landscape.

This logical evolution is particularly persuasive due to its foundation on empirical evidence and a well-defined, rational progression of events that are easy to understand. The numerous failures of the past—whether they manifested as security breaches, catastrophic exchange collapses, or glaring regulatory missteps—served as the raw material from which the forthcoming innovations were constructed. Each lesson learned from these events contributed significantly to the creation of a much more mature market, one that is not only capable of navigating the complexities of global trading but also equipped to innovate and adapt continuously. The analytical framework here is quite straightforward: when a system is granted the opportunity to learn from its past mistakes and evolve accordingly, it ultimately becomes stronger, more efficient, and notably more trustworthy in the eyes of participants. This ability to learn and adapt is crucial for fostering ongoing improvements in operational practices and market resilience.

Persuading the Skeptics: The Case for an Integrated, Secure Future

For those who still remain doubtful and skeptical about the long-term viability of digital currencies, the evolution of the crypto trading ecosystem provides a persuasive and compelling counterargument that cannot be ignored. The progress from what was once a chaotic and unregulated environment to a mature and integrated market is not merely based on anecdotal evidence—it is robustly supported by a wealth of data, rigorous analysis, and a logical sequence of significant technological and regulatory advancements. This transformation highlights the growing acceptance and adoption of digital currencies, reinforcing their potential to thrive in the financial landscape.

The fact that numerous major institutions, various governments, and leading financial experts now actively engage and participate in the ever-evolving crypto market is a powerful and significant testament to its growing legitimacy and acceptance. When influential global regulators, such as those in Japan and Switzerland, take the initiative to create robust frameworks that protect investors and promote transparency within the crypto space, it sends a clear, persuasive signal to the entire world. This indicates that digital currencies are not merely a passing fad or a temporary trend, but rather a foundational and integral element of the future of money and financial systems as a whole. Such developments underline the importance of adapting to new financial paradigms and embracing innovative technologies that are reshaping the landscape.

The robust and intricate networks that underpin modern crypto trading, with their strong emphasis on enhanced security, seamless interoperability, and stringent regulatory compliance, clearly demonstrate that the industry has indeed learned valuable lessons from its early mistakes. Every significant milestone—whether it's the innovative development of advanced security protocols, the emergence of fully regulated exchanges, or the ongoing integration of decentralized finance—reinforces the logical and compelling case for establishing a secure, integrated trading ecosystem that effectively meets the diverse needs of today's rapidly evolving global market. These advancements contribute to building trust and confidence among traders and investors alike, fostering a more stable and efficient trading environment.

The Broader Vision: A New Paradigm for Global Finance

At its core, the transformation of crypto trading represents a significant paradigm shift—a comprehensive rethinking of how money is effectively created, managed, and exchanged on a truly global scale. The ongoing evolution of integrated, secure networks carries profound implications for the future landscape of finance. This groundbreaking movement not only challenges the traditional, centralized model but also actively paves the way for a decentralized, inclusive, and remarkably dynamic financial ecosystem that can empower individuals worldwide.

This new paradigm is characterized by notable transparency, remarkable resilience, and heightened efficiency. It is a world where the immense power to participate in trading is not confined to a select few individuals or institutions, but is instead widely distributed across a global network that includes countless individuals, institutions, and advanced technologies. This significant shift represents a logical and inescapable outcome of decades of innovative thought and continuous improvement across various fields. The persuasive argument in favor of this transformation is abundantly clear: a decentralized, integrated market not only greatly enhances security and boosts investor confidence but also fosters greater economic inclusion and contributes to global financial stability in ways previously unimagined. The implications of such a revolutionary framework are profound and far-reaching, suggesting a future where everyone can access and benefit from financial opportunities.

The integrated networks that now enable seamless global trading represent much more than mere technical marvels—they serve as the essential backbone of an entirely new financial order. These systems connect diverse markets, effectively bridge various regulatory gaps, and empower users to transact with absolute confidence, irrespective of their geographic location. This interconnected network stands as a remarkable example of how technology has the profound ability to dismantle traditional barriers, enabling innovation and creating a more inclusive and resilient global economy for everyone involved. It illustrates the potential for a transformed landscape where opportunities abound, and inclusivity becomes the standard rather than the exception.

Conclusion: Embracing a Future of Secure, Integrated Crypto Trading

The evolution of crypto trading—from the chaotic and largely unregulated days of the early internet era to the sophisticated, highly integrated networks we see and use today—is an intriguing story of remarkable progress, logical reasoning, and relentless innovation within the financial landscape. The key milestones that have shaped this extensive journey are not isolated events; rather, they are all part of a coherent narrative that effectively demonstrates the remarkable resilience and adaptability of the ever-evolving digital asset market. This narrative showcases how, through time, various technologies and user demands have driven the transformation and maturation of crypto trading platforms, leading to the more structured and regulated environment we experience now.

Through a series of enhanced security protocols, significant regulatory overhauls, groundbreaking technological breakthroughs, and a relentless, unwavering commitment to transparency, the crypto ecosystem has undergone a remarkable transformation into a robust, secure platform for global trading activities. This remarkable transformation is not only as shocking as it is logical but also serves as a clear and analytical response to the numerous challenges associated with managing digital assets in our increasingly interconnected world.

For investors, traders, and everyday users alike, the multifaceted journey of crypto trading stands as a compelling argument for the future of money in this evolving digital age. It serves as a powerful testament to the incredible capacities of human ingenuity that a system once characterized by significant vulnerability and chaos can undergo such a remarkable transformation into a stable, secure, and inclusive marketplace. The intricately integrated networks that facilitate seamless global trading are not merely tools; they embody a groundbreaking new financial paradigm. In this innovative landscape, trust is woven into the fabric of every transaction, and security is upheld as a fundamental right for all participants.

As we look ahead to the future, the ongoing evolution of crypto trading will undoubtedly lead to even greater innovations and significant improvements in the market. With constant advancements in blockchain technology, increased regulatory cooperation, and enhanced security protocols, the market is poised to not only become more resilient but also significantly more efficient. The logical and analytical case for establishing a secure, seamlessly integrated crypto trading ecosystem is stronger now than it has ever been before. Moreover, the evidence supporting this transformation is clear and compelling: the future of money is not just digital but decentralized, transparent, and unmistakably global in reach and influence. With these foundational elements in place, we can anticipate a vibrant and dynamic marketplace that fosters trust and enables unprecedented opportunities for investment and economic growth.

In conclusion, the evolution of crypto trading platforms presents a truly mind-blowing narrative of remarkable progress—a fascinating journey that stretches from a time of unregulated chaos to an impressively mature, fully integrated ecosystem that now meets the ever-growing demands of a modern, interconnected world. The significant advancements in security protocols, regulatory measures, and cutting-edge technology have collectively transformed the landscape, providing a persuasive, logical, and incredibly empowering vision for the future of digital finance. It is essential to embrace this new and exciting era, for it is a future wherein global trading is not only secure and accessible but also firmly built on a solid foundation of transparency and trust—a future that holds the promise to completely redefine the way we interact with money on a global scale, enabling individuals and institutions alike to engage in financial transactions with newfound confidence and ease.

www.ingramcontent.com/pod-product-compliance
Lightning Source LLC
LaVergne TN
LVHW090254210926
848480LV00001B/14
9798231030033